150 Years of Popular Musical Theatre

150 Years of Popular Musical Theatre

Andrew Lamb

Yale University Press   New Haven and London

Designed by Sonia Shannon and set in Adobe Garamond type
by Running Feet Books.
Printed in the United States of America by Sheridan Books, Chelsea, Michigan.

Library of Congress Cataloging-in-Publication Data
Lamb, Andrew.
150 years of popular musical theatre / Andrew Lamb.
p. cm.
Includes index.
ISBN 0–300–07538–3 (alk. paper)
1. Musicals—History and criticism.   2. Musical theater—History and criticism.
I. Title: One hundred fifty years of popular musical theatre.   II. Title.
ML1700 .L24 2000
782.1'09'034—dc21   00–025281

A catalogue record for this book is available from the British Library.

The paper in this book meets the guidelines for permanence and durability
of the Committee on Production Guidelines for Book Longevity of
the Council on Library Resources.

10 9 8 7 6 5 4 3 2 1

To my father and my late mother,
who gave me my love of the musical theatre

Contents

Part III
Continental European Round-Up

Part IV
The Musical Since World War II

Preface

"All the world's a stage," wrote Shakespeare; and in this book, for my part, I seek to view musical theatre as a global phenomenon. At the same time, it is almost entirely from Europe and North America that works of international currency have come, and it is thus on those two continents that this book inevitably concentrates.

The book views the modern American (and non-American) musical as a natural development of such nineteenth-century theatrical genres as comic opera, *opéra-comique, opérette,* and *vaudeville.* In his masterly study *Musicals* (Carlton, 1995), my good friend Kurt Gänzl rejects the use of the word *development* as implying some ongoing process of improvement or, at least, movement in a single direction. I see no such problem with the word. The development of the musical simply means a process of evolution which implies positive advances but also, necessarily, backward steps, sideways movements, and most particularly, rediscovery of things from the past. This tendency for trends and subject matter (and even melodies) to reappear down the ages is an important theme of this book.

The history of the musical theatre can, of course, be traced back for many centuries. So why did I make 1850 the starting point for this study? Well, one has to start somewhere; and in the first chapters I shall attempt to set the early works of the period in the context of what went before. But around this time the industrial revolution came into full force, vigorously extending communications and education and thus expanding not only the means of producing theatrical entertainments but also popular awareness of them, which in turn led to an increase in the number of theatres presenting them. Most particularly, it was around 1850 that the composers Hervé and Jacques Offenbach—generally recognised as the founding fathers of the operetta—were working on their first light-opera pieces. With their arrival on the stages first of Paris, then the world, the demand for popular musical entertainment increased. And Offenbach, more than any of his contemporaries, exploited the opportunities to make something recognisably new, providing a basis for the whole of subsequent musical theatrical development.

In referring to the works of Offenbach and Hervé, I should note that composers and their works provide the main narrative thread to the book. This is not to deny the importance of the various other contributors to the success of a work of the musical theatre: librettists, performers, directors, designers, and choreographers. But we traditionally refer to Offenbach's *La Belle Hélène,* Johann Strauss's *Die Fledermaus,* Jerome Kern's *Show Boat,* and Leonard Bernstein's *West Side Story.* The librettists—Henri Meilhac and Ludovic Halévy, F. Zell and Richard Genée, Oscar Hammerstein, and Stephen Sondheim—are not ignored here, but the composers take centre stage. In addition, I mention major performers, producers, and directors along the way.

Inevitably, in absorbing theatrical lore over several decades, I have consciously or unconsciously acquired information from more sources than I could hope to list. There is, however, a group of theatrical researchers and writers to whose work I have frequently referred. All are personal friends, with whom I have had the pleasure of exchanging information and whose help (witting or unwitting) I readily acknowledge. They include Gerald Bordman, Alexander Faris, Kurt Gänzl, Robert Pourvoyeur, Richard Traubner and, sadly in the past tense, the late Antonio de Almeida and Max Schönherr.

My thanks go also to my editor, Harry Haskell, whose idea this book was; to John Dizikes, who helped it through the acceptance stages; and to Lisa Agate, Bridget Burke, and Susan Smits for all their work in providing the illustrations. Last, and not least, I owe thanks to my wife, Wendy, for tolerating all the time and effort that went into the writing.

Part I

Continental European Operetta
from Offenbach to Lehár

Chapter One
Paris and the Rise of Offenbach

By the 1840s, Paris had long enjoyed a tradition of lighthearted *opéras-comiques* that offered spoken texts interspersed with arias, duets, trios, and ensembles. To the modern listener, many of these eighteenth-century pieces seem little different in structure and content from the operettas of a century or so later. The works of Adrien Boieldieu (1775–1834) provide a happy example. His *Le Calife de Bagdad* (The Caliph of Baghdad, 1800) featured a farcical story of romantic intrigue, disguise, and mistaken identity that would scarcely have been out of place in romantic operettas of the late nineteenth century. Its overture, which remained a popular favourite for more than a century and a half, was appropriate for a full-length opera. In fact, the score comprised no more than seven numbers, plus the overture, making up a total of some forty minutes of music, interspersed with dialogue of a similar length.

Boieldieu also composed evening-length works, among which *La Dame blanche* (The White Lady, 1825) was especially successful. However, its proportions and vocal demands were more operatic than was usual for comic operas. More relevant to popular musical theatre developments was the work of Adolphe Adam (1803–56), a pupil and assistant of Boieldieu's who is best known for his ballet *Giselle* (1841). Adam composed several obvious successors to his master's one-act works. *Le Chalet* (1834) had a slight plot, in which a couple of young lovers are besieged in their Swiss chalet by a company of soldiers, and a score adorned by rousing military songs. This brand of one-act comic opera was literally "operetta," in the sense of being a little opera. So was *Les Noces de Jeannette* (Jeannette's Wedding, 1853), a charming opéra-comique composed by Victor Massé (1822–84), produced at the Théâtre de l'Opéra-Comique in Paris. *Les Noces de Jeannette* has become a staple of the French operetta repertory, even though it predates what has generally been considered the birth of operetta as such.

If its antecedents are so clearly evident in such works, what then caused what we nowadays recognise as operetta to emerge in the mid-1850s? Behind the answer lie the increasingly serious and ambitious pretensions of opera in general and of the opéra-comique in particular as they developed during the 1840s. During the 1830s the first productions of Giacomo Meyerbeer's grand operas *Robert le Diable* (1831) and *Les Huguenots* (1836) were staged in Paris. The 1840s saw not only the early operas of Verdi but also the first performances of Wagner's *Rienzi* (1842), *Der fliegende Holländer* (1843), and *Tannhäuser* (1845). During the 1840s the whole operatic movement acquired greater gravitas, causing composers of more traditionally lighthearted works to despair for the production of their output. Seeking a new outlet, Adam founded the Opéra-National, which opened in 1847 but closed (leaving Adam financially ruined) after revolution broke out in Paris in 1848.

The emergence of operetta as a recognisably different genre also needs to be seen against the social background of the time. These were years when the industrial revolution was both changing ways of life and increasing the populations of urban areas. The urban working classes had little interest in the products of the opera house. Rather, they flocked to the dance halls and the *cafés-concerts* (or *cafés-chantants*), the French equivalents of the early British music halls. At the latter they could enjoy catchy songs and hummable, danceable melodies that were readily accessible to the untrained ear and delivered by performers expert in putting such material across.

Thus it was as an antidote to such works as Meyerbeer's *L'Etoile du nord* (The North Star, 1854), as well as to meet a need for less sophisticated, more accessible theatrical entertainment, that the *opérette* evolved in Paris during the 1850s. Posterity has generally awarded the prize for the creation of the genre to Jacques Offenbach, and it was certainly he who established it as something recognisably separate. However, he came onto the scene rather later than another, nowadays less celebrated, exponent.

"Hervé" was the nom de plume of Florimond Ronger (1825–92). Born near Arras in northern France, Ronger became a choirboy at the Saint-Roch church in Paris and studied at the Conservatoire under Daniel-François Auber. At the age of fifteen he was playing the organ in the chapel of Bicêtre and teaching in the neighbouring lunatic asylum. Moving on, he gained the position of organist at the church of Saint-Eustache, which provided him with the security upon which to base his early sorties into the musical theatre. Hervé was not only a composer who often wrote his own lyrics but also a performer. In 1847 he was approached by a French actor with the stage name of Désiré, who requested him to compose a comic work for a benefit performance. *Don Quichotte et Sancho Pança* was tailor-made for the tall, slim Hervé and small, roly-poly Désiré; and in 1848 it was performed at Adam's Opéra-National. With its comic songs and irresistible buffoonery, it may be seen in retrospect as the prototype of the whole new operetta genre.

In 1851, Hervé secured the post of musical director at the Théâtre du Palais Royal, and then in 1854 that of director of the small Folies-Concertantes (soon renamed Folies-Nouvelles) in the Boulevard du Temple, the main Parisian theatrical thoroughfare of the time. There his development of the operetta began in earnest as part of a varied programme of theatrical entertainments. The strict licensing regulations of the time confined him to short one-act pieces for just two performers, and his programmes initially included *pantomimes* (mimed pieces) as well as vocal works. Among them were *Le Compositeur toqué* (The Crazy Composer, 1854) and *Latrouillat et Truffaldini, ou Les Inconvénients d'une vendetta infiniment trop prolongée* (Latrouillat and Truffaldini, or The Drawbacks of a Vendetta Prolonged Infinitely Too Long, 1855). Hervé's enterprise positioned him to grab the attention of the crowds who flocked to Paris for the Exposition Universelle, which was mounted in 1855 as a showpiece for the regime of Napoléon III.

In the event, Hervé's efforts were eclipsed by the entertainments of Jacques

Jacques Offenbach, photographed by Nadar
Author's collection

Offenbach, who had just abandoned a position as musical director of the Comédie-Française in order to open his own Théâtre des Bouffes-Parisiens off the Champs Elysées. Six years older than Hervé, Offenbach (1819–80) had come to Paris from his native Cologne as a teenager and had gained an international reputation as a cello virtuoso before becoming musical director at Paris's leading dramatic theatre. Like Hervé, he composed a few isolated early theatrical pieces, staging them mainly at annual concerts of his music which also included cello and vocal works. In 1847 he produced *L'Alcôve,* and during the years 1853–55 wrote several more one-act pieces. In 1853 his offering was *Le Trésor à Mathurin* (Mathurin's Treasure), a sentimental piece about a young man's discovery of a treasure in the form of the niece of the title character.

Also first performed in 1853—at the Théâtre des Variétés, to which Offenbach would return in later years—was another one-act piece, *Pépito,* set in Spain. Its title character never actually appears, an idea that became a staple of the musical theatre. The major character is an innkeeper, Vertigo, who sings a parody of the "Largo al factotum" aria from Rossini's *Il Barbiere di Siviglia* (1816). In 1855, Offenbach's quirky *Oyayaye, ou La Reine des Iles* (Oyayaye, or The Queen of the Isles) was performed at Hervé's Folies-Nouvelles, with Hervé himself playing the part of a cannibal queen on whose desert island a Parisian double-bass player is shipwrecked.

By this time, however, Offenbach had already opened his own theatre to present works in a similar vein to Hervé's for the crowds of the Exposition Universelle. The theatre was tiny, no more than a flimsy wooden structure, but it could scarcely have been better positioned: just off the Champs Elysées and close to the Exposition grounds. Offenbach's licence limited him to one-act pieces for no more than three performers. His opening programme in July 1855 began with a brief welcoming prologue, *Entrez, Messieurs, Mesdames!* (Come In, Ladies and Gentlemen!), followed by an operetta, *Une Nuit blanche* (A Sleepless Night). In the latter a smuggler's wife receives a visit from her customs-officer cousin, who, to protect himself when the husband returns unexpectedly, agrees to turn a blind eye to what he discovers in the cellar in which he hastily hides. (Amorous intrigue and embarrassment were staples of Offenbach pieces.) These two works were followed by a pantomime, *Arlequin barbier* (Harlequin Barber), with music adapted by Offenbach from Rossini's *Il Barbiere di Siviglia,* and the evening was rounded off by a "bouffonerie musicale," *Les Deux Aveugles* (The Two Blind Men), which featured two lovable rogues posing as blind beggars on a Parisian bridge. It was the hit of the evening and turned Offenbach's venture into one of the successes of the Exposition season.

Changes to Offenbach's programme soon occurred, with pantomimes dropped in the face of the overriding popularity of the one-act operettas. *Le Rêve d'une nuit d'été* (A Summer Night's Dream) featured two English visitors to Paris, *Le Violoneux* (The Violinist) was based on an old Breton legend about a magic violin, and *Madame Papillon* (Mrs. Butterfly) told of an old woman who visited Paris in search of romance. The title role of this last was played by the company's leading actor *en travesti,* that is, in "drag"—another common feature of these early works.

Offenbach chose his performers shrewdly, employing both newcomers from the provinces and café-concert performers. Among his early recruits was Hortense Schneider, recently arrived from Bordeaux and destined to be the brightest star of Parisian operetta in the 1860s and 1870s. Another was Etienne Pradeau, who was the co-star of *Les Deux Aveugles* and played the title role in *Madame Papillon.* His comic antics made him the company's principal attraction, his face being described as "a flexible oval, [which] twists about into any number of grotesque countenances." Offenbach's choice of librettists demonstrated skill as well as good fortune. Above all, there was Ludovic Halévy (1834–1908), a government official who shared Offenbach's taste for the bizarre and turned out numerous witty pieces for him. Halévy was the nephew of Fromental Halévy (1799–1862), composer of the opera *La Juive* (The Jewish Woman, 1835) and Offenbach's former composition tutor.

Offenbach's initial summer season at the unheated and drafty theatre off the Champs-Elysées proved sufficiently successful for him to seek winter premises, which he found in the Théâtre des Jeunes-Elèves in the Passage Choiseul, a covered arcade not far from the Avenue de l'Opéra. This larger theatre became the permanent home of Offenbach's company and (as rebuilt in 1863) has remained the Théâtre des Bouffes-Parisiens to the present day. The new premises opened auspiciously in December 1855 with one of the most successful and enduring of all Offenbach's one-act pieces. *Ba-ta-clan* had a book by Ludovic Halévy that showed both him and the composer at their zany best. Described as a "chinoiserie musicale," it featured a cast of supposedly Chinese characters who all turn out to be Parisians. The score comprised an overture and seven numbers, including a Chinese march (the "Ba ta clan") with nonsensical pseudo-Chinese words, two solos for soprano, a duet, a comic trio, and an "Italian duet" which mercilessly mocked the operatic conventions of Bellini and Donizetti. With this work, Offenbach established himself at his new premises as firmly as he had with *Les Deux Aveugles* at the old.

Among Offenbach's other successes during the next few months were *Tromb-al-ca-zar, ou Les Criminels dramatiques* (Tromb-al-ca-zar, or The Theatrical Criminals, 1856), another absurd piece, this time about a theatrical touring company that is mistaken for a gang of bandits. It featured a fine cast of Pradeau, Léonce (another of Offenbach's staunchest performers), and Schneider. The melodies of two of the numbers—a song about a crocodile and another about a Bayonne ham—are familiar to modern audiences from the ballet score *Gaîté parisienne*, arranged by Manuel Rosenthal on music from various Offenbach stage works. Other themes too may seem vaguely familiar. One anticipates the galloping main theme of Franz von Suppé's *Light Cavalry* overture, another the duet "Love Changes Everything" from Andrew Lloyd Webber's *Aspects of Love*.

Later came *Le 66* (1856), about a peasant who believes he holds the winning number, 66, in a lottery, only to discover that he actually has 99. The following year saw *Croquefer, ou Le Dernier des paladins* (Croquefer, or The Last of the Paladins, 1857), in which Offenbach managed to get round the censor's restriction on the number of speaking characters (only four were allowed at the time) by adding a fifth character in the form of an "incomplete warrior" with one leg, one eye, and no tongue, who grunts his way through his musical number and conveys messages on bandanas. Once again, operatic conventions and themes—most particularly Meyerbeer's—were subjected to ridicule in a comic duet.

Offenbach always balanced the zanier works in an evening's programme with more sentimental pieces, such as *Une Demoiselle en loterie* (A Young Lady Raffled, 1857), in which a former circus bareback rider puts herself up as the prize in a lottery. In similar vein was *Le Mariage aux lanternes* (Marriage by Lantern Light, 1857), a refurbishment of *Le Trésor à Mathurin* with new numbers that included a show-stopping duet for two quarrelling widows. Another important constituent of Offenbach's one-act repertory was the military operetta, exemplified by *Dragonette* (1857), in which, by posing as her soldier twin, the young woman of the title saves her brother from being posted as a deserter. Léonce had one of his drag roles as an army canteen woman.

Though Offenbach's music dominated the productions of the Bouffes, other composers were featured too. In 1856, for instance, Adolphe Adam contributed *Les Pantins de Violette* (Violette's Puppets). Not least the young Léo Delibes (1836–91), having contributed *Deux sous de charbon* (Two Pieces of Charcoal, 1856) to Hervé's Folies-Nouvelles (with Hervé as a character deflected from suicide by a surprise legacy), then found at the Bouffes-Parisiens a stage for his one-act *Deux Vieilles Gardes* (Two Old Nurses, 1856), *Six demoiselles à marier* (Six Girls for Marriage, 1856), *L'Omelette à la Follembuche* (The Follembuche Omelette, 1859), and *Le Serpent à plumes* (The Plumed Serpent, 1864).

Offenbach also swelled the repertory with adaptations of light operatic pieces such as Mozart's *Der Schauspieldirektor* (The Impresario, 1786) and Rossini's *Il Signor Bruschino* (1813). In addition, in 1856, he announced a competition to produce new works from new composers. The contestants were required to set a libretto by Léon Battu (1828–57) and Ludovic Halévy entitled *Le Docteur Miracle*. The joint winners were the twenty-four-year-old Charles Lecocq (1832–1918) and the eighteen-year-old Georges Bizet (1838–75), whose winning versions alternated for a time in the repertory of the Bouffes-Parisiens. Bizet went on to compose the most celebrated French opera of all, *Carmen* (1875), while Lecocq in due course became Offenbach's principal successor in Parisian operetta. Lecocq's setting of *Le Docteur Miracle* follows the operetta conventions of its time more closely, while Bizet's demonstrates a more adventurous spirit.

Having established itself as a recognisable form of popular entertainment, the one-act operetta began to take off in 1858 when Offenbach succeeded in getting the licensing restrictions on the number of performers lifted. The event was celebrated most immediately in the one-act *Mesdames de la Halle* (Ladies of the Market, 1858), in which Offenbach finally enjoyed the luxury of a full chorus and a larger number of characters. His highly colourful piece was set in Paris's main vegetable market, and three of the female market traders were played by Offenbach's leading male comedians—Léonce, Désiré, and Mesmacre. Désiré, whom we have met already as Hervé's Sancho Panza, was one of those performers whose mere appearance was good for a laugh—short in stature and almost as broad as he was tall. The cast also included one of Offenbach's military characters, Drum-Major Raflafla. He and the market woman played by Léonce turn out to be the parents of the heroine Ciboulette, who is finally married to the hero, played by a woman in trousers! The music of *Mesdames de la Halle* is rousing and tuneful, and it too reappears in the ballet score *Gaîté parisienne*.

The removal of the licensing restriction also enabled Offenbach to provide sufficiently varied characterisation to venture into full-length, two-act works. Thus, seven and a half months after *Mesdames de la Halle* came the work with which Offenbach's name is perhaps above all associated: *Orphée aux enfers* (Orpheus in Hell, 1858). *Orphée* is significant not only for venturing beyond the single-act form but for the nature and sharpness of its satirical thrust. This was no idle piece of madcap humour but an unabashed ridiculing of one of the classic legends of mythology that were much revered at the time.

In the myth, Orpheus truly loves Eurydice and is committing an act of genuine self-denial in refraining from turning to look at her as he leads her from the underworld. By contrast, in Offenbach's satire, Orpheus and Eurydice are thoroughly sick of each other. Not only does Orpheus have his own lovers, but Eurydice is being courted by the shepherd Aristaeus who is really the god Pluto in disguise. Offenbach's Orpheus is forced to seek out his wife solely for the sake of public opinion and to satisfy the legend. He would never have turned round if Jupiter hadn't exploded a thunderbolt immediately behind him.

Such reversals of the traditional story abound in this *opéra-bouffe*. Offenbach's musical fun included quoting "J'ai perdu mon Eurydice" from Gluck's revered opera *Orphée et Eurydice* and, more daringly, to represent the revolt of the gods, the "Marseillaise," which was banned during the Second Empire because of its subversive connotations. Although these in-jokes may have appealed to Paris audiences, what gave the score universal and eternal fame was the "infernal galop" —the can-can—that the gods danced in Hell. Other numbers in the piece include a charming violin solo (the creator of Orpheus, Tayau, having been a proficient violinist) that is the centrepiece of the famous overture. As it happens, this

Bache as John Styx and Lise Tautin as Eurydice in Offenbach's
Orphée aux enfers, from a lithograph sheet-music cover
Author's collection

overture was not composed by Offenbach himself but put together by the conductor Carl Binder (1816–60) for the Viennese production, titled *Orpheus in der
Unterwelt,* from which derives the standard, bowdlerised English title "Orpheus
in the Underworld."

The female lead in *Orphée aux enfers* was played by the diminutive Lise
Tautin, while Offenbach's two comics Léonce and Désiré took the parts of her
lover Aristaeus/Pluto and the lecherous Jupiter, respectively. At one point Jupiter
disguises himself as a fly in order to gain access to Eurydice's boudoir and rav-
ish her—a scene that must have been all the more effective for the plump
Désiré's comic appearance. Another key role is Public Opinion, a kind of Greek
chorus who comments on the action and forces Orpheus to keep to the legend for
the sake of posterity. One of the oddest aspects of *Orphée aux enfers* is the underworld character of John Styx, who sings his otherworldly "Quand j'étais roi de

Béotie" (When I was King of the Boeotians). The part was created by Bache, an eccentric actor described as "tall and thin, with an ascetic air," whom Offenbach knew from his days at the Comédie-Française.

With its first evening-length production, the Bouffes-Parisiens hit the jackpot. *Orphée aux enfers* ran for 228 performances, an unprecedented run for that time. The operetta had entered a significant new phase of its growth, developing into a full-length work. Offenbach never fully abandoned one-act works, and for a while they continued to be his prime output. Increasingly, however, they were overshadowed by his full-length pieces. After the success of *Orphée,* Offenbach tried another satire of antiquity, this time a story from the crusades. But even though *Geneviève de Brabant* (1859) starred Tautin, Léonce, and Désiré, it was only a modest success. Nonetheless, Offenbach's stature was by now such that in 1860 he fulfilled commissions from both the Opéra and the Opéra-Comique. For the Opéra he wrote a ballet, *Le Papillon* (The Butterfly), whose "Valse des rayons" (Waltz of the sunbeams) owes its lasting familiarity to having been used by the Théâtre du Moulin Rouge in 1906 as an apache dance (a high-spirited dance, performed by two Parisian underworld characters). For the Opéra-Comique, Offenbach provided the three-act *Barkouf,* whose title character was a dog. The opera too proved a "dog."

On his own, less exalted territory, Offenbach continued to prosper. In January 1861 the Bouffes-Parisiens staged the sentimental *La Chanson de Fortunio* (Fortunio's Song), built around a song that Offenbach had composed ten years earlier for a Comédie-Française production of Alfred de Musset's *Le Chandelier* (The Candlestick, 1851). In it a young man is infatuated with an older woman, who uses him to divert attention from a more serious affair. Years later the play would be the basis for an opera by André Messager, but, for Offenbach's one-act piece, librettists Hector Crémieux and Halévy created a spin-off, in which the song became a sort of musical love potion which caused women to fall in love with the singer.

Then came another evening-length concept with *Le Pont des Soupirs* (The Bridge of Sighs, 1861). Désiré played the Doge of Venice, Bache his servant, and Tautin the Doge's wife Caterina, with the soubrette Lucille Tostée showing off her shapely legs as the page boy Amoroso. The story was set in fourteenth-century Venice and involved much serenading beneath balconies, a fair amount of cuckolding, some absurd disguises, bodies hidden in grandfather clocks, and a hilarious scene featuring Venice's notorious Council of Ten. The most enduring single number was Amoroso's serenade to Caterina in Act 1. In 1919 it achieved renewed success as "Lieblichste aller Frauen" in a German Offenbach pastiche, *Der Gold-schmied von Toledo* (The Goldsmith of Toledo).

For sheer impudence neither *La Chanson de Fortunio* nor *Le Pont des Soupirs* matched their one-act successor, *M. Choufleuri restera chez lui le . . .* (Mr. Cauli-flower Will Be at Home on . . . , 1861). This achieved its première at a gala private soirée in the unlikely surroundings of Paris's Palais-Bourbon, home of the Na-tional Assembly. Offenbach had long been friendly with the comte (later duc) de Morny, illegitimate son of Queen Hortense and half-brother of Napoléon III. The count was himself an amateur composer under the pen name of St. Rémy, and his *Mari sans le savoir* (Husband Without Knowing It, 1860) had already been produced at the Bouffes-Parisiens. *M. Choufleuri restera chez lui le . . .* was con-ceived by Morny and then developed by Offenbach and his regular team of col-laborators into a masterpiece of musical buffoonery. It revolves around the attempts of the culturally ignorant but newly wealthy Choufleuri to gain recognition in Paris by giving a grand soirée. He has invited ministers, ambassadors, and anyone who is anything in Paris to hear a concert performed by the celebrated (real-life) singers Sontag, Rubini, and Tamburini. Tragedy strikes when a message arrives that all three have suddenly become indisposed. The occasion is saved by Chou-fleuri's daughter Ernestine (Tautin), who impersonates Sontag, while her com-poser lover Babylas takes the place of Rubini, and Choufleuri himself (the ro-tund Désiré) stands in for the notoriously rotund Tamburini. The impersonation is successful, and Choufleuri rewards Babylas with his daughter's hand. Along the way Offenbach provides hilarious musical fun, including quotations from Mozart and, above all, a mock Italian trio in which the three impersonators parody the mad scene from Donizetti's *Lucia di Lammermoor* in absurd pseudo-Italian.

Some of Offenbach's works were tried out at the summer theatre at Bad Ems, a German spa near Mainz whose waters were not only deemed advantageous for Offenbach's gout but attracted the wealthy of many nations. There, in the summer of 1862, Offenbach staged an adaptation of a 1624 Cervantes comedy, *Los habladores,* about a pair of incessant gossips. The work was produced that same autumn in Vienna before finally reaching the Théâtre des Bouffes-Parisiens in Paris in early 1863 as *Les Bavards* (The Gossips).

Passing through Bad Ems again in the summer of 1863, Offenbach was challenged to compose and produce an operetta within a week. Paul Boisselot (1829–1905), known primarily as an actor, provided him with a slight sketch en-titled *Lischen et Fritzchen* about a young couple who meet while both are return-ing from Paris to their native Alsace. Their pleasure at discovering that they are both Alsatian is nothing compared with their eventual discovery that they are long-lost siblings. Their initial meeting is charmingly captured in a duet "Je suis alsacienne," whose melody has again remained familiar through the ballet *Gaîté parisienne*. In terms of Offenbach's career, the piece was significant for introducing a young singer named Zulma Bouffar, who was to be one of his two most important female interpreters.

Offenbach's works had also become big business in Vienna, which from now on he was to see as a second field of campaign. His venture bore fruit with a grand romantic opera, *Die Rheinnixen* (The Rhine Nymphs, 1864), for the Court Opera. From it came the "Goblins' Song," which was later turned into the immortal barcarolle in *Les Contes d'Hoffmann* (1881). At the same time, in Paris, he was on the point of breaking with the Bouffes-Parisiens, making complex plans with the Théâtre des Variétés and a new writing partnership for a work that was to lead to a new phase of productivity and theatrical domination.

As operetta librettists, Henri Meilhac (1831–97) and Ludovic Halévy were to prove unchallenged. Moreover, not only did they write the best original operetta libretti but they produced "straight" comedies that were fruitful sources for later operettas, including Strauss's *Die Fledermaus* and Lehár's *Die lustige Witwe* (The Merry Widow). That they also wrote the libretto of Bizet's *Carmen* highlights their mastery. Meilhac was essentially the ideas man, sketching out the plot and the principal scenes, while Halévy was primarily responsible (as he already had been so often for Offenbach) for the lyrics. The dialogue tended to be a joint effort.

Where *Orphée aux enfers* had mocked the classical mythology of Orpheus and Eurydice, *La Belle Hélène* (1864) did something similar for the story of Helen of Troy. Venus has promised the shepherd Pâris (who happens to be the son of King Priam of Troy in disguise) the most beautiful woman on earth for his wife. By common consent, this is Helen, Queen of Sparta and wife of the decidedly dull King Menelaus. For a time Menelaus's fellow kings of Greece—Agamemnon (King of Kings), Achilles (of Phtiotis), and the two Ajaxes (of Salamis and the Locrians)—prevent her from giving in to Pâris's advances, but finally the High Priest Calchas conspires to ensure that she does just that while convincing herself that it is all just a dream. When what has happened is revealed, the kings duly vow to avenge the affront to Menelaus by launching the Trojan War.

To support Hortense Schneider in the title role, the Variétés provided a fine cast, led by the Pâris of José Dupuis, a splendid character actor and singer, along with a formidable team of comedians. Eugène Grenier, who played the read-

Henri Meilhac (right) and Ludovic Halévy in 1865
Author's collection

ily bribable Calchas, was celebrated for his "lump of gristle that served as a nose" and his "bones so brittle that he might break an arm or a leg almost without noticing it." Jean Kopp established in Menelaus a prototype of the Offenbachian henpecked husband, while Henri Couder made much of the less prominent role of Agamemnon. Meilhac and Halévy used this gallery of actors to create a rich vein of comic situations. The charades in Act 1 and the boardgame of Goose in Act 2 were clear allusions to the entertainments of the house parties Napoléon III held every year at Compiègne. Likewise, the gathering of crowned heads at Nauplia in Act 3 mirrored the real-life Second Empire summer gatherings at Biarritz. Yet the piece remains enjoyable today even without the topicality that gave extra weight at the time. The monocled boulevard dandy (Agamemnon's son Orestes) and the bribable public official (Calchas) are still recognisable.

If *La Belle Hélène* did not provide a single number to match the overwhelming popularity of the can-can from *Orphée aux enfers,* it is in almost every respect a superior work. Its libretto is far more "of a piece" and more naturally witty, while Offenbach's music displays not only a more consistent level of inspiration but a finer sense of structure and greater depth of invention. Above all, the solo numbers for Schneider ("Amours divins!" in Act 1, "Dis-moi, Vénus" in Act 2) make every note tell, with words and music lying perfectly on the voice.

José Dupuis as Pâris in Offenbach's *La Belle Hélène*
Copyright Collection Viollet/Roger-Viollet, Paris

Dupuis, too, rejoiced in "Au mont Ida trois déesses," with its "Evohé" refrain that made ideal use of his glorious head-voice. And has there ever been a more beautiful waltz than that sung with deliberate incongruity to the words "un vile séducteur"? In *La Belle Hélène*, Offenbach's music and Halévy's lyrics are throughout used to delightfully humorous effect. There are the couplets in which the gods introduce themselves with chopped-up syllables, culminating in Menelaus's "Je suis l'époux de la reine, poux de la reine, poux de la reine." A mock-operatic ensemble is built on the inane words "L'homme à la pomme," and the Patriotic Trio in Act 3 parodies a piece in Rossini's *Guillaume Tell*.

The Parisian public responded to *La Belle Hélène* with huge enthusiasm, raising Offenbach's reputation to yet a higher plane and making Schneider the darling of Paris. In Vienna, too, it went down well, after the score was modified to include various new numbers and a fine Viennese-style overture to replace the original brief orchestral prelude. To follow, Offenbach looked to the Middle Ages, just as he had after *Orphée aux enfers*. His collaborators came up with the somewhat gruesome subject of Bluebeard and his six wives; but in Offenbach's version the wives ultimately proved to have been merely put to sleep temporarily, thereby enabling the fun to be uninhibited. The title role in *Barbe-bleue* went to Dupuis, as did the best number in the score, his jaunty recital of his repeated bereavements, with its rousing refrain "Je suis Barbe-bleue ô gué! Jamais veuf ne fut plus gai" (I am Bluebeard, oh joy! Never was a widower happier). Schneider played Boulotte, a promiscuous peasant who becomes Bluebeard's sixth wife and in whom he finally meets his match. Henri Couder was Popolani, Bluebeard's alchemist, who gets rid of the wives when Bluebeard no longer needs them, while Jean Kopp was another henpecked King and Eugène Grenier a fawning court chamberlain.

Before 1866 was out, Offenbach and his new librettists had produced another, quite different, piece for the Théâtre du Palais-Royal. To entertain the visitors who were expected to throng to Paris for the Exposition of 1867, they came up with a five-act Paris travelogue, expanded from an earlier short Meilhac and Halévy piece. *La Vie parisienne* expounded the attractions of Paris and poked fun at foreign visitors, including a wealthy Brazilian and a Danish baron and baroness whose impatience to enjoy the pleasures of the city are exploited by a couple of hard-up men-about-town.

Such a full-scale operetta was a new venture for the Palais-Royal company of actors, most of whom had only a modest singing ability, and Offenbach made various stylistic concessions to accommodate them. In addition to importing Bouffar for the role of the Parisian glovemaker Gabrielle, he set the melodies mainly in the orchestra, thus lightening the burden on some suspect singing voices. And what melodies there were! *La Vie parisienne* is Offenbach's most consistently sparkling and tuneful score; its music later formed the core of the ballet score *Gaîté parisienne*. The highlight of Act 1 is the Brazilian's patter-song entrance number "Je suis Brésilien, j'ai de l'or," while the final act contains the delicious slow waltz-rondo of the courtesan Metella, "A minuit sonnant commence la fête." Perhaps the climax of the whole evening is the riotous party at which, in order to divert the Swedish baron so he can pay court to the baroness, Gardefeu stages a glamorous soirée with the servants at his aunt's house posing as Society guests. Bobinet, dressed up as a Swiss admiral (Switzerland being in reality landlocked!), splits his costume, inspiring one of Offenbach's mock-operatic ensembles around the phrase "Votre habit a craqué dans le dot" (Your costume has split down the back). The excitement builds up to a marvellous climax with another famous can-can.

The exhibition season featured yet another success from the Offenbach-Meilhac-Halévy team at the Variétés. *La Grande-Duchesse de Gérolstein* (1867) was a military satire built around the character of the youthful Grand Duchess of a mythical German grand duchy. Her passion for a young soldier named Fritz causes her to promote him to higher and higher ranks before she finally realises that she won't be able to prise him from his sweetheart, Wanda. "Ah, que j'aime les militaires!" sang Schneider in the role of the Grand Duchess, while Dupuis played the naive soldier at whom she sets her cap. There was the usual bevy of baritone character parts, including Couder as the swaggering General Boum, whose rank the Grand Duchess hands over to Fritz in her pursuit of the young man's favours. The real crowned heads who flocked to Paris for the Exposition paid homage at the court of the mythical Grand Duchess in the person of Hortense Schneider, and the visiting public as a whole found the piece irresistible. This exposure to visitors of various nationalities created an international demand for both the work and Schneider herself. Productions in London and New York followed, giving Offenbach a greater popularity in the English-speaking world than he had ever known.

In Paris itself, Offenbach's success led to another commission for the Théâtre de l'Opéra-Comique, which he fulfilled with *Robinson Crusoé* (1867). This was based on the British pantomime version of Defoe's story and mixed some typically Offenbachian humour into a score that was more substantial than that of a typical opéra-bouffe. There was a swirling waltz for the soprano and a superb aria for Man Friday, played by the mezzo-soprano Célestine Galli-Marié, the future creator of Carmen. Several of its melodies also found their way into the ballet *Gaîté parisienne*. Also in 1867 the tiny Théâtre des Menus-Plaisirs produced a substantially revised version of *Geneviève de Brabant,* whose new numbers included a song that achieved fame throughout the British Empire as the

Hortense Schneider in Offenbach's
La Grande-Duchesse de Gérolstein
Author's collection

"Gendarmes' Duet," as well as becoming celebrated in the United States as the Marine Hymn.

For a new work for the Variétés, Meilhac and Halévy now came up with *La Périchole* (1868), a piece that was less satirical and suggestive, more sentimental than usual. Schneider and Dupuis played a pair of Peruvian street-singers, and Schneider had enduring numbers in the Letter Song "O mon cher amant" and the solo "Ah! que les hommes sont bêtes" in which she denounces all men. Grenier was Don Andrès de Ribeira, viceroy of Peru, who thinks to go around Lima incognito, even though everyone knows full well who he is. He was especially effective in a waltz rondo about recalcitrant husbands, in which Halévy and Offenbach once again practised their trick of chopping up words into constituent phrases:

Aux maris ré,
Aux maris cal,
Aux maris ci,
Aux maris trants,
Aux maris récalcitrants.

Offenbach's success was such that he was now producing works at a hectic pace for a range of theatres. *Le Château à Toto* (Toto's Castle, 1868), a follow up to *La Vie parisienne* for the Palais-Royal, was a flop, as was *La Diva* (1869) at the Bouffes-Parisiens, despite a Meilhac and Halévy libretto and a semi-autobiographical role for Schneider. More successful at the Bouffes-Parisiens was *La Princesse de Trébizonde* (1869), whose young lead, Céline Chaumont, made the most of a negligible voice as a female juggler who poses as a wax figure of a princess and falls in love with a real prince. For the Opéra-Comique there was *Vert-Vert* (1869), about a young man forced to take the place of a dead parrot as mascot at a girls' school.

The one full-length work of 1869 that fully maintained Offenbach's reputation was *Les Brigands,* another Meilhac and Halévy collaboration for the Variétés. In the romantic robber tradition of Auber's *Fra Diavolo,* it was set on the (nonexistent) border of Spain and Italy. The score included excellent numbers for the bandit chief Falsacappa (Dupuis) and another for the young farmer Fragoletto, intended for Schneider but ultimately played by Bouffar. Kopp was Falsacappa's second-in-command Pietro, and there was a cameo role for Léonce as the Duke of Mantua's corrupt treasurer, whose witty claim was that "one must steal according to the position one occupies in society." The piece also introduced a talented new comic, Baron, as the leader of a bunch of comic carabinieri who always arrive too late to make an arrest.

Offenbach had been far from alone as composer of such light theatrical entertainments over the previous fifteen years. Indeed, the success of his full-length works at the end of the 1860s was almost matched by that of Hervé's satirical works such as *L'Oeil crevé* (The Pierced Eye, 1867), *Chilpéric* (1868), and *Le Petit Faust* (1869). The Opéra-Comique, too, produced other works that were close to what we would now classify as operetta, notably *Le Voyage en Chine* (The Journey to China, 1865), with a book co-written by the playwright Eugène Labiche (1815–88) and a score by François Bazin (1816–78) that was distinguished by an exhilarating bolero. Delibes's operetta career culminated in 1869 in the three-act *La Cour du Roi Pétaud* (The Court of King Pétaud), which bridged the gap be-

Caricature by André Gill of Hervé when starring in his *Chilpéric,*
from *L'Eclipse* (8 November 1868)
Copyright Collection Viollet/Roger-Viollet, Paris

tween *La Périchole* and *Les Brigands* at the Variétés and had Bouffar in its cast.
And Charles Lecocq, joint winner with Bizet of Offenbach's operetta competition,
had an early success with *Fleur-de-Thé* (1868), a "Chinese" piece with Offenbach's
two comedians Désiré and Léonce in the cast.

Yet, although these other composers prospered, they remained very much
in the shadow of Offenbach's perpetual inventiveness. It was Offenbach who, in
the fifteen years from 1855 to 1870, established a recognisably new style of theatrical entertainment that was to take the general name of "operetta." It is Offenbach,
too, whose works are still frequently revived in theatres and opera houses around
the world. And it was Offenbach who was setting the tone for popular musical
theatre in 1870, when all entertainment in Paris was abruptly halted by the outbreak of the Franco-Prussian War.

Chapter Two
Third Republic Paris

The Franco-Prussian War destroyed the French Second Empire and left the French capital in a state of political and cultural shock. A way of life had gone for ever, and frivolity and gaiety were never again as unrestrained as they had been under the old regime. Now, it appeared, something a little more substantial, a little more romantic was wanted from the musical theatre.

In spite of his German origins, it was still to Offenbach that the public turned first. His old favourites were revived; but now he also sought to retain his audience with a variety of new productions. *Le Roi Carotte* (King Carrot, 1872) was produced at the Théâtre de la Gaîté, which specialised in *féeries*, which we

The poster for Offenbach's *Le Roi Carotte,* from
Le Théâtre (1 September 1904)
Author's collection

would call "spectaculars" or "extravaganzas." But the piece was not all froth: the libretto by Victorien Sardou satirised the folly of idealistic governments in much the same way Gilbert and Sullivan later did in *The Gondoliers.* In line with the policy of the Gaîté, the piece contained a substantial number of scenes, and Offenbach not only provided a large-scale ballet but scored for a much larger orchestra than for the Bouffes-Parisiens or the Variétés. Not least of its attractions was Offenbach's newest leading lady, Anna Judic, whom he had imported from the Eldorado café-concert, where she had come to prominence in the short operettas that were part of an evening's fare.

Meanwhile, *Fantasio* appeared at the Théâtre de l'Opéra-Comique just three days after *Le Roi Carotte.* But not even an established play by the respected Alfred de Musset and the presence of famed mezzo-soprano Célestine Galli-Marié in the leading role (en travesti) were enough to win Offenbach acceptance in serious opera circles. On the other hand, the Théâtre de la Renaissance achieved something like the old Offenbach success with *La Jolie Parfumeuse* (The Pretty Perfumier, 1873). It told of a rich financier's attempt to seduce a newly married woman on her wedding night. Only after much confusion and mistaken identities does the financier's mistress restore the young lady to her husband and marry the financier herself. If Offenbach's music sparkled less consistently than in earlier days, the Parisian public was much taken by the sight of another recruit from the music halls, Louise Théo, starring in various states of dress and undress.

The Théâtre de la Renaissance enjoyed another success with *Madame l'Archiduc* (Madame Archduke, 1874), in which Anna Judic played a hotel worker to whom an Archduke cedes his position in the hope of seducing her. The "Alphabet Sextet" was the big hit. Meanwhile, at the Variétés, *La Vie parisienne* was revived in 1873 with José Dupuis as the Baron de Gondremark, and in the following year a refurbished *La Périchole,* with a whole new act, was put on. This is the form in which we know the work today; it includes "Tu n'es pas beau, tu n'es pas riche," which was the last of the exquisitely shaped songs that Offenbach composed for Hortense Schneider and that rank among the highlights of his musical output.

Henri Meilhac and Ludovic Halévy collaborated with Offenbach again on *La Boulangère a des écus* (The Baker-Woman Has Money, 1875). The piece was designed for Schneider, but the temperamental diva was replaced shortly before the première. It still enjoyed some success with her replacement, Marie Aimée, as a baker who has become rich by dabbling in stocks and shares. The cast also included Dupuis as a hairdresser and Paola Marié, younger sister of Célestine Galli-Marié, as his sweetheart the barkeeper, as well as Offenbach stalwarts Jean Berthelier and Léonce as a pair of comic constables. The run was prolonged when Offenbach added a new role and some extra numbers for the great café-concert performer Thérésa. But it proved the last work on which the three master creators of operetta were to work together.

Offenbach had now taken over the management of the Théâtre de la Gaîté, with the intention of staging expanded versions of earlier successes in the spectacular féerie style. For the revised *Orphée aux enfers* (1874), the four original scenes were turned into four full-length acts, with three interpolated ballets. Several new pieces were added, and the chorus now numbered 120 and the corps de ballet 60. Its success was considerable; but it was also expensive. Offenbach could not keep up this standard of production, although he tried, first with a Sardou play, *La Haine* (Hate, 1874), for which he wrote incidental music, then with a further revised *Geneviève de Brabant* (1875) and the spectacular new *Voyage dans*

Poster by Jules Chéret for the 1874 revival of
Offenbach's *Orphée aux enfers*
Bibliothèque et Musée de l'Opéra,
Bibliothèque Nationale de France, Paris

la lune (The Journey to the Moon, 1875). This last had Zulma Bouffar in trousers as a lunar voyager in a piece inspired by Jules Verne's novel *De la terre à la lune* (From the Earth to the Moon). By now deep in debt (owing to losses suffered on the productions), Offenbach was forced to sell his interest in the theatre and undertake a variety of money-making projects, including a concert tour of the United States in 1876.

Offenbach's financial plight also meant that he was composing for as many theatres as would take his works. Inevitably, he began spreading his genius too thin. At the Bouffes-Parisiens, *La Créole* (1875) came and went; even Judic's presence could not make a success of it. Less successful still was *Le Docteur Ox* (1877), a science-fiction piece which again hoped to capitalize on the public's fascination for the works of Jules Verne. Offenbach's run of modest successes suggested a composer who was played out, especially in comparison with the new French favourite, Charles Lecocq.

We recall that Lecocq had been one of the joint winners of Offenbach's Bouffes-Parisiens competition some twenty years earlier. He it was who now struck the mood of Third Republic audiences most securely, producing a series of operettas that rejected the frivolous 1860s opéra-bouffe style of Offenbach and Hervé in favour of more romantic works. Lecocq had been born in Paris to poor parents and studied at the conservatoire at the same time as Bizet and Camille Saint-Saëns. Crippled from childhood, he spent almost all his life on crutches, a fact that cut him off from close friendships and encouraged his determination to achieve success as a composer.

He had already had several opéras-bouffes staged during the 1860s, but none enjoyed much success until the oriental *Fleur-de-Thé* was produced in 1868. His career began to take off when the Parisian theatres were temporarily closed during the war, and he was commissioned to provide a new piece for the leading operetta theatre in Brussels, the Fantaisies-Parisiennes. He chose a libretto by his regular collaborators, Henri Chivot (1830–97) and Alfred Duru (1829–89). *Les Cent Vierges* (The Hundred Virgins, 1872) was a saucy tale about a colony of men in the South Seas who are sent a consignment of a hundred young women. Unfortunately, the ship is lost at sea, and a second batch is hastily assembled. In the rush to round up the women, two young sightseers, Gabrielle and Eglantine, are mistakenly included. In typical comic-opera style, their husbands disguise themselves among the women, who eventually arrive to provide relief for the colony's frustrated males. Inevitably, the husbands are assigned to the governor and his male secretary, and the situation becomes increasingly confused until the original group of women turns up and all the men are satisfied. Alfred Jolly, a veteran French operetta character actor, shone as Plupersonn, the governor of the colony; but Anna Van Ghell in the role of Gabrielle had most of the evening's big hits. Her nostalgic "O Paris, gai séjour" remains one of the great operetta waltz melodies, receiving appropriately prominent treatment in the ballet *Mam'zelle Angot,* which Gordon Jacob arranged from Lecocq's finest melodies.

Les Cent Vierges enjoyed tremendous international success, even after some of the more "immoral" aspects were toned down for English-speaking audiences. But its success was nothing compared with that enjoyed by Lecocq's next piece for the Fantaisies-Parisiennes. *La Fille de Madame Angot* (Madame Angot's Daughter, 1872) was based upon a series of plays by the dramatist Maillot (1747–1814). It

Lithograph sheet-music cover showing a scene from Lecocq's *La Fille de Madame Angot*
Copyright Collection Viollet/Roger-Viollet, Paris

concerns Clairette, the orphaned daughter of the celebrated Madame Angot, who falls for the dashing political poet Ange Pitou in preference to the adoring but uninspiring wig maker Pomponnet. In the course of the action, Clairette is arrested for singing one of Pitou's revolutionary songs and becomes involved with her friend Mademoiselle Lange's plot to overthrow the government. Eventually, Clairette realises that Ange Pitou and Mademoiselle Lange deserve each other and settles for the humble Pomponnet.

The role of Clairette was created by the young soprano Pauline Luigini, Jolly was Pomponnet, and the rising young star Marie Desclauzas played Mademoiselle Lange. The real delight of *La Fille de Madame Angot,* however, was Lecocq's score, whose melodies pour out in delightful, contrasting succession. Singling out Pitou's lilting admission of Clairette's charms (Certainement, j'aimais Clairette), Clairette's rousing "Chanson politique," and her quarrel duet with Mademoiselle

Lange is merely to scratch the surface. Particular effect was created in the Act 2 finale, one of the greatest scenes in all operetta. As government troops approach, the sotto voce "Chorus of Conspirators" gradually evolves into a swirling waltz, "Tournez, tournez," as Mademoiselle Lange leads the conspirators in a dance at a grand ball (the cover for their meeting). The success of *La Fille de Madame Angot* far surpassed that of anything Offenbach produced in the 1870s, and it has remained a classic of the French operetta repertory. Its melodies made up the bulk of the *Mam'zelle Angot* ballet score, based on the same story.

As if one title role were not enough for Luigini, in the next Lecocq work she created two. *Giroflé-Girofla* (1874) was more in the outrageous, suggestive vein of *Les Cent Vierges* than the historical mode of *La Fille de Madame Angot*. It tells of the twin sisters Giroflé and Girofla (both played by Luigini), daughters of Don Boléro (Jolly), the governor of a Spanish coastal province. Problems begin when Girofla is captured by pirates. Since both girls are due to enter into marriages of considerable pecuniary advantage to their father, Don Boléro prevails upon Giroflé to play the part of both sisters—and marry both husbands—until he and his wife can ransom Girofla from the pirates. If it is not quite as well endowed with extractable numbers as its predecessors, *Giroflé-Girofla* nonetheless has an agreeable score, in which the Act 2 quintet and Giroflé's Drinking Song stand out. And it was more than enough to confirm Lecocq as the new darling of the French musical theatre.

Following his three Brussels successes, Lecocq returned to Paris, where all three works had been equally well received. But he had no great success with either the historical *Les Prés Saint-Gervais* (1874) at the Variétés or the bandit-piece *Le Pompon* (The Tassel, 1875) at the Folies-Dramatiques. Much better received was a piece for the Théâtre de la Renaissance, where Jeanne Granier had risen to stardom in *Giroflé-Girofla*. Originally spotted by Offenbach, Granier was brought to the Renaissance in his *Jolie Parfumeuse*. She was now to become as closely associated with Lecocq as Hortense Schneider had been with Offenbach.

The first new work Lecocq composed for Granier was *La Petite Mariée* (The Little Bride, 1875). This was another piece that satisfied the public's taste for sexual titillation, in this case leaving them wondering what was—or was not—happening on the wedding night. The local magistrate Rodolpho, having caught his wife in flagrante delicto with his friend San Carlo, has vowed to cuckold San Carlo in return as soon as the latter marries. Hence the need for San Carlo to keep secret from the magistrate the fact that he is about to take a "little bride," Graziella (Granier). The ensuing complications kept the public agreeably entertained through two acts. Lecocq's numbers for Granier included the sprightly Act 1 "Je tenais, monsieur mon époux," in which she simultaneously showed off her wedding dress and her figure.

Lecocq struck gold again with *Le Petit Duc* (1878), in which—for the first time—he set a libretto by Meilhac and Halévy. The masculine title role made no difference to the fact that the work was once more built around Granier. This time she was in trousers as the teenaged Duc de Parthenay, who for political reasons has been married to the even younger Blanche de Cambrai. Once again the audience's thoughts of what ought to happen on a wedding night were central to the entertainment; for, though obliged to marry, the two are deemed too young to consummate their union. Naturally, they manage it in the end, but only after three acts of improbable adventures. The delights of Lecocq's score include a tender Act 1 duet for the young couple, "C'est pourtant bien doux"; a catchy little chorus of pages, "Il a l'oreille basse"; the Act 2 singing lesson, "L'amour est le bien suprême"; and an ensemble "Pas de femmes" that recalls the conspirators' music of *La Fille de Madame Angot*. Blanche was played by another future star of the French operetta stage, Mily-Meyer, with Offenbach's old character actor Berthelier as the Duke's tutor Frimousse.

Two modest successes followed, both featuring former Offenbach favourites: *La Camargo* (1878), with Zulma Bouffar as the celebrated eighteenth-century ballet dancer of that name, and *Le Grand Casimir* (The Great Casimir, 1879), starring José Dupuis, Céline Chaumont, and Léonce. The Lecocq-Meilhac-Halévy team then produced *La Petite Mademoiselle* (1879), in which Granier found herself in a variety of disguises, and Mily-Meyer, Desclauzas, and Berthelier rounded out a distinguished cast. All the women had good numbers in a score that ranked among Lecocq's own favourites.

After a few works that added little to Lecocq's reputation, success came again with *Le Jour et la nuit* (The Day and the Night, 1881). Its farcical libretto of lust, liaisons, and mistaken identities was the work of Eugène Leterrier (1842–84) and Alfred Vanloo (1846–1920), who had already teamed up with Lecocq on *Giroflé-Girofla* and *La Petite Mariée*. Set in Portugal, it starred Marguerite Ugalde, fresh from creating the role of Nicklausse in Offenbach's *Les Contes d'Hoffmann*. Jules Brasseur, the original Brazilian, Frick, and Prosper of Offenbach's *La Vie parisienne*, played the Portuguese prime minister, Prince Picratès de Calabazas. In a delightfully tuneful score, he had the major hit number, the rhythmically invigorating "Les Portugais sont toujours gais," a piece that also found its way into the ballet score *Mam'zelle Angot*.

Charles Lecocq in old age
Author's collection

Another fair success was *Le Coeur et la main* (The Heart and the Hand, 1882), with Berthelier heading a strong team of male comics. Perhaps, though, the piece sought too obviously to follow its predecessor, for its setting was again the Iberian Peninsula. Nor did it have the same appeal in its female characters or the same tunefulness of score. *La Princesse des Canaries* (The Princess of the Canary Islands, 1883) enjoyed the benefit of a cast headed by husband-and-wife actors Juliette Simon-Girard and Simon-Max; but it represented the start of a sharp decline in Lecocq's fortunes. He went on composing for almost thirty years, but without achieving anything more of note. He had, however, won a place among classical French operetta composers surpassed only by that of Offenbach himself.

For all its popularity, however, *La Fille de Madame Angot* was only the second-most-successful French operetta of the 1870s. The hit of the decade was written by a young new entrant to the musical theatre, Robert Planquette (1848–1903). A native of Normandy, he studied at the Paris Conservatoire, but found its formalities not altogether to his taste. He preferred composing for the cafés-concerts of Paris. It was in one of these that baritone Lucien Fugère, later an opera star, introduced Planquette's immensely successful march "Le Régiment de Sambre et Meuse" in 1867. For the next decade, Planquette composed a number of one-act operettas for the cafés-concerts. Louis Cantin, manager of the Théâtre des Folies-Dramatiques, finally gave him the opportunity to compose a full-length score, and in *Les Cloches de Corneville* (The Bells of Corneville, 1877), he succeeded beyond anyone's dreams in capturing the public with a romantic story reminiscent of Boieldieu's *La Dame Blanche*. *Les Cloches de Corneville* made a refreshing change from the farcical and suggestive Parisian operettas that had held the stage for so long.

Set in Normandy, the operetta concerns the search for the rightful owner of a manor in the village of Corneville, complicated by the efforts of Gaspard, the steward, to frighten him off by pretending the house is haunted. The Marquis Henri de Corneville enters to a tremendously effective rondeau-valse, "J'ai fait trois fois le tour du monde," in which he tells of the travels from which he has just returned. The greatest impact of the piece was achieved in the "Legend of the Bells," with its refrain "Digue-digue-digue, digue-digue-don," first introduced by Germaine, Gaspard's ward, and liberally reprised throughout the score. Other musical highlights include the Chorus of Servants, which employs a double chorus, in which the two themes are first sung separately and then combined contrapuntally. Not the least pleasing aspects of the production for the original audiences were the performances of the young tenor Simon-Max as Germaine's intended, Grenicheux (with his barcarolle "Va, petite mousse"), and the even younger Juliette Girard as the maid Serpolette. The two married soon afterward and for many years were among Paris's most popular theatre couples.

Les Cloches de Corneville went on to conquer the world and made Planquette's name and fortune, but it was some time before he followed it up with a similar success. Even with Jeanne Granier in the cast, *Les Voltigeurs de la 32ème* (The Light Infantrymen of the 32nd Regiment, 1880) did no great business at the Renaissance in Paris, while *La Cantinière* (The Canteen Girl, 1880) fared no better at the Nouveautés. But then, in the wake of the extraordinary international success of *Les Cloches,* Planquette received a commission to compose a piece for London's Comedy Theatre.

Rip Van Winkle (1882) was an adaptation of Washington Irving's story, with an English libretto by H. B. Farnie based on a French outline by Henri Meilhac and Philippe Gille. It began an exceptionally long run at the Comedy and had an international success that threatened to rival that of *Les Cloches*. Paris saw a heavily rewritten version under the simplified title of *Rip!* in 1884, with Simon-Max and Mily-Meyer. In its French form, the operetta has remained familiar for such numbers as the duet "Aux montagnes de Katskill," Rip's "Vive la paresse!" (added for the French version), his Act 2 Echo Song, and his Drinking Song.

Planquette continued to play the cross-Channel game for some years. London's *Nell Gwynne* (1884) became Paris's *La Princesse Colombine* (1886); even *Les Voltigeurs de la 32ème* was refurbished for London in 1887 as *The Old Guard*. Most successful of these international pieces was a sturdy seafaring operetta which began in Paris as *Surcouf* (1887) and was remodelled for London as *Paul Jones* (1889). Planquette's works graced both French and British stages for many years, but none achieved lasting success. Ultimately, it is on *Les Cloches de Corneville* and, to a lesser extent, *Rip!* that his reputation rests.

As a follow-up to *Les Cloches,* the Théâtre des Folies-Dramatiques turned —somewhat surprisingly—not to Planquette but to the old master, Jacques Offenbach, who used the opportunity to score two of the biggest successes of his later career. *Madame Favart* (1878) featured a book by Chivot and Duru that built an imaginary plot of intrigue and disguise around the real-life actress Justine Favart. The score forswore the frothy texture of Offenbach's earlier opéras-bouffes in favour of something more sturdily opéra-comique. Much of its success was due to the young Simon-Girard as Justine Favart and Simon-Max as Hector de Boispréau, whom Favart helps win a police appointment. The show's two hundred performances represented a considerable achievement for the day.

To prove that *Madame Favart* was no flash in the pan, Offenbach next provided the Folies-Dramatiques with *La Fille du Tambour-Major* (The Drum-Major's Daughter, 1879), which was even more successful than its predecessor. Once again the book was by Chivot and Duru, and its military colour recalled Donizetti's *La Fille du régiment* (1840). The book appealed to nationalistic loyalties in a story set during the French campaign to liberate northern Italy from Austro-Hungary. Juliette Simon-Girard once again had the title role, Stella, and Simon-Max was the love-sick soldier Griolet. Rounding off a remarkable family complement, Simon-Girard's mother, Caroline Girard, took the part of Stella's mother, the Duchesse della Volta. Stella's defiant military song "Petit Français" and the officers' "C'est un billet de logement" linger in the memory from a work that continues to be staged in France.

Offenbach's comeback was all the more remarkable for the fact that these two scores were composed while he was busy with his most ambitious attempt to appeal to serious opera lovers. With the posthumously produced *Les Contes d'Hoffmann* (The Tales of Hoffmann, 1881), Offenbach finally fulfilled his grand-opera ambitions. On a bigger scale than anything he composed for the popular

Act 3 of the 1911 Théâtre Apollo revival of Offenbach's *Madame Favart*
Author's collection

theatre, the opera nonetheless has individual passages that would have been at home in any of his operettas—most obviously, the comic couplets for the servant Frantz. That Offenbach ended his career with two great operetta successes and one of the classics of the opera repertory demonstrates his superiority to all rivals during his quarter-century in the musical theatre.

The one composer who could be said to challenge Offenbach's durability was his old rival Hervé. Having anticipated Offenbach's developments during the 1850s, he had responded during the 1860s with *L'Oeil Crevé, Chilpéric,* and *Le Petit Faust.* At the end of the 1870s, he emerged again, having in the intervening years pursued a comfortable existence on both sides of the Channel, with homes in Paris and London and a wife and family in each. Now he became involved in a series of works by different composers for the Théâtre des Variétés that showed off the talents of Anna Judic, the café-concert singer Offenbach had brought into the musical theatre for *Le Roi Carotte.* Styled *vaudeville-opérette* or *comédie-*

vaudeville, these pieces were a cross between fully-fledged operetta and "straight" comedy with interpolated songs.

The first, *Niniche* (1878), had a slight score by the theatre's musical director, Marius Boullard (1842–91); its main attraction was Judic in a bathing suit, a sight that shocked and excited the public. Hervé was brought in as composer for its successor, *La Femme à Papa* (Daddy's Wife, 1879). José Dupuis played not only the Daddy whose wife Judic was intended to become but also the son she actually married. The next piece was *La Roussotte* (The Redhead, 1881), on whose book Meilhac and Halévy collaborated with Albert Millaud. The score was originally assigned to Lecocq but was completed by Hervé and Boullard. Hervé was sole composer again for *Lili* (1882), in which Judic was required to age forty years, and also for the most significant of the series, *Mam'zelle Nitouche* (Miss Innocence, 1883).

The story might have been based on Hervé's own career, for it told of a convent music teacher, Célestin (played by Baron, erstwhile leader of the carabiniers in Offenbach's *Les Brigands*), who composes somewhat naughty operettas in his spare time. This secret is discovered by his young student Denise de Flavigny (Judic), who contrives to accompany him to the theatre for a first night. There she falls for a handsome young soldier, finds herself performing in the operetta, and is arrested climbing out a window. She is taken to the barracks, disguises herself as a soldier, and finally sneaks Célestin back into the convent, where she contrives a credible story for the Mother Superior. Now contrite, she vows to become a nun—until she discovers that her father has chosen the handsome soldier to be her husband. Hervé had always specialised less in Offenbachian ensembles than in catchy songs and duets, and here he came fully into his own. His simple but tuneful songs, alternately gentle, spirited, and comic, sometimes as much spoken as sung, brought him his most enduring success in the musical theatre. *Mam'zelle Nitouche* is still frequently performed in France.

But Offenbach, Hervé, Lecocq, and Planquette were not the only talents on the scene: Judic's first big break had come in a work composed by Léon Vasseur (1844–1917), who had started out as an organist in Paris. Turning to operetta, he immediately had an enormous success at the Théâtre des Bouffes-Parisiens with *La Timbale d'argent* (The Silver Goblet, 1872). The title referred to the prize in a village singing contest, but there was more at stake: the judge (played by Désiré) had also offered the hand of his niece (Judic) to the winner. Oaths of sexual abstinence, and the breaking thereof, feature prominently in the plot. Vasseur went on to turn out some thirty operettas, most of them similarly saucy, among which *La Cruche cassée* (The Broken Jug, 1875), *Le Droit du seigneur* (1878), and *Le Voyage de Suzette* (Suzette's Journey, 1890) stand out.

Another composer who achieved his period of success was Louis Varney (1844–1908). He was the son of Alphonse Varney (1811–79), who wrote a celebrated revolutionary song, the "Chant des Girondins," and was for some years musical director and manager of the Bouffes-Parisiens. Louis in turn became musical director at the Théâtre de l'Athénée-Comique, for which he composed music for revues. Then he was commissioned to provide a musical adaptation of a successful vaudeville, *L'Habit ne fait pas le moine* (It's Not the Cowl that Makes the Monk). The result was *Les Mousquetaires au couvent* (The Musketeers in the Convent, 1880). This tells of two soldiers, the lovesick Gontran and his friend Brissac, who steal monks' habits to gain access to a convent where Gontran's sweetheart Marie de Pontcourlay and her sister are about to take holy orders against their will. The action advances through a succession of amusing situations and disguises, and the score possesses several agreeably varied numbers, among them the abbé Bridaine's jaunty entrance song, a lilting trio for Brissac, Gontran, and Bridaine, a romance for Marie, Brissac's clever Tipsy Song, and the sprightly galop that ends both the overture and Act 2.

For a first full-length score, it was almost as noteworthy as Planquette's *Les Cloches de Corneville*. Yet Varney never approached similar success again. *Fanfan la Tulipe* (1882), about a popular fictional womanising soldier, and *Les Petits Mousquetaires* (The Little Musketeers, 1885) each ran for some months at the Folies-Dramatiques, and Varney's reputation ensured that in all some forty operettas from his pen were staged. But none achieved the international acclaim or popularity that has made *Les Mousquetaires au couvent* a staple of the French operetta repertory.

The 1870s and 1880s represented perhaps the most prolific period for the French operetta. One composer who contributed briefly to the genre before moving on to more substantial things was Emmanuel Chabrier (1841–94), who earned his living in the Ministry of the Interior but moved in artistic circles by night. He first tried his hand at operetta in the early 1860s; but his collaborations with the poet Paul Verlaine (1844–96) on *Fisch-Ton-Kan* and *Vaucochard et fils 1er* (Vaucochard and Son the First) remained unfinished. He finally achieved a Bouffes-Parisiens stage production with *L'Etoile* (The Star, 1877), a work with a zany, complicated libretto by Leterrier and Vanloo. It describes the efforts of King Ouf and his astrologer Siroco to escape from the prophesy that both are fated to die at the same time as a young peddler named Lazuli, whom the King has condemned to death. Paola Marié played the travesti role of the impoverished Lazuli, whom Chabrier provided with a sparkling rondeau, "Je suis Lazuli," and the delicate romance "O petite étoile." Chabrier's harmonies and orchestration were a little advanced for the time and, apart from Lazuli's two arias, the work was always more admired by connoisseurs than by the general public.

By contrast with the complexities of *L'Etoile,* the follow-up by Chabrier, Leterrier, and Vanloo was the simple one-acter called *Une Education manquée* (A Missing Education, 1879). It was conceived for private performance and proved a delightful treatment of the popular coitus interruptus theme. In this case the education of the two newlyweds has stopped short of knowing what they are supposed to do on their wedding night. Only when they fall into each other's arms during a thunderstorm do they figure it out. The highlight of the score is a big waltz duet, which achieved wider currency when Emile Waldteufel incorporated it into his waltz *España,* based on Chabrier's rhapsody. Thereafter, Chabrier himself wrote only for the Opéra and Opéra Comique.

More consistently successful on the Anglo-French circuit in the 1880s than Planquette, Vasseur, or Varney was Edmond Audran (1840–1901). The son of distinguished Provençal opéra-comique tenor Marius Audran (1816–87), Edmond was born in Lyons (where his father was performing) but began his career in Marseilles. His big step on the road to theatrical fame came when *Le Grand Mogol* (The Grand Mogul) was produced at Marseilles's Théâtre de la Gymnase in 1877. Its libretto was by Henri Chivot, a friend of his father's, and concerned a young Indian prince, Mignapour, who is required to remain a virgin until he becomes mogul. This he succeeds in doing despite the attempts of the Grand Vizier and Princess Bengaline to wrest the crown from him; as mogul, he is rewarded with the hand of the pretty snake charmer Irma. The public loved not only the exoticism of the oriental setting but also Audran's fresh, lilting score, in which Irma's snake-charming song, "Allons, petit serpent," and her enchanting duet with her brother Joquelet, "Dans ce beau palais de Delhi," stand out. The work launched not only Audran but also his leading lady, a native of Marseilles who took the stage name Jane Hading and went on to enjoy prominence as a dramatic actress.

Le Grand Mogol was not produced in Paris for more than seven years, but in 1884 it was revised by Chivot and Duru in the spectacular Gaîté style. By then, Paris already knew Audran as the composer of three unquestioned hits. *Les Noces d'Olivette* (Olivette's Wedding, 1879) appeared at the Bouffes-Parisiens, followed by Audran's most enduring score, *La Mascotte* (The Mascot, 1880). Where Lecocq was apparently fixated with wedding nights that did not go according to plan, Audran was obsessed with virginity, inside and outside marriage. *La Mascotte* tells of a farm girl, Bettina, who, as long as she remains a virgin, will bring luck to anyone to whose household she belongs. In spite of its improbable plot, the operetta's development was so divertingly carried out that Paris remained enchanted throughout an extraordinarily long run of 460 performances. Here Audran's fund of melodic invention flowed just that bit more richly than even he usually managed. The baritone's "Legend of the Mascot" and the racy galop that concludes Act 1 are as good as anything of their type; but the best number is a highly distinctive and celebrated duet in which Bettina and her farm-boy lover Pippo describe their respective passions for turkeys and pigs, with appropriate animal noises thrown in.

Its successor, *Gillette de Narbonne* (1882), was based on one of Boccaccio's tales and set in Audran's native Provence. If not of the same consistently light-hearted standard as *Les Noces d'Olivette,* it has in Gillette's "Ah! quel bonheur" and the duet "Rappelez-vous nos promenades" a pair of songs that display Audran's penchant for melodic phrases and refined orchestration. After reviving a refurbished *Grand Mogol,* the Gaîté followed with *La Cigale et la fourmi* (The Grasshopper and the Ant, 1886), based by Chivot and Duru on La Fontaine's fable. Jeanne Granier was the grasshopper and sang the hit song, "Ma mère, j'entends le violon."

Audran's run of success was then temporarily interrupted; but in 1890 came a show that enjoyed an even longer Parisian run than *La Mascotte. Miss Helyett* (1890) achieved an astonishing 816 performances, due partly to the usual delights of the score but more particularly to the plot's typically delectable Parisian naughtiness. The Miss Helyett of the title is a somewhat prudish American who falls off a cliff while climbing in the Pyrenees. She is saved by a branch, which turns her upside down in the process. Thus suspended, she is sketched by a passing artist, who captures the full impression of the charms beneath her skirt. For Miss Helyett the only solution is to go in search of the man who has seen what only a husband should see. Eventually, she tracks him down and discovers to her delight that he is the young Paul on whom she had already set her heart. Audran's score is distinguished especially by the dance music for the Act 1 casino setting and by the Act 2 duet between Paul and his friend Bacarel in which they breathlessly admire the view of Miss Helyett portrayed in Paul's sketch ("Ah! ah! le superbe point de vue!").

Among Audran's later works, only one recaptured earlier glories. This was the Gaîté's *La Poupée* (The Doll, 1896), which offered a variant of the E. T. A. Hoffmann plot in which a doll is confused for a human (or vice versa). In this case, the abbé of a monastery decides that the novice monk Lancelot (played by Paul Fugère, brother of Lucien) should "marry" in order to get the dowry promised by Lancelot's uncle and thereby restore the monastery's finances. His "bride" will be one of the dolls from the local toyshop, a ruse that ought to fool Lancelot's drunken, half-blind uncle. In the event, Lancelot chooses the dollmaker's daughter Alésia (Mariette Sully) and not surprisingly prefers marriage with her to becoming a monk. One of the abbé's songs enjoyed especial success in England as the baritone solo "A Jovial Monk Am I."

With its richly melodic score, *La Poupée* proved another huge international success, but it was Audran's last. He too experienced the downturn of acclaim that inevitably follows success; but he had established his position alongside Hervé, Lecocq, Planquette, and Varney. The works of these composers may have faded from the international scene, but they are still enjoyed in their native country today.

Chapter Three
The Viennese Waltz Operetta

No less than the French, German-speaking countries had a tradition of light musical theatre stretching back over the centuries. By the time Wagner's operas reached the stage in the 1840s, the comic operas of Albert Lortzing (1801–51) were already well established. The success of *Zar und Zimmermann* (Tsar and Carpenter, 1837) was repeated by that of *Der Wildschütz* (The Poacher, 1842) and *Der Waffenschmied* (The Armourer, 1846), which was produced at the Theater an der Wien in Vienna while the German Lortzing was engaged there as conductor.

     The Theater an der Wien, situated by the tiny river Wien, was one of several Viennese theatres that included occasional operas in repertories specialising in homely Viennese comedies and magic plays with interpolated songs. Written by the likes of Ferdinand Raimund (1790–1836) and Johann Nestroy (1801–62), these plays and their songs became firmly wedged in the Viennese consciousness. "Brüderlein fein," composed by Josef Drechsler (1782–1852) for Raimund's fairy tale *Der Bauer als Millionär* (The Peasant as Millionaire, 1826), and the "Kometenlied" (Comets Song), by Adolf Müller (1801–86) for Nestroy's "magic piece with song" *Lumpacivagabundus* (1833), are two of the most famous.

The Viennese tradition was taken a stage further when the Theater an der Wien engaged a Dalmatian-born musician named Franz von Suppé (1819–95). Like other theatre composers, he wrote for a variety of stage works, but more significantly he prefaced these works with rousing overtures, whose equal had not been heard before—and has scarcely been heard since. Suppé's overtures for *Ein Morgen, ein Mittag, ein Abend in Wien* (Morning, Noon and Night in Vienna, 1844), a "portrayal of Viennese life," and for Karl Elmar's "comedy with song" *Dichter und Bauer* (Poet and Peasant, 1846) became universally popular.

It was into this Viennese performing tradition that Offenbach's works entered during the late 1850s. Almost inevitably, the ever-popular *Les Deux Aveugles* was the first Offenbach piece seen in Vienna, performed by a visiting French company at the Carltheater in April 1856. It was at the same theatre that the first Offenbach works in translation were staged in 1858 and 1859. In fairly rapid succession the Viennese saw versions of six one-act operettas, led by *Le Mariage aux lanternes* as *Hochzeit bei Laternenschein* and *Pépito* as *Das Mädchen von Elisonzo*, all adapted for Viennese tastes by the Carltheater's actor-manager Carl Treumann (1823–77). The scores were adapted and orchestrated from piano scores by the musical director, Carl Binder (1816–60). It was when *Orphée aux enfers* arrived at the Carltheater in March 1860 in a Viennese version by director Nestroy (with an enlarged role for himself as Jupiter) that Binder put together what has come down to us as the overture to *Orpheus in the Underworld*.

Aiming to exploit his success, Offenbach became more directly involved in the Viennese productions of his works. He brought the Bouffes-Parisiens company to Vienna; he helped produce Viennese versions of his Parisian successes; and, beyond this, he composed his pieces with a view toward Viennese productions. In February 1864 his romantic opera *Die Rheinnixen* was produced at the Vienna Court Opera, and in March 1865 *La Belle Hélène* reached the Theater an der Wien just three months after Paris. For this, Offenbach added music to suit the more lyrical style of leading lady Marie Geistinger. The operetta was no less a success in Vienna than in Paris, and Offenbach's individual style ushered in a new era of musical theatre in Vienna, most notably in the work of Suppé, who composed additional numbers for the first Viennese production of Offenbach's *Le Pont des Soupirs*.

Although theatrical success came later to Suppé than to Offenbach, he was actually Offenbach's elder by two months. Born in Spalato (now Split, Croatia), Suppé was the son of a Belgian father and a Czech or Polish mother. After his father's death the family moved to Vienna, where he studied music, played the flute in various orchestras, and served as assistant conductor at the Theater in der Josefstadt. Later he moved to the Theater an der Wien alongside Albert Lortzing and Carl Binder. It was in this capacity that Suppé composed what has come to be regarded as the first Viennese operetta, *Das Pensionat* (The Boarding School, 1860), which was described as a "komische Operette" and presented as a direct response to the Offenbach productions at the rival Carltheater. It told a typically insubstantial Offenbachian story of a law student committed to finding a job within forty-eight hours so he can marry his sweetheart. His heart is set on the position of school administrator, which he duly obtains in return for protecting the good name of the headmistress after trapping her in a compromising situation witnessed by the girls of the school.

Though never threatening to halt the Offenbach bandwagon, the work was sufficiently successful for Suppé to follow it with others. He had by now moved to a second Treumann enterprise, the Kaitheater, which in its short existence (it burned down in 1863) became the principal Viennese home for Offenbach's early works. The indebtedness to French sources that was to permeate Viennese operetta was already evident: the book of *Zehn Mädchen und kein Mann* (Ten Girls and No Man, 1862) was based on Delibes's *Six demoiselles à marier* (1856). Where Delibes had six sisters in search of husbands, Suppé had ten. Their father advertises for husbands, and his eagerness to accept sons-in-law of various nationalities leads to each daughter doing a musical turn in a different national style. This gave Suppé the opportunity to create a number of delightful pastiches, including a Tyrolienne, a mock-Italian aria, an English arietta. In the end, the only suitor who responds is more interested in the housekeeper. To provide the happy ending that was required of all operettas, the father's disappointment is mollified by the discovery that the young man is his son by his first marriage.

The success was repeated by *Flotte Bursche* (Jolly Students, 1863), with a story of student romps and a score filled with student songs. This again produced a popular overture, as did *Pique Dame* (Queen of Spades, 1865), a revision of Suppé's earlier *Die Kartenschlägerin* (The Fortune Teller, 1862). Suppé finally achieved success in a big way with *Die schöne Galathé* (Beautiful Galatea, 1865). Though only one act long, it was, as a "comic mythological operetta," a direct response to Offenbach's *La Belle Hélène*. It concerns the sculptor Pygmalion and his finest creation, Galatea, who comes to life and proceeds to play merry hell before being turned back into stone. The overture is distinguished by an off-centre waltz that never actually appears in the operetta itself. The big vocal numbers include the aria in which Galatea comes to life, and a drinking song, "Hell im Glas." Actor-director Treumann played the wealthy art collector Midas, and Anna Grobecker had an important "trousers" role as Ganymede, Pygmalion's assistant. The work was first performed at a benefit for Grobecker in Berlin, two months before the Viennese première at the Carltheater.

Treumann returned to the Carltheater after the destruction of the Kaitheater, and Suppé dedicated his next significant work to him. This was *Leichte Kavallerie* (Light Cavalry, 1866), which was set in Hungary and, like so many of Suppé's stage compositions, has survived only through its overture. A slightly more durable stage piece was *Banditenstreiche* (Bandits' Pranks, 1867). Again adapted from a French source, it features a merry bandit who helps a pair of lovers outwit the girl's ambitious father. The overture includes a charming serenade with lute accompaniment.

But Suppé was not the only composer providing Vienna with Offenbachian one-acters. A man who briefly challenged Suppé's local success was Giovanni von Zaytz (1832–1914), who, like Suppé, was born on the Adriatic coast, in Rijeka. For the Carltheater he composed two short works that did well. *Mannschaft an Bord* (Crew on Board, 1864) was a nautical operetta set in an English harbour and making use of English sea shanties. Treumann and Grobecker starred, accompanied by a bevy of chorus girls playing sailors. The "magic piece" *Fitzliputzli* (1865) was followed by other Zaytz scores that were less successful. But Zaytz soon returned to Croatia, where, as Ivan Zajc, he created what became the most popular Croatian opera, *Nikola Šubić Zrinjski* (1876).

Yet neither Zaytz nor Suppé could come close to challenging the dominance of Offenbach in Vienna during the late 1860s. After her success in *Die schöne Helena*, Geistinger took the Hortense Schneider roles in *Blaubart* (Barbe-Bleue) and *Die Grossherzogin von Gerolstein* (La Grande-Duchesse de Gérolstein) at the Theater an der Wien, while her rival Josefine Gallmeyer helped make *Pariser Leben* (La Vie parisienne) a hit at the Carltheater. Their success merely heightened the determination of Viennese impresarios to find a local composer to loosen Offenbach's stranglehold over the Viennese no less than the Parisian musical theatre.

In fact, only one local composer was big enough to take on Offenbach, and that was Johann Strauss (1825–99), the Waltz King. Like Offenbach, he was riding a wave of success, with such waltzes as "An der schönen blauen Donau" (1867), "Künstlerleben" (1867), "Geschichten aus dem Wienerwald" (1868) and "Wein, Weib und Gesang" (1869). The major obstacle confronting him was that he had no experience whatsoever of writing for the theatre. But at the urging of the Theater an der Wien management—and that of his wife, the singer Jetty Treffz—he agreed to try.

In fact, composing operettas posed a severe challenge to a man in his mid-forties who had written only dance music, and Strauss did not make the transition to the theatre easily. A projected vehicle for Gallmeyer entitled *Die lustigen Weiber von Wien* (The Merry Wives of Vienna) was abandoned when the management was unable to sign her up. But Geistinger, the Theater an der Wien's leading lady, was free, and for her Strauss composed an Arabian Nights fantasy entitled *Indigo und die vierzig Räuber* (Indigo and the Forty Thieves, 1871). Geistinger's co-star, as Ali Baba, was the Hungarian-born Jani Szika, who had come to prominence opposite her in the Viennese *Grande-Duchesse de Gérolstein*.

The popular jibe that the piece should have been called "Indigo and the Forty Librettists" had some substance and highlighted a recurrent problem in Viennese operetta, namely the dearth of good librettists, who were so prevalent in Paris. *Indigo,* alas, enjoyed little more than a succès d'estime, coming to life most fully with the sweeping waltz to the words

> Ja, so singt man, ja, so singt man,
> In die Stadt, wo ich geboren.
>
> [Yes, they sing so; yes, they sing so;
> In the city where I was born.]

Therein lay the key to Strauss's contribution to Viennese operetta: it depended heavily on dance rhythms in general and the waltz in particular. Viennese operetta thus developed a more romantic style than the sharply satirical French form. Strauss himself was never really comfortable with theatrical composing. He relied to a considerable extent on Richard Genée (1823–95), the Theater an der Wien's conductor and house librettist, who refined the dramatic structure underpinning Strauss's lyrical melodies.

Whatever the shortcomings of *Indigo,* it was a good first effort, and Strauss got another commission on the strength of it. As so often happened, its source was French, Victorien Sardou's 1861 comedy *Piccolino*. In *Carneval in Rom* (Carnival in Rome, 1873), Geistinger played a peasant girl who joins her artist lover in Rome at carnival time. The music varied between light dance tunes for the humorous scenes and more lyrical passages for the romantic, and the play's Italian setting provided Strauss with the opportunity to portray a country he especially loved. Yet the score made no great impression; and this time there was no big waltz to save it.

With his next work, Strauss repaired that omission—and then some. How he received the commission not only tells us something about the way the composing business worked in nineteenth-century Europe but highlights some of the differences in Parisian and Viennese taste. In September 1872, Henri Meilhac and Ludovic Halévy had staged *Le Réveillon* at the Théâtre du Palais-Royal in Paris. The piece was not an operetta but a comedy with interpolated music. As was the custom, the work was then adapted for performance in Vienna. But the initial version, by the playwright Carl Haffner, was deemed unsuitable. This has been attributed to the fact that the *réveillon* (a Christmas Eve or New Year's Eve supper party) was considered too specifically French for Viennese tastes. More likely, the problem lay in the plot: the married hero takes supper with several young women and is seduced by one of them—with champagne being drunk in wholly immodest quantities. This might have been acceptable stage behaviour in Paris, but not in Vienna.

Fortunately, someone came up with an ingenious solution: if *Le Réveillon* was too Parisian, why not transform it into something typically Viennese? More particularly, why not turn the Parisian supper into a Viennese ball? Thus was born *Die Fledermaus* (The Bat, 1874). The original French play, together with Haffner's adaptation, was given to Richard Genée for conversion into an operetta libretto. Though Haffner and Genée are thus credited jointly with the book of *Die Fledermaus,* Genée later claimed that the two never even met and that he made no use of Haffner's translation.

Die Fledermaus details how a notary, Dr. Falke, avenges himself on the wealthy Gabriel von Eisenstein (played by Jani Szika) for a trick Eisenstein had played on him: after a fancy dress ball, Eisenstein had confiscated Falke's clothes, forcing him to walk through the streets dressed as a bat. In Falke's elaborate scheme, Eisenstein and members of his household are brought together at a ball given by the young Russian, Prince Orlofsky (a trousers role, as in the French original). There, Eisenstein is confronted by his maid Adele, disguised as an actress, as well as

Irma Nittinger as Prince Orlofsky in Strauss's
Die Fledermaus at the Theater an der Wien, 1874
Author's collection

by his wife Rosalinde (Geistinger), disguised as a Hungarian countess. Not recognizing her, Eisenstein tries to seduce Rosalinde, who convinces him to give her his distinctive repeater-watch. Having recently committed a minor misdemeanour, Eisenstein then reports to the local jail, where he is surprised to recognise the jailer, Frank, who had been masquerading as a Frenchman at the ball. Worse, he finds his place already taken by his wife's lover, the singing teacher Alfred, dressed in Eisenstein's own smoking jacket and slippers. But he backs off after his wife arrives and produces his watch as evidence of his own attempted infidelity.

With a brilliantly conceived plot centred around the ball, Strauss was here in his element, and he produced a string of immortal arias to supplement the swirling waltzes of Act 2. Chief among them are Rosalinde's csárdás "Klänge der Heimat," with which she "proves" that she is genuinely Hungarian, and Adele's two solos: "Mein Herr Marquis," in which she laughs off Eisenstein's recognition of her, and "Spiel ich die Unschuld vom Lande," in which she shows off her acting prowess. Much of the libretto, including the distinctive scene for the tipsy jailer at the beginning of Act 3, comes straight from the French play, while other details are changed only slightly. (The bat was a bluebird in the original, and Alfred an orchestra conductor.) Elsewhere, the action was built up to allow Rosalinde and Adele to reappear in Acts 2 and 3, rather than disappear after Act 1.

It has been claimed that Strauss composed the score of *Die Fledermaus* in six weeks. In fact, that was the time it took him to sketch the work out; the whole creational process took closer to six months. Another misunderstanding produced the claim that *Die Fledermaus* was originally such a failure that it was taken off after only sixteen performances. Rather, the run was always scheduled to be interrupted by a season of Italian opera. But as soon as that was over, *Die Fledermaus* returned. Next "Prince Orlofsky" was taken ill, forcing a further break after forty-nine performances, but the piece returned yet again, with a slightly altered cast. Ferdinand Lebrecht, the original Falke, had tragically died onstage, and his place was taken by a young actor named Alexander Girardi, the future star of Viennese operetta.

Die Fledermaus was soon beginning the international round that, thanks to its clever situations and scintillating score, made it the most celebrated of all Viennese operettas. Strauss never again matched the success of *Fledermaus,* but he had ensured that his reputation extended beyond the ballroom to the theatre.

His next operetta, *Cagliostro in Wien* (1875), was built around an apocryphal visit to Vienna by the Italian adventurer Count Alessandro di Cagliostro in the 1780s. Carl Adolf Friese, the original Frank in *Die Fledermaus,* sang Cagliostro, with Alexander Girardi as his assistant Blasoni. In this, his first original Strauss role, Girardi sang "Könnt ich mit Ihnen fliegen durch Leben?"—the first of the big waltz songs which quickly became a hallmark of his appearances in Strauss operettas. Geistinger played Cagliostro's wife and Szika a young Hungarian officer. The work represented Strauss's first collaboration with what was to become the leading Viennese librettist partnership of the time—Richard Genée and the former Danube steamship captain Camillo Walzel (1829–95), who wrote under the pseudonym "F. Zell." Walzel customarily concentrated on the situations and the book, while Genée wrote the lyrics.

Neither, though, was involved in Strauss's next operetta, written for the Theater an der Wien's rival, the Carltheater. *Prinz Methusalem* (Prince Methuselah, 1877) was in a very different style, an Offenbachian charade that was translated from a text by the French playwrights Victor Wilder and Alfred Delacour, who had adapted *Indigo* and *Die Fledermaus* for the Parisian stage. But the piece did not come off; satirical comedy was not Strauss's forte. Most successful was a comic number "Das Tipferl auf dem i" (The Dotlet on the I), which became internationally popular in the music halls. Strauss returned to the Theater an der Wien for his next work, *Blindekuh* (Blind Man's Buff, 1878), but it fared no better. Indeed, this was the weakest of his operetta scores to date, though it did contain music that was adapted for the "Nuns' Chorus" in the 1928 pastiche operetta *Casanova*.

Things picked up again with Strauss's next operetta, *Das Spitzentuch der Königin* (The Queen's Lace Handkerchief, 1880). Set in sixteenth-century Portugal, its story was based on an incident in the life of Cervantes, whose song "Wo die wilde Rose erblüht" provided some of the themes for Strauss's ballroom waltz *Rosen aus dem Süden*. If *Rosen aus dem Süden* has proved far more durable than the operetta, the latter was nevertheless a genuine success in its day—above all, in America.

Strauss's theatrical fortunes revived even further with *Der lustige Krieg* (The Merry War, 1881), for whose libretto Zell and Genée again joined forces. With one of the Italian settings Strauss loved, it told the unlikely story of two Italian states at war over a ballet dancer. Not a shot is fired in this "merry" war, probably because the Massa-Carrara army was composed entirely of women. The plot's complications include the appearance of a Dutch bulb seller, Balthasar Groot (Felix Schweighofer), and his wife (Rosa Streitmann), who manage to lose not only each other but Balthasar's store of bulbs. The latter are mistaken for onions and eaten. Somewhat surprisingly, the formula worked—not least owing to a charming quintet "Kommen und gehen" and, above all, the waltz "Nur für Natur," which was thrown in at the last minute for Girardi as the Marchese Sebastiani. Of all the hits Strauss wrote for Girardi over the years, this was probably his biggest. Until well into the twentieth century, the operetta itself remained the third-most successful Strauss operetta, following *Die Fledermaus* and the later *Der Zigeunerbaron* (The Gypsy Baron).

Only during the twentieth century was *Der lustige Krieg* overtaken in popular esteem by Strauss's next operetta, *Eine Nacht in Venedig* (A Night in Venice, 1883). It was staged at the Theater an der Wien after a première at the newly opened Friedrich Wilhelm-Städtisches Theater in Berlin, a temporary transfer of allegiance that probably owed a lot to the fact that Strauss's young second wife, Lilli, had left him for the director of the Theater an der Wien. That *Eine Nacht in Venedig* was initially something of a disaster was due mainly to the book. As with

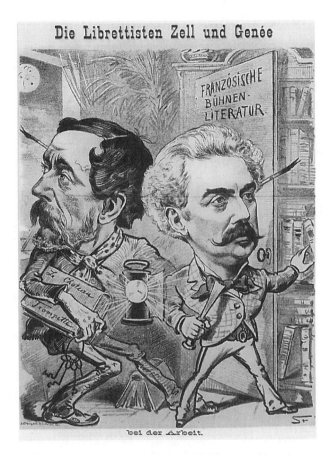

Caricature of the librettists Zell and Genée "at work" stealing
source material for Strauss's *Eine Nacht in Venedig,* from
Der Floh (7 October 1883)
Photo: AKG London

Der lustige Krieg, Zell and Genée had adapted it from an obscure French opéra-comique, but the action virtually expired after the second act, leaving nothing but inanities in the third. Hasty rewriting between the Berlin and Vienna premières helped, without completely curing the problem.

It was the score, however, that explained why managements persevered long after Strauss's death and eventually established *Eine Nacht in Venedig* as a repertory piece. The close of the first act, with night falling over the lagoon in Venice, is Strauss at his melodic and atmospheric best. There are a wealth of delightful set pieces, of which the best known is the first-act "Gondola Song." This was sung in Berlin by Szika and in Vienna by Girardi, in the role of Caramello, factotum to the philandering Duke of Urbino. Another big solo—the "Lagoon Waltz"—at

Poster for Strauss's *Der Zigeunerbaron* at the
Theater an der Wien, 1885
Photo: AKG London

the start of Act 3, belonged to the Duke in the Berlin production, but in Vienna was overhauled, given new words and transferred to Caramello. Unfortunately, this left the Duke without an important solo, a situation that Ernst Marischka and Erich Wolfgang Korngold remedied when they revised the piece in 1923. Other leading characters are Caramello's fisher-girl sweetheart Annina and the comedy pair of cooks Pappacoda and Ciboletta, played in Vienna by Felix Schweighofer and Rosa Streitmann.

The Theater an der Wien première of Strauss's next work, *Der Zigeuner-baron* (The Gypsy Baron, 1885), took place on the eve of his sixtieth birthday. Like Offenbach before him and Lehár after, Strauss now aspired to more than frivolities. He was looking for the prestige that accompanied a success in the opera house. Although not actually first produced in an opera house, *Der Zigeunerbaron* was described as a "Komische Oper" rather than an "Operette," and the piece was more substantial than the usual lightweight work of the popular theatre.

Blaming Zell and Genée for the failure of *Nacht in Venedig,* Strauss had turned for his libretto to a young journalist named Ignaz Schnitzer, who provided an adaptation of a story by the Hungarian novelist Mór Jókai. Set in the mid-eighteenth century, *Der Zigeunerbaron* revolves around Sándor Barinkay (played by tenor Carl Streitmann), whose big entrance aria "Als flotter Geist" marks his return to his native Temesvár to reclaim properties confiscated from his father. There he encounters the illiterate pig-keeper Kálmán Zsupán (Girardi), who introduces himself in the comic "Ja, das Schreiben und das Lesen." Zsupán seeks to interest Barinkay in his daughter Arsena, but Barinkay instead hitches himself to the Gypsy Saffi (Ottilie Collin). In the second act the couple are asked by the authorities for proof of their marriage, which they describe in the duet "Wer uns getraut?" (Who married us?); it appears they were married by the bullfinch, with two storks as witnesses and a nightingale providing the music. (This melting duet was later appropriated by Hollywood as "One Day When We Were Young" in the Strauss film biography *The Great Waltz.*) Meanwhile, in the sensuous "Treasure Waltz," Barinkay and Saffi have discovered Barinkay's family fortune. Their differences of class (a favourite topic of nineteenth-century operetta) are resolved when it is discovered that Saffi is no ordinary Gypsy but the daughter of Hungary's last pasha.

With *Der Zigeunerbaron* Strauss provided Viennese operetta with perhaps its most substantial score; but he never attained the same heights again. After the disappointing reception of *Simplicius* (1887), with Girardi as a peasant caught up in the Thirty Years' War, Strauss finally got his operatic aspirations out of his system with *Ritter Pázmán* (Knight Pázmán, 1892), produced at the Vienna Court Opera House. It was not a success. Thereafter, Strauss resigned himself to composing unpretentious and undemanding operettas. None of his last four stage works for the Theater an der Wien—*Fürstin Ninetta* (Princess Ninetta, 1893), *Jabuka* (1894, for his golden jubilee as a composer), *Waldmeister* (Woodruff, 1895), and *Die Göttin der Vernunft* (The Goddess of Reason, 1897)—went anywhere. Now in his seventies, Strauss finally gave up his struggle with the stage and allowed the conductor-composer Adolf Müller junior (1839–1901) to fashion an operetta out of some of his less familiar dance tunes. Strauss did not live to see the result, but the arrangement proved inspired. *Wiener Blut* (1899), a fast-moving story of amorous intrigue set during the Vienna Congress, became one of his most enduring stage works.

By the 1880s Viennese operettas by other composers were also making the rounds of the world's stages. One of the most successful writers was Strauss's lyricist and amanuensis Richard Genée, who had been a conductor and composer long before he teamed up with Strauss. Genée's greatest success as an operetta composer came with *Der Seekadett* (The Naval Cadet, 1876), whose libretto he co-wrote with Zell. Inevitably, it was based on an old French vaudeville and provided a trousers role for Hermine Meyerhoff as the young Fanchette, who disguises herself as a naval cadet to search for her lover (Szika). Since her lover has secretly married the Queen of Portugal, Fanchette finally ends up with a wealthy Peruvian (Felix Schweighofer). Girardi provided some fun along the way as the royal Master of Ceremonies. The work achieved a Broadway success in 1880 as *The Royal Middy*.

Nanon, die Wirthin vom Goldenen Lamm (Nanon, the Hostess of the Golden Lamb, 1877) was also based on a French original, this time one of the pseudohistorical pieces that cropped up in operetta from time to time. The subject was the seventeenth-century Parisian court beauty Ninon de l'Enclos, and Louis XIV was one of the characters. Szika had the leading male role of the Marquis d'Aubigny, with Girardi and Carl Adolf Friese in supporting roles. Genée's scores are now virtually forgotten, but they are full of sensitivity and style. His other operettas included such unlikely titles as *Im Wunderlande der Pyramiden* (In the Wonderland of the Pyramids, 1877) and *Die letzten Mohikaner* (The Last of the Mohicans, 1878), which owed nothing to James Fenimore Cooper.

Mostly, Genée was content with being half of Vienna's most successful team of librettists, whose composer clients included that same Franz von Suppé who had been instrumental in founding the Viennese operetta years before. Temporarily eclipsed by Strauss, Suppé finally turned to full-length operettas at the Carltheater. Zell and Genée came up with an adaptation of Eugène Scribe's libretto for Auber's 1861 opéra-comique *La Circassienne*. Transformed into *Fatinitza* (1876) and set during the Crimean War, it tells of a young Russian officer, Wladimir Samiloff, who is in love with Lydia (Hermine Meyerhoff) and masquerades as a young woman named Fatinitza in order to hoodwink Lydia's uncle, General Kantschukoff (Wilhelm Knaack). What Wladimir/Fatinitza doesn't plan is that the amorous general will fall for the supposed Fatinitza. The Wladimir/Fatinitza impersonation was, of course, yet another trousers part—this time for the bright young star Antonie Link. And an additional display of scantily-clad women occurs in Act 2, set (on a fairly slim narrative pretext) in a Turkish harem. Only *Fatinitza*'s overture remains in the popular repertory, but the whole score shows Suppé's rousing, melodic style at its best. A particular hit with the public was the march "Vorwärts mit frischem Muth," both for the irresistible swing of its music and for its spectacular staging.

That Suppé achieved such immediate success with the full-length operetta form makes it all the more surprising that he hadn't tried it earlier. Once started, he proceeded to better himself when Zell and Genée delved once more into French sources. They came up with a piece based on the life of Giovanni Boccaccio and the theory that his stories of cuckolds in the *Decameron* were taken from life. The title role of *Boccaccio,* a trousers part, went to Antonie Link, who had meanwhile scored a success in the title role of Strauss's *Prinz Methusalem.* There were key roles also for Rosa Streitmann as Boccaccio's sweetheart Fiametta and veteran comedy pair Karl Blasel and Therese Schäfer as her foster parents, the grocer Lambertuccio and his wife Peronella. The series of tales within a tale won the approbation of the public not only in Vienna but around the world—helped by another swinging score that mixed tender lyric moments with rousing student songs and comic ensembles. It has remained Suppé's best-known full-length operetta, with Fiametta's "Hab' ich nur deine Liebe" showing his more tender side, and the Boccaccio-Fiametta duet "Florenz hat schöne Frauen" (often sung in Italian as "Mia bella Fiorentina") proving that he could, when required, turn out a waltz to match the best.

Suppé's third international success with Zell and Genée had a Spanish setting. *Donna Juanita* (1880) starred Rosa Streitmann as an army cadet who disguises himself as Donna Juanita in order to spy on the English governor of San Sebastián and the local mayor. Blasel and Schäfer again had key roles as the mayor and his wife. The mixture was much as before, and the work was again well received without ousting the earlier works from popularity. Nor did the overture, despite its elegant violin solo. Yet with *Fatinitza, Boccaccio,* and *Donna Juanita,* Suppé had made the Carltheater a formidable competitor to the Theater an der Wien. The response of the latter was to sign him up. Suppé was already turned sixty, however, and neither *Die Afrikareise* (The African Journey, 1883) for the Wien nor such later works for the Carltheater as *Die Jagd nach dem Glück* (The Search for Happiness, 1888) and the posthumous *Das Modell* (The Model, 1895) matched his previous work in either quality or popularity.

Among the other composers whose operettas enjoyed international success during the 1880s was Alphons Czibulka (1842–94), a Hungarian who was successively concert pianist, theatre conductor, and military bandmaster, and who is best remembered today for such salon pieces as the "Stephanie-Gavotte" and "Liebestraum nach dem Balle." Of his half-dozen operettas, the two most popular

Franz von Suppé in 1880
Photo: AKG London

were *Pfingsten in Florenz* (Whitsun in Florence, 1884), with Girardi as the dicta-tor of sixteenth-century Florence, and *Der Glücksritter* (The Soldier of Fortune, 1887). Both libretti were co-written by the ubiquitous Genée. However, Czibulka's operetta scores have succeeded no more than Genée's in holding the stage.

There was in fact only one composer who ranked alongside Strauss and Suppé in the forefront of Viennese operetta composers of the 1870s and 1880s. Carl Millöcker (1842–99) produced neither waltzes to match those of Strauss nor overtures comparable with those of Suppé, but for effective stage writing he was the equal of either, if not their superior. Many years younger than they, he began his career in 1858 as a flautist under the direction of Suppé himself in the orches-tra of the Theater in der Josefstadt. After spells as a conductor in Graz, Vienna, and Budapest, Millöcker became principal conductor at the Theater an der Wien. This obliged him to compose music for all kinds of theatrical pieces. His first big operetta success came with *Das verwunschene Schloss* (The Haunted Castle, 1878). Set in the Austrian Tyrol, it featured several of the theatre's regular performers.

Carl Adolf Friese was Count von Geiersburg, the owner of the haunted castle, with Jani Szika as the young dairyman Sepp and Alexander Girardi as the cowherd Andredl, who finally wins the hand of Josefine Gallmeyer's heroine. The piece has endured because of its catchy waltz "O, du himmelblauer See," which Sepp and Andredl sing at a party given by the count.

The following year Millöcker produced another operetta, which is better known, if not in its original form. Adapted as usual from a French source, *Gräfin Dubarry* (Countess Du Barry, 1879) brought Millöcker into the Zell and Genée fold. A historical piece about the legendary Madame Du Barry, mistress of Louis XV, it achieved no more than modest success. But fifty-two years later it was disinterred and turned into the highly successful *Die Dubarry* (1931). A completely new book was written for this, however, and Millöcker's music (by no means all of it from *Gräfin Dubarry*) was subjected to extensive reconstruction and modernisation. The major song success of the original 1879 piece was the romance "Charmant! Charmant!" which was rewritten in 1931 as "Ich schenk mein Herz."

After *Apajune der Wassermann* (Apajune the Water Sprite, 1880) and *Die Jungfrau von Belleville* (The Maiden from Belleville, 1881) came the work that has remained Millöcker's major claim to fame. The story goes that when Millöcker and Johann Strauss sought successors to *Die Jungfrau von Belleville* and *Der lustige Krieg,* respectively, Zell and Genée had two libretti available. The librettists were aware that the book to *Eine Nacht in Venedig* was by far the weaker and thus needed the genius of Strauss to turn it into a success. Knowing that Strauss was a poor judge of a libretto, they persuaded him that Millöcker was keen to set it. This convinced Strauss that it must be the better book, and he insisted on having it for himself, thus leaving the field clear for Millöcker to set *Der Bettelstudent* (The Beggar Student, 1882). This story is credible, and it may explain why Strauss looked to other librettists after *Eine Nacht in Venedig.*

For *Der Bettelstudent,* Zell and Genée adapted an 1870 Sardou play, *Fernande,* which in turn used ideas from Edward Bulwer-Lytton's 1837 *The Lady of Lyons.* They changed Sardou's Lyons to the Krakow of the early eighteenth century, when it was occupied by Saxon forces. This gave the piece a greater immediacy for Central European stages, as well as opportunities for colourful staging, which Millöcker seized. *Der Bettelstudent* is not only a work of solid dramatic construction and development but is adorned with striking melodies. Millöcker's command of orchestration and harmony make the most of these, while his dramatic pace outdoes even the best of Strauss.

The plot revolves around the revenge of the formidable Colonel Ollen-

Hermine Meyerhoff as Millöcker's Gräfin Dubarry
Photo: AKG London

dorf against the aristocratic Countess Laura Nowalska, who has rejected him. To taunt her, he recruits a poor student to disguise himself as a prince and win her affections, intending to humiliate her by revealing her suitor's unworthiness. Inevitably, the student is ennobled (for helping the Poles overcome the Saxons) and thus becomes an eligible suitor. Felix Schweighofer was the blustering Ollendorf, with Girardi as the student Symon Rymanowicz. Josef Joseffy played his fellow student Jan Janicki, Caroline Finaly was Laura, and Therese Schäfer was her mother, Countess Palmatica. The hit of the show was the waltz refrain "Ach, ich hab' sie ja nur auf der Schulter geküsst," in which Ollendorf complains that when he merely kissed Laura on the shoulder, she slapped him in the face. The score's other superbly crafted numbers include the exhilarating entrance duet for Symon and Jan, "Die Welt hat das genialste Streben"; Symon's song in praise of Polish women, "Ich knüpfte manche zarte Bande"; and his declaration of allegiance to the Polish cause, "Ich hab' kein Geld, bin vogelfrei."

In German-speaking countries, *Der Bettelstudent* remains one of the three or four most performed classical Viennese operettas. Building on its success, Millöcker turned out another work that initially showed signs of matching its popularity. *Gasparone* (1884) featured a Zell and Genée book that for once did not have an obvious French source, other than that general body of bandit tales that had inspired such works as Auber's *Fra Diavolo* and Offenbach's *Les Brigands*. It is also one of those stage works in which (as with Offenbach's *Pépito*) the title character never appears. Indeed, he does not even exist, being an illusionary figure on whom all the misdeeds in Syracuse can be blamed. Maria Therese Massa as Countess Carlotta and Rosa Streitmann as Sora were the leading female characters, with the usual team of male leads—Girardi as the innkeeper Benozzo, Joseffy as Count Erminio, and Schweighofer as the mayor Nasoni. There was a popular duet for Erminio and Carlotta, the former of whom has won her favours by staging her rescue from the clutches of the nonexistent Gasparone. As usual, Girardi had the big number—"Er soll dein Herr sein," a lilting waltz in Act 3 that became a popular street song in Berlin, "Mutter, der Mann mit den Koks ist da."

Though twenty-three years younger than Suppé, Millöcker scarcely outlasted the older man professionally. In 1894, at the age of fifty-two, he suffered a stroke and completed only one operetta thereafter. His 1890s output comprised just one lasting success, *Der arme Jonathan* (Poor Jonathan, 1890). Again based on a French comedy, it displayed Millöcker's usual inventiveness. Alexander Girardi played Jonathan, the cook of an American millionaire. Each, in despair, is about to commit suicide, when they decide instead to let Jonathan take over the millionaire's fortune, on condition that, if things don't work out, they will kill themselves after all. Needless to say, the piece ends with millionaire and cook happily restored to their original positions. Girardi sings one of his ubiquitous waltz songs, "Ich bin der arme Jonathan," and there is engaging music for Harriet (Ottilie Collin), an operatic prima donna whose marriage to the millionaire is largely instrumental in restoring his happiness.

None of the major creative talents of the so-called golden age of Viennese operetta of the 1870s and 1880s survived into the twentieth century. Suppé died in 1895, in the same year as both of the unchallenged masters of nineteenth-century Viennese operetta libretti, Zell and Genée. Strauss and Millöcker died in 1899, the latter on the last day of the 1890s. But among them, they created operettas that can still be seen on German stages today, as well as pieces that live through their overtures (Suppé) and their dance arrangements (Strauss). Above all, Strauss's *Die Fledermaus* is a work that has transcended the confines of operetta and gained a universally acknowledged place in the international operatic repertory.

Chapter Four
Fin de Siècle

Changes in fashion or the rise of a new star have always accentuated the natural artistic peaks and troughs in the musical theatre. The early 1890s represented a watershed for European operetta. Many of its founders seemed content to rest on their reputations, while newcomers evinced an interest in bringing the genre up to date.

In Paris the younger composers were well represented by Victor Roger (1853–1903). A graduate of the Ecole Niedermeyer in Paris, he wrote unashamedly jolly music for works that were not so much full-fledged operettas—in which dialogue linked the musical numbers—as comedies with operetta-ish songs inserted. Two of his *vaudevilles-opérettes* are still occasionally performed on French stages. In *Joséphine vendue par ses soeurs* (Josephine Sold by Her Sisters, 1886), the biblical Joseph underwent a sex change and became Joséphine, an aspiring singer who is Madame Jacob's favourite of her twelve daughters. Her frustrated sisters conspire to "sell" her to an Egyptian pasha for an engagement at the Cairo Opera; instead, she finds herself in a harem. Fortunately, her mother and sisters, realizing their mistake, pursue her; the twists of the plot end with all twelve daughters happily married off. The soubrette part of the youngest sister, Benjamine, was played by one of the bright young stars of the Parisian musical theatre, the vivacious Mily-Meyer, while Madame Jacob was Marguerite Macé-Montrouge, the original Public Opinion in Offenbach's *Orphée aux enfers* twenty-eight years earlier.

Roger's other enduring success, *Les 28 Jours de Clairette* (Clairette's 28 Days, 1892) had one of those military settings that were so popular in operetta (and opera too) because of their opportunities for military rhythms and colourful costumes. The twenty-eight days of the title represent the duration of French military service, which is due to be performed by Clairette's husband, Vivarel. On his way to report, he meets an old flame, Bérénice, who follows him to the barracks. When Clairette shows up there, she discovers Bérénice ensconced as Vivarel's "wife" and herself assumed to be his mistress. Making use of the martial-arts training given her in childhood by her father, who had always wanted a son, she ends up posing as a missing soldier and doing service herself to keep an eye on her husband. Complications over sleeping arrangements add typical piquancy to the piece. The role of Clairette was created by Marguerite Ugalde, the original Nicklausse in *Les Contes d'Hoffmann*. Among her best numbers in Roger's bright, uncomplicated style was the Act 1 "En tierce, en quarte, en quinte, en prime," in which she explains her expertise in the martial arts.

Roger's music adorned several other Parisian successes of the 1890s, most notably *L'Auberge du Tohu-Bohu* (The Topsy-Turvey Hotel, 1897) and *Les Fêtards* (The Revellers, 1897). But these were more plays than strict operettas, and Roger's music was often cut when the pieces were adapted for production abroad. His early death added him to the list of French operetta composers who barely survived the turn of the century.

Two who did were André Messager and Louis Ganne, creators of the most long-lasting operettas of the period. Messager (1853–1929) was only five months younger than Roger, but their periods of major success were consecutive rather than concurrent. Moreover, the styles of their works were profoundly dif-

André Messager, from *Musica* (September 1908)
Author's collection

ferent. Where Roger contributed bright, bubbly songs to comical plots, Messager composed scores of immense refinement for light comedies that hearkened back to genuine opéra-comique. Few composers in the history of operetta matched him for delicacy and polish of vocal and orchestral writing. Even without his operetta successes Messager would have been a significant musical personality as conductor, impresario, and composer of more serious operas.

Educated—like so many French operetta masters—at the Ecole Niedermeyer, Messager initially combined composing serious works with conducting at the Folies-Bergère and other music halls. His publisher gave him his first chance in operetta when the composer Firmin Bernicat (1843–83) died unexpectedly, leaving the score for *François-les-Bas-Bleus* (1883) unfinished. Though Bernicat had evidently composed a good deal of the work, Messager's graceful personal style shines through at various points of this piece about a public scribe and his street-singer lover during the French Revolution. He followed it with two fair successes produced within a month of each other: *La Fauvette du temple* (The Songbird of the Temple, 1885) had various military elements and an action partly set in Algeria, and *La Béarnaise* (The Girl from the Béarn, 1885) featured familiar confusion in which a young woman dressed as a man goes through a form of marriage ceremony. The former show had Juliette Simon-Girard and Simon-Max in leading roles, the latter Jeanne Granier (in trousers) and Mily-Meyer.

Messager had so many irons in the fire—including composition of the ballet *Les Deux Pigeons* (The Two Pigeons, 1886) for the Opéra—that he never produced the flood of operettas that would have been expected of a composer more heavily dependent on the popular musical theatre. *La Basoche* (The Bar, 1890) confirmed his standing; but this was a more substantial score written for the Opéra-Comique company during its temporary housing in the Théâtre-Lyrique after the destruction of the Salle Favart by fire in 1887. *Madame Chrysanthème* (Madame Chrysanthemum, 1893), an oriental piece based on a story by explorer-writer Pierre Loti, was even more ambitious.

Messager's breakthrough into the operetta big-time finally came when the Bouffes-Parisiens staged *Les P'tites Michu* (The Little Michus, 1897). The piece concerns two girls—Blanche-Marie and Marie-Blanche—who are brought up by a shopkeeper and his wife as twins, though in fact one is their own child and the other a general's daughter they have fostered since infancy. With operetta in-evitability (shades of Gilbert and Sullivan's *Gondoliers!*), the two are mixed up. Once they are grown up, therefore, nobody knows which one is really engaged to Gaston, the aristocrat the general had long ago chosen for his daughter. So they try each pairing in turn. When Marie-Blanche takes up the aristocratic life and leaves Blanche-Marie to work in the shop, things are a mess; when they switch, everything works out happily. The most delectable number is the song where they introduce themselves as "Blanche-Marie et Marie-Blanche"; but the insinuating trio "Michu! Michu! Michu!" between Gaston and the two girls, and Blanche-Marie's Act 3 solo with its touching refrain "Ah, soeurette!" (Ah, little sister!) are not far behind.

It was, however, with his next piece for the Bouffes-Parisiens that Messager created one of the classics of the operetta repertory. The story of *Véronique* (1898)—with a book by Albert Vanloo (1846–1920) and Georges Duval (1847–1919)—was more consistently original than its predecessor, and its love interest more credible and affecting. Set in 1840, its heroine is the aristocratic Hélène de Solanges, who by royal decree is to be married to Vicomte Florestan de Valain-court, a renowned libertine. The two have never met, but Hélène chances upon him when she is visiting the flower shop of Agathe Coquenard, who happens to be Florestan's current mistress. She overhears him telling Agathe of the "petite dinde" (little turkey) he is due to marry. To teach him a lesson, Hélène and her aunt Ermerance disguise themselves as "Véronique" and "Estelle" and take jobs in the shop. Florestan promptly falls for the supposed Véronique. Their romance de-velops during an Act 2 picnic at Romainville, but the complications are stretched out until pretences are finally set aside and the two are happily united. Messager's score is one of infinite grace and charm, and its two second-act duets—both in

The Donkey Duet from Messager's *Véronique,* with Jean Périer
as Florestan and Mariette Sully as Hélène
Copyright Harlingue-Viollet/Roger-Viollet, Paris

the picnic scene—rank as all-time operetta favourites. In the Donkey Duet, Florestan and Hélène/Véronique appear riding on donkeys and have some fun urging one of the donkeys to "Trot here, trot there" (De ci, de là). Then they entertain themselves on a swing in the lilting Swing Duet (Poussez, poussez l'escarpolette). The piece confirmed the reputations of Mariette Sully and the baritone Jean Périer as the lovers and of Anna Tariol-Baugé as the flighty Ermerance.

    Like Leonard Bernstein half a century later, Messager now found himself subjugating his talent for composition to his work as musical director of the Opéra-Comique, where in 1902 he conducted the first production of Debussy's *Pelléas et Mélisande* with *Véronique* star Périer as Pelléas. Then he took up the position of director of Covent Garden Theatre, London, and later of the Paris Opéra. Until 1914 his only further operetta was *Les Dragons de l'impératrice* (The Empress's Dragoons,

1905), a modest success at the Théâtre des Variétés that was full of melodic grace and charm. Yet if Messager's contributions to the musical theatre were rationed, a result was that his inspiration and fame did not so readily burn out. Perhaps only Richard Rodgers wrote so successfully for so long. And like Rodgers, Messager had two distinct periods of creativity, the second of which I shall discuss later.

Messager's contemporary Louis Ganne (1862–1923) was a student of César Franck's and Jules Massenet's at the Conservatoire. Like Messager, he began his career at the Folies-Bergère, where the first of his many ballets was performed when he was only twenty. He went on to compose popular orchestral music; the "Valse des Blondes" and the marches "Le Père, la victoire" and "Marche lorraine" are among the best known. Also like Messager, he made a career as conductor (albeit in less exalted circles); his contributions to the operetta repertory were thus similarly infrequent and all the more appreciated.

It was with *Les Saltimbanques* (The Circus Artists, 1899), produced at the Gaîté on the penultimate day of the 1890s, that Ganne achieved operetta immortality. The work was a natural for the French theatre in that it set a simple love story in a circus background, which has always had a particular fascination for the French. The circus in question belongs to the tyrannical Malicorne, and the artists are the juggler Paillasse, his lover Marion, the strong man Grand Pingouin, and Suzanne, the Malicornes' adopted daughter. While the circus is at Versailles she leaves, along with her three colleagues, because of the harsh treatment they have received. Forming a company called the Gigoletti, they perform in Normandy for the Comte des Etiquettes. Suzanne sings a song she heard in her childhood that turns out to have been composed by the count himself, who recognises her as his long-lost daughter. This makes her worthy of the handsome Lieutenant André for whom she previously felt herself too humble.

The story is slight, but the circus background provides a rich setting. And what Ganne's music lacks in refinement compared with Messager's, it makes up for in rhythmic vitality. It is replete with captivating melodies, including the invigorating circus music and André's second-act military song "Va, gentil soldat." But all else falls short of the waltz "C'est l'amour" in the Act 1 finale. The extent to which this has penetrated the French consciousness can readily be gauged from the air of eager anticipation that radiates from theatre audiences as the orchestra pauses before moving into its irresistibly haunting melody.

Ganne's next operetta, *Hans le joueur de flûte* (Hans the Flute Player, 1906), came some six years later and was staged in the distinguished surroundings of the Opera House in Monte Carlo, where Ganne was conductor. It was worth the wait.

The opening scene from Ganne's *Les Saltimbanques* at the Théâtre de la Gaîté
Copyright Harlingue-Viollet/Roger-Viollet, Paris

The story is a variant of the Pied Piper legend, set in a town named Milkatz, which has controversially been pursuing its grain business at the expense of its artistic traditions. Hans the flute player leads the town's cats to the river, where they drown, leaving the grain supply at the mercy of mice. He stops only when the town resumes its subsidy for the traditional festivals and, in particular, its competition for life-sized dolls. This is won by the poet Yoris, who also gains the hand of the burgomaster's daughter Lisbeth with a doll made in her image. *Hans le joueur de flûte* may have lacked the hit numbers of *Les Saltimbanques,* but its leading singers Jean Périer and Mariette Sully (the stars of *Véronique*) made it a success, and its score is scarcely less endearing overall. But none of Ganne's later scores attained anything like the same success.

Very different in style were the works of Claude Terrasse (1867–1923), who sought to revive the topsy-turvy burlesque style of Offenbach and Hervé. Terrasse's first hit came at the Bouffes-Parisiens with *Les Travaux d'Hercule* (The Labours of Hercules, 1901), based on the premise that Hercules had not actually performed the celebrated labours. Then the Variétés staged *Le Sire de Vergy* (Lord de Vergy, 1903), which drew on the mediaeval legend of Gabrielle de Vergy (who killed his wife's lover and served her his heart on a plate), and *Monsieur de la*

Act 1 of Terrasse's *Monsieur de la Palisse* at the Théâtre des Variétés
Author's collection

Palisse (1904), a comedy of amorous intrigue. Albert Brasseur, son of the original Brazilian in Offenbach's *Vie parisienne,* took the male lead in the two Variétés works. Each was a considerable success at the time, though the fashion for Terrasse's frothy pieces proved a passing phase.

In Vienna, meanwhile, the creators of what later came to be called the golden age of Viennese operetta were likewise succeeded by younger writers less concerned with elaborate comic-opera structures than with more immediately appealing numbers. This was the case with Carl Zeller (1842–98), without doubt the outstanding Viennese operetta composer of the 1890s. Zeller was a soprano in the Vienna Boys' Choir before studying law and music and going into the Austro-Hungarian civil service. Composition was strictly part time, and his operettas were consequently few and infrequent. *Joconde* (1876) offered a somewhat confused story about one of Oliver Cromwell's generals and was another in the long line of trousers roles. Neither *Die Carbonari* (1880), set in Italy, nor *Der Vagabund* (1876), set in Russia, left any enduring trace. However, their successor most certainly did.

Alexander Girardi as Adam in Zeller's *Der Vogelhändler,* 1891
Photo: AKG London

Der Vogelhändler (The Bird Seller, 1891) was produced at the Theater an der Wien, with a book by Moritz West (1840–1904) and Ludwig Held (1837–1900) that was set in the Rhineland Palatinate and based on a French vaudeville. Its leading character, Adam, is a travelling bird seller from the Austrian Tyrol modelled on Papageno in Mozart's *Zauberflöte.* The role provided Alexander Girardi with one of his most distinctive creations. The story involves the usual romantic misunderstandings, as Adam seeks the hand of the village postmistress Christel but also gets involved with the Electress of the Rhineland province.

The longevity of the piece rests on its charm, which encompasses not only the rural setting and lightly romantic story, but Zeller's score, which is sweetly melodious from start to finish. The best number is the duet "Schenkt man sich Rosen in Tirol," in which Adam explains to the Electress Marie that anyone who gives roses in the Tyrol gives his heart as well. Other songs that have survived independently are Adam's two big solos in Tyrolean dialect—"Grüss enk Gott, alle mit einander" and the second-act Nightingale Song ("Wie mein Ahnl zwanzig Jahr"). Christel's entrance, "Ich bin die Christel von der Post," has also had a life outside the theatre. Yet those who know only the arias for the leading characters miss the wonderful ensemble and comedy numbers. The way the extended opening builds up into the revelation that the Elector's wild boars have been shot just as the Elector is due to arrive for a hunt is irresistible, as is the comedy duet "Ich bin der Prodekan" for two eccentric professors sent to test Adam's suitability for the post of Royal Menagerie Keeper.

If the success of *Der Vogelhändler* could hardly be surpassed, the extent to which it has overshadowed its successor *Der Obersteiger* (The Mine Foreman, 1894) does little justice to the latter, whose music continues in the same delightful mode. Indeed, the later work has perhaps the most widely known single number of the two, the ravishing waltz "Sei nicht bös." After it was recorded by Elisabeth Schumann, this became the province of sopranos, but it originated as the big tenor number for Girardi. Perhaps the close similarity of the story to that of *Der Vogelhändler*—by the same librettists—has kept managers from alternating the two in repertory today. Zeller later suffered a mental decline: convicted of perjury and imprisoned, he was forced to resign his civil-service post. His final operetta, *Der Kellermeister* (The Cellarman, 1901), was completed by others after his death; it produced one more hit song for Girardi in the hero's "Lass dir Zeit."

After Zeller's downfall, the spotlight fell on other composers, among them Richard Heuberger (1850–1914), who began life as an engineer before becoming a music critic, choral conductor, and opera composer. He was nearly fifty when he tried his hand at operetta, but the result was another work that has lasted to the present. *Der Opernball* (The Opera Ball, 1898) was another of those seemingly interminable French adaptations, in this instance the popular vaudeville *Les Dominos roses* (The Pink Dominoes), by Alfred Hennequin and Alfred Delacour, produced in Paris in 1876.

The operetta concerns a pair of married men out for adventure at the Paris Opéra Ball. Accepting an invitation for an assignation with some unknown women disguised in pink dominoes, they never suspect that they are being tricked by their own wives. Henri, the young nephew of one of the two, also receives an invitation. At the ball the action develops into a series of comical comings-and-goings, in the course of which the pairings change as the pink dominoes are passed around. Instead of making advances to their own wives, as the women had intended, both husbands end up flirting with the maid Hortense, who had been intended to educate the shy Henri in life. Further complications arise when everyone attempts to explain things the following morning. In best operetta tradition, all finally declare that no real damage has been done.

Curiously, for an operetta whose central act is set in the very public surroundings of the Opéra Ball, there is only one chorus number, and even that has traditionally been dropped in more financially strapped times so the operetta can be produced with a small cast. That Heuberger's ultra-sweet score has survived so well is due partly to its overture, which still turns up in concerts of Viennese music, and more particularly to the insinuating waltz *"Im chambre séparée,"* in which Hortense attempts to lure Henri into a private box. It was written as a duet for two female voices, since Henri was played by a mezzo-soprano. Of Heuberger's further operettas, *Ihre Excellenz* (Her Excellency, 1899), based on Hennequin and Millaud's *Niniche,* was the most successful. Of the others, *Das Sechsuhrzug* (The Six O'Clock Train, 1900) was based on a play by Henri Meilhac and *Das Baby* (1902) on a work by the British playwright Arthur Wing Pinero. Neither had any great success.

Prime among minor Viennese operetta composers of the time was Carl Michael Ziehrer (1843–1922). He achieved distinction originally as a military bandmaster and dance composer, becoming the only non-Strauss to hold the official Habsburg title of k.k. Hofballmusikdirektor (Imperial and Royal Court Ball Music Director). Of his early stage works, two for the Carltheater were of greatest significance—*Wiener Kinder* (Viennese Children, 1881) and *Ein Deutschmeister* (1888). Their very titles show their Habsburg narcissism, the "Deutschmeister" being the crack regiment of whose band Ziehrer was bandmaster.

The course of Ziehrer's career began to change when *Der schöne Rigo* (Handsome Rigo, 1898) was produced at Venedig in Wien (Venice in Vienna), an open-air summer operetta theatre in the Prater. It was sufficiently well received for a successor to be required the following summer, and this was an even bigger hit. *Die Landstreicher* (The Tramps, 1899) tells of a couple of tramps who are arrested for stealing jewels. Not only are they innocent, they manage to find the lost jewels. Or do they? The complication is that there are two sets of jewels—the real ones and a set of paste copies. Ziehrer's rousing marches and homely dances helped the operetta hold the stage for many years, transferring nicely to the dance orchestra and military band repertory as well.

None of Ziehrer's subsequent operettas was as successful on first production, though some of their titles—*Die drei Wünsche* (The Three Wishes, 1901),

Der Fremdenführer (The Tourist Guide, 1902), and *Der Schätzmeister* (The Treasurer, 1904)—have remained familiar to lovers of Viennese dance music for the tunes Ziehrer extracted from them. *Der Fremdenführer's* initial modest reception came in spite of the presence in the cast of Alexander Girardi as Corporal Ratz. Yet *Der Fremdenführer*—a sort of Viennese equivalent of *La Vie parisienne*—achieved a significant afterlife, with major revivals in Vienna in 1943 and 1978. Its final act, set in the Hotel Bristol, has many of the elements of a Feydeau farce.

Another composer who dabbled in the musical theatre was Josef Hellmesberger (1855–1907), a member of an eminent Viennese musical family. His father, also Josef (1828–93), was a violinist and conductor whose orchestral composition *Ballszene* (Ball Scene) is still played in Viennese concerts. The younger Josef, popularly known as Pepi, became a violin professor at the Vienna Conservatory and ultimately conductor of the Vienna Philharmonic. His compositions were primarily ballet scores and operettas, early examples of the latter including *Der Graf von Gleichen und seine beiden Frauen* (The Count of Gleichen and His Two Wives, 1880) and *Das Orakel* (1889). His greatest operetta success came with *Das Veilchenmädel* (The Violet Girl, 1904), which starred Louis Treumann as a travelling conjurer and Mizzi Günther as his wife. Together with the success of *Wien bei Nacht* (Vienna by Night, 1905), *Das Veilchenmädel* saved Hellmesberger from financial ruin after he had lost his official positions following an indiscrete affair with a married dancer at the Court Opera.

While Vienna was successfully challenging Paris as a source of internationally performed operettas, Berlin remained largely a secondary outlet for popular Viennese and Parisian shows. Yet Germany's own operetta output was far from negligible. During the 1850s and 1860s the one-act works of August Conradi (1821–73) were especially popular. Operettas such as *Die Braut des Flussgottes* (The Bride of the River God, 1859) and *Das schönste Mädchen im Städtchen* (The Prettiest Girl in Town, 1868) drew on local colour and offered a Berlin counterpart to Suppé's Viennese pieces.

Later came Rudolf Dellinger (1857–1910), who also achieved an international reputation. Originally from Bohemia, Dellinger moved first to Hamburg and then to Dresden as musical director of the Residenz-Theater. His first operetta successes were staged at the Carl-Schultze Theater in Hamburg. The most important of these was *Don Cesar* (1885), based on a French play, *Don César de Bazan,* by Philippe Dumanoir and Adolphe d'Ennery, that was also the source of Vincent Wallace's English ballad opera *Maritana* (1845). *Don Cesar* had a hint of Offenbach's *La Périchole* and Gilbert and Sullivan's *The Yeomen of the Guard* in the way the plot required the leading lady to go through a marriage ceremony. In Dellinger's operetta she is ostensibly marrying the King of Spain; but, since he is already married, he arranges for the captive Don Cesar to take his place. Inevitably, everybody is honourably partnered off by the final curtain. By that time, too, Dellinger's Spanish-influenced melodies had created a success that not only challenged Viennese works on their own territory but also crossed the Atlantic to New York. The tenor hero's serenade "Komm herab, o Madonna Theresa" was especially popular.

Dellinger never quite repeated this success, but two of his later operettas made the rounds of Austrian, as well as German, stages. *Kapitän Fracassa* (1889) was based on Alexandre Dumas's *Les Demoiselles de St. Cyr* and had a libretto by Zell and Genée, into whose orbit Dellinger had been propelled by his first big success. Next, for Dresden, came *Die Chansonette* (1894), set in contemporary Turin and Milan.

The major turning point for the creation of a specifically German operetta school came with the rise of Paul Lincke (1866–1946). Lincke played bassoon in Berlin theatre orchestras before becoming a conductor at the Apollo-Theater in the Friedrichstrasse. This was one of the variety theatres that had long provided a home for one-act operettas as part of an evening's entertainment. Their emphasis was primarily on spectacle, but Lincke's exceptional melodic and rhythmic invention not only enhanced the genre as a whole, it brought such pieces a wider celebrity than they previously enjoyed. His one-act *Venus auf Erden* (Venus on Earth, 1897) owed something to Offenbach's *Orphée aux enfers,* not to mention Gilbert and Sullivan's *Thespis,* in using a classical setting and portraying Venus, Jupiter, Mars, and Diana disporting themselves amongst the mortals. Its staging allied plenty of attractive women to a saucy, topical book by Lincke's friend Heinrich Bolten-Baeckers (1871–1938) and some splendid songs—above all the catchy "Schenk mir doch ein kleinen bisschen Liebe."

Lincke was promptly tempted away for a couple of seasons at the Folies-Bergère in Paris, but on his return to the Apollo he produced the work that has come to be regarded as the epitome of Berlin operetta. As a "burlesque-fantastic-spectacular operetta in 1 act and 4 scenes," *Frau Luna* (1899) was very much a revue-style sequence of scenic attractions rather than a sustained narrative piece. Such plot as there was concerned the inventor Hans Steppke (played by popular Berlin comedian Robert Steidl), who leaves his lover Marie and travels to the moon with two friends and their landlady in a home-made balloon. There they engage in various amorous adventures with Frau Luna—the woman-in-the-moon—as well as

with such other lunar characters as Prince Shooting-Star. The spectacular staging embraced a grand ballet and showstoppers such as the waltz "Schlösser, die im Monde liegen," the swinging march "Lasst den Kopf nicht hängen," and the land-lady's lilting "O Theophil," in which she reminisces over her affair with the moon-minder Theophil. Even in its original form, *Frau Luna* had sufficient oomph to ex-cite audiences not just in Berlin but in Austria, France, and England. It has since become a rather different animal, being expanded to an even greater extent than Offenbach expanded *Orphée aux enfers*. In Lincke's case the adaptation in 1922 to a full evening's entertainment was achieved by inserting hit numbers from his other shows.

Lincke's other shows enchanted Berlin audiences for a few more years. *Im Reiche des Indra* (In the Realm of Indra, 1899) had a durable overture and a bari-tone hit in the dreamy "Es war einmal." Later came *Lysistrata* (1902), which of-fered Offenbachian tilts at Aristophanes' story of a sex strike. It produced Lincke's greatest international hit — the Glow-Worm Idyll, which was later picked up by the ballerina Anna Pavlova for a short performance piece. Then, from *Berliner Luft* (Berlin Air, 1904), came the swaggering march "Das ist die Berliner Luft," which became something of a Berlin rallying song and was one of the numbers later incorporated into the enlarged *Frau Luna.*

The Lincke–Bolten-Baeckers successes sparked off a period of great popularity for revue-operettas in Berlin before World War I. Lincke's most significant challenger in the field was Walter Kollo (1878–1940), born Elimar Walter Kollodzieyski in what was then East Prussia and is now Poland. Kollo worked as a theatre conductor in Königsberg (now Kaliningrad) before contributing songs to Berlin's cabarets and revue theatres. His scores for the Berliner Theater were usually padded out with contributions by the theatre's musical director, Willi Bredschneider (1889–1937). Such was the case with *Filmzauber* (Film Magic, 1912), which courted topicality by dealing with the infant silent film industry. It contained one of the marches so beloved of Berliners—"Untern Linden, untern Linden." The show's nature is best indicated by its description as "Posse mit Gesang" (farce with song): it concentrated on popular variety songs rather than attempting the traditional integrated comic opera.

The following year Kollo and Bredschneider enjoyed even greater success with *Wie einst im Mai* (As Once in May, 1913), a diverting piece which followed two families through four scenes and four generations, with a romance between them thwarted in the first three scenes before finally coming to fruition in the fourth. The score's best pieces were the swinging "Das war in Schöneberg im Monat Mai" and the scornful "Die Männer sind alle Verbrecher." The show was adapted for Broadway as *Maytime* (1917), for which it was given a wholly new score by Sigmund Romberg. In Germany, *Wie einst im Mai* has remained Kollo's passport to immortality. As with *Frau Luna,* its score was later reinforced (and Bredschneider's contribution removed) by adding numbers from others of Kollo's works as well as new songs by his songwriter son Willi Kollo (1904–88). The work's durability has been further ensured by the advocacy of Willi's son, the opera tenor René Kollo (b. 1937).

The third big name in the Berlin musical theatre in the years before the First World War was that of Jean Gilbert (1879–1942). This was the stage name of Max Winterfeld, who came from a musical family and was a theatre conductor in Bremerhaven, Hamburg, and Berlin before taking up operetta. Success came first with *Polnische Wirtschaft* (Polish Housekeeping, 1909), followed by the even more popular *Die keusche Susanne* (Chaste Suzanne, 1910). This was yet another work derived from a successful French comedy—in this case *Fils à Papa* (Daddy's Boy), by Antony Mars and Maurice Desvallières. Its plot revolved around various supposedly virtuous individuals who are caught visiting the infamous Moulin Rouge.

The show was a huge international success and is still performed today, though once again usually in a version strengthened by the composer's son, the successful lyricist Robert Gilbert (1899–1978).

For the next few years Jean Gilbert held a position alongside Kollo as composer of shows with catchy songs and snappy titles such as *Autoliebchen* (Motor Love, 1912), with its song "Ja, das haben die Mädel so gern"; *Puppchen* (Little Doll, 1912), with "Puppchen, du bist mein Augenstern"; and *Die Kinokönigin* (The Movie Queen, 1913), with "In der Nacht." Like Kollo, too, Gilbert went on composing after World War I. But by then the world and operetta had both undergone a radical transformation. Although turn-of-the century works from Paris, Vienna, and Berlin still grace the stages of their respective countries today, the period was essentially a transitional phase from the comic-opera pieces of the nineteenth century to the rather different styles that prevailed in the twentieth.

Chapter Five
Habsburg Twilight

If the leading composers of nineteenth-century Viennese operetta had been almost entirely superseded by the start of the twentieth, a link between the two eras was provided by the partnership of librettists Victor Léon (1858–1940) and Leo Stein (1861–1921). Viennese born Léon began as a journalist before turning to operetta books. Besides preferring a French nom-de-plume to his real name of Viktor Hirschfeld, he had the traditional Viennese librettist's taste for French sources. His early libretti included Johann Strauss's *Simplicius* (1887) and, in collaboration with Heinrich von Waldberg (1860–1942), Alfons Czibulka's *Der Bajazzo* (1892), Rudolf Dellinger's *Die Chansonette* (1894), and Richard Heuberger's *Der Opern-*

ball (1898) and *Ihre Excellenz* (1899). It was when he teamed up with railway-official-turned-playwright Stein (né Rosenstein) that he formed his most significant writing partnership.

Their first collaboration was the book for the Johann Strauss pastiche *Wiener Blut* (1899), followed, among others, by adaptations of Henri Meilhac's *Décoré*—for Heuberger's *Das Sechsuhrzug* (1900)—and *L'Attaché d'ambassade* (1862). The latter concerned the efforts of a small, impoverished German principality to prevent the widow of its chief banker from marrying a Frenchman and taking her inherited wealth to France with her. Léon and Stein had first suggested the well-established Heuberger as its composer, but when he tried out his initial ideas for them, they were unimpressed. It was then suggested that the piece should be offered to the young Franz Lehár, with whom Léon and Stein had already collaborated on a couple of minor, forgotten works. Contracts were signed, and the result was *Die lustige Witwe* (1905), perhaps the most famous, most perfect operetta ever composed.

Franz Lehár (1870–1948) was born in the Danube port of Komáron in Hungary (now Komarnó in Slovakia). His father was a military bandmaster, and his own musical education included a period of study at the Prague Conservatory, where he acquired a first-rate orchestral and harmonic technique. He took a job as violinist in a theatre orchestra and then spent many years as a military bandmaster, while unsuccessfully trying his hand at operas. He next moved to Vienna, where in 1902 he enjoyed acclaim for his "Gold und Silber" waltz, which demonstrated at once his supreme melodic gift and the refinement and elegance of his orchestration. His theatre career proper began that same year, when he was appointed conductor at the Theater an der Wien and received commissions to compose operettas for both that theatre and its rival the Carltheater.

The title of his first piece for the Theater an der Wien, *Wiener Frauen* (1902), was misleading to the extent that it was primarily a vehicle for a man, the legendary Alexander Girardi, now in his fifties, who played the piano tuner Nechledil. The work fell short largely in its libretto: Lehár's score contains some delightful waltz melodies as well as a march refrain, "Nechledil, du schöner Mann," that brought the house down. The show has a splendid overture, distinguished by a piano solo that evokes the piano tuner at work. It then eases into one of the score's best waltzes before concluding with the Nechledil march theme.

Der Rastelbinder (The Tinker, 1902), with a libretto by Léon, followed at the Carltheater less than a month later. It starred the popular light tenor Louis Treumann as the onion seller Wolf Bär Pfefferkorn and the soprano Mizzi Günther as Suza. It concerns the triumph of their love over such obstacles as Suza's childhood betrothal to the tinker Janku. Set partly in Slovakia, it offered Lehár an opportunity to make use of local colour, at which he was particularly adept. It also included some of the sensuous love music that became Lehár's trademark in the popular musical theatre, just as Puccini had made it his speciality in opera. The exquisite duet "Wenn zwei sich lieben" in *Der Rastelbinder* is perhaps Lehár's earliest demonstration of his skill.

The piece was a big success, and Léon followed it with a reworking of the legend of Amphitryon, whose wife Alcmene gave birth to Hercules after Jupiter came down to earth and seduced her. In Léon's reworking as *Der Göttergatte* (The God Husband, 1904), Jupiter's efforts are thwarted by Juno's disguising herself as Alcmene, thus re-creating the *Fledermaus* situation in which a husband seduces his own wife. Treumann and Günther again had leading roles, and there were some first-rate waltzes. However, a mythological satire was less suited to Lehár's sensuous style than it might have been to that of Offenbach or Paul Lincke. Nor did he find any greater joy with the farcical *Die Juxheirat* (The Joke Marriage, 1904), in which Girardi played a chauffeur. Indeed, it was one of the biggest flops in the careers of both Girardi and Lehár.

Perhaps it was with this in mind that Léon and Stein turned first to Heuberger when seeking a composer for *Die lustige Witwe*. Yet even with Lehár finally on board, not all was initially plain sailing. Some of his music caused consternation in the mind of the Theater an der Wien's manager, Wilhelm Karczag, who was apparently unable to appreciate its more innovative style. The piece finally opened at the tail end of 1905 with Günther as the widow, Hanna Glawari, and Treumann as the Pontevedrin embassy attaché Danilo, who is deputed to keep her from marrying a Frenchman. The initial reception of the work was mixed, and there were political demonstrations from Montenegrin students who took offence at their homeland (only thinly disguised as Pontevedro) being the subject of operetta satire. But the Balkan connections gave Lehár important opportunities to introduce national colour in Act 2, in which Hanna's tale of a Pontevedrin mountain sprite named Vilja is woven into a sequence of party music using the rhythm of the Balkan kolo folk dance and the sound of the tamburizza, a local string instrument. Productions in other countries soon followed, and the operetta's reception in London in 1907 began the attention that was to turn it into a world sensation. New York followed suit that same year, with a production helped on its way with sundry commercial appendages such as Merry Widow hats, cigars, and cocktails. Paris took it to its heart in 1909.

Act 2 of the original production of Lehár's *Die lustige Witwe*, with Louis Treumann and Mizzi Günther
Photo: AKG London

So familiar are we with Lehár's score today that it is difficult to appreciate the effect it must have had on first hearing, or to recognise how much was new about it. It is not just that it is so full of ravishing melodies from start to finish, but that the emotional depth of its love music, the colour and harmonic sophistication of the orchestral writing were unprecedented. As befits a work created in the era of Sigmund Freud, it penetrates deeply into human psychology. It begins not with a conventional overture but with a brief prelude that immediately evokes a Parisian embassy party. The rakish Danilo then arrives to a number that is no conventional set of verses but just a single verse and chorus that say all that is needed. Hanna in turn enters to music that immediately conveys her glamour and the complete captivation of the men of the embassy. The sheer eroticism of the love music is noteworthy not just in the writing for the leading characters but also in that for the secondary couple, the ambassador's wife Valencienne and her lover Camille de Rosillon, which scales almost Wagnerian heights in the summerhouse scene in Act 2. The principal march is no "Forward into Battle!" stereotype but an expression of male bafflement over the ways of women. Lehár also includes what was a very up-to-date acknowledgement of the dance trends of the time with the introduction of a cakewalk into Act 3.

The growing reputation of *Die lustige Witwe* ensured that Lehár's next works would be eagerly anticipated. Unfortunately, *Der Mann mit den drei Frauen* (The Man with the Three Wives, 1908) failed to fulfil expectations. The story of a man who had wives in Vienna, London, and Paris, it was written by the same librettist (Julius Bauer, 1853–1941) as the earlier *Die Juxheirat* and suffered much the same fate. For *Das Fürstenkind* (The Prince's Child, 1909), Lehár went back to Léon for the libretto, and the piece was much better received. Set in Greece and America, it enabled Lehár once more to provide Balkan colour, and once again it starred Treumann and Günther in the leading roles.

With his next work, *Der Graf von Luxemburg* (The Count of Luxembourg, 1909), Lehár challenged the international success of *Die lustige Witwe*. The book had a curious history: it had originated as the libretto by Alfred Maria Willner (1859–1929) for Johann Strauss's unsuccessful *Die Göttin der Vernunft* (1897). As was his wont, Strauss had contracted to set the book without reading it, and he subsequently regretted it. Only the threat of legal action persuaded him to go through with the commission, and he never even attended a performance. Later, the score and libretto were legally separated. Willner felt that his book had further mileage and reworked it with Robert Bodanzky (1879–1923; brother of conductor Artur Bodanzky, 1877–1939) as the story of an arranged marriage between an impoverished count and an opera singer, who is in need of a title in order to marry her aristocratic lover. During the ceremony, the couple are kept apart by a screen, but subsequently they meet and fall in love. Eventually they realise that they are already married to each other.

Der Graf von Luxemburg followed the formula of *Die lustige Witwe* closely. Both are set in Paris, and the situations, characters, and distribution of musical numbers bear close similarities. Whereas in the earlier work the hero and heroine are former lovers, in the later they are unknowingly married to each other. René, the Count of Luxembourg, is cast in the rakish mould of Danilo. In addition, Act 2 of *Der Graf von Luxemburg* begins with a party at the heroine's home, just as the same act in *Die lustige Witwe* does, and once again the idea of marrying for money is a central theme. Not least of the resemblances is in the music: the beguiling strains of "Bist du's lachendes Glück" replace the seductiveness of the Merry Widow Waltz; and the music's intense eroticism again reveals hidden love, as when Angèle pretends to reject René in "Lieber Freund, man greift sich nach den Sternen." Similarly, the swirling violins in "Es duftet nach *Trèfle incarnat*" catch not only emotion but even a scent, in this case Angèle's perfume *Trèfle in-*

carnat (pink clover), which awakes in René the memory of the hand he touched through the screen at the arranged marriage ceremony.

That Lehár settled for a book so reminiscent of an earlier work was probably due to his composing *Der Graf von Luxemburg* under tight time pressure. Usually, Lehár strove for something new, as in *Zigeunerliebe* (Gypsy Love, 1910), a passionate love story involving Transylvanian Gypsies. It featured a lengthy dream sequence and had a more sombre tone. This limited its success with international audiences who expected something lighter, though they were well pleased with the swinging waltz refrain "Nur die Liebe macht uns jung." The csárdás "Hör' ich Cymbalklänge" that has come to be linked with the operetta was actually written as a separate piece and only added to *Zigeunerliebe* many years later.

For *Eva* (1911), Lehár again trod unconventional operetta ground with a work that, as its subtitle "Das Fabriksmädel" indicates, is about a factory worker. Eva was played by Mizzi Günther, with Louis Treumann as the boss from whose attentions her fellow workers seek to extricate her. Eva is a foundling, whose vague memory of her mother inspires the most oft-performed number, with its sensuous refrain "Wär' es auch nichts als ein Traum von Glück." This is only one of many lovely waltz melodies in the score.

As he was to do throughout his career, Lehár next sought to make a success of an earlier score that he felt deserved a better fate. He provided a great deal of new music for a revised version of his Amphitryon piece, *Der Göttergatte*, which now had a very different libretto, by the up-and-coming team of Julius Brammer (1877–1944) and Alfred Grünwald (1884–1951). The revised piece dealt with new characters in a modern Spanish setting, which provided the opportunity to introduce the currently popular tango rhythm. In its new form as *Die ideale Gattin* (The Ideal Wife, 1913), it starred Günther as the wife and gave leading parts to Theater an der Wien stalwarts Hubert Marischka as the husband, and the comedy pair of Ernst Tautenhayn and Louise Kartousch. Alas, it achieved little more success than the first version.

Nor was there much joy from Lehár's next two pieces—*Endlich allein* (Alone at Last, 1914) and *Der Sterngucker* (The Stargazer, 1916)—the former continuing Lehár's quest for new challenges by placing the two central characters alone on a mountaintop for the whole second act.

Lehár was to return to both works later, but for the present he was showing signs of being played out. Moreover, his opportunities were limited by the

Louise Kartousch and Ernst Tautenhayn in Lehár's *Eva*
Kurt Gänzl Collection

outbreak of the First World War, which denied central European operettas their accustomed export opportunities to French and British theatres in particular. In due course, moreover, the war led to the breakup of the Habsburg empire, in which the Viennese operetta had flourished and which had provided so much of its geographical settings and subject matter and had shaped its style. Viennese operetta in particular, and European operetta in general, was never again to be the international theatrical force after World War I that it was before.

In the few years immediately before World War I, however, the success of *Die lustige Witwe* created a demand for Viennese operetta which was satisfied by a flood of works by composers who for a time were almost as popular as Lehár. Among them was Lehár's contemporary Oscar Straus (1870–1954), the son of a wealthy Viennese banker who had studied serious musical composition in Berlin before taking a job as pianist and composer for a cabaret. His first operettas included two much-praised collaborations with the satirist Fritz Oliven, known as "Rideamus" (1874–1956). *Die lustigen Nibelungen* (The Merry Nibelungs, 1904) was a witty burlesque of Wagner's *Ring,* while *Hugdietrichs Brautfahrt* (Hugdietrich's Bridal Journey, 1906) was an equally imaginative comic fairy tale. The young soubrette Mizzi Zwerenz played the hero Hugdietrich, and the audience was treated to the sight of her both in male and female garb, for the hero disguises himself as a girl during his quest for a bride.

The success of *Die lustige Witwe* encouraged Straus to abandon satirical material in favour of sentimental and romantic works. The story goes that his librettist Leopold Jacobson (1878–1943) had been so taken by a women's orchestra at a Vienna restaurant that he decided to weave the idea into an operetta libretto. The result was *Ein Walzertraum* (A Waltz Dream, 1907), the story of Lieutenant Niki of the Viennese hussars, who marries Princess Helene of Flausenthurn but yearns so much for his native Vienna that on his wedding night he is seduced both by the sound of a Viennese orchestra and by Franzi, its conductor. The conflict is resolved when Franzi selflessly helps the Princess rearrange her quarters in the Viennese manner to make Niki feel at home. Zwerenz played Franzi, with Fritz Werner as Niki.

The story was unlikely, to say the least; but in the wake of the international triumph of *Die lustige Witwe* the title itself was almost enough to ensure success. *Ein Walzertraum* proved the biggest success the Carltheater had ever known, and a new generation of Viennese operetta was thus established at Vienna's two major operetta theatres. Straus's score was the real reason for its appeal. It was full of catchy numbers, including a lilting comic duet in polka tempo, "Piccolo! Piccolo! Tsin-tsin-tsin," and, above all, "Leise, ganz leise, klingt's durch den Raum," celebrating the appeal of the Viennese waltz. The show's Viennese success was repeated in theatres around the world.

For their next show Straus and Jacobson collaborated on *Der tapfere Soldat* (The Brave Soldier, 1908) for the Theater an der Wien. This was an adaptation of George Bernard Shaw's comedy *Arms and the Man,* about a chocolate-loving Swiss mercenary in the Serb army who is fighting in Bulgaria. When the fighting gets too hot, he takes refuge in the bedroom of a stranger who, despite being the daughter of a Bulgarian colonel and engaged to a Bulgarian soldier, falls for the handsome intruder. The ensuing intrigue revolves around the fact that the mercenary knows that the woman's father and fiancé are by no means the heroes she believes them to be. The show was not particularly popular in Vienna, although it did make a hit of the languorous waltz "Komm', komm', Held meiner Träume," in which the heroine Nadina sings of her absent, purportedly heroic fiancé. However, the show travelled to America and Britain, where it received considerable acclaim under the catchier title of *The Chocolate Soldier*. Despite having given permission for the adaptation, the play's author felt so ill-disposed to the operetta that he refused to accept royalties and insisted on a disclaimer being printed in the programme: "With apologies to Mr. Bernard Shaw for an unauthorised parody on one of his comedies." Shaw later regretted his resultant financial loss.

Thereafter, Straus was able to enjoy the fame occasioned by these two works, although the new pieces he wrote during the next decade did not do as well. There was much attractive music in *Didi* (1909, based on Sardou's *La Marquise*) and *Mein junger Herr* (1910), but as a whole they were undistinguished. The one operetta that really caught the Viennese public's attention was *Rund um die Liebe* (About Love, 1914), with Mizzi Günther and Fritz Werner in the leading roles. Serving as an antidote to the depression created by the war, it achieved a better initial run than even *Ein Walzertraum,* but it was unable to travel outside central Europe. Its overture is still heard, as are the heroine's tipsy song "Ein Schwipserl möcht' ich haben" and the tenor's "Es gibt Dinge, die muss man vergessen."

The other composer to achieve international prominence along with Lehár and Straus was Leo Fall (1873–1925). Born in Olmütz in Moravia, he was, like Lehár, the son of a military bandmaster. Indeed, he and Lehár played together in his father's band. Like Straus, Fall established himself in Berlin cabaret before gravitating to Vienna. But he was a true original, in some ways the most naturally inventive and fascinating of the three composers. His shaping of melodic line had an individual cast, in which musical phrases were extended over an unusually long span and bent into intriguing shapes that reflected natural speech to an unprecedented extent. Moreover, where most composers of the time relied on professional orchestrators (among them Arnold Schoenberg and Alexander von Zemlinsky), Fall (like Lehár) always did his own. His orchestration has a delicacy reminiscent of chamber music and is littered with delightful touches.

Fall's first operetta, *Der Rebell* (1905), was a flop at the Theater an der Wien, being taken off after five performances just a month before the première of *Die lustige Witwe*. His next, *Der fidele Bauer* (The Merry Peasant, 1907), produced at an operetta festival in Mannheim, was a rustic romp. The book by Léon concerned the problems that arise when Matthäus Scheichelroither, the son of an

Leo Fall (right) with Oscar Straus (left) and
Franz Lehár in Bad Ischl, ca. 1915
Photo: AKG London

ambitious peasant, becomes a doctor and marries into a higher social stratum.
The piece was extremely successful and is still performed in German-speaking
countries, especially for the father's two big dialect songs, and his son's expressive
"O frag' mich nicht, mein süsser Schatz."

It was his next work that put Fall in the international ranks. *Die Dollarprinzessin* (The Dollar Princess, 1907) had a book by A. M. Willner and Fritz
Grünbaum (1880–1941) that broke new ground in various ways. It was set in
America and opened with a chorus of secretaries working at their typewriters,
their tapping exquisitely captured in Fall's music. The secretaries work for millionaire businessman Couder, whose daughter and deputy Alice proclaims herself "ein echtes Selfmademädel." These revolutionary feminist attitudes delay
—although ultimately they don't prevent—her inevitable engagement to Fredy,
the young German she has appointed her secretary. Mizzi Günther and Louis

Treumann were the creators of these leading roles, with Louise Kartousch as Couder's niece Daisy and Hans Meister as another German worker, Hans. Alice and Fredy hum a big waltz hit in Act 1, while Daisy and Hans have their moment with the captivating "Wir tanzen Ringelreih'n" in Act 2. Then all four sing the title waltz, "Das sind die Dollarprinzessin." Together with the American setting—an original feature—these numbers served to make the work another huge Viennese operetta hit around the world.

Scarcely less successful was *Die geschiedene Frau* (The Divorcée, 1908), written by Léon and featuring Anny Dirkens as Gonda, Mizzi Zwerenz as Jana, and Hubert Marischka as Karel. The first act is set in a Dutch courtroom, where Jana is seeking a divorce from Karel, who has been forced by a jammed door to share a railway sleeping compartment with the flirtatious Gonda. In an ending that owed something to Gilbert and Sullivan's *Trial by Jury*, Gonda ends up with the judge, while the divorced couple are reunited. Fall's score contained some exquisite waltzes, among them Gonda's "O Schlafcoupé," the duet "Gonda, liebe kleine Gonda" in which the accused husband seeks to do the decent thing for his co-respondent by offering to marry her, and the lively "Kind, du kannst tanzen wie meine Frau," a duet for the divorcing couple.

Die schöne Risette (Beautiful Risette, 1910) was well-liked in Vienna but was less successful abroad, and Fall had two further relative failures in *Das Puppenmädel* (The Doll Girl, 1910) and *Die Sirene* (1911). Then he returned to his early flop *Der Rebell*. Revised for Berlin as *Der liebe Augustin* (Dear Augustin, 1912), it now proved a great success and did the rounds internationally. Vienna-born Fritzi Massary, who had built up a local reputation as a soubrette in revue and operetta, played Princess Helene, who can resolve her dynasty's financial plight by marrying the wealthy Prince Nicola of Mikolics. Fortunately for her, she has been involved in another operetta mix-up of babies, which means that she is really the Princess's maid. This allows her to marry her beloved piano teacher Augustin, leaving the Prince to her former maid, the real Princess. Fall's score was once again captivating, especially Augustin's jaunty philosophising in "Lass' dir Zeit" and the love duet "Und der Himmel hängt voller Geigen," another of Fall's conversationally shaped melodies.

A further series of failures followed—*Die Studentengräfin* (The Student Countess, 1913) with Massary, *Der Nachtschnellzug* (The Night Express, 1913) with Girardi, *Jung England* (Young England, 1914), set in England and featuring the suffragist movement, and *Der künstliche Mensch* (The Artificial Man, 1915). But then came two works which, although limited internationally by the war, restored

Fritzi Massary in Fall's *Die Kaiserin,* in the Berlin production
Photo: AKG London

Fall's standing in central Europe. *Die Kaiserin* (The Empress, 1915) had its première in Berlin but had to be revised for Vienna, where it was not permitted to
portray the empress, Maria Theresia, in a musical show. Thus, for the Carltheater,
it became *Fürstenliebe* (Princely Love), with Mizzi Zwerenz as a less specifically
identified leading character. "Du, mein Schönbrunn," her celebration of Schönbrunn Palace, was the highlight of a score that Fall is said to have considered his
personal favourite.

Posterity has preferred the following year's *Die Rose von Stambul* (1916).
Here Hubert Marischka, darling of the Theater an der Wien, had one of his most
rewarding roles as Achmed Bey, son of the Turkish prime minister. He is be-
trothed to the pasha's European-educated daughter, Kondja Gül (played by Betty
Fischer), who is corresponding with a writer, one André Lery, who supports Western rights for Turkish women. In true operetta style, the resultant dilemma over
Kondja Gül's future course is resolved when it turns out that Lery is the pen name

of Achmed Bey himself. Besides the irresistible title waltz, the score included another, "Ein Walzer muss es sein," that typifies Fall's ability to deck out dance rhythms with melodic lines of gossamer lightness. No less good is another tenor favourite, "Ihr stillen, süssen Frau'n," in which Achmed Bey serenades the silent women of the harem, with bubbling clarinet effects in the orchestra. Louise Kartousch and Ernst Tautenhayn had superb comedy numbers. Fritzi Massary took over the title role in Berlin, and the work was sufficiently highly regarded to be produced in New York after the war was over.

The relative standing in their home city of the Viennese operetta composers of this time can be gauged by a 1914 cartoon. In an allusion to Lehár's *Endlich allein,* with its second act set on a mountaintop, Lehár is depicted sitting triumphantly on a mountain peak bearing the description *genius.* Below him, beside the word *talent,* are Oscar Straus, striving for the peak, and Leo Fall, seemingly losing his footing. (This was during his slump.) Lower down still, contentedly resting and pouring out a drink from one of several bottles in his knapsack, is a fourth composer—Edmund Eysler (1874–1949).

Eysler certainly never achieved the success of the other composers on that cartoon mountain, and he did seem content to go on producing unchallenging works in a folksy Viennese idiom. A local boy, he was the son of a Jewish businessman and first achieved success with *Bruder Straubinger* (Brother Straubinger, 1903). This had a rewarding role for Girardi as a man who, when his identity papers are stolen, attempts to use those of his late grandfather. The work's success was largely due to the waltz "Küssen ist keine Sünd," which was typical Girardi material.

For Girardi, too, Eysler provided a second hit with the Cherry Song in *Pufferl* (1905), in which he played a hairdresser, and another in the Mutterl-Lied (Mother Song) in *Die Schützenliesl* (Rifle-Shooting Liesl, 1905). Several other Eysler shows were produced abroad, among them *Künstlerblut* (Artist's Blood, 1906), the one-acter *Vera Violetta* (1906), *Der Frauenfresser* (The Woman Hater, 1911), and *Ein Tag im Paradies* (A Day in Paradise, 1913). The most successful was *Der lachende Ehemann* (The Laughing Husband, 1913), a Brammer and Grünwald piece that also played (in English) in London and New York and sported as hit number the drinking song "Fein, fein schmeckt uns der Wein." However, Eysler's reputation has largely been restricted to his native Vienna.

Other composers who, like Lehár, gravitated to Vienna from the farther reaches of the Austro-Hungarian empire were more ambitious than Eysler. Prominent among them was Oskar Nedbal (1874–1930), who was born in Tábor in southern Bohemia and studied at the Prague Conservatoire at the same time as Lehár. An eminent string player and conductor, he was founding violist of the Bohemian String Quartet and conductor of both the Prague (later Czech) Philharmonic and the Tonkünstler Orchestra in Vienna. Much of his composing was done while travelling between engagements. His most individual works were his ballets-pantomimes; the "Valse triste" from his *Pohádka o Honzovi* (The Tale of Honza, 1902) remains especially treasured today.

Nedbal's first venture into operetta came with *Die keusche Barbara* (Chaste Barbara, 1910), first produced in Prague. Set in nineteenth-century Britain, it did so well that the Carltheater in Vienna produced the première of his next and greatest operetta, *Polenblut* (Polish Blood, 1913). This concerns a Polish count, Bolesláw Baránski (known to his friends as Bolo), whose estates are so run down that marriage to a wealthy woman appears to be his only salvation. His friends suggest Hélena, daughter of a local landowner; but Bolo is more interested in Wanda, a ballet dancer at the Warsaw Opera. His friends solve the dilemma by installing Hélena (her true identity unknown to Bolo) as his housekeeper "Marynia." Her management of his estate is such a success that he ultimately realises that Hélena/Marynia is the right woman for him. Zwerenz created the part of Hélena.

Polenblut owed much of its success to some big waltz duets—"Hören sie, wie es singt und klingt" for Bolo and Wanda at a ball in Act 1, and "Ihr seid ein Kavalier" and "Mädel, dich hat mir die Glücksfee gebracht" for Bolo and the disguised Hélena in Act 2. There was also an effective gambling scene in Act 2, during which Bolo and his friends continue to play cards as the bailiffs seize his furniture item by item.

After World War I began, Nedbal never achieved the same success he had with *Polenblut,* although *Die Winzerbraut* (The Vineyard Bride, 1916) was much admired. Its settings of a Croatian vineyard for Act 2 and Vienna for Act 3 were preceded by a first act in Zagreb. That proved a sad pointer for Nedbal's own untimely end. Plagued by depression, he threw himself from an upstairs window of Zagreb's National Theatre, where he was due to conduct a ballet performance on Christmas Eve 1930.

The major Austro-Hungarian operetta centre outside Vienna was not Prague but Budapest. There Viennese works gained early Hungarian-language stagings in repertory with native works. Of these, *János vitéz* (Hero John, 1904), produced at the Király Szinház (King's Theatre), has achieved the status of a Hungarian national folk operetta. It contains important fairy dream sequences

Sári Fedák and Miska Papp in Kacsóh's *János vitéz*
Kurt Gänzl Collection

and has a book by Károly Bakonyi based on a dramatic poem by Sándor Petöfi. The score by Pongrác Kacsóh (1873–1923) includes some simple folk numbers that have become part of Hungarian culture. The title role of János, a young shepherd who becomes a hero when he saves the French from defeat by the Turks, was created by the popular Hungarian leading lady Sári Fedák.

Budapest also produced a group of composers whose works more closely imitated the Viennese style. Jenö Huszka (1875–1960) was born in Szeged, studied music in Budapest and Paris, and worked as a violinist before taking up operetta composition. *Bob herceg* (Prince Bob, 1902) had a libretto by Bakonyi and Ferenc Martos (1875–1938) that was set in London and featured the Queen of

England and her son, Prince George (Sári Fedák). He spends his time roaming the streets under the name of Bob and ends up triumphing over the barber Plumpudding for the hand of glamorous student Annie. The score begins with a rousing chorus of guards outside Buckingham Palace and features an entrance for Bob in which he hymns the narrow alleyways in which he loves to roam.

Huszka went on composing operettas for another fifty years, without achieving significant notice outside Hungary. *Gül Baba* (1905) had a Turkish setting, and *Lili bárónö* (Baroness Lili, 1919) followed George M. Cohan's *Little Johnny Jones* (1904) and Lionel Monckton's *The Arcadians* (1909) in featuring a jockey who, against all odds, rides an unknown horse to victory. Both had books by Martos, the most successful Hungarian operetta librettist of the time. The Cigarette Waltz and a love duet from *Lili bárónö* proved particularly popular.

One Hungarian composer whose work certainly did reach beyond the Hungarian border was Viktor Jacobi (1883–1921). Trained at the Budapest Conservatory, he had his first big international success with *Leanyvásár* (Girl Market, 1911), which deliberately pandered to the lucrative transatlantic stage by having a book—by Miksa Bródy (1875–1924) and Ferenc Martos—with a Wild West setting. Lucy Harrison, a millionaire's daughter, goes off with her maid Bessy to a California village where they chance upon an annual ritual in which women are auctioned off to the local men. Unaware that they are watching real marriages being performed, they decide to take part, and Lucy finds herself paired off with handsome stranger Tom. He turns out to be the son of a man her father had ruined in business, and she begins to suspect that he is seeking revenge. She wishes she had settled for the wealthy but boring suitor her father had intended for her, but ultimately she decides that Tom is the right man for her.

Leanyvásár was exported first to Germany and Austria as *Mädchenmarkt* and then around the English-speaking world as *The Marriage Market*. Its score is light and sparkling, with captivating turns of melodic phrase and rhythm. Lucy's swirling entrance waltz, a ravishing waltz duet for Lucy and Tom, invigorating duets for the comedy pair, and bright choral numbers are just some of its highlights.

In the original production the two leading female roles were taken by prominent singing actresses of the Hungarian stage. Sári Fedák played Bessy, while Lucy was created by Sári Petráss, the niece of Ilka von Pálmay, a Hungarian prima donna who had created starring roles in Vienna in Zeller's *Der Vogelhändler* and in London in Gilbert and Sullivan's *The Grand Duke*. Petráss followed *Leanyvásár* onto the international circuit but met an untimely end when she drowned in Belgium in 1930.

Having thus successfully tapped the international market, Jacobi, Bródy, and Martos did just as well with *Szibill* (Sybil, 1914). Set in Russia, it features an opera singer (played by Fedák) who is mistaken for a visiting Grand Duchess—a mistake she is happy to go along with. Jacobi again mixed romantic and comic numbers to delightful effect, as in the love duet "Illuzió a szerelem." The war put a temporary halt to Jacobi's arrangements for a London production. Instead, he took the show to America, where he settled and became an American citizen. He died all too early at the age of thirty-eight.

Another Hungarian who rose to prominence in the first decade of the century was destined to follow Lehár's triumphant route to Vienna and climb to a position on that cartoonist's mountain only a little below the peak reached by Lehár himself. Emmerich (Imre) Kálmán (1882–1953) was born in Siófok on the shore of Lake Balaton. He originally intended to become a pianist, but persistent neuritis forced him to turn his attentions first to music journalism and then to composition in various forms, including cabaret songs. He made an auspicious operetta debut with *Tatárjárás* (Tatar Campaign, 1908), about the love of a wealthy widowed baroness and a lieutenant colonel whose regiment is on manoeuvres near her home. Apart from the inevitable waltzes, the big hit was the song "Adj egy édes csókot" for a shy young military recruit. The directors of Vienna's Theater an der Wien went to see the show and signed up both it and the composer. They produced a revised version called *Herbstmanöver* (Autumn Manoeuvres, 1909) that was highly successful, with newcomer Louise Kartousch winning favour as the young cadet.

A more folksy Hungarian work by Kálmán, *Az obsitos* (1910), was similarly transported to Vienna, refurbished by Victor Léon as *Der Gute Kamerad* (The Good Comrade, 1911). By then Kálmán was sufficiently well established in Vienna to be commissioned to set an original German libretto, albeit a story with a Hungarian subject to suit the distinctive Hungarian cabaret rhythms that were his strength. *Der Zigeunerprimás* (The Gypsy Virtuoso, 1912) told of a clash of generations. Pali Rácz, a real-life Gypsy violinist and the father of sixteen children, is cynical about his son Laczi's preference for modern music over the traditional melodies he himself favours. When the elderly Rácz gives a concert in Paris, he misses his cue and is saved by his son's intervention. Since it is the younger Rácz whose music is now appreciated by the audiences, the old man finally realises it is time to retire. Alexander Girardi, as the elderly violinist, had another in his string of waltz hits with "Mein alter Stradivari," in praise of his violin, while the lilting "Du, du, du, lieber Gott schaust du" and "O komm' mit mir und tanz mit mir ins Himmelreich hinein" found a life outside the theatre. They feature prominently in Kálmán's popular orchestral waltz *Dorfkinder* (Village Children).

For a while Kálmán divided his time between Budapest and Vienna, and it was in the former that his next significant creation appeared. *Zsuzsi kisasszony* (Miss Susi, 1915) had a Bródy and Martos libretto about a young woman whose excitement over the return of a local-boy-made-good is dashed when he turns out to be an imposter (an idea that became familiar later through *Martin Guerre*). Budapest took the highly rhythmic numbers to its heart, and the show was snapped up for America, where it appeared (much revised) as *Miss Springtime*. For Vienna, Kálmán chose to attach the score to a completely new book as *Die Faschingsfee* (The Carnival Fairy, 1917). Set in Munich at carnival time, it now concerned an artist who wins a prize that is withdrawn when he inadvertently offends the donor at the presentation party. Mizzi Günther played the young widow Countess Alexandra Maria, the "Carnival fairy" who ensures that, despite everything, the artist will not only keep the prize but win her hand into the bargain. For Berlin the piece was revised yet again for Fritzi Massary, who had a big hit with the slow waltz "Lieber Himmelsvater, sei nicht bös."

Meanwhile, Vienna had staged the work that was above all to ensure Kálmán's international reputation. *Die Csárdásfürstin* (The Csárdás Princess, 1915), with a libretto by Leo Stein and Béla Jenbach (1871–1943), was produced at the Johann-Strauss-Theater and proved one of the greatest Viennese operetta hits of all time. The Princess is not, as its later British title was to suggest, a *Gypsy* princess, but a variety-theatre singer whose speciality is the csárdás. She is Sylva Varescu (another Günther creation), who becomes engaged to Edwin Ronald, son of Prince Leopold Maria von und zu Lippert-Weylersheim. The father naturally opposes such a socially unequal marriage, until it transpires that Edwin's mother had herself once been a chorus girl.

The story is conventional; but Kálmán's is one of those scores in which just about every number is a hit. Among the best are "Die Mädis vom *Chantant*," in which Edwin's friend Count Boni Káncsiánu and man-about-town Feri von Kerekes reminisce about the girls of the cafés-chantants; Boni's rueful "Ganz ohne Weiber geht die *Chose* nicht"; and some romantic waltz numbers—most notably "Tausend kleine Engel singen." The whole is decked out with the sort of exotic orchestral sounds that Kálmán favoured, trading on almost nonstop rhythm and counterrhythm, demonstrated most vividly in the Act 1 finale by a csárdás version of Mendelssohn's Wedding March, complete with cimbalom!

But for all its wonderful melodies, Kálmán's operetta exemplifies what had now become the stock formula of Viennese operetta. Gone are the varied lists of characters and the quasi-operatic ensembles of the nineteenth century. Instead, romantic numbers for soprano and tenor alternate with song-and-dance comedy routines for buffo and soubrette; the other characters don't sing at all. The finales to each act have prominent choral contributions and move the action along with the help of reprises of earlier numbers.

This more-restricted musical ambition and recourse to stock formulas was probably a factor in the decline of European operetta as an international musical force. The suddenness of its decline was exacerbated by the First World War, which divided the musical theatre along political lines and destroyed the Habsburg monarchy that had fostered it. Yet the formula had served uncommonly well in its time. It was through the romantic operettas of Lehár, Straus, Fall, and Kálmán that European operetta achieved its greatest popular success, and their works epitomise the glamour that is still associated with operetta. Even today, these four composers feature prominently in the operetta repertory. And in *Die lustige Witwe,* Lehár gave the world a work that, like Strauss's *Die Fledermaus,* has transcended its humble origins to become an acknowledged masterpiece of the lyric theatre.

Part II

Comic Opera and Musical Comedy:

Britain and America

Chapter Six
Gilbert and Sullivan and
British Comic Opera

Britain never achieved a native grand opera tradition to rival that of France or Germany. Until the nineteenth century British musical stage entertainment had come most notably in the form of ballad opera, which sometimes set existing music to an original text, as in John Gay's *Beggar's Opera* (1728). The genre developed via the masques and operas of Thomas Arne (1710–78), among them *Alfred* (1740), which contained the chorus "Rule, Britannia," *Thomas and Sally* (1760), and *Love in a Village* (1762). Later came Charles Dibdin (ca. 1745–1814), whose works included most notably *Lionel and Clarissa* (1768). The nineteenth century then brought sub-Verdian romantic operas such as *The Bohemian Girl* (1843), by Michael Balfe (1808–70), *Maritana* (1845), by Vincent Wallace (1812–65), and *The Lily of Killarney* (1862), by Julius Benedict (1804–85). Smaller-scale operettas were also produced for drawing-room entertainment.

It was London's receptiveness to imported material, coupled with Offenbach's relationship by marriage to London producer and ticket agent John Mitchell, that made the British capital one of the first places outside Paris to enjoy Offenbach's operettas. The Bouffes-Parisiens company, led by Offenbach himself, performed a two-month season at the St James's Theatre between May and July 1857. During the 1860s, English versions of the Offenbach one-acters became popular fare in the music halls. But it took longer for English versions of the full-length works to become established. The British had their own idea of what constituted burlesque: a satirical treatment of a familiar opera or story, replete with puns and song parodies. London audiences had little need for the Parisian humour of *Orphée aux enfers*. Moreover, British moral standards militated against such works as *La Belle Hélène*, in which adultery was seen to triumph. Not until the end of the 1860s were the defences breached, partly through guest appearances by Hortense Schneider and other leading Parisian performers in the French versions but also by English-language productions of *The Grand Duchess of Gerolstein* in 1867 and *Geneviève de Brabant* (with its celebrated Gendarmes' Duet) in 1871.

As the French one-acters were gaining acceptance among the working classes in the music halls, they were also appealing to the middle classes as private drawing-room diversions; and it was through the drawing-room that Britain first began to establish its own national equivalent. Offenbach's *Les Deux Aveugles* was so popular at the Saturday-evening smoking parties held by the industrialist Arthur Lewis at his home in Kensington that his guests began devising similar entertainments of their own. Two of these guests were *Punch* contributor Francis Cowley Burnand (1836–1917) and composer Arthur Sullivan (1842–1900), the white-hot hope of the London musical establishment. They responded by adapting a currently popular stage play, John Madison Morton's *Box and Cox,* to private use. The action concerns a landlady, Mrs. Bouncer, who finds a way to charge double rent for the same room, by letting it out to two gentlemen at once. Since Box works by day and Cox by night, the two meet only on the stairs, the one leaving for work as the other returns, until one day they finally come face to face in what each thinks is his own room.

For their all-male gatherings, Burnand and Sullivan transformed Mrs. Bouncer into Sergeant Bouncer, interpolated solos, duets, and trios, and reversed the title. *Cox and Box* was performed privately with piano accompaniment in 1866, and then orchestrated the following year for a charity performance. Its enthusiastic reception led to its being taken up by the Royal Gallery of Illustration, a place of entertainment that resembled a hall more than a theatre and which sought to avoid the less respectable associations of theatres by using the term *illustration* in preference to *play*. In keeping with the general moral tone, the accompaniment was provided by piano and harmonium. There *Cox and Box* shared the bill with two Offenbach one-acters, *Croquefer* and *Ching-Chow-Hi* (*Ba-ta-clan*). Once again, the piece was a hit, running to well over two hundred performances, a remarkable achievement for the time. Its success persuaded Sullivan to collaborate with Burnand again, this time on a full-length comic opera, *The Contrabandista, or The Law of the Ladrones* (1867), commissioned for the newly opened St George's Opera House. A somewhat innocuous piece in both its humour and its music, it tells of a Spanish bandit tribe (the Ladrones) who capture an English photographer, who, according to an obscure law, is required to become their new chief.

Sullivan considered such pieces no more than light relief from his real work as a composer of symphonic and choral works. However, he could not escape the precedent they had set. When in 1871 the theatre manager John Hollingshead required a Christmas piece for his recently opened Gaiety Theatre, he teamed Sullivan with the playwright and humorous writer W. S. Gilbert (1837–1911). The result was *Thespis, or The Gods Grown Old* (1871), and it cannot have been coincidence that it featured encounters between gods and mortals that were reminiscent of *Orphée aux enfers*. In the Gilbert and Sullivan work, the mortals are actors, who meet the gods on Mount Olympus and change places with them. *Thespis* served its immediate purpose well but was considered of purely ephemeral importance. Indeed, only one song, a chorus, and some ballet music have survived.

Gilbert and Sullivan went back to their separate interests until 1875, when they were brought together again by impresario Richard D'Oyly Carte, who needed a one-act afterpiece for Offenbach's *La Périchole*. The resultant *Trial by Jury* (1875), styled a "dramatic cantata," is through-composed and is one of the most perfect small pieces in any branch of musical theatre. It portrays a trial for breach of promise, which is ultimately resolved when the judge decides to marry the plaintiff himself. The whole piece shows both Gilbert and Sullivan at their best. Gilbert's book is full of delightful comic touches, not least of which is the

The cast of *Trial by Jury,* in a contemporary engraving
Mander and Mitchenson Theatre Collection

inability of judge and jury to retain even a semblance of impartiality (the judge falls in turn for the principal bridesmaid and the plaintiff; the gentlemen of the jury frequently express their anger at the defendant), while Sullivan's music is light, unassuming, and hummable. The solos of the Defendant, Plaintiff, Counsel, and Learned Judge retain their freshness to this day. The staging, too, featured such original touches as the plaintiff's appearance in bridal dress accompanied by her bridesmaids and the defendant accompanying himself on the guitar as he gave his testimony. Sullivan's elder brother Frederic followed up his minor role as Apollo in *Thespis* by creating the leading comic character, the Learned Judge.

Perhaps surprisingly, composer and lyricist split up immediately after writing *Trial by Jury,* working with other collaborators for a time. Sullivan and B. C. Stephenson (1838–1906) produced the one-act *The Zoo* (1875), which was set in the currently fashionable London Zoo, while Gilbert returned to Frederic Clay (1838–89), with whom he had already created various one-acters for the Royal Gallery of Illustration. These included *Ages Ago* (1869), whose score Clay dedicated to Sullivan and at whose rehearsals Gilbert and Sullivan first met. Now Gilbert and Clay collaborated on a piece in what was to become the traditional

Caricature of Gilbert and Sullivan by Alfred Bryan, 1878
Mander and Mitchenson Theatre Collection

British two-act format (rather than the continental three). *Princess Toto* (1876) re-counted the marital fortunes of a somewhat eccentric princess.

But it was not long before Richard D'Oyly Carte brought Gilbert and Sullivan together again, when he formed his Comedy Opera Company for the express purpose of producing British comic opera. Gilbert set about developing a love-potion story that he had already used in *Dulcamara,* a burlesque of Donizetti's *L'Elisir d'amore.* Now it became *The Sorcerer* (1877), in which a member of a family firm of sorcerers creates havoc by distributing an aphrodisiac amongst the inhabitants of a village. For the Opera Comique Theatre, Carte put together the basis of what was to prove, as the D'Oyly Carte Opera Company, one of the longest-lived theatrical companies of all time.

Over the years of Gilbert and Sullivan's creativity, members of Carte's company would come and go, but the performance styles established in their initial two-act work remained essentially unchanged. By far the most experienced member of Carte's early company was Mrs. Howard Paul, a mezzo-soprano in her forties whose background included playing the title role in one of London's first productions of Offenbach's *The Grand Duchess of Gérolstein*. As Lady Sangazure, "a lady of ancient lineage," she provided the prototype of what may be the most questionable target of Gilbert's humour—the ageing female who is looking for a husband. Meanwhile, as her elderly beau Sir Marmaduke Pointdextre, Carte engaged the thirty-year-old baritone Richard Temple, already a veteran of both opera and operetta. He and two performers who had only recently arrived on the London stage were to become irrevocably associated with the Gilbert and Sullivan operettas. Twenty-four-year-old Rutland Barrington, a member of Mrs. Howard Paul's touring company, played the village curate Dr. Daly, while a twenty-nine-year-old concert entertainer named George Grossmith took the title part of the sorcerer, John Wellington Wells. The latter role had been intended for Sullivan's brother Frederic, who had died a few months earlier. Grossmith possessed a modest singing voice, but he knew how to put across a comic song.

The Sorcerer was received with warm approval. Gilbert's book was deemed witty and amusing, and Sullivan's music sparkled and charmed. Rutland Barrington's sentimental ballad "Time was when Love and I were well acquainted" proved one of the most popular numbers in the score, and George Grossmith racked up a major success with a rapid-fire patter song, "My name is John Wellington Wells." The show settled in for a highly respectable run of 175 performances.

By the time it closed, the collaborators had a successor ready. This was "an entirely original nautical comic opera" entitled *HMS Pinafore* (1878). Its story stretched credulity, since the tenor lead, Ralph Rackstraw, presented throughout as a young man, turns out to have been swapped at birth with his sweetheart Josephine's father (the captain of the *Pinafore*). However, nobody seems to have minded much, and the lifelike setting of a man-of-war moored off Portsmouth, with even the rigging meticulously reproduced, appealed no less than Gilbert's topsy-turvy humour and his swipes at class consciousness and privilege. Much fun is made of the character of the First Sea Lord, Sir Joseph Porter, whose complete lack of experience at sea makes him ideal—in political terms—for the position. This was an undisguised dig at W. H. Smith (of the London stationery chain), a man with similar lack of experience who had been appointed by Prime Minister Disraeli as First Lord of the Admiralty. As Sir Joseph, George Grossmith made much of his entrance song, "I am the monarch of the sea," in which he described his progress up the political ladder and culminated bitingly with:

Stick close to your desks and never go to sea,
And you all may be Rulers of the Queen's Navee.

All the major comic roles in *HMS Pinafore* were designed for the company of *The Sorcerer*. In addition to Grossmith, there was Rutland Barrington, who played Captain Corcoran and sang the sentimental number, "Fair moon to thee I sing"; Harriet Everard, as the Portsmouth bumboat woman Little Buttercup, the elderly woman who is still looking for love; and Richard Temple as the crippled, trouble-making sailor Dick Deadeye.

The first of many immortal Gilbert and Sullivan catchphrases comes in Captain Corcoran's opening song, where he makes his emphatic claim: "I'm never, never sick at sea"; it is greeted by his crew's retort, "What *never?*" which forces from him the qualified, "Well, *hardly* ever!" But Gilbert's comedy went beyond lyrics: in an inventive touch, he provided a female chorus of Sir Joseph Porter's "sisters and his cousins and his aunts" as a counterpart to the male chorus of sailors. At their head as Cousin Hebe was the young Jessie Bond, who in due course became another Gilbert and Sullivan stalwart.

Sullivan's score is even sprightlier and brighter than the music for *The Sorcerer,* and altogether more assured in the way it responds to Gilbert's clever lyrics. There are solos of great beauty in Josephine's "Sorry her lot who loves too well," Captain Corcoran's serenade, and Little Buttercup's simple entrance in waltz tempo, "I'm called Little Buttercup." Perhaps the greatest advance lies in the exuberance Sullivan gives to comic numbers such as the trio "Never mind the why and wherefore."

Yet *HMS Pinafore* was by no means an unalloyed success at first. London was suffering from a heat wave that made stuffy theatres the last place the public wished to be. More than once, closure notices were posted for the show, and the salaries of the company were cut. At about that time, Sullivan conducted one of Covent Garden's Promenade Concerts, where he included a selection from the piece. This gave the music a new audience, who flocked to the Opera Comique. For a short time there was even a rival, unauthorised production seeking to cash in on *Pinafore's* popularity. The Opera Comique run eventually stretched to 571 performances—an unprecedented total for that time.

Yet even this success was nothing compared with the piece's reception in the United States. Because there was no international copyright agreement (that didn't come until 1891), productions of *Pinafore* could spring up at will—and they did, all bearing varying degrees of fidelity to the original but all having in common that Gilbert and Sullivan didn't make a penny from them. The result was that Gilbert, Sullivan, and Carte not only took their own, official version of *Pinafore* to New York, but they determined to stage their next work there before it even appeared in London. Purely to secure the British copyright, *The Pirates of Penzance* (1879) was staged once by a touring *Pinafore* cast in the modest surroundings of Paignton, Devon, but the real première came in New York. Since Gilbert and Sullivan were already in America putting the finishing touches on the work, the Paignton production was a makeshift effort—the cast wore their *Pinafore* costumes and read from scripts—that bears a questionable relation to the finished product.

In *The Pirates of Penzance,* Gilbert's humour centred around a paradox: a man who is born on 29 February (Leap Year Day) is deemed, after twenty-one years, to be only five years old because he has celebrated only five birthdays. Frederic is the literal-minded hero who accepts this proposition; his dilemma is compounded by the earlier actions of his nursemaid Ruth, who, being hard of hearing, apprenticed him as a boy to a pirate instead of a pilot (of a ship). Because his apprenticeship lasts until his twenty-first birthday, Frederic considers himself bound to serve the eighty-odd years it will take.

George Grossmith played Major-General Stanley, who describes himself in Grossmith's now-traditional patter song as "the very model of a modern Major-General." It is his attractive chorus of daughters who eventually deflect the pirates from their evil ways. The pirates are not all evil, however; as orphans themselves, they refuse to take advantage of others in a similar condition—which all their intended victims consequently claim to be.

Major-General Stanley's daughters are first encountered arriving at the beach for a picnic, singing a delightful chorus whose music had previously appeared in *Thespis.* The heroine, Mabel (who in due course falls in love with Frederic), then offers a coloratura waltz that burlesques the stylistic extravagances of grand opera, in particular Juliette's "Je veux vivre" in Gounod's *Roméo et Juliette.*

Richard Temple was the Pirate King, and a highlight of the score is the Paradox Trio in which he points out to Frederic and Ruth that Frederic's birthdate ties him to the pirate band until 1940. Rutland Barrington was the Sergeant of Police, whose ballad "When a felon's not engaged in his employment" is eternally quoted for its refrain, "A policeman's lot is not a happy one." The relationship of police and pirates is strikingly similar to the one between carabiniers and brigands in Offenbach's *Les Brigands;* like their Offenbachian predecessors, the Penzance policemen always arrive too late to apprehend their prey. The similarity cannot have been coincidental, for Gilbert had once translated the Meilhac and Halévy text for the publishers Boosey and Company.

The success of Gilbert and Sullivan's collaboration now ensured a regular flow of commissions. *Patience* (1881) was a satire on the fashionable aesthetic movement and the otherwordly poses adopted by its adherents, who included the Irish poet Oscar Wilde. Patience is a village milkmaid, and she and her fellow village maidens are wooed not only by the aesthetic poet Reginald Bunthorne (played by Grossmith) and her childhood sweetheart Archibald Grosvenor (Barrington) but by the entire 35th Dragoon Guards under Colonel Calverley (Temple). Patience and Grosvenor have a particularly charming duet ("Prithee, pretty maiden"), and Grosvenor sings a swinging anti-aesthetic number ("A magnet hung in a hardware shop"). Sullivan's score gains much from the contrast between the languorous music of the village maidens ("Twenty love-sick maidens we") and the vigour and swagger of the martial music for the Dragoon Guards ("The soldiers of the Queen") and Colonel Calverley ("When I first put this uniform on"). Alice Barnett took over the contralto roles that Mrs. Howard Paul had originated; here she was the middle-aged Lady Jane, who embraces aestheticism to attract a man. She accompanied herself on the cello for "Silver'd is the raven hair," in which she bemoans the ravages of time.

So profitable had the Gilbert and Sullivan operettas now become that Carte was able to abandon the outdated, cramped, stuffy Opera Comique and transfer *Patience* to his newly built Savoy Theatre. The first theatre in London to be lit by electricity rather than gas, it was a venue in which the cream of London society were all the happier to be seen. In *Iolanthe* (1882), the first new piece staged there, developments in electricity even permitted him to set battery-powered stars in the hair of the fairy characters, creating a sensation. *Iolanthe*, like most fairy operettas, involves its fairies with mortals, and it was a stroke of daring on Gilbert's part to make the latter members of the House of Lords. Jessie Bond achieved star status in the mezzo-soprano role of Iolanthe, who has been outlawed by the fairies for marrying the Lord Chancellor (played by Grossmith). The pair have a son, Strephon (Temple), who is a fairy from the waist up but a mortal from the waist down.

Gilbert here set up various windmills to tilt at — the British aristocracy, the hereditary and political system, and the topsy-turvydom of a son who looks no younger than his immortal fairy mother and whose lower half threatens to age while the upper half remains immortal. The tenor and soprano leads are the Earl

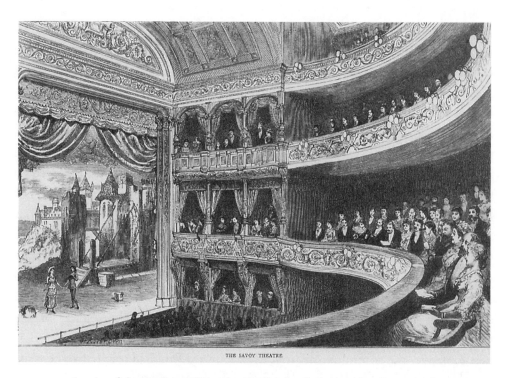

Interior of the new Savoy Theatre in 1881, showing the inaugural performance of
Patience there (the meeting of Patience and Bunthorne in Act 1)
Mander and Mitchenson Theatre Collection

Tolloller and an Arcadian shepherdess and Ward in Chancery named Phyllis
(Leonora Braham). Rutland Barrington played Tolloller's counterpart the Earl of
Mountararat, and Alice Barnett now took the contralto role of the Queen of the
Fairies. The score was Sullivan's most polished and musicianly to date. It included
a symphonic overture instead of the orchestral medleys that he was inclined to
leave assistants to put together; the fairy music was up to the standards of his incidental music for productions of *The Tempest* and *The Merry Wives of Windsor;*
and the March of the Peers was one of his most majestic. The staging was equally
spectacular.

In its characterisation and orchestration, Sullivan's score is one of the most
cultured in the musical theatre repertory. Even its stock numbers surpassed their
predecessors. Grossmith's Nightmare Song was easily his most testing and effective patter song, ending with the apt words, "The night has been long—ditto,
ditto my song—and thank goodness they're both of them over!" Strephon, complete with panpipes, sings an engaging duet with Phyllis, "Good morrow, good
lover," while Mountararat recalls Britain's past glories in "When Britain really

ruled the waves." The bouncing trio "He who shies at such a prize" calls to mind *Pinafore's* "Never mind the why and wherefore." Another big hit was the song for the sentry stationed in front of the House of Lords, where he reflects on the "astonishing" fact that "ev'ry boy and ev'ry gal that's born into the world alive is either a little Liberal or else a little Conservative." The role was created by the Irish bass Charles Manners, who later became a Covent Garden opera singer and formed the Moody-Manners Opera Company with his wife, Helen Moody.

Up to that point Gilbert and Sullivan had experienced unbroken success, but their next collaboration proved a disappointment. *Princess Ida* (1884) featured rival kings and satirised education for women. It contained some typically inspired music from Sullivan, including a soprano role for the Princess with coloratura demands, as well as such sprightly numbers as the quintet "The woman of the wisest wit" and a marvellous sequence in which Prince Hilarion and two male companions climb over the walls of Princess Ida's college dressed in female robes. But Sullivan was ill when he composed the score, and he derived limited inspiration from the book and lyrics, which Gilbert had adapted from an existing stage piece. In three acts rather than the usual two, and in blank verse, *Princess Ida* did not flow in the way Savoy audiences had come to expect. Worse, it did not provide balanced roles for the team of Savoy favourites. As Princess Ida's father, old King Gama, Grossmith did not appear until the second act, and Temple had an even smaller role as Gama's son Arac. Leonora Braham, the creator of Patience, had the title role, with Barrington as King Hildebrand, and Durward Lely as Cyril, a friend of Hildebrand's son Hilarion (Henry Bracy). Succeeding Alice Barnett in the contralto role, Rosina Brandram played a college professor, while Jessie Bond was her daughter Melissa.

Princess Ida was a failure only by the Savoy's high standards; but it closed after only 246 performances, making it necessary for Carte to revive a revamped *Sorcerer* while Gilbert and Sullivan hastily finished their next piece. They came up trumps, producing the work that worldwide has ever after been most closely associated with their names. Just as the topicality of the aesthetic movement had inspired *Patience,* so a vogue for things Japanese inspired *The Mikado* (1885). The show's success was fanned by the popularity of a Japanese Village that was then an attraction of an exhibition of Japanese customs in Kensington. Even if much about the piece and its characters remains resolutely British, the mere fact that it had a Japanese setting, poses, and costumes brought in the public in 1885. As is usual in Gilbert and Sullivan's works, the actual story was less important than Gilbert's humorous situations and witty dialogue and lyrics, together with espe-

Sybil Grey, Leonora Braham, and Jessie Bond as
the Three Little Maids in *The Mikado*
Mander and Mitchenson Theatre Collection

cially rewarding parts for the Savoy regulars. Grossmith was Ko-Ko, Lord High
Executioner of Titipu, a position the character attained when he was due to be executed for flirting, a capital offence. In typical Gilbertian logic, the best way to
circumvent the Mikado's oppressive law was to appoint as executioner the man
who was next in line to be killed; for he could not "cut off another's head until
he's cut his own off." Ko-Ko's "Taken from a county jail," in which he relates his
history, followed by "I've got a little list," which describes people whose loss would
be a distinct gain to society, are masterpieces of verbal and rhythmic ingenuity.

Ko-Ko's peace of mind in his seemingly invulnerable position is shattered
by the news that the Mikado (Temple), anxious to know why no executions have
taken place, is planning a visit to Titipu. Somewhat surprisingly, someone volun-
teers to help Ko-Ko out by letting him behead him. This is Nanki-Poo (Durward
Lely), the Mikado's son, who has disguised himself as a wandering minstrel in
order to escape the clutches of the ageing Katisha (Rosina Brandram, now en-

sconced in the contralto roles). On learning that his sweetheart, Yum-Yum, is engaged to Ko-Ko, Nanki-Poo prepares to commit suicide, and he doesn't mind if
Ko-Ko does the job instead. But Ko-Ko finds he doesn't have the guts to perform
the execution, and so he merely pretends to have done so—which proves just as
well, when the Mikado and Katisha arrive and discover just who he's supposed to
have killed. For Grossmith the character of Ko-Ko was the creation of a lifetime,
as was Pooh-Bah, Lord High Everything Else, for Rutland Barrington. The high
official's readiness to accept bribes carries as much sting today as it did in 1885.
Leonora Braham, Jessie Bond, and Sybil Grey were the "three little maids from
school" whose innocence Sullivan deliciously captured in his music. Individual
musical delights are Nanki-Poo's ballad "A wandering minstrel I," with its pastiches of various types of popular songs; his duet with Yum-Yum, "Were you not
to Ko-Ko plighted," in which the two demonstrate—at length—the embraces
they would exchange if it weren't improper; the ingenious patter trio "I am so
proud," in which Pooh-Bah, Pish-Tush (a nobleman), and Ko-Ko explain why
they must altruistically decline to be executed; Yum-Yum's eloquent (and egotis-
tical) hymn to her own beauty "The sun whose rays"; the rollicking trio "Here's a
how-de-do" and the equally lively quintet "The flowers that bloom in the spring";
and, perhaps the most famous of all, Ko-Ko's mock elegy "Tit Willow," on the
death from unrequited love of a tom-tit. *The Mikado* ran for almost two years and
has been a part of British culture ever since.

It was perhaps inevitable that its successor would fail to reach the same
standard. Even the title of *Ruddigore* (1887) was problematic; in its original form
of *Ruddygore* it offended Victorian susceptibilities in view of the association with
ruddy as an expletive. The play is set in the Cornish village of Rederring, and the
idea of a female chorus of professional bridesmaids and a male chorus of ghostly
ancestors in a picture gallery is Gilbert at his brilliant best. Yet, as a burlesque of
British melodrama with a story about a family curse, the piece lacked the gaiety of
its predecessor. Moreover, the ending, in which the ancestors turn out—on a
very convoluted piece of reasoning—to be alive, and pair off with the professional bridesmaids, was a somewhat unsatisfactory denouement.

Sullivan nevertheless turned out some inspired numbers, above all the
ghost music which, with Sir Roderic Murgatroyd's "When the night wind howls"
as its climax, shows the composer at his descriptive best. George Grossmith played
Sir Ruthven Murgatroyd, the current baronet, who is disguised as a farmer to
avoid the family curse, and Durward Lely was his sailor foster-brother, Richard
Dauntless, who makes his entrance with a jaunty hornpipe. Rutland Barrington

played Sir Despard Murgatroyd, who has become the twenty-second "wicked baronet" of Ruddigore following the disappearance of his brother Ruthven. It was as their late father, Sir Roderic Murgatroyd, that Richard Temple stepped down from his picture frame. Leonora Braham was the innocent village maiden Rose Maybud, who consults her book of etiquette on all occasions, while Rosina Brandram played her aunt, Dame Hannah. Jessie Bond was Sir Despard's somewhat demented companion "Mad Margaret," and the two sing a particularly droll duet, "I once was a very abandoned person," after both have "reformed."

Though falling short of Gilbert and Sullivan's greatest hits, *Ruddigore* ran for a healthy 288 performances. But by now Sullivan was feeling frustrated by the comic opera formula, and it was to assuage his feelings that Gilbert provided a more serious piece, *The Yeomen of the Guard* (1888). It even had a sad ending. Ever original in his settings, Gilbert this time chose the Tower of London during the sixteenth century. The story revolves around Lieutenant Fairfax (played by Courtice Pounds, by now the Savoy company's leading tenor), who has been condemned to death on a charge of sorcery trumped up by a relative who wants to inherit his wealth. He is set free by the sympathetic yeoman, Sergeant Meryll (Temple), who convinces his daughter Phoebe (Bond) to seduce the stupid jailer Wilfred Shadbolt (W. H. Denny) and obtain the keys to the condemned man's cell. To confound his scheming relative, Fairfax secretly marries a strolling player, Elsie Maynard (Geraldine Ulmar), intending to leave his estate to her. Fairfax is finally reprieved, and he and Elsie find they love each other after all. At this, her erstwhile partner and lover, the jester Jack Point (Grossmith), falls senseless to the stage, his heart broken.

Even in this more serious mode, Gilbert still provided Sullivan with perfect material, resulting in the most carefully worked of all Sullivan's comic opera scores. Its overture is a minor symphonic masterpiece, with an imposing Tower motif that recurs throughout the work and helps lay the shadow of the prison over the whole work. Elsie Maynard's soprano aria "'Tis done! I am a bride!" is of operatic stature, and Fairfax's "Is life a boon?" and "Free from his fetters grim" make the role meaty enough for any leading tenor. There is an exquisitely worked number for the two strolling players (Elsie and Point) in "I have a song to sing, O!" and a haunting, solemn march intended to preface Fairfax's execution. Phoebe's "When maiden loves," with its orchestral evocation of a spinning-wheel, and her teasing "Were I thy bride" show Gilbert and Sullivan at their collective best. There are also moments of humour, notably the passage in the Act I finale when Fairfax, now disguised as Sergeant Meryll's son

George Grossmith as Jack Point in *The Yeomen of the Guard*
Mander and Mitchenson Theatre Collection

Leonard, is introduced to his supposed sister, Phoebe, without having the faintest idea who she is.

If *The Yeomen of the Guard* occupies a special pinnacle in Gilbert and Sullivan's oeuvre, their next piece, *The Gondoliers* (1889), challenged *The Mikado* for popularity. By this time Sullivan's more serious ambitions were being satisfied by a commission for a grand opera, *Ivanhoe* (1891), which left him in the mood to turn out some of his sunniest music for the Savoy. The opening twenty minutes of *The Gondoliers* offer an unbroken stretch of music, containing one glorious melody after another, as the two carefree gondoliers Marco and Giuseppe Palmieri (played by Courtice Pounds and Rutland Barrington) choose their partners Gianetta and Tessa in a Venetian piazza. The Grand Inquisitor, Don Alhambra del Bolero (W. H. Denny), explains in "I stole the Prince" that *either* Marco or Giuseppe is actually king of the island of Barataria, but it takes until the final curtain to discover that in fact *neither* is the king thanks to mix-up in infancy. Shades of *HMS Pinafore!* Until the final revelation the two have reigned jointly, initially denied the company of their wives but having a high old time putting their republican theories into practice.

There is rich humour in the character of the hen-pecked Duke of Plaza Toro, who "led his regiment from behind" because "he found it less exciting." But the great glory is Sullivan's music, with such rare delights as Tessa's tender "When a merry maiden marries," Gianetta's appealing "Kind sir, you cannot have the heart," Giuseppe's buoyant "Rising early in the morning," and the lyricism of Marco's "Take a pair of sparkling eyes." And how joyously the score lights up when the two brides arrive at the island kingdom! Not least, the unique inventiveness of Gilbert and Sullivan is captured by the moment when Marco and Giuseppe, having been told that they will reign jointly, once more take this to its literal extreme, replying as one individual and singing alternative bars:

> *Marco:* Replying, we
> *Giuseppe:* Sing as
> *Marco:* One indi-
> *Giuseppe:* Vidual. As I
> *Marco:* Find I'm a
> *Giuseppe:* King, to my
> *Marco:* Kingdom I
> *Giuseppe:* Bid you all.

It might have been more satisfactory if the Gilbert and Sullivan partnership had ended with *The Gondoliers,* leaving Sullivan to pursue his serious musical ambitions and a faithful public wanting more. In fact, the pair, whose collaboration had prospered because of the creativity sparked by their very contrasted natures, quarrelled over the mundane matter of expenditures for the Savoy Theatre. Though they collaborated again on *Utopia Limited* (1894) and *The Grand Duke* (1896), neither of these two works ranks with the earlier operettas in quality or popularity.

There was, anyway, far more to English comic opera than just the work of Gilbert and Sullivan. In addition to Frederic Clay, already mentioned, London-born Edward Jakobowski (1856–1929) had a hit with *Erminie* (1885), which, although it ran for only three months in London, toured the provinces and the empire for many years. Its tale of a couple of comic thieves had its biggest success in the United States, where several songs became popular, notably the lullaby "Dear Mother, in dreams I see her." But none of Jakobowski's later work did very well; the best received was *Mynheer Jan* (1887), which had a Dutch setting. His *Die Brillanten-Königin* (1894) was produced at the Carltheater after he sought to revive his career in Vienna.

In reality, there were just two British composers who came at all close to rivalling Sullivan. Alfred Cellier (1844–1891) first gained note as a composer of comic operas with *The Sultan of Mocha* (1874), whose score he dedicated to Sullivan. He hit the big time with *Dorothy* (1886), which ran in London for 931 performances—far longer than anything by Gilbert and Sullivan. *Dorothy* boasted a strong cast: Marion Hood in the title role, Ben Davies as principal tenor, and handsome matinée idol C. Hayden Coffin in the baritone lead. The score appealed for its simple yet refined rusticity, especially in Coffin's serenade "Queen of my heart," an adaptation of an existing Cellier song that was added in London while the composer was away in Australia. Cellier retained his claim to be Sullivan's strongest rival with another rural English piece, *Doris* (1889), which boasted an attractive tenor number, "I've sought the brake and bracken," as well as with the posthumous *The Mountebanks* (1892). This latter benefited from a libretto by W. S. Gilbert with some appealing innovations, including a popular number for two automatons, "Put a penny in the slot"; but it also suffered from its re-use of the magic-potion idea Gilbert had already employed in *The Sorcerer*.

The other challenger to Sullivan—and at one stage his most likely successor—was Edward Solomon (1855–95). A prolific writer of popular songs, he attracted attention on both sides of the Atlantic as a composer of comic operas with his nautical *Billee Taylor* (1880), which contained the hit "All on account of Eliza." During the 1880s he turned out a string of stage pieces whilst pursuing a somewhat irresponsible personal life that saw him in the courts for debt and bigamy. His big moment artistically came when Gilbert and Sullivan quarrelled and the Savoy management commissioned him to write *The Nautch Girl* (1891), an "Indian comic opera." With more than two hundred performances, it succeeded reasonably well in its Sullivanesque style, notably with the comic song "The Rajah of Chutneypore" (for Rutland Barrington) and the leading lady's ballad "Near thee once more." For a follow-up, Solomon revised his *Vicar of Bray* (1882), which, as it had done first time round, was popular enough, without filling the gap left by Gilbert and Sullivan.

Solomon's early death at the age of thirty-nine conformed to the pattern followed by all Sullivan's potential challengers. Clay died at fifty (having been paralysed since he was forty-four), Cellier at forty-seven. In the final reckoning, Gilbert and Sullivan were unique, with the sometimes cruel edge of Gilbert's brilliant wit softened by Sullivan's graceful music. The latter's style owed more to the classical masters and to English balladry than to the dance rhythms that pervaded European operetta. This, together with Gilbert's very individual humour, set them apart from the continental tradition; it also made their operettas less accessible to non-English speakers. The unique style and unparalleled popularity of the Gilbert and Sullivan operettas has also had the unfortunate side effect that their British contemporaries have undeservedly suffered virtual oblivion.

Chapter Seven
Gaiety Girls

At his death, Sullivan left half finished *The Emerald Isle* (1901), a comic opera with an Irish setting. Its book was by Basil Hood (1864–1917), perhaps the most talented of the librettists to whom Sullivan turned after his working relationship with W. S. Gilbert finally collapsed. The first Hood and Sullivan collaboration, for the Savoy Theatre, had been *The Rose of Persia* (1899), based on the Arabian Nights story of Abu Hassan. The next was *The Emerald Isle* and, to complete it, a composer was chosen who had no experience in writing comic opera beyond a single student work. But he had long been seen as a composer in the Sullivan mould because of his musical education (at London's Royal Academy of Music),

Henry Lytton as the Earl of Essex and Rosina Brandram as Queen Elizabeth
in German's *Merrie England,* from *The Playgoer* (April 1902)
Author's collection

his symphonies and songs, and, most particularly, the incidental music he had
written for a number of theatrical productions.

Edward German (1862–1936) was born German Edward Jones in Whit-
church, on the English-Welsh border. He made such a good job of completing
The Emerald Isle (1901) in Sullivan's style that he and Hood were immediately
commissioned to produce another piece. This time it was a quasi-historical pag-
eant, featuring among its characters Queen Elizabeth (played by Gilbert and Sullivan's contralto Rosina Brandram) and Sir Walter Raleigh (tenor Robert Evett),
as well as evoking the spirit of Robin Hood and his Merry Men in the Act I finale.
The story revolves around the Queen's jealousy at Raleigh's love for her lady-in-
waiting Bessie Throckmorton (soprano Agnes Fraser), while the Queen herself
is the target of the affections of the Earl of Essex (baritone Henry A. Lytton).
Comic contributions come from a troupe of strolling players. German lacked
Sullivan's flair for dramatic writing, but he rivalled him in melodic inspiration.

Merrie England has remained the best-known British comic opera by someone other than Sullivan, and several songs survive on the concert platform: Raleigh's beautiful tribute to "The English Rose," Essex's stirring "The yeomen of England," Bessie's waltz "Oh, who shall say that love is cruel?" and the Queen's imposing "O Peaceful England."

Hailed as the heirs to Gilbert and Sullivan, Hood and German had much less joy with their next work. *A Princess of Kensington* (1903) was in the mould of Gilbert's fairy pieces; the novelty was that this time the fairy characters become involved with a crew of sailors. It gave German the opportunity to create music in varied styles, including impressive ensembles, a charming tenor ballad, "My heart a ship at anchor lies," and a lively male quartet, "We're four jolly sailor men." But the play's modest run helped to bring home that the traditional comic opera format was now somewhat dated. It brought to an end the era of new Savoy operas and the brief collaboration of Hood and German.

Although writing for the popular theatre, German retained his musicianly ideals, and an invitation by producer Robert Courtneidge to compose a work for the two-hundredth anniversary of the birth of Henry Fielding produced a comic opera score that is generally acknowledged his best. *Tom Jones* (1906) was a much-trimmed-down version of Fielding's novel—and a lot of its bawdiness went too—but German was the ideal composer to catch the rustic elements of the story, as well as to portray its sturdy hero Tom Jones (played by baritone Hayden Coffin), whose somewhat wild adventures ultimately lead him to respectability and the hand of his beloved Sophia (Ruth Vincent). Sophia's coloratura waltz "For Tonight" arguably surpassed Mabel's "Poor wandering one" in Sullivan's *Pirates of Penzance* and gained a lasting place in the concert repertoire. The daintier aspects of the score are well represented by her reflective "Dream o' Day Jill" and her maid Honor's "The Green Ribbon," while the comic baritone's dialect song "On a Januairy Morning" is in keeping with the pastoral setting. Tom's dashing nature is equally well captured in "West Country lad" and "A Scarlet Coat." But the muted reception to even so outstanding a score as this carried the same message that greeted *A Princess of Kensington*: comic opera was no longer to the public taste. German composed just one more, in collaboration, as it happened, with the elderly W. S. Gilbert. Alas, *Fallen Fairies* (1909) represented a sad decline for both, and it was their swan song.

The truth is that, since the early 1890s, London had been undergoing changes in theatrical fashion no less than Paris, Vienna, and Berlin, favouring a lighter, brighter, snappier style of show that incorporated contemporary manners and songs, with routines and spectacle lifted from the variety theatre. In fact, by the 1890s the term "musical comedy" was being used on both sides of the Atlantic as a general description of song-and-dance shows held together by a loose plot.

The credit for establishing modern-dress musical comedy as a specific genre belongs to London theatre manager George Edwardes. Since 1885 he had been associated with the Gaiety Theatre, where the regular fare comprised burlesques with such titles as *Faust up-to-Date* (1888), *Ruy Blas and the Blasé Roué* (1889), *Carmen up-to-Data* (1890), and *Cinder-Ellen up-too-Late* (1891), with scores by the theatre's German-born musical director Wilhelm Meyer Lutz (1829–1903). The shows modernised and satirised familiar stories, with lively comic scenes, catchy songs and dances, and plentiful female figures on display. When the taste for burlesque began to wear thin, Edwardes set about producing a variant, a show that retained the songs, the dances, and the girls but was no longer dependent on satire and punning titles.

Thus, at the Prince of Wales's Theatre, Edwardes produced a "musical farce," *In Town* (1892), with a loose plot about London backstage life. It had song-and-dance numbers composed by F. Osmond Carr (1858–1916) and featured popular performers of the comic-opera and variety stage along with a galaxy of female beauties. Reflecting the sharper title, the main novelty lay in the topical subject and fashionable costumes. The experiment was sufficiently successful for Edwardes to follow it up with *A Gaiety Girl* (1893), this time described simply as a "musical comedy." Again, the piece had a minimal plot (about a stolen comb) and concentrated on the marital manoeuverings of theatrical and society figures. A contemporary report described the show as "sometimes sentimental drama, sometimes comedy, sometimes almost light opera, and sometimes downright 'variety show'; but it is always light, bright and enjoyable." Sidney Jones (1861–1946) composed the score, which featured a fine ballad, "Sunshine Above," for Hayden Coffin.

After this, Edwardes installed the new musical comedy formula at his Gaiety Theatre in place of the somewhat tired burlesque. *The Shop Girl* (1894) had an undemanding plot about the misunderstandings and confusion that arise from attempts to determine which of a group of shopgirls is a lost heiress. Its sumptuous dresses, contemporary dialogue, youthful cast, and lively tunes established it as the paradigm for Gaiety musical comedy for years to come.

The score was by Ivan Caryll (1861–1921) and Lionel Monckton (1861–1924), who collaborated on ten musical comedies for the Gaiety between 1894 and 1909, almost all of which ran for a year or more. The two were a study in contrasts. A bon vivant and larger-than-life character who sported a carefully groomed beard, Caryll, born Félix Tilkin in Liège, had been educated at the Paris Conservatoire before settling in London in the mid-1880s as a music teacher, musical director, and composer. He was soon adding his own music to imported French operettas. His breakthrough as a theatre composer came with a modern burlesque called *Little Christopher Columbus* (1893) and led directly to his appointment as musical director and house composer at the Gaiety. By contrast, the introspective Monckton was the son of a London town clerk and an amateur actress. Educated at Charterhouse School and Oxford University, where he took part in amateur theatricals himself, he began a career in the law, with a sideline as a theatre and music critic. But when George Edwardes used some of Monckton's songs in his productions, Monckton decided to concentrate full time on the theatre. Where Caryll could produce impressive-sounding but largely forgettable ensemble numbers, Monckton had the supreme gift of providing melodies that caught and retained the public's attention.

Thus, for *The Shop Girl,* Caryll composed the bulk of the score but Monckton produced the hits, most notably "Beautiful, Bountiful Bertie" for juvenile comic lead George Grossmith junior, the son of the Gilbert and Sullivan star. *The Shop Girl* established two other practices that became a feature of Edwardesian musical comedy. First, the composers introduced new songs from time to time to entice audiences back, and, second, the principal performers occasionally introduced numbers by other composers. Thus, the real hit of *The Shop Girl* ended up being a song by Felix McGlennon, "Her Golden Hair Was Hanging Down Her Back," which had been performed in British music halls and American vaudeville before being appropriated (with new words) by Gaiety leading man Seymour Hicks.

The emphasis on female glamour and a chorus of "Gaiety Girls" chosen for their looks and their ability to wear smart clothes was reflected in a sequence of "girl" titles now produced by the Gaiety. *The Circus Girl* (1896) was set in Paris during the festivities of Mi-Carême (the third Thursday in Lent) and featured a group of English tourists who become mixed up with a troupe of circus artists. A principal attraction was the first scene of Act 2, set in a circus ring viewed from the rear. Monckton's two big hits were "A Simple Little String," for leading lady Ellaline Terriss (the wife of leading man Seymour Hicks) as one of the English visitors, and "Not the Way to Treat a Lady," sung by plump Connie Ediss in the role of the circus-owner's wife.

For *A Runaway Girl* (1898) the setting was Corsica for Act 1 and Venice for Act 2. (Exotic settings were, of course, de rigeur.) The girl of the title (Terriss) is an Englishwoman at a Corsican convent, from which she runs away to avoid an arranged marriage with a man she's never met. She joins up with a group of "musicians" who—this being Corsica—turn out to be bandits. She escapes with a handsome Englishman (W. Louis Bradfield), with whom she has fallen in love, and the two flee to Venice. Inevitably, he turns out to be the man she had been contracted to marry. The show had roles for the actors who had become the established Gaiety favourites: Connie Ediss as a member of the minstrel/bandit troupe with a penchant for Spanish dancing, and comics Harry Monkhouse as her admirer and Edmund Payne as a Cockney manservant. The big number was a swinging march, "Soldiers in the Park," whose refrain "O listen to the band" made it one of Monckton's most enduring creations.

The next Gaiety show offered a superficial change of formula: the "girl" of the title became a "boy." Although *The Messenger Boy* (1900) thus centred its story around Edmund Payne as a messenger entrusted with delivering a promissory note to a woman in Egypt, the show's mixture was basically the same as in the "girl" comedies. The writer of the note discovers that, by mistake, he has given the messenger a compromising letter, which necessitates sending various Gaiety favourites in pursuit. The songs were not up to Monckton's standard, but the show was nonetheless a big success, and it was produced in Budapest and Vienna.

Even more popular was the next "boy" show—*The Toreador* (1901), in which the road to Egypt became a road to Spain. Edmund Payne became embroiled not only in Spanish politics but with a Spanish woman—first in the real town of Biarritz and then in the imaginary Villaya. Monckton provided several engaging numbers, including the jaunty "When I marry Amelia" for Pettifer (Fred Wright), a dealer in wild animals, "Archie" for man-about-town Sir Archibald Slackitt, Bart., a lieutenant in the Welsh Guards (played by the younger Grossmith) and, above all, "Keep off the Grass," for supporting character Cora Bellamy. This last was performed by a vivacious newcomer named Gertie Millar, who made such a sensation that her part was gradually built up, with Monckton adding "Captivating Cora," another hit, for her. Millar soon afterward became Monckton's wife, and over the years she enjoyed Gaiety stardom with an increasing number of her husband's best songs.

For *The Orchid* (1903) a new Gaiety Theatre had been built to replace the old. The show's story concerned pupils and staff of a horticultural college who congregate in Nice where rival British and French horticulturalists are trying to

4883 M ROTARY PHOTO. E.C. FOULSHAM & BANFIELD
MR. & MRS LIONEL MONCKTON.
(MISS GERTIE MILLAR).

Gertie Millar and Lionel Monckton
Mander and Mitchenson Theatre Collection

get their hands on a precious orchid. Edmund Payne was a gardener at the college and Gertie Millar a pupil. Her hits included "Little Mary," which made fun out of a euphemism for the stomach, and "'Liza Ann," which celebrated Millar's own Yorkshire origins.

The Spring Chicken (1905), *A New Aladdin* (1906), and *The Girls of Gottenberg* (1907) were Caryll-Monckton shows for the Gaiety that in various ways sought to strike out along different paths. The first was an adaptation of a French farce, *Coquin de Printemps,* and thus had more plot than usual. The second was an

The new Gaiety Theatre during the run of
The Spring Chicken, 1905
Author's collection

unsuccessful attempt to revive the old burlesque formula. The third was a drama-
tised version of a historical event—the so-called Köpenick Incident, in which a
German shoemaker successfully posed as a senior official. Payne, Grossmith, and
Millar starred in all three shows; Monckton's "Two Little Sausages" from the last
was probably the most popular single number.

This experimentation was a prelude to the longest-lasting Caryll-Monckton
show. *Our Miss Gibbs* (1909) brought the Gaiety musical comedies full circle. Like
The Shop Girl fifteen years earlier, the story concerned a shop assistant who enters
high society. Millar had star billing as the Yorkshire girl who works in a depart-

Mr. Amalfy, the Director General (Mr. H. B. Burcher) of the White City receiving the Earl of St. Ives (Mr. O. B. Clarence).

Act 2 of *Our Miss Gibbs,* set at the White City Exhibition
Author's collection

ment store called Garrod's (cf. Harrod's). Considerable effect was achieved by the second-act setting in London's recently opened White City Exhibition grounds, which in 1908 had staged the Olympic Games. But what really made the show were the musical numbers. In "Mary," the heroine introduced herself as a little Yorkshire lass who wished that people "wouldn't call me Mary when my name's Miss Gibbs." The highlight of the show—of the whole Gaiety series—came when she sang "Moonstruck," for which she was bewitchingly attired in a Pierrot costume. Grossmith, who didn't have any Monckton numbers, nonetheless made a sensation with the American comedy song "Yip-I-Addy-I-Ay," by Will D. Cobb and John H. Flynn. *Our Miss Gibbs* proved to be the last of the Caryll-Monckton collaborations. Caryll, feeling squeezed out by Monckton's songs on the one hand and American interpolations on the other, left to seek new fame in America.

The Monckton-Caryll shows at the Gaiety were matched by an equally significant series at Daly's Theatre. The indefatigable George Edwardes was responsible for these as well; but for Daly's he developed a variant formula. An equal emphasis on elegant modern dress and picturesque settings was tied to a more consistent romantic operetta plot in which the comedy was restricted to the secondary characters. The scores were also more substantial, and the interpolated numbers were more likely to be ballads than American vaudeville routines. Indeed, the Daly's shows had little to do with musical comedy as the term later came to be understood, and were closer to operettas in the continental sense. The series started after *A Gaiety Girl* transferred from the Prince of Wales's Theatre to Daly's in late 1894 and continued with *An Artist's Model* (1895), in which the title character, now a wealthy widow, renews her youthful romance with a poor Parisian artist. The score was by Sidney Jones, who had composed *A Gaiety Girl,* and the romantic leads were played by Marie Tempest and Hayden Coffin, with comedy supplied by popular song-and-dance performer Letty Lind, whose "The Gay Tom Tit" was a big hit.

Book author Owen Hall (1853–1907), lyricist Harry Greenbank (1865–99), and composer Jones worked also on the next three Daly's shows, of which the first was one of the most successful British productions in any musical theatre genre. *The Geisha* (1896) is a typical West-meets East tale. In this case the Westerner is British sailor Reginald Fairfax (played by Coffin), who, while on duty in Japan, spends time at the Teahouse of Ten Thousand Joys, run by the comic character Wun-Hi (Huntley Wright). There he is smitten by the geisha O Mimosa San (Tempest), to the consternation of his fiancée Molly Seamore (Letty Lind), who responds by dressing up as a Japanese to see whether she can lure him back. Thus attired, she becomes mixed up in the sale of the teahouse and its geishas, and only after the usual operetta confusion is she finally reunited with Fairfax.

The Geisha had an opening chorus worthy of Sullivan himself; but Jones's score also paid greater homage than Sullivan ever did to continental European musical styles—most obviously in O Mimosa San's lilting waltz "A Geisha's Life." Other delights of the score included her engaging tale of "The Amorous Goldfish" and Fairfax's fine baritone ballad "Star of My Soul." The comedy numbers included Wun Hi's "Chin-Chin-Chinaman" and Molly's song-and-dance "Chon-Kina" and "The Interfering Parrot." Along the way, the score picked up songs by other composers that became famous, including Monckton's "Jack's the Boy," James Philp's "The Jewel of Asia," and J. M. Capel's "Love, Could I Only Tell Thee."

First announced in London as a "comedy opera" (a common alternative to "comic opera," used, for instance, to describe Cellier's *Dorothy*), *The Geisha* finally bore the designation "musical play," a description often used thereafter for works with a more consistent plot and more substantial score than "musical comedies." *The Geisha* became a hit not only throughout Britain, the empire, and America, but around the world. On German stages it was performed more often than any German-language operetta of its time; and its international currency is further demonstrated by references to it in Anton Chekhov's story "The Lady with the Lapdog." *The Geisha* continued to enjoy popularity in continental Europe until well after World War II.

Jones's next score, *A Greek Slave* (1898), was set in Ancient Greece. Marie Tempest played Maia, daughter of soothsayer Heliodorus (Huntley Wright), and her slaves included the handsome Diomed (Hayden Coffin) and jolly Iris (Letty Lind). Rutland Barrington, the original Pooh-Bah, was the appropriately named prefect Pomponius. In some ways more ambitious than *The Geisha,* the work ran for a year without rivalling its predecessor's appeal. This prompted, in *San Toy* (1899), a return to the winning formula of *The Geisha.* Instead of Japan, *San Toy* was set in China, with Barrington as mandarin Yen How, whose daughter San Toy (Tempest) has been brought up as a boy to avoid being drafted into the emperor's all-female army. This creates problems when she falls in love with English Captain Bobby Preston (Coffin). Barrington had a hit with a song about his "Six Little Wives" and Tempest another with "The Petals of the Plum Tree." The parallels with *The Geisha* extended to another "comic" oriental portrayal by Huntley Wright as Li, who sang of a "Chinee Sojeman."

In London, *San Toy* ran for even longer than *The Geisha,* and longer than any London musical to that time except *Dorothy.* But despite the proven success of his formula, a number of external circumstances now forced Edwardes to change it. Letty Lind had left the company after *A Greek Slave,* and, not long into the run of *San Toy,* Tempest did likewise after a quarrel over the length of her costume. Book author Owen Hall had moved on to other things, and lyricist Harry Greenbank had died at the young age of thirty-three. His brother Percy Greenbank (1878–1968) now took over the lyric writing. Most important, composer Sidney Jones had left in search of a management that would permit him to compose integrated comic-opera scores without the interpolations that were a feature of Edwardes's productions. Jones never had a success that matched his Daly's works, however, whether with the old-fashioned, rustic "comedy opera" *My Lady Molly* (1903) or with the more up-to-date *The Medal and the Maid* (1903).

Back at Daly's, Edwardes turned to the ever-reliable Lionel Monckton. This time Monckton was commissioned to compose not just the big numbers but the major part of the score for a new musical play. The book, by James T. Tanner (1858–1915), was set in England, although Eastern visitors were welcome there.

Hayden Coffin played Geoffrey Challoner, squire of a Devonshire village, with Huntley Wright as his manservant Barry, and Rutland Barrington as the supposed Rajah of Bhong, who turns out to be an Englishman in disguise. The plot's complications have Barry dressing up as a dowager before Geoffrey is finally reunited with his childhood sweetheart Marjorie. As so often with these musicals, the story was decidedly thin; but the score of *A Country Girl* is a fine one. Monckton rose to his challenge with excellent concerted writing, especially in the Act 1 finale, which concludes with a rousing waltz chorus. The solo numbers are no less delightful, among them the Rajah's introduction, "The Rajah of Bhong"; "Under the Deodar," an Indian princess's memories of home; and Geoffrey's spirited shanty "Yo ho, little girls, yo ho!" Edwardes still allowed interpolated numbers, but the ones for *A Country Girl* were particularly good: the love duet "Coo" for Geoffrey and Marjorie and the comic duet "Two Little Chicks," by Paul A. Rubens (1875–1917), who was almost as gifted a melodist as Monckton himself.

The son of a wealthy London stockbroker, Rubens had been a nineteen-year-old Oxford University undergraduate when George Edwardes accepted one of his songs for *The Shop Girl* in 1894. Later he and his younger brother Walter Rubens (1877–1920) collaborated on the score for *Great Caesar* (1899). Whereas Walter then concentrated on the family stockbroking business, the appeal of the theatre was too great for Paul. His natural talent made him ever ready to toss off a lyric or song melody, and we shall find him as contributor to shows by various other composers before encountering those shows for which he was sole composer and lyricist and sometimes book author too.

The creative partnership of *A Country Girl* was retained for the next piece, set now in Ceylon. *The Cingalee* (1904) tells of a local girl, Nanoya (played by Sybil Arundale), who was engaged in childhood to a pompous Kandy nobleman Boobhama Chettur Bhoy (Rutland Barrington). To avoid marrying him she runs away to a tea plantation, where she falls in love with planter Harry Vereker (Hayden Coffin). Complications involving a crooked lawyer, Chambhuddy Ram (Huntley Wright), and a stolen pearl are finally overcome, which enables the lovers to marry. The Monckton-Rubens score had many of the virtues of its predecessor, including the baritone hero's "Pearl of Sweet Ceylon" and the soprano's "My Cinnamon Tree." But, although the show ran for a year, it was not the hit its predecessors were, and Edwardes looked to the continent for his next production. In Messager's *Les P'tites Michu* and later Lehár's *Die lustige Witwe* he found shows that continued to keep the Daly's public well entertained.

British musical shows continued to flourish, however. At the Lyric The-

Leslie Stuart
Author's collection

atre the big success was *Florodora* (1899), composed by Leslie Stuart (1863–1928), who had been imported from the variety theatre, where he had composed song hits such as "Soldiers of the Queen," "Lily of Laguna," and "Little Dolly Daydream." The book of *Florodora,* by former Daly's stalwart Owen Hall, was set in the Philippine Islands, and the title referred to an exotic perfume whose rightful ownership provides the major prop of such plot as there was. But plot was irrelevant, especially in a piece that had such numbers as the soprano's "The Silver Star of Love," the baritone's "The Shade of the Palm," and the rousing "I Want to Be a Military Man"—not to mention interpolated hits by the ubiquitous Paul Rubens, among them "The Queen of the Philippine Islands," for leading lady Evie Greene, and "Tact," for imported variety star Ada Reeve. What really made *Florodora* a smash hit on both sides of the Atlantic was a showstopping production number in which six handsome men ask six elegant women the question, "Tell me, pretty maiden, are there any more at home like you?" This exchange was set to an intricate, ongoing rhythm seemingly adapted from the American cakewalk. In large part owing to this number, *Florodora* made Stuart and the show's backers wealthy, and Stuart embarked on a string of successors. *The Silver Slipper* (1901), *The School Girl* (1903), *The Belle of Mayfair* (1906), and *Havana* (1908) all enjoyed good runs; but ultimately Stuart's musical style proved too stereotyped for him ever to reproduce the success of *Florodora*.

The last of the half-dozen composers who became pre-eminent in the British musical play of the first decade of the twentieth century was Howard Talbot (1865–1928), an American by birth who had been brought up in Britain and had studied medicine before entering the musical theatre as conductor and composer. He experienced indifferent success until he became involved with one of the unexpected triumphs that the theatre throws up from time to time. *A Chinese Honeymoon* (1899) was originally no more than a low-budget touring musical, but its oriental story and music-hall songs caught the public fancy. In 1901 it settled down in London, where its very unpretentiousness attracted all types of audiences, with the result that it became the first musical anywhere to run for a thousand performances. The success may have been freakish, but Talbot was a consummate musician, who was at home with more ambitious ensemble writing. This made him an ideal collaborator for Lionel Monckton and Paul Rubens, who specialised in adding the showstoppers.

It was with Rubens that Talbot worked first. With Talbot composing the ensembles and extended sequences, Rubens further established himself variously as book author, lyricist, and composer of three works. *Three Little Maids* (1902) had a lightweight story about three daughters of a country vicar who finally woo their lovers away from a trio of town ladies. The three leading men were all notable performers: comedian G. P. Huntley; romantic, Turkish-born, French-accented Maurice Farkoa; and handsome Bertram Wallis. The score for *Lady Madcap* (1904), again with Maurice Farkoa and G. P. Huntley, was largely the work of Rubens, with Talbot's extended contributions in short supply. For another oriental piece, *The Blue Moon* (1905), Talbot supplied stirring ensemble music that included an especially fine opening chorus and first-act finale to balance Rubens's more popular numbers.

For *The Dairymaids* (1906), Rubens collaborated with Frank E. Tours (1877–1963) rather than Talbot and had a hit with "The Sandow Girl," sung in a gymnasium by a group of young women wielding dumbbells to promote physical fitness. His success emboldened him to branch out in a series of shows for the Prince of Wales's Theatre. In these (apart from some collaboration on the books)

G. P. Huntley as Hook in Rubens's *Miss Hook of Holland,*
from *The Play Pictorial* (vol. 9, no. 56), 1907
Author's collection

he was sole author and composer. The first, *Miss Hook of Holland* (1907), was an
unassuming piece full of engaging melodies that went on to a considerable international career. Described as a "Dutch musical incident," the play concerned a
liqueur called Cream of the Sky, for which the creator, wealthy widower and dis-
tiller Hook (G. P. Huntley), loses his recipe. The various mix-ups in the distillery
are prolonged long enough for two acts to pass before Sally, the daughter of the
out-of-work Slinks, retrieves the lost recipe and with it wins the love of bandmaster Van Vuyt—a part created by future Wagnerian tenor Walter Hyde. The public came for the glamour of Isabel Jay as Sally, the comic antics of Huntley, and
the charming musical numbers. Prime among these are Sally's lyrical "Fly Away,

Kite," her rhythmic "Little Miss Wooden Shoes," the comedy maid's saucy "A Pink Petty from Peter" (about the petticoats she receives from admirers), and Van Vuyt's "The Violoncello."

Miss Hook of Holland also began a sequence of works at the Prince of Wales's Theatre starring Jay, who was also the wife of the theatre's impresario, Frank Curzon. None quite reached the standard of *Miss Hook of Holland*. Rubens's *My Mimosa Maid* (1908) placed her on a mimosa plantation on the French Riviera, with Huntley as a chimneysweep who falls in love with her, and Farkoa as a French café proprietor who is Huntley's rival. Then came *King of Cadonia* (1908), a show set in Ruritania, in which Jay played Princess Marie, daughter of the Duke of Alasia, the heir-presumptive to the ill-fated throne of Cadonia. For this piece the theatre turned to composer Sidney Jones, interpolating additional numbers by Frederick Rosse (1867–1940). The book was by the rising young playwright Frederick Lonsdale (1881–1954). *King of Cadonia* closed after a year's run, and the Prince of Wales's returned to Rubens for *Dear Little Denmark* (1909) and *The Balkan Princess* (1910), neither of which achieved the same success, even with Jay in the lead.

Still only in his mid-thirties, Rubens was already suffering from the consumption that soon killed him. But, as his output declined, the tenderness in his music increased—never more so than in the soaring "Violin Song," written for Phyllis Dare in the show *Tina* (1915), on which he collaborated with Haydn Wood (1882–1959).

As author and composer, Rubens made one further, especially important contribution to the evolution of the operetta into the musical. Between *The Blue Moon* and *The Dairymaids* he had staged *Mr Popple (of Ippleton)* (1905), with G. P. Huntley as Mr. Popple, a country innocent in London. The work was described as "comedy with music" and was, indeed, much more a comedy with songs than an integrated operetta. Rubens had always emphasised the modest pretensions of his music, using such disclaimers as "jingles and tunes" to describe it; here he went out of his way to stress that his aim had been to write a comedy with a consistent story, "without wanting a string of musical numbers, a large chorus, and scenery and dresses which are so costly that only a very long run can compensate the management for its lavish expenditure." Therein lay much of the philosophy of the musical comedy that was to prevail in the United States. Ten years later, *Mr Popple (of Ippleton)* appeared in New York, rewritten and with a completely new score by Jerome Kern. As *Nobody Home* (1915), it has been hailed as a precursor of the specifically American musical comedy for precisely those more intimate features that had always been present in Rubens's piece.

Only Lionel Monckton consistently outcomposed Rubens, and to Monckton fell the major compositional credit for the two musical comedies of the Edwardian era that have proved most durable. *The Arcadians* (1909) departed from the standard formula of the time in being a "fantastic musical play," whose first act was set in Arcadia, land of ideals, where a stray aviator gives the Arcadians an unfortunate idea of what Londoners are like. In the second act, the Arcadians come to London to "improve" the inhabitants. Not only do they find the natives incorrigible, but they discover that they envy their "wicked" ways and start to emulate them. The show featured such topical touches as an aeroplane and a scene at Askwood (Ascot-cum-Goodwood) racecourse. Howard Talbot as co-composer produced some fine concerted numbers, plus the highly successful "My Motter" (Cockney for "My Motto") for the lugubrious jockey Doody (Alfred Lester), whose motto was that he was "always merry and bright." Talbot also composed the lilting duet "Half-Past Two" and, in a number added later, acknowledged one of the latest dance crazes in the invigorating "The Two-Step." But the majority of the hits came, inevitably, from Monckton. Phyllis Dare as Eileen introduced herself with an Irish lilt as "The Girl with the Brogue" and sang a duet, "Charming Weather," with Harry Welchman as Jack Meadows. Dan Rolyat, as the errant aviator whom the Arcadians convert into their own Simplicitas, had a stirring march, "All down Piccadilly"; but most enduring of all were "The Pipes of Pan" and "Arcady Is Always Young" for the coloratura Florence Smithson as Sombra, the lead Arcadian.

Running a close second to *The Arcadians* as the work by which this era of British musical theatre is best remembered is *The Quaker Girl* (1910), with words by James T. Tanner (book) and Adrian Ross and Percy Greenbank (lyrics), all longtime Edwardes contributors. Gertie Millar played the title role of Prudence, who is thrown out of the Family by the strict Quakers when caught taking a sip of champagne. The settings moved between the English countryside and Paris, where Prudence's grey dress and bonnet become the height of fashion. As ever, Millar introduced some of her husband's best numbers, including "A Quaker Girl," "The Little Grey Bonnet," and "Tony from America," in which she expressed her admiration for American attaché Tony Chute, played by Joseph Coyne (the original Danilo in the London production of *The Merry Widow*). Hayden Coffin played Captain Charteris, the King's Messenger; but it was Georges Carvey, as Prince Carlo, who had the show's most widely sung number in the waltz "Come to the Ball."

Increasingly squeezed between Viennese operetta of the *Merry Widow* era on the one hand and American ragtime revue on the other, British musical comedy thereafter lost ground. No less than Jones, Stuart, and Rubens, Monckton felt the change in the relative failures of *The Dancing Mistress* (1912) and, with Howard Talbot, *The Mousmé* (1911) and *The Boy* (1917). Only the coming of World War I kept the London theatre British, and two native musical works that provided similarly safe, escapist entertainment were particular hits.

Chu Chin Chow (1916) was a version of the Arabian Nights tale of Ali Baba and the Forty Thieves written by actor-director Oscar Asche (1872–1936) as a vehicle for himself and his wife, Lily Brayton. Asche played robber chief Abu Hasan and Brayton the captive Zahrat al-Kulub, whom he disguises as a slave to spy on the home of rich merchant Kasim Baba. Thanks to Kasim's shiftless brother Ali Baba, the plot is uncovered and Zahrat herself helps stab Abu Hasan to death and dispose of his band of thieves in boiling oil. All this was done, of course, in the jolly fashion that traditionally ensured that virtue emerged triumphant in family entertainments. The score of *Chu Chin Chow* was entrusted to Frederic Norton (1869–1946), hitherto known primarily as a performer of his own songs and as a composer of a children's entertainment called *Pinkie and the Fairies* (1908). His easily assimilated score achieved classic status around the British Empire through the robbers' chorus "We Are the Robbers of the Wood," the love duet for Ali Baba and his brother's widow Alcolom, "Any Time's Kissing Time," and especially the bass-baritone Cobbler's Song for the rich merchant Kasim Baba. The part of Ali Baba was created by Courtice Pounds, the original Fairfax in *The Yeomen of the Guard* and Marco in *The Gondoliers,* with the composer himself standing in at times during the show's long run.

Staged as a spectacular extravaganza, with a number of scenery changes and a lot of incidental music, *Chu Chin Chow* became one of those freak successes that the theatre occasionally produces. It ran for 2,235 performances, a London record that was to stand for almost forty years.

In a fundamentally different vein was the more traditional *The Maid of the Mountains* (1916), whose 1,352 performances simultaneously clocked up the record for runs of romantic musical plays. It was another in the long line of pieces about mountain bandits, with a book by Frederick Lonsdale concerning a bandit, Teresa, who frees her lover, bandit chief Baldasarre, from an island prison. Baldasarre was a non-singing role, the principal male singing part going to the bandit Beppo. The score was by a virtual newcomer, former shipowner Harold

Fraser-Simson (1872–1944). It had two fine waltzes for the leading lady, "Farewell" and "Love Will Find a Way," the latter's main theme being, in effect, the Merry Widow waltz with each of the first four notes repeated. In spite of rewarding duets for the supporting comic couple, the show was felt to lack hit numbers when it was tried out in Manchester. Leading lady José Collins consequently brought in her stepfather, James W. Tate (1875–1922; older brother of operatic soprano Maggie Teyte), who provided four first-rate numbers for the leading pair that gave the piece its romantic aura and its enduring appeal: "My Life Is Love" for Teresa, the virile "A Bachelor Gay" for Beppo, and the duets "A Paradise for Two" and "When You're in Love."

Chu Chin Chow and *The Maid of the Mountains* provided their creators with the great successes of their respective careers. Norton, in particular, achieved little with his next piece, *Pamela* (1917), and pretty much disappeared. Fraser-Simson did better with a succession of pieces written after World War I that carried the flame for the British romantic tradition for a few more years—particularly *A Southern Maid* (1917), with a South American setting and another romantic role for José Collins; *The Street Singer* (1924), with Phyllis Dare as a French Duchess who disguises herself as a street singer to woo a young painter; and *Betty in Mayfair* (1925), with glamorous Evelyn Laye as a modern woman who disguises herself in demure Victorian garb to win her man.

Moreover, the post–World War I period met the residual demand for works in the light-opera tradition of Sullivan and German with one outstanding piece, *The Rebel Maid* (1921). Set in 1688, the story of a lady assisting William of Orange to overcome the rule of King James II of England was unconvincing, but the score by Montague Phillips (1885–1969), a graduate of the Royal Academy of Music, was most accomplished: lushly conceived, it featured fine traditional dances and vocal numbers. The composer's wife, soprano Clara Butterworth (who died in 1996, aged 108), created the title role of Lady Mary Trefusis, singing the delightful "Are My Lanterns Shining?" and, above all, "Sail My Ships." However, the song that brought the house down was the rousing ballad "The Fishermen of England" for her childhood sweetheart Derek Lanscombe, played by baritone Thorpe Bates, the original Beppo in *The Maid of the Mountains*.

We have seen that British comic operas and musical plays of the post–Gilbert and Sullivan period included some international successes. Thus, around the turn of the century one could see *A Runaway Girl* at the Theater an der Wien and *Florodora* at the Bouffes-Parisiens, while *The Geisha* swept the world. Before long, however, new British musical plays found themselves trapped between the enduring popularity of Gilbert and Sullivan on the one hand and the emergent Viennese operettas and American musical comedies on the other. Their largely ephemeral books make stage revivals unlikely today; but it is a pity that their fine, tuneful music is similarly unknown and unappreciated.

Chapter Eight
The American Melting Pot

During the nineteenth century the works of Offenbach, Johann Strauss, and Gilbert and Sullivan had scarcely less success in the New World than in the Old, whether performed by visiting companies from Europe or by local performers. Immigration to the United States was high, and, although the country had its own native works, it was European theatrical imports that were most widely welcomed. Indeed, because of the varied national origins of the immigrants, foreign-language productions were commonplace. Only four months after *La Grande-Duchesse de Gérolstein* was first seen in Paris in 1867, it was staged in New York, in French, with Bouffes-Parisiens performer Lucille Tostée in the title role. This helped ensure that, for the next decade and more, America was in the grip of opéra-bouffe. Parisian stars made their reputation (and in some cases a fortune) in America, though none quite matched the acclaim of Marie Aimée, whose popularity served to make a success of the American tour of the debt-ridden Offenbach in 1876.

Likewise, during the early 1880s, Viennese leading ladies Marie Geistinger and Josephine Gallmeyer brought Viennese operettas to America. By then, though, the fashion for both French opéra-bouffe and Viennese operette had been superseded by the rage for Gilbert and Sullivan. The success of *HMS Pinafore* became a cause célèbre, with purportedly no fewer than 150 companies performing versions of the show around America—a mixed blessing that led its unpaid authors to mount their next work, *The Pirates of Penzance,* in New York before London.

An early step in the creation of a repertory of native American works was *The Doctor of Alcantara,* produced in Boston in 1862. Even here the European influence was strong: the libretto was by British-born Benjamin E. Woolf (1836–1901) and the music by German-born Julius Eichberg (1824–93). Described as an opéra-bouffe, it used the familiar idea of two young people rebelling against marriages arranged for them by their fathers, only to discover that the partners they have rejected are their true loves. Many of the plot devices were equally familiar from the European theatre, and the score was in the direct line of ballad and comic opera. The work was frequently revived and also played in London and Australia.

More specifically American was *The Black Crook,* produced in 1866 at Niblo's Garden, New York, at the junction of Broadway and Prince Street. Less tightly integrated than *The Doctor of Alcantara,* it was termed an "extravaganza" and relied on spectacle more than cohesive story, after the fashion of the French *féerie.* The musical numbers were songs, choruses, and dances both new and old, written by various composers. Therein lay a more specifically American element, for the native entertainment of the time was more closely linked to vaudeville and minstrel shows than to operetta or European extravaganzas. The show's songs and routines frequently changed over its fifteen-month run, the most admired musical number being "You Naughty, Naughty Men," written by G. Bicknell and T. Kennick and sung by the English soubrette Millie Cavendish.

Even against the competition of *La Grande-Duchesse de Gérolstein,* the big New York success of 1868 was a native work. But *Humpty Dumpty,* staged at the Olympic Theatre and written by and starring George Lafayette Fox (ca. 1825–77),

Marie Majilton in *The Black Crook*
Crawford Theatre Collection, Manuscripts and Archives,
Yale University

was really little more than a pantomime with music. The next major landmark in the development of the native American musical show was *Evangeline, or The Belle of Acadia,* staged at Niblo's Garden in 1874. In the extravaganza tradition of *The Black Crook,* it was a burlesque of the poem by Henry Wadsworth Longfellow; the expulsion of the heroine and her beloved from their village provided the excuse for travels to various exotic locations. The piece did at least boast a score (comprising ballads, sentimental songs, and choruses) written by a single composer, Edward Everett Rice (1848–1924), a theatrical producer from Brighton, Massachusetts. The most noteworthy number was probably "My Heart." Rice was also the producer of the burlesque extravaganza *Adonis* (1884), which this time used the output of various composers. The show gave the burlesque treatment to the story that Franz von Suppé had already set to music in *Die schöne Galathé*. A vehicle for handsome Henry E. Dixey, it became the first native musical show to pass 500 performances, eventually bowing out after a total of 603.

The evolution of the American musical was also advanced by the performing partnership of Edward (Ned) Harrigan and Tony Hart. After appearing in minstrel and variety shows on the West Coast, Harrigan (1845–1911) began writing his own material with music by his English-born father-in-law and musical director David Braham (1838–1905). After Hart became his performing partner in 1871, Harrigan developed an ever-expanding series of sketches featuring himself as immigrant Irishman Dan Mulligan, Annie Yeamans as his ambitious wife Cordelia, and Hart as both their son Tommy and their black maid Rebecca Allup. Hart's diminutive stature and almost feminine appearance made him ideal for such drag roles. His blackface was an obvious evocation of American minstrel shows.

The action usually centred around the conflict between Harrigan's own Mulligan Guards and the black Skidmore Guards, together with the family's social struggles with immigrants of various nationalities, particularly German. The action generally involved the Mulligan Guards in mock-military parades and general fisticuffs, and they were so popular that they gave their name to the succeeding shows. The one-act *The Mulligan Guards* (1874) was no more than a brief sketch, but it introduced a song of the same title that was reprised in the full-length shows that developed from it. All staged at the Theatre Comique, *The Mulligan Guards' Picnic* (1878) and *The Mulligan Guards' Ball* (1879) were followed by five more Mulligan Guards shows before 1881, as well such later Harrigan and Hart extravaganzas as *Cordelia's Aspirations* (1883) and *Dan's Tribulations* (1884). The series ended when the Theatre Comique burned down in 1884, and Harrigan and Hart's partnership failed to survive the transfer to the Park Theatre.

Meanwhile, another noteworthy American extravaganza was touring the country. *Fun on the Bristol, or A Night on the Sound* (1879), put together by playwright George Fawcett Rowe (1834–89), was primarily a vehicle for the actor John F. Sheridan, cast in the drag role of Widow O'Brien, and secondarily a peg for variety sketches, comic songs, minstrel songs, dances, and even opera selections. A minor hit in New York, it toured America for years, went around England in 1882, and reached as far afield as Australia in 1884. With hindsight, we can say that its most significant aspect was its designation as a "musical comedy oddity." This aptly described the way musical and comedy constituents had been loosely thrown together in the piece. As we have seen, it was not until the 1890s that the term "musical comedy" was given a more specific meaning by British impresario George Edwardes.

For a quarter of a century or so, from 1880 onwards, the development of the American musical theatre may best be considered in two parts. The looser type of show that continued the vaudeville and extravaganza tradition we shall pick up again later. We consider first the increasing number of shows that sought to follow the European operetta tradition. In this category the most successful American work of the 1880s was *The Little Tycoon* (1886), by Willard Spenser (1852–1933). A simple piece, it exploited the fashion for oriental subjects with a story concerning a young man who pretends to be "His Royal Highness Sham, the Great Tycoon of Japan" in order to win the approval of his fiancée's father. A particular hit was the waltz "Love Comes Like a Summer Sigh," and the show toured America profitably for years. However, Spenser, who came from a well-to-do New York family, never penetrated beyond the fringe of the American theatrical establishment or the American consciousness in this or his later works.

The first American composer to do so was Reginald De Koven (1861–1920). Born in Connecticut but educated in Europe, he married well, which gave him financial independence and enabled him to concentrate on composition. With librettist Harry B. Smith (1860–1936), he came to public attention with *The Begum* (1887), a work that was something of a sex-change version of the Bluebeard story: the Begum of Oude is trying to get rid of her latest husband, Howja-Dhu, of whom she has tired just as she did his predecessors. But just as Boulotte survived in Offenbach's opéra-bouffe, so did Howja-Dhu—perhaps inevitably since the part was played by the popular De Wolf Hopper. The show mixed elements of extravanganza and low comedy with those of opéra-bouffe, but in possessing a solid, cohesive score it took a significant step in the development of American musical theatre.

That this development progressed further owed much to the Bostonians, an opera company set up in Boston to promote native comic opera. For them De Koven and Smith produced a version of *Don Quixote* in 1889 that enjoyed no more than local success; but they followed it up with the work that really set American comic opera on its international feet. *Robin Hood* (1890) featured England's outlaw hero and sought to portray some of the olde-worlde Englishness that De Koven had picked up during his British years. Its score contained several elaborate ensembles, as well as more straightforward numbers, including the solo "Oh, Promise Me!" sung by contralto Jessie Bartlett Davis in the travesti part of

Allan-a-Dale. The song was actually interpolated into *Robin Hood* from elsewhere in order to build up Davis's part; but it stole the show and survived for many decades as a popular wedding song.

The partnership of De Koven and Smith continued with *The Fencing Master* (1892). This was produced at New York's Casino Theatre, which impresario Rudolph Aronson had opened ten years earlier as a varied entertainment centre. The piece was set in early fifteenth-century Italy, and the fencing master's daughter Francesca was played by the visiting Marie Tempest. As she was later to do in Sidney Jones's *San Toy* in London, she spent a good deal of time in trousers. De Koven returned to British settings with *Rob Roy* (1894), based on the legend of Bonnie Prince Charlie and the Highland chief Rob Roy. Britain also served as the background for *The Highwayman* (1897), a show that was one of De Koven's more successful after *Robin Hood,* with an admired love duet, "Do You Remember?" De Koven was never short of critical admiration for the scholarliness of his writing, but his shows achieved greater frequency than real success. He sought to recapture old glories with a *Robin Hood* sequel, *Maid Marian* (1902), whose hit "Tell Me Again, Sweetheart" (for Allan-a-Dale) was itself an obvious sequel to "Oh, Promise Me!" Thereafter, De Koven's shows made little mark, for styles of theatrical entertainment were on the move.

By this time two composers whose reputations were to prove vastly more durable had established themselves on the scene. John Philip Sousa (1854–1932), best known as a band composer, made his musical theatre bow by contributing numbers to a musical comedy, *Our Flirtation* (1880), and then producing the entire score for an operetta called *The Smugglers* (1882). As musical director of a touring opera company, Sousa had conducted (and reorchestrated) *HMS Pinafore* and also Sullivan's *The Contrabandista,* and it was on the book of the latter that *The Smugglers* was clearly based. However, neither this, its successor *Desiree* (1884), nor the one-act *The Queen of Hearts* (1886) made much impact. Much more effective was his work as leader of the U.S. Marine Band, for which he composed "The Gladiator" (1886), "Semper Fidelis" (1888), "The Washington Post" (1889), and other marches that ensured his fame.

Sousa, though, was not one to restrict his energies to a single medium. A novelist as well as composer, he returned to the stage and achieved success in Boston and then New York with *El Capitán* (1896). Book, lyrics, and score again showed their indebtedness to European operetta, with echoes of Offenbach's *La Périchole* in the comical and cowardly Don Medigua, viceroy of Peru, who is disguised as the rebel bandit of the title. The role was played by the popular comedy bass De Wolf Hopper, who also produced, and whose current wife, tiny Edna Wallace, was in the cast. His appearance in ill-fitting armour and a plumed helmet, together with his individual singing voice, were enough to send the audience into raptures, not only in New York but later in London, where the show ran for 140 performances. If much of Sousa's score was unremarkable, he did give Hopper a rousing entrance song in march tempo, "You see in me, my friends," which later became part of the concert march Sousa adapted from the operetta. In fact, the popularity of the concert march has ensured that the operetta, too, is occasionally revived by those curious to sample Sousa's stage output.

None of Sousa's later operettas achieved the same success. *The Bride Elect* (1897) reused some of the music of *The Smugglers* as well as material from an unperformed operetta called *The Wolf;* it too had a march that was to outlive the stage piece. The far-fetched story concerned a war between two fictitious kingdoms over a goat belonging to one king that the other king shoots. The libretto, which Sousa wrote, was considered a drawback, though not enough to prevent a tour of some months. For *The Charlatan* (1898), set in Russia, Sousa once again called on the librettist (Charles Klein) and star (De Wolf Hopper) of *El Capitán*. He was rewarded by a success second only to that hit, as well as by another tour in London, where the piece was retitled *The Mystical Miss*. As with De Koven, Sousa's subsequent operettas achieved little more than a succès d'estime. *Chris and the Wonderful Lamp* (1899) was a lavishly staged fairy-tale spectacular; *The Free Lance* (1906) a somewhat outdated operetta with a book by De Koven's old partner Harry B. Smith; and *The American Maid* (originally *The Glass Blowers,* 1913) a more serious, patriotic work. It proved to be Sousa's theatrical swansong.

For the other major American composer of the era, the theatre proved a more natural milieu. Victor Herbert (1859–1924) was born in Dublin but brought up in Stuttgart, where he trained as a cellist at the conservatory. In 1886 he emigrated to America with his wife, an operatic soprano. He worked for a time as a cellist at the Metropolitan Opera, as a military bandmaster, and as an orchestra conductor, all the while composing. In fact, he produced two concertos for his own instrument, in addition to other orchestral works. When Herbert's technical expertise was allied with his remarkable gift for melody, it is hardly surprising that he came to tower over his contemporaries in American operetta.

His first score to be staged was *Prince Ananias* (1894), which was composed for the Bostonians and ran for less than two months. His next, *The Wizard of the Nile* (1895), was staged at the Casino in New York and went on to achieve productions in London, Vienna, and all over continental Europe, something later

Herbert works—including *Babes in Toyland* and *Naughty Marietta*—were never able to match. This was his first collaboration with the prolific Harry B. Smith, and it was a vehicle for the diminutive comic Frank Daniels as a phoney rainmaker who manages to land up in a variety of comical predicaments. The climax comes when he is unable to stop the rain and is entombed alive. The score was tuneful enough, without producing any lasting Herbert hits. Most admired was the waltz "Star Light, Star Bright."

By now established on Broadway, Herbert followed up at the Casino with *The Gold Bug* (1896) and at the Knickerbocker Theatre with *The Serenade* (1897). The latter was once more composed for the Bostonians and was one of Herbert's finest scores, parading the established talents of Jessie Bartlett Davis and comic Henry Clay Barnabee along with those of soprano newcomer Alice Nielsen. The hit numbers included the title serenade "I Love Thee, I Adore Thee" and a waltz trio, "Dreaming, Dreaming." *The Idol's Eye* (1897), another Middle Eastern vehicle for Frank Daniels, was less popular, while the historical *Peg Woffington* (1897) failed to reach New York. But the following year Herbert enjoyed by far his biggest success to that date. *The Fortune Teller* (1898) was staged by Alice Nielsen's own opera company and had a book by Harry B. Smith concerning the confusion of identities between a Gypsy fortune teller named Musette and her heiress double Irma —both played, of course, by Nielsen. The picturesque Hungarian settings and costumes inspired Herbert to one of his best scores. Musette's entrance csárdás "Romany Life" became one of his best-loved creations, although the bass's Gypsy love song "Slumber On, My Little Gypsy Sweetheart" was almost as popular.

Four more Herbert shows appeared and disappeared in rapid succession. *Cyrano de Bergerac* (1899) was a burlesque of Edmond Rostand's recent Paris success; it failed despite the presence of popular comedian Francis Wilson in the title role. *The Singing Girl* (1899) was better suited to Herbert's romantic style and was mildly successful as a star vehicle for Alice Nielsen. *The Ameer* (1899) played down to the vaudeville talents of Frank Daniels and provided him with profitable touring material. Lacking a star of similar magnitude, *The Viceroy* (1900) never went anywhere. At this point, Herbert apparently paused to take stock of his career, concentrating on his work as conductor of the Pittsburgh Symphony Orchestra. Not until 1903 did he return to Broadway with a pair of new works, the first of which remains one of his most celebrated. *Babes in Toyland* (1903) was an extravaganza populated by children's characters. Its tuneful score included not only the celebrated March of the Toys but also the lullaby "Go to Sleep, Slumber Deep," the dreamy "Toyland," and the sparkling "I Can't

Poster for Herbert's *The Fortune Teller*
Prints and Photographs Division, Library of Congress, Washington, D.C.

Do the Sum." *Babette* (1903), by contrast, was a genuine operetta that made little impression beyond introducing to the popular musical theatre the former Metropolitan Opera singer Fritzi Scheff, for whom Herbert was to compose some of his best soprano numbers.

It Happened in Nordland (1904) created some acclaim for popular comedy star Marie Cahill and for a hit number called "Absinthe Frappé"; but *Miss Dolly Dollars* (1905) and *Wonderland* (1905), in the vein of *Babes in Toyland,* were only modest successes. Then, at the Knickerbocker Theatre, Herbert struck gold with *Mlle Modiste* (1905). Its setting, a Parisian hat shop, recalled works by Victor Roger and André Messager; but in this case the milliner torn between rival marriage proposals leaves the shop to become a singing star before everything is sorted out. Designed as a vehicle for Viennese-born Scheff, its book was the work of Herbert's most successful later librettist, Henry Blossom (1866–1919). The hit numbers included "The Time and the Place and the Girl," "I Want What I Want When I Want It" and, above all, "Kiss Me Again," which was used in an audition scene reminiscent of *Die Fledermaus* and was perhaps the most seductively winning number Herbert ever composed.

For all the show's success, its popularity was to be eclipsed by Herbert's next piece. *The Red Mill* (1906), produced at the Knickerbocker, was created for the musical comedy team of David Montgomery and Fred Stone, who played two impoverished Americans in Holland. Herbert slipped into waltz-time as readily as Sousa into march-time; and the jaunty "The Streets of New York," "The Isle of Our Dreams," and the shimmering "Moonbeams" are still sung today. Neal McCay had a big hit as the amorous governor of Zeeland, with his declaration that "Every Day Is Ladies' Day with Me." *The Red Mill* was Herbert's longest-running Broadway show, and it achieved productions in Britain and Australia as well.

Several further works intervened before Herbert came up with what was to prove his passport to stage immortality. *Naughty Marietta* (1910) was a "Creole comic opera" commissioned by impresario Oscar Hammerstein for the soprano Emma Trentini and other singers of the failed Manhattan Opera House, with which Hammerstein had sought to rival the Metropolitan Opera. Set in eighteenth-century New Orleans, the plot tells of the efforts of Captain Dick, the head of a band of rangers, to track down the pirate Bras-Priqué. Unknown to everyone, Bras-Priqué is actually the son of the governor of New Orleans. The diminutive Trentini played Marietta, Countess d'Alténa, who arrives by ship from Europe escaping an unwanted suitor and who declares that she will marry the man who can complete a melody that has come to her in a dream. After much intrigue in which Dick and Bras-Priqué compete for her hand, Dick completes the melody and wins her love. Some of Herbert's most ingratiating music helped make this silly story acceptable, with no fewer than five showstoppers: "'Neath the Southern Moon," the march "Tramp, Tramp, Tramp," the dreamy waltz "I'm Falling in Love with Someone," the lively "Italian Street Song," and, of course, the dream song itself, "Ah! Sweet Mystery of Life."

Of Herbert's subsequent operettas, *The Enchantress* (1911) was notable for the leading lady's entrance, "The Land of My Own Romance," and the showpiece "I Want to Be a Prima Donna." *Sweethearts* (1913), which has remained celebrated despite a relatively short original run, concerned mistaken identities, this time of a princess who was raised by a Belgian laundress. Its enduring fame is tied largely to the title waltz, also known as "Every lover must meet his fate." *The Only Girl* (1913) was a lighthearted musical comedy that included the lovely "When You're Away" and brought Herbert one of his longest Broadway runs and a rare British production.

Emma Trentini in Nedbal and Friml's *The Peasant
Girl* (an adaptation of Nedbal's *Polenblut*), 1915
Crawford Theatre Collection, Manuscripts
and Archives, Yale University

Herbert's stage works continued to alternate between the semi-operatic
and the primarily comic, according to the producers and performers for whom
they were written. He even collaborated with Irving Berlin (1888–1989) on the
score for a spectacular revue called *The Century Girl* (1916), in between two
more ambitious efforts, the comic opera *The Princess Pat* (1915) and the light
opera *Eileen* (1917), which celebrated Herbert's native Ireland. A particular vein
of tenderness was notable in this piece, especially in the song "Thine Alone."
Up until his death Herbert went on producing songs that remain familiar today: "I Might Be Your Once-in-a-While," from *Angel Face* (1919), and "A Kiss in
the Dark," from *Orange Blossoms* (1922). But the shows themselves were less successful; for Herbert's style had had its day.

Herbert's chief competitors were also European-born and also wrote in a
style that owed much to European influences. Gustav Luders (1865–1913) emigrated from Germany in his twenties, first to Milwaukee and then to Chicago,
where he produced a series of musical comedies around the turn of the century.
The Burgomaster (1900) drew on the Rip Van Winkle story; in this case, Peter
Stuyvesant, burgomaster of New Amsterdam (New York), falls asleep in 1600 and

wakes up in 1900. Henry E. Dixey, the star of *Adonis,* played the leading role. Luders followed it with *King Dodo* (1902), which provided comedian Raymond Hitchcock (Charley in the first American *Charley's Aunt*) with a popular topical song, "They Give Me a Medal for That." But the work for which Luders and regular librettist Frank Pixley (1867–1919) became best known was *The Prince of Pilsen* (1902). This was very much in the vein of British musical plays of the time, with an exotic setting (Nice, where the American and European characters go on holiday) and mistaken identities (a Cincinnati brewer who is mistaken for a prince). The numbers that enabled the work to survive on the road in America for many years included a students' chorus, "Heidelberg Stein Song"; a waltz-duet, "The Message of the Violet"; and a *Florodora*-style cakewalk, "The American Girl," which was also known as "Song of the Cities," because each verse referred to a different American city.

Another popular composer, Gustave Kerker (1857–1923), was born in Westphalia, Germany, and taken to America as a boy. Like Herbert, he progressed from orchestral cellist to theatre conductor and composer. In 1888 he took a job at New York's Casino Theatre, then the home of imported operetta. In traditional musical-director fashion, he provided occasional music for shows, achieving domestic success with the revue-style *The Whirl of the Town* (1897). International success came with his next work for the Casino, whose story of a Salvation Army girl, Violet Gray, and a wealthy boy gone wrong, Harry Bronson, to some extent anticipated Frank Loesser's *Guys and Dolls. The Belle of New York* (1897) made no particular impact in New York itself; but it arrived in Britain with its original cast in 1898, when the new-style musical comedy was all the rage. London took to pretty leading lady Edna May in a big way, as well as to the catchy title waltz, together with the heroine's lively "The Purity Brigade" and the neatly turned duet "When We Are Married." The American settings, which included New York's Chinatown, the interior of Grand Central Station, and the casino at Narragansett Pier, were exotic for Europeans, and the London success was repeated at the Carltheater in Vienna in 1900 and the Moulin Rouge in Paris in 1903. Even with another Edna May vehicle, *The Girl from up There* (1900), Kerker never again did as well.

Somewhat similar was the case of Ludwig Englander (ca. 1851–1914), who was also a one-hit wonder. A native of Vienna, he arrived in New York as a young man and was engaged as conductor at the German-language Thalia Theater. His earliest works there were composed to German texts, including the American historical *1776* (1884), which starred Vienna's Marie Geistinger. Like Kerker, Englander began providing occasional music for various shows and, also like Kerker, tended to cobble together lightweight musical comedy scores rather than compose complete operetta or musical play scores as De Koven and Herbert had. In many cases, he was responsible merely for coordinating a score containing songs by a number of other composers. Such was the case with his sole international success, *The Casino Girl* (1900), a Casino Theatre counterpart of the type of show favoured by London's Gaiety. Its book was by the ubiquitous Harry B. Smith and concerned a Casino chorus girl pursued as far as Cairo by an English earl with the suitably comic name of Percy Harold Ethelbert Frederick Cholmondeley. Like the Gaiety shows, it underwent several changes of musical content during its three shortish seasons. Presumably fearing that the caricature of an earl would seem less amusing in London, the character was there changed to an American called Percy Harold Ethelbert van Stuyvesant. The revamping was successful, and the show found favour with audiences who had previously loved *The Belle of New York*.

A younger immigrant from Central Europe was Karl Hoschna (1877–1911), who hailed from Bohemia. A wind player in an Austrian band, he emigrated to America at the age of nineteen and played for a time in Victor Herbert's orchestra. Anxious to give up the ardours of performing, he got a job with the Witmark publishing firm and teamed up with a would-be lyricist named Otto Hauerbach (1873–1963; later Otto Harbach), a member of an immigrant Danish family who had worked in insurance and advertising before turning to the theatre. With *Three Twins* (1908) the two hit the jackpot. Much of its success was due to two numbers that in different ways touched a chord with American audiences. "The Yama-Yama Man" was a children's cautionary tale made popular by former vaudeville dancer Bessie McCoy, who sang the number in harlequin costume. Her "Cuddle up a Little Closer" appealed even more for its comforting lyric and ingratiatingly simple melody.

An even greater success for Hoschna came with a work that had originated in Berlin with a quite different score, by Viennese-born Hugo Felix (1866–1934). *Madame Sherry* was produced with Felix's score in Berlin in 1902 and at New York's New Amsterdam Theatre with Hoschna's in 1910. Its diverting story concerned a young man who funds his bachelor lifestyle by donations from a rich uncle to whom he pretends he has a wife and children to support. Complications inevitably arise when the uncle decides to visit. The show provided Hoschna with his greatest single success in "Every Little Movement," whose rhythmically distinctive melody soon made it an international hit. Alas, Hoschna's death at the age of thirty-four cut his career untimely short.

At this time Europeans regarded America as the land of enterprise and opportunity, and a number of composers who had already made reputations in Europe decided to try America next. One of these was Ivan Caryll, the house composer of London's Gaiety Theatre who had been squeezed out by the husband-and-wife partnership of Lionel Monckton and Gertie Millar. In New York, he built up a respectable following with a sequence of shows that were based—as so many of his works were—on French plays. His biggest single hit from any of these was the waltz "My Beautiful Lady," in *The Pink Lady* (1911). A string of later scores did nicely: they included *Oh! Oh! Delphine* (1912), *The Little Café* (1913), a trio of pieces for the comedian Fred Stone in *Chin-Chin* (1914), *Jack o' Lantern* (1917), and *Tip-Top* (1920). A collaboration with lyricist P. G. Wodehouse (1881–1975) played on Broadway as *The Girl Behind the Gun* (1918), and, in war-conscious London, opened at the West End under the more peaceful title of *Kissing Time*.

A similar move was made by Hungarian composer Viktor (Americanised to Victor) Jacobi on the heels of the international success of his *Leányvásár* (The Marriage Market) and *Szibill* (Sybil). Like Hoschna, Jacobi died in his thirties, and his brief American career did not have a chance to take off. *Apple Blossoms* (1919) and *The Love Letter* (1921) were notable mainly for introducing song-and-dance brother and sister Fred and Adele Astaire (who had hitherto appeared chiefly in vaudeville) to book musicals. Jacobi composed the score of the former in collaboration with the famous violinist Fritz Kreisler (1885–1962), himself living in America. If it was Jacobi's "You Are Free" and "Little Girls, Goodbye" that most attracted attention, it was one of Kreisler's numbers that proved most enduring. Although it didn't get much attention at the time, Kreisler's waltz "Who Can Tell?" later resurfaced in his Viennese musical comedy *Sissy* (1932) and as "Stars in Your Eyes" in the Hollywood movie *The King Steps Out*.

In such a way did the European operetta tradition of romantic, escapist works endure in the American theatre well into the twentieth century. Yet a comparison of the Berlin and New York scores of *Madame Sherry* shows clearly how two different styles were developing. Whereas the German original was marked by elaborate ensemble writing, Hoschna's American numbers were crisp and to the point. Caryll and Jacobi, too, adapted their styles to the needs of ragtime-conscious America. In other shows, interpolated vaudeville songs helped to bridge the transition from traditional European outpourings to the snappier products that typified the mood of a youthful nation.

The evolution of a more indigenous form had progressed also from more loosely constructed shows such as *Evangeline* and *Adonis* via the extravaganza *A Trip to Chinatown,* which toured the United States for a full year before reaching New York in 1891 and establishing a new record for the longest New York theatre run, with 657 performances. Set in San Francisco, it concerned the embarrassment of an ageing gentleman who goes out for a night in Chinatown believing he has a date with a vivacious widow, only to find himself alone and becoming increasingly drunk and embarrassed in front of various younger couples. The authors of the piece were librettist-lyricist Charles Hoyt (1860–1900) and his musical director-composer Percy Gaunt (ca. 1852–96), and the songs included "The Bowery," one of the most famous evocations of old New York. But in the manner of such works, much of the show's success lay in the songs that were interpolated from time to time, among them Charles K. Harris's "After the Ball."

During the 1890s the shows of Harrigan and Hart, too, found successors in the burlesque extravaganzas of Joe Weber (1867–1942) and Lew Fields (1867–1941). The two New Yorkers had paired up as ten-year-olds in 1877 and developed an act in which the stocky Weber and the lanky Fields, gaudily suited and bewhiskered, traded German-accented banter. Their later acts revolved around slapstick humour and repartee full of malapropisms, and they were fond of doing take-offs of current theatrical shows. They are said to have originated one of the most famous pieces of stage repartee:

"Who vass the lady I seen you with last night?"
"That was no lady, she vass my wife!"

In 1896 they opened the Weber and Fields Music Hall on 29th Street, off Broadway, where they presented a series of extravaganzas over the next eight years. These incorporated all manner of speciality acts into the evening's entertainment, performed by many of the greatest vaudeville names of the era, including the buxom first lady of the American comic opera, Lillian Russell. The shows' titles reflected the slapdash nature of the entertainments: *Hurly Burly* (1898), *Whirl-i-Gig* (1899), *Fiddle-Dee-Dee* (1900), *Hoity Toity* (1901), and *Twirly Whirly* (1902). The music was composed by John Stromberg (1853–1902) and included such enduring numbers as "Ma Blushin' Rosie," sung by Fay Templeton in

Lew Fields in 1906
Crawford Theatre Collection, Manuscripts
and Archives, Yale University

Fiddle-Dee-Dee, and "Come Down Ma Evenin' Star." This last was sung by Lillian Russell in *Twirly Whirly;* the manuscript had been found in Stromberg's pocket after he committed suicide in his dressing room because of ill-health and financial problems.

Significant, too, was the career of George M. Cohan (1878–1942), who was born into a vaudeville family. From 1888 young George and his sister toured the country with their parents as the Four Cohans, and in due course he began contributing his own material, including songs such as "I Guess I'll Have to Telegraph My Baby" (1898). An early musical celebration of the telegraph, this won popular acclaim when sung by vaudeville comedienne Ethel Levey, who later became Cohan's wife and joined the family act.

Little by little, Cohan expanded his vaudeville sketches. In 1901 he produced *The Governor's Son* (1901), a three-act piece containing a dozen songs and dances. It proved more successful as touring than as Broadway material, but it encouraged Cohan to write a successor, *Running for Office* (1903). This in turn was followed by *Little Johnny Jones* (1904), which in retrospect proved epochal. It is the

Sheet-music cover for "The Yankee Doodle Boy"
from Cohan's *Little Johnny Jones*
Historical Sound Recordings Collection, Yale University

piece that most obviously provided the foundation of American musical comedy: vernacular American songs and dialogue woven into a lighthearted song-and-dance piece. Cohan played Johnny Jones, a jockey who goes to England and rides in the Derby. He is accused of throwing the race and undergoes various disgraces before finally being cleared. Cohan's philosophical monologue "Life's a Funny Proposition" won the public's favour; but what have endured above all are Cohan's entrance-song, "The Yankee Doodle Boy," and "Give My Regards to Broadway," in which he draped an American flag around himself and strutted around the stage.

It was as a creator of flag-waving material that Cohan was thereafter renowned. *Forty-Five Minutes from Broadway* (1906) was set in New Rochelle, a wealthy suburb of New York, and featured comedienne Fay Templeton as Mary Jane, housemaid to a recently deceased millionaire. The show contained another pair of Cohan hit numbers—"Mary's a Grand Old Name" and "So Long, Mary." Then, in *George Washington, Jr.* (1906), Cohan starred as an ordinary citizen whose patriotism is such that he adopts the name of America's first president. The principal song was "You're a Grand Old Flag." Cohan brought out further shows in the next few years—*The Honeymooners* (1907), *The Talk of New York* (1907), *Fifty Miles from Boston* (1908), *The Yankee Prince* (1908), *The American Idea* (1908), *The Man Who Owns Broadway* (1909), and *The Little Millionaire* (1911), in which his parents made their final appearance as performers. His activities then expanded into production and revue, and his creative talent became somewhat diluted as his ambitions expanded. Yet he brought to the American musical show a specifically American identity, with characters who spoke the American language and sang songs with a specifically American rhythm.

A further factor in the evolution of the American musical theatre was the popularity of black entertainers such as the team of Bert Williams (1874–1922) and George Walker (?–1911). Among their vehicles was Broadway's first black musical comedy, *In Dahomey* (1903), in which they played, respectively, the comical Shylock Homestead ("Shy" to his friends) and Rareback Pinkerton, his friend and adviser, who become involved in a plan to colonise the African country of Dahomey (Benin). The show had an all-black cast, and the songs were written largely by the poet Paul Dunbar (1872–1906) and composer Will Marion Cook (1869–1944). Originally designed for black audiences, it failed to excite white theatre-goers on Broadway, but it did a great deal better in London, where energetic performances of the cakewalk and other black material proved a welcome novelty after years of minstrel shows by whites in blackface.

Whether through shows that followed European patterns or developed a more specifically native style, the American theatre by World War I had produced a wealth of important works. In Victor Herbert and George M. Cohan, especially, it had outstanding composers in the two fields. If American shows were still not regarded as important internationally, where traditional European material held sway, that situation was about to change.

Chapter Nine
America Ascendant

The route to American domination of the musical stage on both sides of the Atlantic was smoothed by a New York composer who served a youthful apprenticeship in London. Jerome David Kern (1885–1945) studied harmony, theory, and piano at the New York College of Music. But his first jobs were as a song-plugger for the publisher T. B. Harms and a rehearsal pianist in Broadway theatres, where he began contributing songs to American versions of European imports. The earliest notable example was "How'd You Like to Spoon with Me?" (1905), interpolated into Ivan Caryll's *The Earl and the Girl*. At the same time, Kern began regular visits to London, where his connections gave him valuable introductions to important theatrical figures. He met and collaborated with P. G. Wodehouse, and composed interpolated numbers for George Grossmith junior in *The Spring Chicken*. His most significant meeting was with an American, the impresario Charles Frohman, who engaged Kern to provide additional songs for the European shows Frohman was importing to New York. By World War I, more than a hundred Kern songs had been interpolated into some thirty shows, most particularly "They Didn't Believe Me" for Sidney Jones and Paul Rubens's *The Girl from Utah* (1914). More than any work of its day, "They Didn't Believe Me" symbolised the emergence of American theatrical song, in which swirling melodies, lush orchestration, and the romantic doings of palaces and princes were replaced by simple, gently tripping melodic lines and lyrics that expressed the workaday sentiments of ordinary people.

In 1915 Frohman, on one of his regular scouting missions to London, went down with the *Lusitania* when it was torpedoed by the Germans in the Atlantic. Kern found further commissions from the Shubert brothers, East Prussian Jewish immigrants who controlled a number of New York theatres. For them Kern composed scores for the musical comedies *The Red Petticoat* (1913) and *Oh, I Say!* (1913), as well as *Ninety in the Shade* (1915) for comedian Marie Cahill. He was next commissioned to provide additional numbers for New York's Princess Theatre, which was owned by a partnership that included the Shuberts but which was controlled by the management team of F. Ray Comstock and Elisabeth Marbury.

The particular significance of the Princess Theatre lay in its tiny auditorium, which held only 299 persons with a correspondingly tiny orchestra. Works produced there had necessarily to be on a small scale. Accordingly, Comstock and Marbury chose an adaptation of a work that, though European, had sought to break away from the inflated operetta manner and to present a more logically developed comedy interspersed with integrated songs. This was the 1905 Paul Rubens musical comedy *Mr Popple (of Ippleton)*, with which Kern was familiar from his visits to London. The American reworking was by the English-born Guy Bolton (1884–1979), Kern's librettist on *Ninety in the Shade,* and Kern contributed an almost completely new score for the piece, which was renamed *Nobody Home* (1915).

If Rubens's ideas had been somewhat too advanced for Edwardian England, they proved ideal for the America of a decade later and, more particularly, for Kern's intimate song style. *Nobody Home* was reasonably successful, and it led to *Very Good Eddie* (1915), also for the Princess Theatre, and even better received.

Very Good Eddie features two pairs of honeymooners, Eddie and Georgina Kettle, and Percy and Elsie Darling, who are about to board a Hudson River boat at Poughkeepsie. Percy and Georgina are accidentally left behind, which means that tiny, henpecked Eddie and demure Elsie are thrown together on board ship. There, embarrassed by the chance presence of Eddie's former schoolmate Dick Rivers, they pose as husband and wife. The resultant complications are compounded when Percy and Georgina rejoin the party. The cleverly contrived story delighted the public no less than Kern's unassuming and tuneful songs. The lilting "Some Sort of Somebody" was taken over from Kern's earlier *Miss Information* (1915), while other successes were the quartet "Isn't It Great to Be Happily Married?"; the diminutive Eddie's comedy song, "When You Wear a Thirteen Collar"; Dick Rivers's "Old Boy Neutral"; and the charming duet for Eddie and Elsie, "Babes in the Wood."

Very Good Eddie was significant not only in itself but because it led to the reunion of Kern and P. G. Wodehouse. Together they proceeded to write a number of songs to enliven shows by the newly fashionable Emmerich Kálmán. For *Miss Springtime* (1916; originally *Zsuzsi kisasszony*) there was "My Castle in the Air," and for *The Riviera Girl* (1917; a heavily adapted *Die Csárdásfürstin*), "Bungalow in Quogue" (rhymes with "log"), whose fast-moving melody and witty lyric typified the Wodehouse-Kern style:

> Let's build a little bungalow in Quogue,
> In Yaphank, or in Hicksville or Patchogue . . .

The new partnership of Bolton, Wodehouse, and Kern was also seen with an original show, *Have a Heart* (1916), which revolves around a couple's attempts to save their troubled marriage by going on a second honeymoon, which is complicated by the arrival of an old flame of the husband's. And the same team produced the next Princess Theatre show, *Oh, Boy!* (1917). This enjoyed an even longer run than *Very Good Eddie,* with a story built around amorous misunderstandings among a group of prudish and not-so-prudish characters. Once again, Kern combined rhythmically engaging numbers ("Rolled into One"), comic take-offs ("Nesting Time in Flatbush"), and lyrical songs, among which the duet "Till the Clouds Roll By" became a Kern classic. *Oh, Boy!* achieved a run of 463 performances, a remarkable achievement for the time. It further inspired *Oh, Lady! Lady!* (1918), which took its title from a catch-phrase of black comedian Bert Williams. The show failed to catch on to quite the same extent as its predecessors,

Scene from Kern's *Oh Lady! Lady!* at the Princess Theatre, 1918, from *The Stage* (October 1934)
Yale University Library

however; even its subsequently immortal "Bill" (later of *Show Boat*) had to be dropped in out-of-town tryouts.

Almost simultaneously with *Oh, Boy!* at the Princess, Ray Comstock produced another piece by the Bolton, Wodehouse, and Kern partnership that did equally well for the Longacre Theatre. *Leave It to Jane* (1917) belonged to a genre that was to become particularly popular in America—the college sports show. The Jane of the title is Jane Witherspoon, daughter of the president of Atwater College. To help Atwater win the big football game against arch rival Bingham College, Jane seduces star Bingham player Billy Bingham, son of the president, who transfers to Atwater and wins the game for them. Of course, the essence of these pieces lies not in the plot but in the characters and comic situations it engenders. And, as always, Kern's graceful melodies and Wodehouse's witty lyrics move the story along. Outstanding are the bouncy title song, the duet "The Crickets Are Calling," and, above all, a cabaret-style "Cleopatterer," concerning the activities of the legendary Egyptian queen.

While Kern busied himself with other projects, Bolton and Wodehouse teamed up with Louis Achille Hirsch (1881–1924) for the Princess Theatre's *Oh! My Dear* (1918). Hirsch had followed a similar career path to Kern's, interpolating songs into imported Viennese shows before gradually creating entire scores for revues and musicals. Like Kern, too, he made a mark in London, creating the scores for London Hippodrome revues that exploited the current ragtime fashion. Among his book musicals, *Going Up* (1917) was an especial success, boasting a topical story about aviation and songs ranging from the modern dance number "The Tickle Toe" to the lyrical ballad "If You Look in Her Eyes." Later, for the Knickerbocker Theatre, Hirsch produced another international hit in *Mary* (1920), from which came the popular song "The Love Nest." But Hirsch lacked Kern's genius, although his death at the age of forty-two may have prevented him from producing his best work.

If Hirsch has suffered posthumous eclipse, the role of the Princess Theatre has increasingly been recognised as pivotal in the development of modern American musical theatre. The shows' basic plots and situations weren't particularly original, but their success proved that there was a public for everyday characters in everyday dress using everyday language, singing simple songs about nothing in particular to light, lilting melodies. Another composer in this style was Harry Tierney (1890–1965), who likewise made an early impression in London with songs for ragtime revues at the Alhambra Theatre before trying his hand at book musicals in New York. In America he teamed up with lyricist Joseph McCarthy (1885–1923) for *Irene* (1919), whose book was adapted by James Montgomery from his play *Irene O'Dare*. A previous Montgomery play had been adapted for Hirsch's *Going Up,* whose glamorous leading lady Edith Day here reappeared as Irene O'Dare, a poor New York Irish shop assistant. When Irene is sent to the mansion of a wealthy Long Islander, Donald Marshall, to do an upholstering job, he arranges for her and two of her friends to work as models in a New York fashion house. At an elegant party they are passed off as society ladies, as a result of which Irene is pursued by ambitious J. P. Bowden. When Bowden discovers her true origins, however, he backs away, leaving her to discover love with Donald.

Irene was hugely successful and, together with Hirsch's *Mary,* set a fashion in the Broadway musical theatre for modern Cinderella stories. Edith Day had two especially appealing numbers in the title song and the classic "Alice Blue Gown," while another notable item was "Castle of Dreams," which appropriated a theme from Chopin's Minute Waltz. (This kind of musical borrowing was currently popular on Broadway. McCarthy had teamed with Harry Carroll [1892–1962] in the most notorious borrowing of all, "I'm Always Chasing Rainbows," based on Chopin's "Fantasie-Impromptu" for the Vanderbilt Theatre's *Oh, Look!* [1918].) McCarthy and Tierney collaborated again on *Up She Goes* (1922), *Glory* (1922), and *Kid Boots* (1923) and had another major success with *Rio Rita* (1927), a colourful and extravagantly staged piece which opened the new Ziegfeld Theatre. Set in Mexico, its story concerned Texas ranger Jim Stewart, who is simultaneously chasing a bandit and the glamorous leading lady. Jim's "Following the Sun Around" was the big hit.

But during the 1920s it was still Jerome Kern who led the way in the American musical theatre. His post–Princess Theatre shows continued to capture the spirit of the age, as can be seen from such titles as *Toot-Toot!* (1918), *Rock-a-Bye Baby* (1918), *Head over Heels* (1918), *She's a Good Fellow* (1919), *Zip Goes a Million* (1919), and *The Night Boat* (1920). Only the last was a real hit, especially with the songs "Whose Baby Are You?" and "Left All Alone Again Blues." But with *Sally* (1920), Kern made another major advance in the emergent song-and-dance musical comedy. It was by far the longest-running show ever staged at the New Amsterdam Theatre, the grand Art Nouveau building on 42nd Street, surpassing even the runs of *The Merry Widow, Madame Sherry, The Pink Lady,* and *Sweethearts,* as well as successive editions of those phenomenally successful revues, the *Ziegfeld Follies.*

Like *Irene* and *Mary, Sally* was a rags-to-riches story, about an orphan who starts out washing dishes in a Greenwich Village restaurant and ends up a star of the *Follies,* acquiring a wealthy husband into the bargain. The piece was commissioned by flamboyant impresario Florenz Ziegfeld (1867–1932) as a vehicle for his latest leading lady, diminutive blonde Marilyn Miller, real-life star of his own spectacular *Follies.* Miller's prowess as a dancer led to the later interpolation of the Butterfly Ballet, composed by Victor Herbert; but Kern's own contributions needed little help, including as they did the lively "Whip-Poor-Will" and a song that was to become another Kern standard, "Look for the Silver Lining." Both were rescued from the unsuccessful *Zip Goes a Million* (1919).

Of subsequent Kern shows, *Good Morning, Dearie* (1921) and several others brought in the crowds for a while without attaining hit status. Even a final reunion with Bolton and Wodehouse failed to make much of *Sitting Pretty* (1924), despite a score full of such delights as a bewitching production number, "The Enchanted Train." But Kern was not finished; he now produced another Marilyn Miller vehicle for the New Amsterdam Theater that soon ranked with *Sally* as an international success. In *Sunny* (1925) Miller played Sunny Peters, a circus rider. The circus background was added more to drag in various speciality acts than to advance the plot. To offer a further range of colourful settings, the action moved from the circus to an ocean liner (pandering to the current fashion for transatlantic travel) and featured a fox hunt and an elegant ball. Book and lyrics were by Oscar Hammerstein II and Otto Harbach, and the score was Kern at his graceful best in the plaintive "D'Ye Love Me?"; the comic "Two Little Bluebirds"; and, above all, the shifting rhythms of "Who?"

Sally's significance had lain not only in its 570 Broadway performances but also in its London success, achieved without the local adaptation or changes that were customary with imported shows. It was the younger George Grossmith who was instrumental in mounting *Sally* in London, and such was its success that he commissioned new works directly from Kern for his Winter Garden Theatre. Even if neither *The Cabaret Girl* (1922) nor *The Beauty Prize* (1923) was top-drawer, both enjoyed significant runs and confirmed the fashion for the American musical on both sides of the Atlantic. Thereafter American musical comedies were almost as much at home in Britain as in America itself.

The next show at London's Winter Garden Theatre was provided not by Kern but by another composer, who regarded Kern as his mentor and who was rapidly establishing an important reputation in his own right. George Gershwin (1898–1937) came from an immigrant family in New York, and he followed the conventional songwriter's route to the musical theatre by acting as pianist and song-plugger for the publishing firm of Jerome H. Remick. He scored his first major song hit with lyricist Irving Caesar (1895–1996) when the exhilarating "Swanee" was performed by Al Jolson in the show *Sinbad* (1918). His first book show, *La La Lucille* (1919), made little impact; he achieved far more success with the individual numbers "Stairway to Paradise" (1922) and "Somebody Loves Me" (1924) that he composed for successive versions of *George White's Scandals,* a rival revue series to the *Ziegfeld Follies.*

For all his inexperience with book musicals, Gershwin had impressed Kern and Grossmith, who commissioned him to write *Primrose* (1924). Perhaps unnecessarily, Gershwin toned down his naturally ebullient style in favour of music he considered more English; but there were some characteristic numbers in the rhythmically engaging "Wait a Bit, Susie" and "Boy Wanted," reused from a Broadway show. And, though *Primrose* may have been unusual, London and the world would soon become familiar with the "real" Gershwin in song hits written with his lyricist brother Ira (1896–1983).

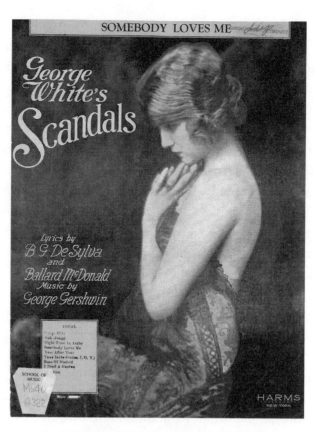

Sheet-music cover for *George White's Scandals* of 1924
Yale University Music Library

The first book show on which the brothers worked together for New York saw them springing onto the scene virtually fully developed. *Lady Be Good!* (1924) was designed for Adele and Fred Astaire, who had begun with dance turns in revues and musical comedies such as Victor Jacobi's *Apple Blossoms* and *The Love Letter* and had attained top billing in such book musicals as Kern's *The Bunch and Judy* (1922). In *Lady Be Good!* they played Susie and Dick Trevor, an impoverished sister and brother who are thrown out of their lodgings. They find themselves embroiled in a series of highly unlikely incidents (at one point, Susie has to impersonate a Mexican) before justice and true love prevail. The now-celebrated title song was sung by the comical lawyer Watty Watkins (played by Walter Catlett), and there were solo spots for ukelele-playing Cliff Edwards, who sang "Fascinatin' Rhythm" and "Little Jazz Bird." The Astaires had two delightful duets,

"Hang on to Me" and "So am I," and Fred had the slow blues "The Half of it Dearie, Blues." But Adele's "The Man I Love" suffered the fate of "Bill" and other songs that eventually became classics when it was dropped during out-of-town tryouts for holding up the action.

The Gershwins' next show was first titled *My Fair Lady* but reached Broadway's Gaiety Theatre as *Tell Me More!* (1925). It had nothing like the same success, despite producing the song "Kickin' the Clouds Away." *Tip-Toes* (1925) did a little better, continuing the Cinderella tradition with the tale of a music-hall dancer named Tip-Toes who marries a millionaire glue manufacturer. The score confirmed the supremacy of the Gershwin song with such numbers as "Looking for a Boy," "Sweet and Low Down" and "That Certain Feeling." More successful still was *Oh, Kay!* (1926) (originally *Cheerio!*), which demonstrated the 1920s Broadway passion for shows with short, snappy titles. Its racy, amusing book was by the veteran team of Guy Bolton and P. G. Wodehouse; it consisted of an old French comedy extensively altered to produce a thoroughly American plot. This was the era of Prohibition, and the revised story concerned a gang of rum runners who take over a Long Island home while the owner is away. Among the bootleggers is Lady Kay, a part created by English star Gertrude Lawrence. Kay is looking for "Someone to Watch Over Me," and after the usual series of misadventures and misunderstandings she eventually finds him in the person of Jimmy Winter, the owner of the house. Along the way, the romantically entwined couple sing the softly romantic "Maybe" and the mutual exhortation to "Do, Do, Do (What You've Done, Done, Done Before, Baby)."

The Gershwins were next reunited with the Astaires for a piece that began life out of town as *Smarty* but reached Broadway as *Funny Face* (1927), taking its revised title from one of the principal songs. It was produced at the newly opened Alvin Theatre (which took its name from its owners, Philadelphians Alex A. Aarons and Vinton Freedley, producers of *Tip-Toes, Lady Be Good!*, and *Oh, Kay!*). On its way to Broadway, *Funny Face* had undergone the sort of drastic overhaul that was typical of shows that depended less on a consistently developed plot and score than on a finely balanced mix of situations, songs, characters, and performers. The cast included comedian Victor Moore as one of a pair of comic jewel thieves after a string of pearls. This has been locked up by one Jimmy Reeve (Fred Astaire), along with a compromising diary belonging to his ward Frankie Wynne (Adele Astaire). Once again, what mattered were the songs, which included the title song (for Jimmy and Frankie), Jimmy's "My One and Only," and two beautiful duets, "He Loves and She Loves" and "'S Wonderful," for Frankie and her aviator boyfriend Peter. Among the songs dumped on the road was the later celebrated "How Long Has This Been Going On?"

The 1920s were the years in which the American song came of age and several "classic" American songwriters came to the fore. One who enjoyed enormous, if short-lived, success was Vincent Youmans (1898–1946). Another New Yorker, he followed the traditional route of song-plugger and rehearsal pianist, making his mark with songs such as "Oh Me! Oh My!" for *Two Little Girls in Blue* (1921), on which composer Paul Lannin and lyricist Ira Gershwin also worked. Youmans's next collaboration was with composer Herbert Stothart (1885–1949) on *Wildflower* (1923). The piece was notable not least for its team of librettists— Oscar Hammerstein II and Otto Harbach. Hammerstein (1895–1960) was the grandson of the Oscar Hammerstein whose failed Manhattan Opera project had led him to stage Victor Herbert's *Naughty Marietta*. Oscar Hammerstein II turned from law to playwriting and songwriting, finally teaming up with the established Otto Harbach, with whom he had written *Sunny*. It may be recalled that, under his original name of Hauerbach, the latter had been lyricist for Karl Hoschna on *Three Twins* and *Madame Sherry*. Under his modified name he had collaborated with Louis Achille Hirsch on *Going Up* and *Mary*.

As usual with Stothart shows, *Wildflower* was an ambitiously composed piece, satisfying the lingering public taste for the older operetta style. Its poor-girl-makes-good story was set in Lombardy, where hotheaded farmgirl Nina Benedetto (played by Edith Day) stands to inherit a fortune if she can keep her temper for six months. This she finally succeeds in doing despite all the efforts of her cousin Bianca, who is next in line for the inheritance. Youmans provided the more modern song interpolations, which included the two hits, the title song and the tripping "Bambalina," about an old man who played the fiddle for dancing.

Meanwhile, Youmans had also created the first score that was entirely his own. *No, No, Nanette* (1923) took almost two and a half years to move from its Detroit première to Broadway's Globe Theatre, having undergone extensive rewriting and having enjoyed a twelve-month run in Chicago along the way. It had also begun a run of almost two years in London, which was now only too ready to lap up the latest American successes. The story concerns a successful bible publisher, Jimmy Smith, who overcomes the frustrations of a penny-pinching wife by spending money from his bible business on entertaining a trio of young women. Eventually, the three become too demanding, and Jimmy brings in his lawyer friend Billy for a showdown in Atlantic City. But not only are Jimmy and his ward Nanette present, so are Jimmy's wife Sue and Billy's wife Lucille. The cleverly contrived set of misunderstandings, estrangements, and reconciliations keep the piece rolling merrily towards the final curtain, in which marital harmony is restored, and Nanette is paired off with Billy's assistant Tom.

No, No, Nanette has since become the paradigm of the 1920s song-and-dance musical. Its attributes include not only a cleverly alliterative title and a suitably unpretentious story but songs that illustrate perhaps more than those of any other show how far the essence of American popular songwriting lay from the extravagant vocalising of nineteenth-century operetta. For Youmans, especially, the secret lay in straightforward phrasing, limited vocal and melodic range, and simple variations of rhythms, which offset the deliberately under-played lyrics of Irving Caesar. These were features of "I Want to Be Happy," sung by Nanette, Jimmy, and the company, and "Tea for Two," featuring Nanette, Tom, and the company. Both were admirably complemented by the sprightly title song for Nanette, and the charming "Too Many Rings Around Rosie" for Lucille and the chorus.

No, No, Nanette was a sensation not only in the United States and the British Empire but also on the European continent, where it established more than any other work the taste for American musical comedy. Yet Youmans, apparently on the verge of a successful career, next suffered a string of failures or near failures: *The Left Over* (1923), which was revised for New York as *Lollipop* (1924); *Mary Jane McKane* (1923); *A Night Out* (1925); and *Oh, Please!* (1926). Only *Hit the Deck* (1927) came close to matching *No, No, Nanette*. This new work was a naval piece, produced by Lew Fields (of Weber and Fields) and adapted by his son Herbert Fields (1897–1958) from the play *Shore Leave*. Dockside café-owner Looloo Martin comes into money and decides that she wants to share it with visiting sailor Bilge Smith, who has by now gone back to sea. She follows his trail all the way to China, where she eventually tracks him down and learns that he isn't interested in her wealth. Only when he thinks she is poor again does he consent to marry her. Neither of the two big hit numbers was entirely new. Looloo and Bilge's "Sometimes I'm Happy" (another Youmans-Irving Caesar song built up from simple rhythmic phrases) was borrowed from the unsuccessful *A Night Out,* having even earlier still been dropped from *Mary Jane McKane,* where it had the lyric "Come on and pet me." In quite a different vein was the upbeat "Hallelujah!" a revivalist number for Looloo's black friend Lavinia, which Youmans had composed, but not used, years earlier.

Another team of American popular songwriters had a big success—their first—in 1927: lyricists B. G. ("Buddy") De Sylva (1895–1950) and Lew Brown (1893–1958), and composer Ray Henderson (1896–1970). De Sylva had been Jerome Kern's lyricist on "Look for the Silver Lining" and "Whip-Poor-Will," while Brown and Henderson had first collaborated in 1925 on "Don't Bring Lulu." After joining up in 1925, the three wrote "The Birth of the Blues" and "The Black Bottom" for *George White's Scandals of 1926,* before going on to write songs for the book musical *Good News* (1927).

Good News has been described as "probably the quintessential musical comedy of the era of wonderful nonsense." Like Kern's *Leave It to Jane,* it featured a college football story. This time Tom Marlowe, pride of the Tait College team, will be banned from the big game if he doesn't pass his exams. He does, of course, thanks to the tutoring of fellow student Connie Lane, with whom he duly pairs up at the final curtain. These two sing the most lasting song, "The Best Things in Life Are Free." Much of the show's strongest effect was achieved by an incidental character named Flo, who not only sang the title song but led the assembled students in "The Varsity Drag," described as a kind of riotous cakewalk and performed to the strains of George Olsen's Band, which was in the pit in place of the usual theatre orchestra. The uninhibited mood of the evening was established as the audience entered the theatre, where ushers (dressed in college jerseys) and the band rushed down the aisles to the orchestra pit chanting college cheers. Subsequent stage musicals by De Sylva, Brown, and Henderson included two more sports shows. *Hold Everything!* (1928) featured boxing, made a star of comic Bert Lahr, and introduced the song "You're the Cream in My Coffee." *Follow Thru* (1929) dealt with golf and contained "Button up Your Overcoat." Thereafter, the trio mainly wrote songs for films.

Of the teams of songwriters for book musicals that emerged during the early 1920s, one especially was to have a major effect on both American musical theatre and American popular song. Composer Richard Rodgers (1902–79) and lyricist Lorenz Hart (1895–1943) joined up when Rodgers was writing songs for amateur and college shows. They wrote seven songs that were interpolated into *Poor Little Ritz Girl* (1920), but, like so many other songwriters, their first real notice came with a revue when "Manhattan" made its debut in *The Garrick Gaieties* (1925). They then rapidly churned out a series of book shows. *Dearest Enemy* (1925), with a book by Herbert Fields, was an operetta-ish costume piece set during the American Revolution; its musical highlight was the love duet "Here in My Arms." In musical comedy mode came the song-and-dance piece *The Girl*

Chorus of *Garrick Gaieties* of 1925, with Libby Holman
Theatre Guild Records, Beinecke Rare Book and Manuscript Library, Yale University

Friend (1926), which introduced "The Blue Room." Like other promising musical comedy teams, they also set sail for London, where they produced the unremarkable *Lido Lady* (1926), before returning to the New York stage with *Peggy-Ann* (1926). By featuring a dream sequence, this gave a hint of the more serious approach to musical comedy they were to develop. *Peggy-Ann* ran for an impressive 333 performances.

These early Rodgers and Hart successes of the mid-1920s had, like Youmans's *Hit the Deck*, been produced by veteran Lew Fields. The same team was also responsible for three further works. *A Connecticut Yankee* (1927) was an adaptation of Mark Twain's novel and contained several fine songs: "Thou Swell," "On a Desert Island with Thee," and "My Heart Stood Still," which was taken over from a 1927 London revue, *One Dam Thing After Another*. *Present Arms* (1928) was a marine-military piece that introduced "You Took Advantage of Me." *Chee-Chee* (1928) had an unlikely plot about the son of the Grand Eunuch of ancient China seeking to avoid inheriting his father's position. If this show failed to leave behind

Richard Rodgers and Lorenz Hart in 1925
Theatre Guild Records, Beinecke Rare Book and Manuscript Library, Yale University

any standard numbers, it may have been because the public found the story dis-
tasteful, for there were melodic and poetic beauties a-plenty in such numbers as "I
Must Love You" and "Moon of My Delight."

While such songs contributed to a growing school of distinctively American popular songs, America's continuing importation of composers from Central
Europe also made the New World the dominant source in the 1920s of romantic
works with characters, attitudes, and vocal styles rooted in the European tradition. The two prime exponents of the genre were Rudolf Friml and Sigmund
Romberg. Friml (1879–1972) began his musical career as a pianist, touring the
world as accompanist to the violinist Jan Kubelik. He settled in America in 1906
and received his first opportunity to compose for the stage when Victor Herbert
fell out with prima donna Emma Trentini. Friml was brought in to compose the
score for *The Firefly* (1912), with book by Otto Harbach, in which Trentini (as
in her previous smash hit, *Naughty Marietta*) played a street singer who dresses

in boy's clothes—this time as a cabin boy on a yacht. The opportunity was doubly fortunate for Friml. He not only began a love affair with Trentini but also established his musical reputation with such numbers as "Giannina Mia," "Love Is Like a Firefly," and "Sympathy."

No less successful was Friml's more lighthearted score for the musical farce *High Jinks* (1913), which used the familiar theme of a magic potion that causes various unlikely romantic entanglements. "Something Seems a Tingle-ingle-ingling," was how the hero described the effects of the potion. The play was successful not only in New York but in London, where wartime sensibilities decreed that the Central European names of Otto Harbach and Rudolf Friml should be disguised as "Ogden Hartley" and "Roderick Freeman." *Katinka* (1915), their third collaboration, did equally well. If it harked back to European operetta in its Viennese and Turkish characters and settings, this was tempered by the appearance of a comical American widow whose "I Want to Marry a Male Quartet" was the score's hit number.

In subsequent works Friml varied his style with mixed success. *The Blue Kitten* (1922), an adaptation of a 1920 Parisian comedy, had genuinely American ragtime dance numbers far away from the mood of *The Firefly*. It was no less successful in its day than the two following works, today much better known, which helped to establish New York as the international centre of not only modern dance musicals but also high-flown romantic works. *Rose Marie* (1924) had many of the ingredients of operetta, but looked westwards, to the Canadian Rockies, for its exotic setting. Operatically trained Mary Ellis created the role of Rose Marie la Flamme, sister of a French-Canadian trapper. Much to the distress of her city suitor Edward Hawley, she is in love with miner Jim Kenyon. When Hawley's former mistress Wanda stabs her Indian lover to death, Hawley seeks to pin the murder on Kenyon, who is forced to flee. Kenyon's comic friend Hard-Boiled Herman finally extracts the truth from Wanda, who interrupts Hawley's wedding to Rose Marie to reunite the heroine with Jim. Friml collaborated on the score with Herbert Stothart, who provided the comedy numbers and incidental music while Friml concentrated on the lyrical bits: Jim's ardent declaration "Oh, Rose Marie, I love you," the "Indian Love Call" duet ("When I'm calling you, oo-oo, oo-oo-oo!"), Rose Marie's "Pretty Things," and the bridal music, "The Door of My Dreams."

Rose Marie enjoyed an instant success in English-speaking countries; along with *No, No, Nanette*, it helped the American musical show gain acceptance around the world. Friml predictably followed it up with another show in similar

Jane Carroll as Huguette in Friml's *The Vagabond King*
White Studio Collection, New York Public Library
for the Performing Arts

vein. *The Vagabond King* (1925) was based on the age-old plot of a commoner who is king for a day, the immediate source being the 1901 play *If I Were King*. Dennis King, the original Jim Kenyon in *Rose Marie,* played swaggering poet-thief François Villon, who is made king for a week, defeats the Duke of Burgundy, and wins himself not only a royal pardon but the hand of aristocratic Katherine de Vaucelles. Friml's score was in the virile, romantic vein of its predecessor, at its best in the march-time "Song of the Vagabonds" and the duet "Only a Rose," which came to epitomise romantic Broadway.

After a couple of relative flops with *The Wild Rose* (1926) and *The White Eagle* (1927), Friml turned once more to swashbucklers in a musical version of Alexandre Dumas's *The Three Musketeers* (1928). P. G. Wodehouse wrote some of the lyrics, and Dennis King again starred, as D'Artagnan. It did well enough, without matching its romantic predecessors. Nor was either of Friml's last two Broadway stage shows—*Luana* (1930) and *Music Hath Charms* (1934)—a success. Friml was thereafter happy to concentrate his attention on Hollywood adaptations of *Rose Marie, The Vagabond King,* and *The Firefly* that helped secure his place in theatrical musical history.

The second major exponent of American romantic operetta during the 1920s was Sigmund Romberg (1887–1951), who studied violin in his native Hungary and found the lure of the theatre greater than that of his intended career of engineering. After moving to New York in 1909, he worked as a pianist and orchestra leader and began composing songs for revues produced by the Shubert brothers, including material for the young Al Jolson. He proved the ideal person to adapt imported Central European operettas to local taste, a task that increasingly meant providing not just topical interpolations but writing a largely new score for the imported plots. This was a role he filled for Edmund Eysler's *Ein Tag im Paradies,* produced in America as *The Blue Paradise* (1915), and Emmerich Kálmán's *Gold gab ich für Eisen,* produced as *Her Soldier-Boy* (1916).

This process was taken to its ultimate extreme when Romberg provided a completely new score for *Maytime* (1917), the American adaptation of Walter Kollo's four-generation saga *Wie einst im Mai.* The piece was now set in New York rather than Berlin, with Romberg's richly romantic "Will You Remember?" (with its refrain "Sweetheart, sweetheart, sweetheart") playing the same recurrent role in the American version as Kollo's "Das war in Schöneberg im Monat Mai" did in the German original. No less successful was Romberg's adaptation of music by Franz Schubert for *Blossom Time* (1921). This was the American version of what had originated in Vienna as *Das Dreimäderlhaus* (1916), whose Schubert melodies were arranged by Heinrich Berté (1857–1924). Romberg's American version helped give the pseudo-biography of Schubert an enduring place in the musical theatre that was further consolidated in 1922 by a quite different British adaptation (by Australian composer George Howard Clutsam, 1866–1951) as *Lilac Time.*

Like Friml, Romberg by no means confined himself to music in the European style. His thoroughly American creations are exemplified by "I Love to Go Swimmin' with Women" for *Love Birds* (1921). He produced at least as many flops as successes before he finally consolidated his reputation with a show that owed more to the European than the native American musical tradition. *The Student Prince in Heidelberg* (1924; later shortened to *The Student Prince*) boasted a book by Dorothy Donnelly (1880–1928), who had also been responsible for *Blossom Time.* Based on the 1901 German play *Old Heidelberg,* it featured Howard Marsh as Prince Karl-Franz, who leaves his palace at Karlsberg with his tutor Dr. Engel to study in Heidelberg. Among the attractions of the Three Golden Apples Inn, the greatest is the innkeeper's pretty daughter Kathie. The two fall in love, but their idyll is shattered when Karl-Franz is summoned back to succeed his grandfather and marry the princess chosen for him.

For the Shubert brothers, who produced it, it was something of an innovation to have the focus on a male, rather than female, chorus; but the drinking song "Drink, Drink, Drink!" and the students' rousing "Come, Boys, Let's All Be Gay Boys" provided ample compensation for any shortage of female flesh. So did such well-remembered numbers as Dr. Engel's nostalgic "Golden Days," the serenade "Overhead the Moon Is Beaming," and the love duet "Deep in My Heart, Dear." In a manner that was becoming increasingly prevalent, these numbers were reprised shamelessly throughout the evening to ensure that the audiences went home humming.

The Desert Song (1926) took the highflown romantic operetta style to French North Africa, exploiting the much discussed exploits of Lawrence of Arabia as well as popular songs such as "The Sheik of Araby" and the films *Beau Geste, The Sheik,* and *The Son of the Sheik* (starring Rudolph Valentino). In the book by Oscar Hammerstein II and Otto Harbach (with the collaboration of Frank Mandel), French authorities fighting the local guerrillas in Morocco are plagued by the mysterious Red Shadow. He turns out to be none other than the governor's son Pierre Mirabeau. At home Pierre affects an air of slow-wittedness that means he has no chance of attracting beautiful Margot Bonvalet; but, clad in Arab garb as the daring Red Shadow, he carries her romantically off into the desert. When the governor rides out to rescue her, the Red Shadow cannot bring himself to kill his own father. He gives up the leadership of his rebel band and, claiming to have killed the bandit, hands over the bandit's clothes to his father. Forewarned that the Red Shadow is his own son, the governor is only too happy to accept the story. What mattered more than this improbable book was the combination of the exotic Moroccan setting and Romberg's luxuriant melodies, heard at their best in the Red Shadow's title song, with its refrain "Blue Heaven, and you and I," and his "One Alone," Margot's rhapsodic dream "Romance," and the rousing "Riff Song" for the male chorus. Scottish baritone Robert Halliday played Pierre, with Vivienne Segal as Margot. Thanks to film versions and stage revivals, *The Desert Song,* even more than *Rose Marie,* defines American musical theatre romanticism.

Romberg's subsequent work included the modest success *Rosalie* (1928), a

Sheet-music cover showing Marilyn Miller in
Romberg and Gershwin's *Rosalie*
Yale University Music Library

vehicle for Marilyn Miller at the New Amsterdam, for which he shared the composing credits with George Gershwin. Then came the third of his big romantic
successes, *The New Moon* (1927), for which Romberg revisited the New Orleans
of Victor Herbert's *Naughty Marietta*. It is based on the story of eighteenth-
century French aristocrat Robert Misson (played by Robert Halliday), who is
taken on as steward by the wealthy shipowning Beaunoir family when he is on the
run because of his Revolutionary sympathies. By the time the French police arrest
him at the end of Act 1, he has fallen in love with the daughter of the house, Marianne. Act 2 opens on board ship (the *New Moon* of the title), with Robert under
arrest and Marianne dreaming of him. Robert's supporters pursue them and enable him to take over *The New Moon* and sail it to an unoccupied island. There
they establish a new colony of which, when the French royalty is overthrown in
the French Revolution, Robert is appointed governor.

The New Moon shows Romberg at his inventive peak, with beautifully crafted romantic numbers that are genuinely touching, as well as being most effectively orchestrated by Romberg's regular assistant Emil Gerstenberger. Even more than in Marianne's "One Kiss" and Robert's "Lover, Come Back to Me," Romberg's romantic invention shines out in the the exquisite duet "Wanting You." Also in the rich score is the trademark male chorus, "Stout-Hearted Men," the beautifully tender "Softly, as in a morning sunrise," sung by Robert's Revolutionary friend Philippe, and the best of Romberg's light-comedy numbers, "Try Her Out at Dances."

The New Moon completed Romberg's trio of important shows, but he proved more durable than Friml. *Nina Rosa* (1930) was a South American romantic piece that had an international career, most particularly in France, which also appreciated *Forbidden Melody* (1936) when it appeared in translation as *Le Chant du Tzigane* (Gypsy Song). Like Friml, Romberg flirted with Hollywood, but successfully, with new hit songs such as "When I Grow Too Old to Dream" for *The Night is Young* (1935). Moreover, he had further significant stage success with *Up in Central Park* (1945), whose utterly American song style is typified in "Close as Pages in a Book." Indeed, Romberg remained active to the end: *The Girl in Pink Tights* (1954), a piece about the creation of the 1866 American musical comedy *The Black Crook,* was produced after his death.

For all their successes, Friml and Romberg represented the end of one line of American musical theatre during the 1920s. Far more significant in the longer run were the less ambitious, but more idiosyncratically American, song-and dance musicals. Their overwhelming importance lay not in the shows as integrated scores but as immeasurably rich sources of vernacular popular songs. Helped especially by the development of sound recording and radio, the new songs entered the popular consciousness in a way never achieved by musical theatre songs of earlier decades.

Chapter Ten
The Musical Comes of Age

Not the least significant aspect of mid-1920s musicals such as Kern's *Sunny* was the way the score incorporated incidental music, underscoring, melodrama, and reprises that kept the piece flowing from scene to scene. This was a particular feature of Kern's scores, and it reached its apogee in a collaboration with Oscar Hammerstein that became one of the great milestones of the American theatre. *Show Boat* (1927) brilliantly integrated vernacular song and dance, as well as anticipating film techniques in its use of underscoring of dialogue.

The play, based on a novel by Edna Ferber, follows the show-business family of Cap'n Andy Hawkes and his wife Parthy Ann, who run a Mississippi

Sheet-music cover for "Why Do I Love You?" from
the 1946 revival of Kern's *Show Boat*
Beinecke Rare Book and Manuscript Library, Yale University

show boat, over a period of thirty years. When the boat is docked at Natchez, the leading lady Julie La Verne (played by Helen Morgan) is forced to flee the state with her husband Steve when it is revealed that she is of mixed blood. Meanwhile, handsome gambler Gaylord Ravenal (tenor Howard Marsh) seduces the Hawkeses' young daughter Magnolia (Norma Terriss), and by the end of Act 1 they have married and left the river. Ravenal's luck as a gambler comes and goes, and eventually he gives up the uneven struggle of supporting Magnolia and their daughter. Magnolia takes to the stage and becomes a Broadway star, a process later repeated by their daughter Kim (named after the three states, Kentucky, Illinois, and Missouri, that converge at the Mississippi River). In the end, Magnolia and Ravenal are reunited; Julie, on the other hand, is destroyed by drink.

The show broke new ground in a number of ways. Although time passes at a bewildering rate in an attempt to condense thirty years into three hours, the characters are credible and the action deals with American racial issues in a serious fashion. In the book and lyrics, Hammerstein showed his supreme ability to capture emotion through natural images, as in Julie's song that betrays her Negro ancestry (Queenie notes that "Ah didn't hear anybody but colored folks sing dat song"):

> Fish got to swim and birds got to fly,
> I got to love one man 'til I die.
> Can't help lovin' dat man of mine!

The score includes a varied succession of numbers, gloriously scored by Broadway's leading orchestrator Robert Russell Bennett. The opening chorus portrays blacks at work on the Mississippi, after which Ravenal and Magnolia tentatively make each other's acquaintance in "Only Make Believe." Leading comedy player Ellie May Chipley sings about "Life Upon the Wicked Stage," and Ravenal displays his virile approach to life in "Till Good Luck Comes My Way." When he and Magnolia declare their feelings for each other in the duet "You Are Love," we have something on a scale above anything heard up to then in a specifically American musical show. Act 2 brings another duet—"Why Do I Love You?"—and the night-club song "Bill" that Julie sings in a rare moment of sobriety. After it was dropped from the 1916 *Oh, Lady! Lady!* "Bill" was revised by Kern and Hammerstein; it now took its place as one of the definitive songs of *Show Boat*. There was also one more song whose like had not previously been heard in a Broadway show. This was the philosophical bass musing "Ol' Man River," sung by Joe, the shiftless husband of the black maid Queenie. The song was written for Paul Robeson, who later made it his own, but, owing to delays in production, it was introduced by Jules Bledsoe.

    Show Boat was a success from the start of its out-of-town tryout, above all for the lavish staging that was typical of a Ziegfeld production, but also for Kern's parade of hit numbers and the overall scale of his musical contribution. Such changes as were made to the show before it reached New York were primarily to trim it from more than four hours to nearer three. London took to the show just as readily as New York. However, *Show Boat* was never going to set a pattern for other large-scale concepts. The particularly lavish extravagance to which Ziegfeld committed himself for the launch of his new theatre was never intended to be repeated even if the show's post–New York tour had not been cut short in 1930 by the Depression.

Show Boat's popularity ensured its adaptation for films and for theatre revivals, with new songs added each time. However, such revivals increasingly concentrated on set numbers at the expense of Kern's extensive musical underscoring. Not until the original performance material again came to light during the 1980s was the extent and originality of Kern's writing appreciated afresh by a new generation. The show's full importance as a precursor of the integrated, more serious Broadway musical was even more keenly recognised, not least the near-operatic scale of its musical concept.

It was some years before anything on a similar scale was even attempted, and Kern contented himself with a variety of less ambitious works. For London he composed *Blue Eyes* (1928) before collaborating again with Hammerstein on *Sweet Adeline* (1929), in which Helen Morgan, specialist in tragic roles, played the daughter of a beergarden proprietor in 1890s Hoboken, New Jersey. Unlucky in love, she expresses her unhappiness in the show's plaintive hits "Why Was I Born?" and "Don't Ever Leave Me." The show's successful Broadway run was halted by the 1929 Wall Street crash. It was then Otto Harbach's turn to collaborate with Kern on *The Cat and the Fiddle* (1931), which returned to the old operetta ambience. Set in Brussels, it revolved around a romance between American singer Shirley Sheridan and Romanian composer Victor Florescu, played by Romanian actor George Metaxa. The memorable songs were Shirley's "She Didn't Say 'Yes,'" and the serenade "The Night Was Made for Love," sung by street singer Pompineau.

Kern was back again with Hammerstein for *Music in the Air* (1932). Staged at the Alvin, it was even more pronouncedly in operetta style than *The Cat and the Fiddle*. The action moved between a Bavarian village and theatrical Munich, its three leading characters being playwright Bruno Mahler and the two rivals for his affections: operetta prima donna Frieda Hatzfeld and would-be star Sieglinde Lessing. Walter Slezak, son of opera tenor Leo Slezak, played the village music teacher Karl Reder, who introduces "I've Told Every Little Star." Other hits were the leading man's elegantly shaped "The Song Is You," the prima donna's gentle "I'm Alone," and the lilting "Egern on the Tegern See" for a supporting character.

Kern returned to Harbach for *Roberta* (1933), about a Parisian fashion shop. The book was no great shakes; but the New Amsterdam Theatre paraded a distinguished cast with Ray Middleton as leading man, veteran Fay Templeton as the aunt from whom he inherits the shop, and vaudeville performer Bob Hope in a comedy role. Kern's score too was a gem, including such beautiful

Natalie Hall as Frieda in Kern's *Music in the Air*
Crawford Theatre Collection, Manuscripts
and Archives, Yale University

numbers as "You're Devastating" (reusing a melody from *Blue Eyes*), "The Touch of Your Hand" and, best of all, the exquisite "Smoke Gets in Your Eyes." The stage show evolved into a film for which Kern contributed more material: "Lovely to Look At" and the syncopated "I Won't Dance," which was taken from *Three Sisters* (1934), an unsuccessful show written with Hammerstein for London's Drury Lane Theatre.

Kern thereafter concentrated his efforts on Hollywood, contributing some of the most sophisticated American popular songs ever written, in such movies as *Swing Time* (1936) and *Cover Girl* (1944). His two final stage shows were undisguised flops. *Gentlemen Unafraid* (1938) was a collaboration with Hammerstein and Harbach but died in tryouts. *Very Warm for May* (1939) played briefly at the Alvin. It is remembered for "All the Things You Are," a masterpiece of harmonic

Ira Gershwin (left) and Jerome Kern working on their film songs
Copyright Underwood and Underwood/CORBIS

and lyrical refinement and one of the finest creations either Kern or Hammerstein ever produced. Kern's last contribution to the Broadway theatre was two
new songs for a 1946 revival of the perennial *Show Boat,* which opened eight
weeks after his fatal collapse in a New York street at the age of sixty.

Meanwhile, George and Ira Gershwin had followed up 1927's *Funny Face*
with several more modestly successful pieces. For *Rosalie* (1928) they tempered the
romantic contributions of Sigmund Romberg with sprightly numbers such as
"How Long Has This Been Going On?" The Alvin Theatre's *Treasure Girl* (1928)
had Gertrude Lawrence in the lead and was notable for "I've Got a Crush on
You," while the Ziegfeld Theatre's *Show Girl* (1929) contained the haunting "Liza."
Like Kern, the Gershwins were seeking to develop their song-and-dance musical
comedies into something more substantial. In its original form, *Strike up the
Band* (1927) was an antiwar, antibusiness political satire by George S. Kaufman
about a trade war with Switzerland over import duties on cheese. As a musical, it

proved too ambitious for its audience, and neither the rousing title song nor "The Man I Love" (rescued from *Lady Be Good*) was able to save it.

Not until 1930 did *Strike up the Band* resurface, with the sharper satiric points of Kaufman's book smoothed down and broader comedy touches added by Morrie Ryskind. The trade war had now been relegated to a dream sequence, and its cause was now chocolate rather than cheese. A chocolate manufacturer, Horace J. Fletcher, promotes the war to boost his business and—in a biting commentary on American commercialism—even offers to pay for the war if it's named after him. Lovers Jim Townsend and Joan Fletcher finally blackmail him into dropping his support, but not before the country has become so excited by the business possibilities of war that top strategists begin planning a caviar war with Russia. The Broadway cast included veteran performer Blanche Ring in a minor role. "The Man I Love" had by now become too well known as an individual song to be included again; but the lovers had the beautiful "Soon," and "I've Got a Crush on You" was taken over from *Treasure Girl*. In the orchestra pit was Red Nichols's Band, which included Benny Goodman, Gene Krupa, Glenn Miller, Jimmy Dorsey, and Jack Teagarden, who gave full value to the title march.

The same distinguished jazz players were present later that same year for what was to prove an even bigger hit. *Girl Crazy* (1930) had no political pretensions, but instead followed *Lady Be Good, Tip-Toes, Oh, Kay!, Funny Face,* and *Treasure Girl* in the tradition of unashamedly lighthearted song-and-dance musicals produced by Alex Aarons and Vinton Freedley at the Alvin Theatre. It tells of fun-loving New Yorker Danny Churchill, who is dispatched by his wealthy father to the supposedly more sober attractions of Custerville, Arizona, only to turn the town into a provincial fun spot. The story was unambitious; but the score possessed the finest collection of songs in any Gershwin musical comedy. The cast, too, featured names that were to shine in lights for years to come. The teenaged Ginger Rogers, as the Custerville postmistress Willie Gray with whom Danny finds love, was blessed with "But Not for Me" and "Embraceable You," while Ethel Merman as the daughter of Custerville saloonkeeper Slick Fothergill showed off her siren voice in the jazzy "I Got Rhythm." Other attractions were a male quartet, who harmonised on "Bidin' My Time" in different ways throughout the evening.

The success of the revised *Strike up the Band* encouraged the Gershwins to collaborate again with Kaufman and Ryskind on another political satire, *Of Thee I Sing* (1931), this time focused on the American presidency. William Gaxton played John P. Wintergreen, who is running for president, with Victor Moore as his nondescript running mate Alexander Throttlebottom. To capture the support of the American public, the pair decide to base their campaign on love, which means that bachelor Wintergreen has to find a wife. A contest is held, won by glamorous Diana Devereaux; but Wintergreen has in the meantime fallen in love with and married his secretary Mary Turner. After he becomes both the president and a father, Wintergreen faces an international incident when Devereaux returns and insists on her right to marriage. The dilemma is solved when Vice President Throttlebottom recognises his constitutional obligation to step in when the president is unable to fulfil his duties.

Of Thee I Sing had music in the traditional Gershwin style, but it was more ambitiously structured into continuous sequences. In addition to the title song and the campaign march "Wintergreen for President!" it boasted the duet "Who Cares?" for Wintergreen and his wife Mary. What attracted most praise, though, was the book, whose groundbreaking qualities were recognised when it became the first American musical comedy book to win the coveted Pulitzer Prize for drama. In truth, the satirical bite in *Of Thee I Sing* was little more than gentle fun compared with what had been typical of such Offenbach pieces as *La Grande-Duchesse de Gérolstein*. In relation to the lightheartedness of earlier American musical comedies, however, *Of Thee I Sing* stood out as significantly different.

The Gershwins had little success with one final song-and-dance score for Aarons and Freedley. *Pardon My English* (1933) had a book by Herbert Fields and songs that included "Isn't It a Pity?" and "My Cousin in Milwaukee," but it proved the least successful of the series. Nor did they have much better fortune with *Let 'Em Eat Cake* (1933), a sequel to *Of Thee I Sing* with the same characters and the same principal performers. Again, the president and his wife had a lasting hit number ("Mine"), but overall there was nothing to match the quality of its predecessor. Undeterred, and striving for greater artistic distinction, the Gershwins devoted themselves to a work that was more ambitious than anything yet attempted in the American musical theatre.

As Kern and Hammerstein had done for *Show Boat,* the Gershwins now turned to a successful novel, which in this case had already spawned an equally distinguished stage play. Where the Kern and Hammerstein chef-d'oeuvre included black characters among what was predominantly a cast of whites, the Gershwins took a story that exclusively concerned blacks. Moreover, unlike the Kern and Hammerstein source, DuBose Heyward's novel *Porgy* was a story of un-

J. Rosamond Johnson (left) as Lawyer Frazier, Todd Duncan as Porgy,
and Anne Brown as Bess in Gershwin's *Porgy and Bess*
James Rosamond Johnson Papers, Yale University Music Library

relieved human suffering which left little scope for the humour that had lightened
Show Boat.

Heyward (1885–1940) had been working as an insurance salesman in
his native Charleston, South Carolina, when he set out to write a novel based
on a real-life crippled beggar who was a familiar sight around the town, travelling

around on a hand-made cart pulled by a malodorous goat. The novel was published in 1925, after which Heyward's wife Dorothy turned it into a play that became a Broadway hit when it was produced by the Theatre Guild in 1927. George Gershwin had been interested in the possibilities of the book as early as 1926, but it was only in 1932, when his aspirations as a serious composer were increasingly bearing fruit, that he approached DuBose Heyward with the suggestion of setting it. Ira Gershwin collaborated with Heyward on the libretto of what was to be a through-composed score.

In its essentials the story of *Porgy and Bess* (1935) is simple enough. The crippled Porgy is hopelessly in love with Bess, mistress of the uncouth Crown. When Crown is forced to flee after killing a man in a brawl, Porgy and Bess are thrown together and, when Crown returns to reclaim Bess, Porgy murders him. Finally released from prison, Porgy returns and discovers that Bess has gone to New York with the drug peddler Sportin' Life. The work ends with Porgy hopelessly setting out after her in his donkey cart. *Porgy and Bess* was far more than a simple story, however, for it depicted black characters and dramatic situations in a way totally foreign to the Broadway musical. In its concept, its structure, and the scale of its vocal and orchestral writing, *Porgy and Bess* was unequivocally an opera, though it contained songs in the Broadway show tradition and used performers from the musical theatre (John W. Bubbles as Sportin' Life, veteran songwriter-performer J. Rosamond Johnson as Lawyer Frazier) along with opera singers Todd Duncan as Porgy, Anne Brown as Bess, and Warren Coleman as Crown. But, unlike operas or near-operas by Offenbach, Johann Strauss, and Lehár, *Porgy and Bess* was produced as a musical in Broadway's Alvin Theatre. Like Sullivan's *Ivanhoe,* it achieved a run (124 performances) that was remarkable for a serious operatic piece, but inadequate for commercial success.

From the operatic standpoint, *Porgy and Bess* contains as many favourites as *Carmen,* among them Bess's delicately spun "Summertime," Porgy's satisfied "I Got Plenty o' Nuttin'," the soaring duet "Bess, You Is My Woman Now," and Porgy's determined "I'm on My Way." In more obviously popular style are Sportin' Life's "It Ain't Necessarily So" and "There's a Boat Dat's Leavin' Soon for New York." Like *Carmen,* the work took time to be widely accepted; but its operatic stature is now acknowledged. Though *Show Boat* (like *Die Fledermaus* and *Die lustige Witwe*) is admitted into the repertory of opera companies as a special concession, *Porgy and Bess* is there by right.

Cruelly, if in some ways fittingly, *Porgy and Bess* was to be George Gershwin's last stage score. Like Kern, he went west and wrote marvellous songs for

Hollywood musicals; but he was only thirty-eight when he died of a brain tumour in July 1937.

While Kern and Gershwin sought to create musical theatre works that stood out from the norm, other major creators remained true to the concept of the song-and-dance musical comedy plot as a peg on which to hang appealing songs and display the talents of individual performers. One who took longer than most to come to the fore was lyricist and composer Cole Porter (1891–1964). Born into a wealthy Indiana family, he was for a while content to parade his talents as a writer of revue songs and performer of his own work in social gatherings in America and Europe. *See America First* (1916), an initial Broadway commission from producer Elisabeth Marbury, failed after two weeks, and not until 1928 did he attract major attention with six songs written for the small-scale *Paris* (1928). They included the suggestive "Let's Do It," sung by French revue artist Irene Bordoni.

Porter's reward for this success was a commission to set the Herbert Fields book for *Fifty Million Frenchmen* (1929), a loosely constructed piece about wealthy and socially ambitious tourists in Paris. In a manner reminiscent of both Offenbach's *La Vie parisienne* and Ziehrer's *Der Fremdenführer*, playboy Peter Forbes (played by William Gaxton) adopts the disguise of a tourist guide in order to win Looloo Carroll away from the Russian Grand Duke for whom she is intended. The two declare their mutual attraction in one of Porter's lasting hits, "You Do Something to Me," in which his distinctive rhythmic style comes across in the internal rhyming of "do do," "voodoo" and "you do":

> Let me live 'neath your spell,
> Do do that voodoo that you do so well.

The show confirmed a popular taste for Porter's sophisticated songs and led to a series of shows that made him one of the hottest properties on Broadway. *The New Yorkers* (1930) shifted back to an American location, with Jimmy Durante, the gravel-voiced comedian with the outsize nose, playing a gangster. Among the songs were "I Happen to Like New York" and "Love For Sale," whose lyric, expressing the feelings of a prostitute on her beat, was too strong for the moral guardians of the time; the song was banned from the airwaves and condemned to circulate for a while as an instrumental piece.

Porter's star rose still higher with his next show. Fred and Adele Astaire had followed their Gershwin successes with another triumphal appearance in the revue *The Band Wagon* (1931), before Adele retired to marry Lord Charles

Clare Luce and Fred Astaire in Porter's *Gay Divorce*
Cole Porter Papers, Historical Sound Recordings Collection,
Yale University

Cavendish. In Porter's *Gay Divorce* (1932) Fred Astaire made a last Broadway appearance before moving on to even greater triumphs in Hollywood. Now that the leading lady wasn't his real-life sister, he could play a romantic lead. His co-star was Clare Luce, playing unhappily married Mimi Pratt, who is so desperate to divorce her husband that she hires someone to act as her co-respondent. Astaire played young novelist Guy Holden, who is in love with Mimi and takes the job. Inevitably, he ends up marrying her. Porter's score was crowned with two big Astaire successes—"After You, Who?" containing a typical Porter internal rhyme, and "Night and Day," whose insistent rhythm ("Like the beat, beat, beat of the tom-tom . . . ") was reportedly inspired by a Mohammedan call to worship.

Porter had long been as much at home in London as in New York, and his next musical was London's *Nymph Errant* (1933), based on a novel with the same sexually suggestive title. Gertrude Lawrence played the lead, Evangeline, who travels around the world, going from one romantic partner to another but never managing to lose her virginity. This is despite the advice to "Experiment" provided by her teacher Miss Pratt and her amorous feelings towards "The Physician" who treated her for measles. Elisabeth Welch played the young black American Haidee Robinson; she sang about "Solomon" and his thousand wives, a song that remarkably she repeated for the first recorded performance of the show (a concert performance) fifty-five years later.

Porter's next Broadway score achieved the prestigious surroundings of the Alvin Theatre and marked his greatest success of the interwar years. *Anything Goes* (1934) was in the best tradition of the Alvin and featured several of the creators of *Girl Crazy*. Its book was originally by the team of P. G. Wodehouse and Guy Bolton and included a comical shipwreck; but the real-life sinking of the *S.S. Morro Castle* forced producer Vinton Freedley to get a rewrite by Howard Lindsay and Russel Crouse. In revised form it concerns evangelist-turned-nightclub-singer Reno Sweeney, who, with her Sixteen Angels back-up group, is sailing to London. Also on board is stowaway Billy Crocker, on whom Reno has a crush but who currently has eyes only for the beautiful Hope Harcourt. Complications abound before Billy finally wins Hope's hand and Reno makes do with gormless (but titled and wealthy) Sir Evelyn Oakleigh. If the plot could be difficult to follow, the songs were anything but. Ethel Merman, as Reno, had the lion's share with "I Get a Kick Out of You" (a catalogue of the things that fail to turn her on, while Billy does), the rousing title song, and her gospel number with the Angels, "Blow, Gabriel, Blow." She also sang the duet "You're the Top" with William Gaxton; in typical Porter fashion, it was filled with references to various real-life celebrities. Gaxton as Billy and Bettina Hall as Hope had the more restful duet "All Through the Night," while Victor Moore played the comic gangster disguised as a clergyman, Reverend Dr. Moon. Such were the riches of the score of *Anything Goes* that it was even possible to drop Billy's "Easy to Love," which became a Porter standard after resurfacing in the 1936 film *Born to Dance*.

Anything Goes has been described as "the quintessential musical comedy of the thirties," and it was certainly one of the shows that did the most to raise the spirits of the Depression years. No other Porter score of the 1930s could match it, though all the shows that followed produced their classic songs. *Jubilee* (1935) revived the idea of disguised royalty wandering among the general public, with romantic attachments between three couples: the Queen and a movie star, Princess Diana and a successful writer, and Prince James and a dancer. The nation they ruled was unnamed; but 1935 was the year of King George V's Silver Jubilee over in England. The movie star, writer, and dancer, moreover, were readily identifiable with current popular idols. What endured were two outstanding songs for the Prince and the dancer, "Begin the Beguine" and "Just One of Those Things."

Red, Hot and Blue! (1936) was designed as a successor to *Anything Goes,* with the same theatre (Alvin), producer (Freedley), book authors (Lindsay and Crouse) and leading lady (Merman). Comedian Jimmy Durante shared top billing, along with Bob Hope as the young lawyer Bob Hale, whose search for a lost love with the imprint of a hot waffle-iron on her backside provides the meat of the plot. It was Merman and Hope who had the show's top number, "It's De-Lovely," a duet in the same mould as "You're the Top." Then came *You Never Know* (1938) and *Leave It to Me* (1938), which followed within a few weeks of each other. The former, with Clifton Webb introducing "At Long Last Love," had but a short run. The latter did better, with a cast that included William Gaxton, Victor Moore, revue-artist Sophie Tucker, and up-and-coming Mary Martin and Gene Kelly. Tucker introduced "Most Gentlemen Don't Like Love," while "My Heart Belongs to Daddy" helped Mary Martin launch a distinguished stage and film career.

If it is thanks in good measure to Porter that the 1930s is remembered as a great decade for witty, sophisticated American songs, he didn't do it alone. Such virtues were also present in the work of several other noteworthy songwriters. Many of these preferred the medium of the revue, with only occasional sorties into genuine musical comedy. Such was the case with Russian-born Irving Berlin (1888–1989), whose only book musical of the 1930s was the New Amsterdam Theatre's *Face the Music* (1932). So it was, too, with composer Arthur Schwartz (1900–1984) and lyricist Howard Dietz (1896–1983), who wrote the revue *The Band Wagon* (1931), in which Fred and Adele Astaire made their final appearance. Schwartz and Dietz's one significant musical comedy of the thirties was *Revenge with Music* (1934) at the New Amsterdam. Set in Spain, the musical was based on Pedro de Alarcón's comedy *El sombrero de tres picos* (The Three-Cornered Hat); Charles Winninger played provincial governor Don Emilio, who gets his come-uppance after unsuccessfully attempting to woo Maria from her husband Carlos on their wedding night. The score bequeathed the enduring "You and the Night and the Music," sung as a duet for the married couple, played by Libby Holman and George Metaxa. After World War II, Schwartz went on to compose two highly regarded musicals, with Lew Fields's daughter Dorothy Fields (1905–74) as lyricist, that starred comedian Shirley Booth. But both *A Tree Grows in Brooklyn* (1951) and *By the Beautiful Sea* (1954) expired after 270 performances. Whether together, or with other collaborators, neither Schwartz nor Dietz ever enjoyed major success with a book musical.

The most consistently inventive of 1930s musical comedy songwriters were undoubtedly Richard Rodgers and Lorenz Hart. Even when their shows were relative failures compared with their 1920s hits for Lew Fields, each contained stylish songs. Thus, two Aarons and Freedley commissions for the Alvin Theatre, *Spring Is Here* (1929) and *Heads Up* (1929), produced "You Took Advantage of Me" and the gentle "Ship Without a Sail." Likewise, the lavishly staged Ziegfeld show *Simple Simon* (1930) gave Ruth Etting a hit with "Ten Cents a Dance," while a song that was cut from the show, "Dancing on the Ceiling," found its definitive home in their London musical *Ever Green* (1930), where it was sung by Jessie Matthews. Then, after a spoof of silent films entitled *America's Sweetheart* (1931), starring Jack Whiting and Harriette Lake (later known as Ann Sothern), Rodgers and Hart spent some unproductive and depressing years in Hollywood.

Major success returned when they reappeared on Broadway with their enthusiasm rekindled by their Hollywood experiences. The vehicle they chose was a New York Hippodrome circus spectacular with Jimmy Durante leading a cast of ninety humans and almost as many animals. Appropriately entitled *Jumbo* (1935), it was the first show to be staged by the extraordinary (and extraordinarily long-lived) George Abbott (1887–1995), who was to become a significant force in the development of the musical. Such was the extravagance of its staging by showman Billy Rose that it failed to produce a profit from 233 performances, though it did produce a hit song in "The Most Beautiful Girl in the World."

Thereafter Rodgers and Hart took a more active interest in the whole structure and production of their musicals, resulting in several works of rare invention and consistency. In collaboration with George Abbott, they wrote their own book for *On Your Toes* (1936), a celebration of the dance form featuring amorous and comic happenings in a ballet company. Broadway dance star Ray Bolger played Junior Dolan, a vaudeville performer-turned-teacher whose pupils include the composer of a jazz ballet. Junior manages to get it staged, with himself in the starring role opposite ballerina Vera Barnova (Tamara Geva). Out of jealousy, her classical ballet partner hires a gunman to shoot Junior; but by his energetic dancing he avoids the would-be assassin's bullets until the police arrive. The jazz ballet "Slaughter on Tenth Avenue," one of the two ballet sequences in the show choreographed by George Balanchine, became a detachable classic. In addition, the score had a fine title song, as well as "It's Got to Be Love," "Quiet

Night" and "There's a Small Hotel." Not least of the attractions were its dance-band orchestrations by Hans Spialek, featuring the piano duo of Edgar Fairchild and Adam Carroll.

The next Rodgers and Hart work, *Babes in Arms* (1937), again featured a theatrical company, but this time it was a group of teenagers putting on an amateur musical. The young cast members were relative unknowns, though several later achieved prominence, notably Alfred Drake and Robert Rounseville. Choreography was again by Balanchine, and the score was full of endearing numbers: "Where or When," "I Wish I Were in Love Again," "My Funny Valentine," "Johnny One Note," "The Lady Is a Tramp," and "Imagine." Then, with *I'd Rather Be Right* (1937), written in conjunction with librettists George S. Kaufman and Moss Hart, the team followed the Gershwins into the field of political shows. The leading character of the president of the United States, who bore a striking resemblance to Franklin D. Roosevelt, was played by veteran showman George M. Cohan. The story, such as it was, concerned his comical attempts to balance the federal budget and thereby enable a pair of young lovers to earn enough money to marry. Cohan treated the show as a vehicle for his vaudeville routines, and the show produced no number more enduring than "Have You Met Miss Jones?"

More productive was *I Married an Angel* (1938), for which Rodgers and Hart again provided their own book, this time in conjunction with director Joshua Logan. It was based on an abandoned film adaptation of a Hungarian play and starred Dennis King as a philandering Budapest banker and Vivienne Segal as his scheming sister. The dancer Vera Zorina played an angel who comes to earth as the banker's wife and creates havoc with her all-too-honest revelations about his banking business. Walter Slezak was also in the cast. The songs included "Spring Is Here," "At the Roxy Music Hall," and the delightful "A Twinkle in Your Eye," and there was once again a Balanchine ballet.

The songwriting team was back to its very best for its next Alvin show, a clever adaptation of Shakespeare's *Comedy of Errors*. The project originated in the strong resemblance between Lorenz Hart's actor brother Teddy and the diminutive comedian Jimmy Savo, which made the pair ideal to play a set of twins. George Abbott was book adaptor, director, and producer of the piece, which was reset in Syracuse, New York, and became *The Boys from Syracuse* (1938). There were outstanding hits in "Falling in Love with Love" and the insistent "This Can't Be Love," plus some only slightly less noteworthy numbers in "You Have Cast Your Shadow on the Sea" and the trio "Sing for Your Supper."

Two lesser achievements followed, *Too Many Girls* (1939) and *Higher and Higher* (1940), the former introducing the charming "I Didn't Know What Time It Was," the latter "It Never Entered My Mind." Then came the biggest show of the entire partnership, *Pal Joey* (1940), based by John O'Hara on his own short stories. What it did that had seldom been done in musical comedy before was set its story among the low-life of Chicago. Gene Kelly starred as the cabaret host Joey Evans, who drops faithful girlfriend Linda English for the predatory Vera Simpson, played by Vivienne Segal. To keep Joey's attentions, Vera promotes his club, but she drops him when blackmailers appear. The Rodgers and Hart songs were consistently up to the pair's highest standard, among them "You Mustn't Kick It Around," "I Could Write a Book," and above all "Bewitched, Bothered, and Bewildered." Together with "Zip!"—an account of the random thoughts of a stripper as she takes off one piece of clothing after another—the songs demonstrated Hart's way with words and Rodgers's sympathetic settings at their brilliant best.

But Hart's erratic life and heavy drinking made him an increasingly unsuitable partner for the more disciplined Rodgers. They completed just one more show together, *By Jupiter* (1942), a tale set in ancient Greece, that tells of Hippolyta, Queen of the Amazons, who rules the country while her consort Sapiens (played by Ray Bolger) and the other husbands stay at home. Thereafter, their only further songs together were for a revised version of *A Connecticut Yankee* (1943), which produced one final hit in the darkly humorous "To Keep My Love Alive," in which Vivienne Segal as Morgan le Fey explains why she disposed of one husband after another. Within three weeks of the revival's first night, Hart was dead at the age of forty-eight.

Britain, meanwhile, was not only continuing to welcome the major American shows but also trying to meet the American invasion on its own terms. Bespectacled comedian and dancer Laddie Cliff followed up his appearance in the London production of the Gershwins' *Tip-Toes* by appearing in a series of similarly intentioned British shows variously featuring his wife Phyllis Monkman, comedians Leslie Henson and Lupino Lane, and Australian dancing pair Madge Elliott and Cyril Ritchard. The craze for everything American was such that the scores of *Lady Luck* (1927), *So This Is Love* (1928) and *Love Lies* (1929) were attributed to "Hal Brody," a name that sounded more American than those of the real songwriters, H. B. Hedley (1890–1931) and Jack Strachey (1894–1972). The later Cliff shows—*The Millionaire Kid* (1931), *Sporting Love* (1934), and *Over She Goes* (1936)—had scores by Billy Mayerl (1902–59), better known for syncopated novelty piano pieces such as "Marigold." The shows helped keep British audiences entertained, but they faded quickly after Cliff's early death in 1937.

Somewhat similar was the fate of another series composed jointly by impresario Jack Waller (1885–1957) and his musical director Joseph A. Tunbridge (1886–1961). As impresario, Waller had been largely instrumental in acquiring *No, No, Nanette* for London before it even appeared in New York, and his long list of scores with Tunbridge included such titles as *Virginia* (1928), *Dear Love* (1929), *Silver Wings* (1930), *For the Love of Mike* (1931), *Tell Her the Truth* (1932), *Yes, Madam?* (1934), and *Please, Teacher!* (1935), many of them staged at the London Hippodrome with comedian Bobby Howes.

Easily the most successful British composer in contemporary vein was classically trained Vivian Ellis (1903–96), who got his big opportunity when he was asked to supplement songs by American Richard Myers (1901–77) for a sex-reversed variation of the Cinderella story. *Mr Cinders* (1928) starred Bobby Howes as Jim and Binnie Hale as Jill, the rich man's daughter with whom Jim falls in love. True to the Cinderella story, Jim is oppressed by a stepmother and two stepbrothers, but he turns up disguised as a South American explorer at a ball given by Jill's father. This is the cue for a hilarious description of adventures "On the Amazon," though the most enduring hit in a delightful score was Jill's "Spread a Little Happiness," which has been much revived over the years. *Mr Cinders* established something of a record for length of evolution when, for a West End revival in 1982, Ellis and co-lyricist Greatrex Newman (1892–1984) added a new song, fifty-four years after the show's creation.

Ellis's subsequent shows were also sometimes composed in collaboration with others, among them *Follow a Star* (1930), *Little Tommy Tucker* (1930), the larger-scale *Song of the Drum* (1931), *Blue Roses* (1931), *Stand up and Sing* (1931), and *Out of the Bottle* (1932). His next significant success started as the touring show *Jack and Jill* (1933) before being revamped for London as *Jill Darling* (1934). The lighthearted plot concerned a by-election fought by two candidates who are supported by two gentlemen with conflicting views but played by the same actor, Arthur Riscoe. The resultant complications were less important than the opportunity to parade glamorous Frances Day's little-girl voice, big eyes, and shining blond hair. The score was notable for the lilting duet "I'm on a See-Saw," sung by the song-and-dance couple John Mills and Louise Browne. Ellis continued to turn out unassuming scores for the rest of the decade—*Going Places* (1936), *Hide and Seek* (1937), which had another hit, "She's My Lovely," for Bobby Howes, *The Fleet's Lit Up* (1938), *Running Riot* (1938), and the long-running *Under Your Hat*

(1938), for husband-and-wife comedy team Jack Hulbert and Cicely Courtneidge. None achieved the durability of *Mr Cinders*.

Indeed, only one other British song-and-dance musical comedy of the interwar years survived to achieve modern revival. Its composer, Noel Gay (1898–1954), was born Reginald Armitage and had been a church organist before adopting his snappier pen name. He wrote popular songs such as "The King's Horses," "There's Something About a Soldier," "Who's Been Polishing the Sun?" and "Round the Marble Arch" for revues and films before being commissioned to provide a handful of numbers for a show that would feature the acrobatic singing comedian Lupino Lane. *Me and My Girl* (1937) followed Cockney Bill Snibson's progress with his girlfriend Sally from lowly Lambeth to an incongruous succession to an earldom. As originally staged in London, the piece had just seven numbers; but these included two huge hits in the lilting title song and the jolly dance, "The Lambeth Walk." The uninhibited gaiety of the latter was to provide a huge boost for a British public beset by wartime troubles.

Otherwise, the major British products of the period sought to recapture the escapist operetta mood. A playwright and performer as well as lyricist and composer, Noël Coward (1899–1973) made a name with revue songs that included the sophisticated numbers "Parisian Pierrot" for *London Calling* (1923), "Poor Little Rich Girl" for *On with the Dance,* "A Room with a View" and "Dance Little Lady" for *This Year of Grace* (1928). However, Coward had grown up with a love of Edwardian musical comedy, and it was a performance of *Die Fledermaus* that persuaded him to try his hand at a book musical that reinterpreted Viennese operetta for the Britain of the 1920s. *Bitter-Sweet* (1929) foreshadowed Kern's *Music in the Air,* with its story of a young English girl, Sarah Millick, who rejects the husband chosen for her and flees to Vienna with her handsome music teacher Carl Linden. There reality takes over and, after becoming famous as singer Sari Linden, she finally settles for the kind of loveless marriage that she had rejected at the start. Peggy Wood and George Metaxa had the leading roles. Coward's score ran the range of emotions, balancing the romantic love song "I'll See You Again" against the sprightly ensemble "Ladies of the Town," and the rousing drinking song "Tokay" against the dreamy "If Love Were All." This last contains the phrase that has so often been used to describe Coward's own "talent to amuse."

Bitter-Sweet was the most successful of three Coward book musicals written for the prestigious His Majesty's Theatre. In *Conversation Piece* (1934), Coward himself stepped in at the last minute to star opposite French performer

Yvonne Printemps. Specially tailored to the fact that Printemps spoke little English, the plot had Coward as the impoverished Duc de Chaucigny-Varennes who takes young French singer Melanie to Brighton to find a wealthy husband who can support them both. Ultimately, of course, Melanie and the Duke realise that their hearts lie with each other. "Regency Rakes" did for the men of Brighton what "Ladies of the Town" had done for the females of Vienna in *Bitter-Sweet;* but the big number was the romantic waltz, "I'll Follow My Secret Heart." Coward's final continental confection likewise brought the illustrious Fritzi Massary to appear as a Viennese singing star in *Operette* (1938). The show-within-a-show device enabled Coward to re-create a turn-of-the-century musical comedy in which Peggy Wood appeared as Rozanne Grey, promoted from the chorus to a star role. Alas, the score was generally undistinguished, with the exception of the male quartet "The Stately Homes of England."

Among other British composers who sought to reinterpret the traditional operetta in more modern terms was George Posford (1906–76), who collaborated with radio executive and lyricist Eric Maschwitz (1901–69) on *Goodnight Vienna* (1932). Originally a romantic musical play for radio, it featured a successful title song in tango rhythm. The two then tried their hands at a stage piece about a tsarist aristocrat and a Russian ballerina. This finally reached London as *Balalaika* (1936), with additional Eastern European colour provided by Viennese émigré composer Bernard Grün (1901–72). Another romantic tango-rhythm title song, "At the Balalaika," helped send the piece across the Atlantic as well as to France, where it is still performed today. A successor with a Hungarian story failed twice, first as *Paprika* (1938) and then in revised form, as *Magyar Melody* (1939).

What inspired the Maschwitz-Posford-Grün excursion into the London theatre was the huge success of a series of works by Ivor Novello (1893–1951) that sought to recapture the opulence of former days. As early as 1916, Novello had collaborated with Jerome Kern on *Theodore & Co* for London's Gaiety Theatre. He likewise had a hand in romantic musical play collaborations with Howard Talbot on *Who's Hooper?* (1919) and Harold Fraser-Simson on *Our Nell* (1924), as well as being sole composer for a P. G. Wodehouse libretto, *The Golden Moth* (1921). For a decade thereafter he concentrated on his career as stage and silent-screen idol before promoting a revival of the lush, spectacular Ruritanian musical show at London's Drury Lane Theatre.

Novello himself appeared as non-singing leading man in pieces for which he wrote the book and (to Christopher Hassall's lyrics) the music. *Glamorous Night* (1935) offered a vast cast, opulent costumes, and a spectacular shipwreck.

Ivor Novello in the Gypsy wedding scene of his *Glamorous Night*
Kurt Gänzl Collection

Novello played young inventor Anthony Allen, who is on a cruise holiday when, during an operetta performance at the Krasnian Opera House, he foils an attempt on the life of prima donna Militza Hájos (played by Mary Ellis), mistress of the Krasnian King Stefan. She seeks refuge on the cruise ship, and romance with Anthony develops before her republican enemies blow up the ship. Escaping via a Gypsy encampment, the two marry in a Gypsy service before returning to Krasnia, where Anthony shoots the villain and restores Militza to the lonely King. This was escapism in the extreme; but the public loved it—not least for Novello's opulent operetta melodies, among them the duet "Fold Your Wings," sung by Ellis with contralto Olive Gilbert; the romantic "Shine Through My Dreams," sung by tenor Trefor Jones; and the jazz-tinged "Shanty Town," sung by Elisabeth Welch as a stowaway entertainer.

The successor, *Careless Rapture* (1936), featured Novello as one of two brothers in love with musical comedy star Penelope Lee, played by Dorothy Dickson. The action takes place in settings as varied as Hampstead Heath and China before the hero gets the girl. The most successful numbers were the soprano's "Music in May" and Olive Gilbert's "Why Is There Ever Goodbye?" *Crest of the Wave* (1937) did rather badly, despite the patriotic tenor number "Rose of England"; but it was followed by the most popular of all Novello's musical plays.

The story of *The Dancing Years* (1939) followed in the tradition of *Bitter-Sweet* and *Music in the Air,* but with daring references to contemporary Nazi repression. Prima donna Maria Ziegler (Mary Ellis) brings fame to impoverished composer Rudi Kleber (Novello) by singing one of his songs; she also becomes his mistress. Since he cannot marry her because of a promise to a childhood friend, Maria marries her old admirer Prince Metterling. But she is able to pay one final homage to the Jewish Rudi by using her influence to save him when he is arrested by the Nazis. The score was Novello's richest, with the show-within-a-show ploy providing the opportunity for the soprano's "Waltz of My Heart," Novello's customary soprano-contralto duet "The Wings of Sleep," and the tenor's "My Life Belongs to You." Other hits were the soprano's "I Can Give You the Starlight," the "Leap Year Waltz," and the sprightly "Primrose" for Kleber's childhood sweetheart.

With the works of Coward, Novello, Ellis, Gay, and Posford the British musical theatre was still able to provide a few bright spots even after London's theatre lights were temporarily dimmed at the outbreak of World War II. But the predominant trends in musical theatre were incontrovertibly set by American shows, most particularly as the source of popular song material that reached a vast public through nightclub singers and the ubiquitous dance bands. In such shows as Porter's *Anything Goes* and Rodgers and Hart's *On Your Toes,* the song-and-dance musical was itself attaining new levels of sophistication; but in the Kern-Hammerstein *Show Boat* and the Gershwins' *Porgy and Bess,* the American musical concept was also becoming ever more inventive and ambitious.

Part III

Continental European Round-Up

Chapter Eleven
The 1920s: The "Années Folles"

Just as the European operetta style faced a challenge in the 1920s from the new-fangled American song-and-dance musical in Britain and America, so it did on the continent, although it inevitably showed greater resistance on its home ground.

In France, one of the transitional composers was Charles Cuvillier (1877–1955), a student of Massenet's and Fauré's whose readily accessible and undemanding music adorned some thirty stage works over a thirty-year period starting in 1905. His first success was *Son P'tit Frère* (Her Little Brother, 1907), a typically sexy French burlesque set in classical antiquity that was staged at Paris's tiny

Théâtre des Capucines. In similar vein was the successor piece of Cuvillier and his librettist André Barde (1874–1945). *Afgar, ou Les Loisirs andalous* (Afgar, or The Andalusian Leisures, 1909) starred two leading figures of the French stage of the time, Marguerite Deval and Henri Defreyn, the latter Paris's first Danilo in *Die lustige Witwe*.

Both works hit the international stages, leading to one of those quirkish situations where a work does little in its own country but becomes a smash hit abroad. Cuvillier fulfilled a commission from Leipzig with *Der lila Domino* (The Lilac Domino, 1912), which was a flop in Germany and was not even staged in France. On the other hand, it was well received in New York in 1914 and became a huge success in London in 1918, the sensuous title waltz becoming especially treasured. The story concerns a young heiress who wears a lilac domino to a ball, at which she meets a young man with whom she soon falls in love. Complications arise from her discovery that he has arranged to share with two cronies the proceeds of their bet that he can win the hand of an heiress. Finally, of course, she discovers that his affection for her is real. If such romantic material was what London favoured as World War I came to an end, it was another Cuvillier-Barde work that fuelled Paris's victory celebrations. *La Reine joyeuse* (The Merry Queen, 1918) was a revision of *La Reine s'amuse* (The Queen Is Amused, 1912), whose title was a play on Victor Hugo's *Le Roi s'amuse*. The revision produced the Cuvillier song that has remained his best remembered in France, the sensual waltz "Oh! la troublante volupté!"

The most potent symbol of France's emergence from the war lay in another work, whose composer, Henri Christiné (1867–1941), was born in Switzerland of French parents. Initially a schoolteacher, he married a café-concert singer for whom he began writing songs. After producing a few unimportant early stage works, he was commissioned to compose the score for one of Paris's ever popular classical burlesques. *Phi-Phi* (1918) was conceived for small forces and a small theatre but at the last minute was transferred to the prestigious Théâtre des Bouffes-Parisiens, where it opened the day after the Armistice. With its witty situations, cast of six toga-clad characters, sexual innuendoes, and anachronisms, along with a superb portfolio of songs in fox-trot, one-step, and slow waltz tempos, this light entertainment turned out to be just what Paris wanted to celebrate the ending of hostilities. Set in 600 B.C., it starred light comedian André Urban as the sculptor Phidias, alias Phi-Phi, and Alice Cocéa as the attractive Aspasie, whom he brings home ostensibly as a model for his new sculpture *Love and Virtue*. This explanation cuts little ice with his wife, but she is herself involved with a handsome

André Urban and cast in Christiné's *Phi-Phi*
Copyright Harlingue-Viollet/Roger-Viollet, Paris

young man, Ardiméon, and she offers him as the model for the other half of the sculpture. Complications are resolved when Pericles puts up the cash to acquire Aspasie. The sheer fun of the piece can be found in such catchy melodies as Phi-Phi's exposition of Aspasie's charms, "C'est une gamine charmante," the duet "Ah! tais-toi" (a seduction number between Phidias's wife and Ardimédon in the manner of the Dream Duet in *La Belle Hélène*), and the "Duo des souvenirs," in which the same couple reminisce the morning after the night before.

Phi-Phi ran for more than 1,000 performances and set the tone for a racy new French musical comedy style that was to adorn the 1920s, the so-called Années Folles, or "Crazy Years." Many of the successes of the period bore the name of lawyer-turned-writer Albert Willemetz (1887–1964), co-librettist of *Phi-Phi* and collaborator also on *Dédé* (1921), Christiné's next work for the Bouffes-Parisiens. This was another jazz-age piece, set in a shoe store and taking its title from the nickname of proprietor André de la Huchette, again played by André Urban. His adoring assistant Denise was Alice Cocéa, also of *Phi-Phi;* but this time much of the fun came from the first operetta appearance of Maurice Chevalier as an overbearing shop assistant. It was Chevalier who had the pick of the songs, with the philosophical "Dans la vie faut pas s'en faire," his thoughts on selling shoes in "Pour bien réussir dans la chaussure" in the Act 1 finale, and the Act 2 duet "Ah! Madame."

Christiné produced many more operettas over the next seventeen years, among which the Bouffes-Parisiens's *P.L.M.* (1925) resurrected the railway-carriage romance idea of Leo Fall's *Die geschiedene Frau,* here set in the Paris-Lyon-Méditerranée railway, with music-hall star Dranem as the ticket collector. But none of these later works matched the success of *Phi-Phi* and *Dédé,* which are both frequently staged in France to this day.

Among other composers of similarly lighthearted entertainments was Polish-born, Warsaw Conservatoire-trained Joseph Szulc (1875–1956), whose big success, *Flup..!* (1913) started out in Brussels and reached Paris in 1920 with Dranem in the title role. Another was Marseilles songwriter Raoul Moretti (1893–1954), who, before turning to films and gaining international fame with the song "Sous les toits de Paris," composed the scores of *En chemyse* (In Nightwear, 1924), *Troublez-moi* (Excite Me, 1924) and *Trois jeunes filles . . . nues!* (Three Young Girls . . . Naked! 1925), all produced at the Bouffes-Parisiens with Dranem as star and with Albert Willemetz and/or Yves Mirande (1875–1957) as librettist.

Of all these composers, the one who stood out alongside Christiné was Maurice Yvain (1891–1965), another Conservatoire-trained musician, who as a young man had been a pianist in Louis Ganne's orchestra at the Monte-Carlo casino. While serving in the war he met up with Maurice Chevalier, as well as fellow music-hall star Mistinguett, who achieved a huge success with Yvain's song "Mon homme" (1921). On the heels of this, Yvain was commissioned to provide the score for the satirical *Ta Bouche* (Your Mouth, 1922), whose three acts trace the amorous and pecuniary adventures of three couples—an impecunious roué and a fake countess, their respective children, and their servants—over a period of a year at three different seaside resorts. The son was played by comedian Victor Boucher, and the male servant by Eugène Gabin, father of future French music-hall and movie star Jean Gabin. Yvain's songs became so popular that during the run the theatre introduced the practice of lowering lyric sheets from the flies so the audience could join in the refrains. The biggest hit was an irresistibly lilting title waltz for the children Bastien and Eva.

The success of *Ta Bouche* was sufficient to spawn a couple of sequels by Yvain and André Barde—*Pas sur la bouche!* (Not on the Mouth!, 1925) and the larger-scale *Bouche à bouche* (Mouth to Mouth, 1925). Both produced their quota

Sheet-music cover for Yvain's *Pas sur la bouche!*
Author's collection

of hits and confirmed the musicianly cut of Yvain's writing. *Pas sur la bouche!* featured dancer-vocalist Régine Flory, who became a star not only in Paris but in London and was shortly to provide her own real-life drama. Having failed at an attempt at drowning herself in the Seine, she put a gun to her head in the manager's office at London's Drury Lane during a performance of *Rose Marie* in 1926.

Yvain's non-*bouche* scores included *La Dame en décolleté* (The Lady in the Low-Cut Dress, 1923), *Gosse de riche* (Rich Man's Kid, 1924) and *Yes* (1928); but only one rivalled *Ta Bouche* in its success and survives in French theatres today. This was the Bouffes-Parisiens's *Là-Haut* (Up There, 1923), a collaboration with Yves Mirande and Albert Willemetz whose story anticipated *Carousel:* the lead male character dreams he is in heaven and comes back to earth to discover what his widow is up to. The role was written for Maurice Chevalier, who had a fair quota of hit numbers, including the title song, the big waltz, and "C'est Paris," a fox-trot in praise of the French capital. Yet Chevalier was less than pleased with his part. In the role of the guardian angel was comedian Dranem, whose antics won such enthusiastic applause that Chevalier walked out of the show with his current flame Yvonne Vallée. He was never seen again in a theatrical piece.

In spite of these native successes, Paris still had time for the best of the new generation of American musicals. And, just as Parisians loved the song-and-dance *No, No, Nanette* and the operetta-style *Rose Marie* and *Desert Song* equally, so Paris continued to balance its lighter native fare with more traditional operettas. Like Planquette's *Rip!* some forty years earlier, Messager's *Monsieur Beaucaire* (1919) had an English libretto (by Frederick Lonsdale) and was first produced in Britain; but, as with *Rip!*, it is the French who have treasured it most. Based on a romantic novel and drama by the American Booth Tarkington about an exiled heir to the French throne living incognito in Regency Bath, its light-opera stature was confirmed when diva Maggie Teyte was brought in for the leading role of Lady Mary Carlisle. A last-minute addition for Teyte, the waltz "Philomel," together with the baritone's "Red Rose," helped ensure the work's enduring success.

When Paris first welcomed *Monsieur Beaucaire* in 1925, with André Baugé in the title role, Messager was already in his seventies. Yet more than forty years after his first shows, he could still produce shows that hold the stage in France even now. *Passionnément!* (Passionately, 1926), described as a "comédie-musicale," had the ubiquitous Willemetz as joint book author and concerned an American millionaire and his business deals over oil-rich land in Colorado. Messager's last completed work, *Coups de roulis* (Roll of the Waves, 1928), was another Willemetz piece. Produced when the composer was seventy-four, it was a shipboard romance with more than a touch of *HMS Pinafore* about it. The leading character was a pompous politician, who is accompanied by his daughter on a fact-finding mission to Egypt. The hit number was a march, "En amour, il n'est pas de grade," that asserted that love levels all ranks. Messager died during the original run, and the work's success provided a happy exit for one of the musical theatre's most elegant composers.

Messager's postwar eminence in more traditional Parisian musical theatre pieces was shared with another, younger classically trained composer. Reynaldo Hahn (1874–1947) was born in Venezuela of a German father, was educated at the Paris Conservatoire, and became the darling of the fin-de-siècle Parisian salons. He entered the ranks of operetta composers with a work for the Théâtre des Variétés that deliberately set out to recapture the spirit of the old opéra-comique and the era of Lecocq's *La Fille de Madame Angot*. This it did through its setting in Paris's Les Halles market, with references to Henry Murger's *Scènes de la vie de bohême*, and a third act in the salon of Third Republic waltz composer Olivier Métra. What was different was the more modern harmonic language that Hahn brought to his score.

Ciboulette (1923) was luxuriously cast. Jean Périer, Debussy's original Pelléas and the first Florestan in Messager's *Véronique*, played Rodolphe Duparquet, who was once the poet Rodolphe of Murger's novel and is now comptroller of Les Halles. Matinée idol Henri Defreyn played young Vicomte Antonin de Mourmelon, and former Opéra-Comique soubrette Edmée Favart had the title role of a naive country girl who comes to the market to sell her produce. The story concerns the somewhat far-fetched fulfilment of a fortune-teller's prediction that Ciboulette will find her husband-to-be under a cabbage-leaf, after causing him to leave a woman capable of turning white in a split second, and after receiving a farewell letter in a tambourine. All these things duly come to pass when Antonin is picked up from under a pile of vegetables after he has fallen asleep in Ciboulette's cart, his fiancée Zénobie has a bag of flour poured over her in an argument with Ciboulette, and a suicide letter he has previously written to Ciboulette is handed to her inside a tambourine at the moment he proposes to her. *Ciboulette* was the last great success of the classical French operetta tradition. It has charm in abundance, exquisite harmonic touches, and inventive orchestral effects. Individual highlights are Ciboulette's entrance "Dans une charette," her introductory "Moi, je m'appelle Ciboulette," her Act 2 duet with Duparquet, "Nous avons fait un bon voyage," Duparquet's showstopping "C'est tout ce qui me reste d'elle," and a delicious last-act waltz, "Amour qui meurt, amour qui passe."

Hahn next attempted a modern song-and-dance musical comedy, *Le Temps d'aimer* (The Time for Love, 1926). However, his other successful score of the 1920s was for a different type of musical theatre piece altogether. The productions of actor-playwright-director Sacha Guitry (1885–1957) were styled "comédie-musicale" but represented something very different from American song-and-dance musical comedy. Designed as vehicles for Guitry himself, who never sang, and his wife Yvonne Printemps, they were not dance pieces but plays with scores that essentially comprised brief songs and underscoring designed to further the all-important dramatic action.

The series started with *L'Amour masqué* (Masked Love, 1923), whose score

Act 2 of Hahn's *Ciboulette,* with Henri Defreyn as Antonin and
Edmée Favart in the title role, at the Théâtre des Variétés, 1923
Copyright Harlingue-Viollet/Roger-Viollet, Paris

was by André Messager and whose principal characters were named simply Elle
(She) and Lui (He). She falls for the subject of a portrait in a photographer's studio and then meets a man who resembles the portrait but is much older. She believes that the portrait's subject must be his son, only to discover that it is actually
He, photographed many years before. Messager's score was written with typical
restraint and discrimination for a small orchestra. Its hit number was Printemps's
first-act "J'ai deux amants," in which she describes her two current protectors, of
whom she has now tired. The refrain, in which she mocks the stupidity of men
with the words "Mais, mon Dieu, que c'est bête, un homme," recalls a similar
outburst in Offenbach's *La Périchole.*

Guitry sought Messager's services again for a fictional piece about Mozart,
to be played by Printemps en travesti. However, Messager balked at Guitry's re-
quirement that he adapt music by his revered Mozart into the score. Hahn, who
had already composed pastiches that evoked an earlier age, was more accommo-
dating, and themes from Mozart's ballet music *Les Petits Riens* are woven into his
score for *Mozart* (1925). Printemps's Letter Song "Depuis ton départ, mon amour"
was the highlight, together with the final duet "Alors, adieu donc, mon amour"

between Mozart and the countess d'Epinay, with whom the young Mozart has fallen in love. Guitry played the Baron Grimm, Mozart's sponsor in Paris, who finally tires of the young man's amorous adventures.

The farther east one looks, the longer it took after World War I for American rhythms to penetrate Europe. In Berlin an outstanding demonstration of the longevity of traditional operetta values came with *Schwarzwaldmädel* (Black Forest Girl, 1917). Its score was by Léon Jessel (1871–1942), a theatre conductor who had already enjoyed international success with the orchestral novelty pieces "Parade of the Tin Soldiers" and "The Wedding Procession of the Rose." Picturesquely set in Germany's Black Forest, the operetta tells of a romantic intrigue involving two friends, Hans and Richard; Hans's girlfriend Malwine; and Bärbele, the orphaned maid of ageing village organist Blasius Römer. As befitted its Komische-Oper staging, *Schwarzwaldmädel* had a musical solidity that recalled the classical operettas of Carl Millöcker. An opening country polka gives way to Römer practising on his organ ("O Sancta Cäcilia"), after which the melodies cascade delightfully one after another—a trio on the attractions and drawbacks of women ("Die Weibsleut, die sind eine Brut—aber gut!"), Malwine's affecting love song ("Muss denn die Lieb' stehts Tragödie sein?"), the catchy quintet ("Mädel aus dem schwarzen Wald"), Richard's admission of affection for Malwine ("Malwine, ach Malwine"), and Bärbele's infectious invitation to the dance ("Erklingen zum Tanze die Geigen"). *Schwarzwaldmädel* represented all that was best in continental operetta. Sadly, Jessel never came near to repeating its triumph in subsequent operettas.

Generally, the tendency in Berlin was to incorporate the new American dance styles into the traditional operetta mode rather than to strive for anything fundamentally new. Walter Kollo's long list of locally successful works followed this pattern, from *Wenn zwei Hochzeit machen* (When Two People Marry, 1915), which contained the diverting "Alle Englein lachen," and *Marietta* (1923), with the lovely "Was eine Frau im Frühling träumt," to *Die Frau ohne Kuss* (The Lady Without a Kiss, 1924) and *Drei arme kleine Mädels* (Three Poor Little Girls, 1927). Similarly, Jean Gilbert achieved his biggest success since *Die keusche Susanne* with the romantic *Die Frau im Hermelin* (The Lady in Ermine, 1919), a period piece set near Verona during the Russian invasion of 1810. Like Millöcker's *Gasparone*, this is a piece whose title character does not exist. The "lady in ermine" is actually a ghost. Gilbert's next major international success was first seen in Vienna, with Mizzi Günther playing the title role of *Katja, die Tänzerin* (Katja, the Dancer, 1922). This tells of deposed Princess Katja Karina, who has ended up working as a dancer in a Paris nightclub. There she falls in love with Prince Eusebius von Koruga, only to find out that he is the prince who deposed her. The show's big hit was a comedy duet "Komm, Liebchen, wander mit deinem Leander." Gilbert's *Annemarie* (1925) introduced another of his enduring songs in praise of the Berlin capital, "Durch Berlin fliesst immer noch die Spree," but his career thereafter went downhill. It ended with his retreat from the Nazis and exile in South America, where he died.

International success attended another Berlin piece, whose composer, Eduard Künneke (1885–1953), had studied with Max Bruch and written a couple of operas before turning to more popular fare. The historical *Das Dorf ohne Glocke* (The Village Without a Bell, 1919) brought a series of commissions from Hermann Haller, director of the Theater am Nollendorfplatz, beginning with *Der Vielgeliebte* (The Much-Loved One, 1919) and *Wenn Liebe erwacht* (When Love Awakes, 1920). But it was with his third offering that Künneke hit the big time. *Der Vetter aus Dingsda* (The Cousin from Nowhere, 1921) was an intimate family piece with just nine characters (including two servants) and no chorus. Set in Holland, it starred Lori Leux as Julia de Weert, who has formed a passion for her cousin and childhood sweetheart Roderich, who emigrated to the East Indies. She refuses all offers of marriage and is delighted when a handsome stranger arrives whom she mistakenly believes to be Roderich. When she discovers that he isn't, she turns him away, regretting her decision when a second, less attractive, stranger appears and turns out to be the real Roderich. All is satisfactorily resolved in the end.

More than anything, what gave the show wide appeal was the strangely alluring tenor aria "Ich bin nur ein armer Wandergesell" (I'm only a poor vagabond), with which the first stranger enigmatically answers Julia's questions about his identity. But there are other captivating numbers in the score, as well, notably "Strahlender Mond," Julia's appeal to the moon to convey her love to her distant lover. Both demonstrate Künneke's ability to spin out a vocal line. Other numbers acknowledged the current popularity of dances such as the Boston, the tango, and the fox-trot. The show was an international success, enabling Künneke to seek riches in America. There he arranged Offenbach melodies into a pseudo-biographical piece entitled *The Love Song* (1925), but it failed to captivate New York audiences. He returned to Germany and continued to turn out quality works that gave him a status in his home country that he never matched elsewhere.

After World War I had destroyed the Austro-Hungarian Empire, Berlin also increasingly became the outlet for former Viennese operetta exponents. Thus it was in Berlin where Oscar Straus's highly successful *Der letzte Walzer* (The Last Waltz, 1920) was staged. Its book by Julius Brammer and Alfred Grünwald tells of Polish Countess Vera Lisaweta's efforts to save the life of handsome Count Wladimir Dimitri Sarasow, who has been condemned to death for rescuing her from the unwelcome advances of a vindictive prince. Straus's score intersperses light-comedy numbers with sugary waltz tunes, with the romantic title duet "Das ist der letzte Walzer" emerging as the big hit of a show that helped confirm Viennese-born Fritzi Massary as Berlin's leading lady of the 1920s.

Massary's other star roles included several other works by Straus—*Die Perlen der Kleopatra* (Cleopatra's Pearls, 1923), *Die Teresina* (Little Teresa, 1925), *Die Königin* (The Queen, 1926)—that were much less successful. Straus's commissions also included the music for one of Sacha Guitry's Parisian "comédies-musicales." *Mariette, ou Comment on écrit l'histoire* (Mariette, or How One Writes History, 1928) had Yvonne Printemps as a hundred-year-old actress recalling her life for a journalist. Guitry played not only the journalist but also the Emperor Napoléon III, with whom the centenarian invents a romance to spice up her narrative. Straus's involvement helped bring the piece in a much revised version to Berlin, with popular singing actress Käthe Dorsch in the Printemps role and operatic bass-baritone Michael Bohnen as Napoléon III; it also made it to Vienna with Rita Georg and Hubert Marischka.

Fritzi Massary's starring roles also included two works composed by Leo Fall, both with libretti by the team of Rudolf Schanzer (1875–1944) and Ernst Welisch (1875–1941). *Die spanische Nachtigall* (The Spanish Nightingale, 1920) was a modest hit; but *Madame Pompadour* (1922) proved to be Fall's most enduring international success. In spite of its historical leading character, the plot had little factual basis, being the story of one René, Comte d'Estrades, who comes to Paris looking for a good time and finding it in the arms of the royal mistress, who is herself having a night out in disguise. The leading comic character is Joseph Calicot, a singer of satirical songs about Pompadour, and his shimmy-rhythm duet with her, "Joseph, ach Joseph," proved the hit of the evening. Pompadour's entrance, "Heut' könnt einer sein Glück bei mir machen," once more demonstrated Fall's mastery in setting a conversational vocal line. The whole score remains a fine epitaph for a composer who is all too little remembered today.

By contrast with Straus and Fall, Franz Lehár remained in Vienna for some time after the war. *Die blaue Mazur* (The Blue Mazurka, 1920), *Frasquita* (1922), and *Die gelbe Jacke* (The Yellow Jacket, 1923) all provided rewarding material for the Theater an der Wien's regular leading couple of tenor Hubert

Marischka and soprano Betty Fischer, along with the supporting comedy pair of Ernst Tautenhayn and Louise Kartousch. The latter were also given a chance to star in the musical farce *Cloclo* (1924), an atypical Lehár work about a Parisian revue performer.

That Lehár's career once more went into overdrive was due to the Austrian tenor Richard Tauber (1891–1947). Born in Linz, Tauber had made a reputation in Dresden as one of the leading operatic tenors. But he loved operetta, and in 1920 and 1921 he appeared as Józsi in Lehár's *Zigeunerliebe* in Berlin and Salzburg. This began a period of mutual admiration and mutual dependence for Lehár and Tauber that lasted the rest of their lives. In 1922 Tauber took over from Hubert Marischka in *Frasquita,* thrilling audiences with his delivery of the serenade "Schatz, ich bitt' dich, komm heut nacht." Thereafter, Tauber's association with Lehár became increasingly fruitful. Always keen to develop operetta along more ambitious lines, Lehár felt threatened by the genre's increasing absorption of popular dance rhythms. Tauber, for his part, needed something to spotlight and test his operatic voice. Thus emerged a new, very personal style of Lehár operetta, in which the writing for Tauber and his leading lady was more operatic and a more serious tone prevailed, including a rejection of the traditional contrived happy endings.

Lehár's first work for Tauber envisaged him as the violinist Nicolò Paganini, who was entangled in a historically unfounded romance with Anna Elisa, Duchess of Lucca and sister of Napoléon. The book was by the Viennese publisher Paul Knepler (1879–1967), who originally intended to compose the music himself. But Lehár saw the opportunities it offered not only for Tauber but also for Italian orchestral colouring and virtuoso writing for his own instrument, the violin. The operetta opens with a miniature violin concerto, supposedly played offstage by Paganini. It is this that first attracts Princess Anna Elisa, who is passing by. Because her husband is carrying on an affair with the singer Bella, Anna Elisa begins one of her own with Paganini and uses her influence to install him at court in Lucca. When in the final act Napoléon sends a general to break up the scandalous affair, Anna Elisa recognises that she must renounce Paganini so he can continue with his artistic career.

Theatrical schedules decreed that *Paganini* (1925) was first staged not with Tauber but with Carl Clewing. Emma Kosáry played the Duchess. Tauber took over the role in Berlin opposite the opera singer Vera Schwarz. The tenor's big number is "Gern hab' ich die Frau'n geküsst," in which Paganini teaches the court chamberlain Pimpinelli how to woo. Other important pieces are Paganini's entrance "Schönes Italien," the Princess's joyous "Liebe, du Himmel auf Erden," and the love duets, which were both passionate ("Was ich denke, was ich fühle") and gentle ("Niemand liebt dich so wie ich"). They were complemented with dances in each act for the comedy duo Bella and Pimpinelli—a waltz ("Mit den Frau'n auf du und du"), a fox-trot ("Einmal möcht ich was Närrisches tun"), and a quickstep ("Wir gehen ins Theater"). The formula for the late Lehár works was here established: a showy leading tenor role, a parting of the lovers at the final curtain, and numbers that were divided between more "serious" choruses and arias for the leading couple and comic dances for the supporting pair.

The success with Tauber in Berlin also ensured that Lehár thereafter looked to that city rather than to the financially strapped Theater an der Wien for the staging of his works. His next operetta had a libretto by Béla Jenbach (1871–1943) and Hans Reichert (1877–1940), adapted from a World War I play by the Polish writer Gabriela Zapolska. Set in the late nineteenth century, it was based on the youthful affair of the last Russian Tsar, Nicholas, with the ballerina Mathilde Kschessinskaia. Presumably because those leading characters were still alive when the play was staged, the source was disguised by intertwining a sanitised version of the life of the early eighteenth-century Tsarevich Alexei, son of Peter the Great. In the operetta the young Tsarevich is a fitness fanatic who disdains girls. Because he must marry, the Tsar's advisers seek to overcome his resistance by smuggling a young dancer named Sonja into his apartment. The ruse succeeds beyond expectations, and the Tsarevich and the dancer fall deeply in love. Unable to marry a woman of her low station, he flees with her to Naples. But, after his father dies, he realises that he must return to St. Petersburg and take up his responsibilities as the new Tsar.

Der Zarewitsch (The Tsarevich, 1927) has remained highly popular in German countries, without arousing the same affection in other countries. It gave Lehár a welcome opportunity to add Russian colour through the use of balalaikas, but much of the music is characterised more by Russian melancholy and gloom. The Act 1 Volga Song is a case in point, as is Sonja's big solo "Einer wird kommen," in which she anticipates her first meeting with the Tsarevich. The mood brightens in the dances for the Tsarevich's servant Iwan and his wife Mascha, and there is some sprightly party music at the start of Act 2 as well as the glorious duet "Hab' nur dich allein," but the ending reverts to melancholy in the sad but exquisitely beautiful "Warum hat jeder Frühling, ach, nur einen Mai?"

Next, in *Friederike* (1928), Lehár featured Tauber as another historical figure, the poet Johann von Goethe, with Käthe Dorsch as an Alsatian pastor's daughter, Friederike, who finally realises that she must forgo her love so that Goethe can take up a post in Weimar. This was not strictly an operetta; it was specifically styled a "Singspiel" (play with songs), and its development came in the spoken text. The big Tauber song was the rhapsodic "O Mädchen, mein Mädchen!" but Lehár also invited comparisons with Schubert in his setting of the Goethe text "Sah' ein Knab' ein Röslein steh'n." Friederike had the tender solo "Warum hast du mich wachgeküsst?" in which she asks why her heart had to be aroused so fruitlessly by her love for the poet.

If neither *Der Zarewitsch* nor *Friederike* offered the gaiety one would expect from an operetta, there was rich compensation in Lehár's next piece. It was not a new work but a revision of his 1923 Chinese piece *Die gelbe Jacke,* which had never been seen in Berlin. Victor Léon's original text was subjected to a thorough revision by Ludwig Herzer (1872–1939) and Fritz Löhner (1883–1942), with the now-standard separation of the lovers at the final curtain and some more ambitious numbers that emphasized the basic theme of the clash of Western and Eastern cultures. As *Das Land des Lächelns* (The Land of Smiles, 1929), it provided Tauber with his greatest Lehár role and his finest Lehár song, "Dein ist mein ganzes Herz." The show opens brightly at a Viennese ball given in honour of Lisa, a nobleman's daughter. During the evening she finds she has an admirer in the person of Chinese nobleman Sou-Chong, and by Act 2 she has gone to China to live with him. Alas, the relationship founders on the oriental view of man as master and woman as his servant. In spite of Sou-Chong's love for Lisa and his efforts to keep her in China, he must eventually allow her to return to Vienna with Gustav, an old flame whose flirtation with Sou-Chong's sister Mi provides the subplot. The setting gave Lehár further opportunities to provide the sort of local colour he loved; and the score was full of fine numbers, whether taken over from the original *Die gelbe Jacke* (Sou-Chong's entrance "Immer nur lächeln," his expression of Chinese philosophy "Von Apfelblüten einen Kranz," Lisa's homesick "Ich möcht wider einmal die Heimat seh'n") or newly composed (Lisa's waltz "Gern, gern wär' ich verliebt," Sou-Chong's "Dein ist mein ganzes Herz," and their passionate duets "Bei einem Tee à deux" and "Wer hat die Liebe uns ins Herz gesenkt?").

While Straus, Fall, and Lehár were reaping the financial benefits to be found in Berlin, Emmerich Kálmán remained faithful to his adopted Vienna. His postwar works had begun with *Das Hollandweibchen* (The Little Dutch Woman, 1920); Maggie Teyte played the lead in the London production later that year. More lastingly successful was *Die Bajadere* (The Bayadère, 1921), a pseudo-oriental piece with Louis Treumann as Prince Radjami, heir to the throne of Lahore. Rather than give the operetta a wholly Indian setting, in which modern dance styles would have been incongruous, librettists Julius Brammer and Alfred Grünwald hedged their bets through the device of the play-within-a-play. Thus the leading lady with whom Radjami falls in love is the French singer Odette Darimonde, who is playing the title role in an oriental operetta called *La Bayadère* at the Théâtre du Châtelet, Paris. Obliged by Indian law to find a bride in a hurry, the Prince settles on Odette. He manages to marry her not only after the usual misunderstandings and quarrels but also after she has undergone a brief period in a trance. Christl Mardayn played Odette, with Louise Kartousch and Ernst Tautenhayn as the comedy pair. Kálmán's romantic music was climaxed by the tenor waltz "O Bajadere," and both the Parisian setting and current dance crazes were acknowledged in such comedy numbers as "Die kleine Bar dort am Boulevard" and "Fräulein, bitte woll'n sie Shimmy tanzen?" The show was also staged with considerable success in Paris and in America, where the setting was localised and the title became *The Yankee Princess*.

For all his success with settings in Germany, Holland, and France, Kálmán remained fascinated with Hungarian rhythms. This now led to what was to become his most popular work after *Die Csárdásfürstin. Gräfin Mariza* (Countess Maritza, 1924) again had a Julius Brammer and Alfred Grünwald book, this time about the impoverished Count Tassilo Endrödy-Wirttenburg (Hubert Marischka), who is reduced to taking paid employment as manager of his former estate. The current owner is the Hungarian Countess Maritza (Betty Fischer), who arrives ostensibly for a party to announce her engagement. In fact, this is merely a device to keep her many suitors at bay; and the name of Baron Koloman Zsupán that she gives as her fiancé is one she lifted from the cast list of Johann Strauss's *Der Zigeunerbaron*. Imagine her surprise and embarrassment, therefore, when a genuine Baron Zsupán (Max Hansen) turns up at the party and claims her hand! But he turns out to be more taken by Tassilo's sister Lisa (Elsie Altmann), while the Countess marries Tassilo and thus enables him to regain his former estate. Like *Die Csárdásfürstin, Gräfin Mariza* has a succession of fine songs, but they have more depth and substance than those in the earlier score. The big solos are Maritza's csárdás "Höre ich Zigeunergeigen" and Tassilo's vibrant "Komm' Zigány!" Scarcely less appealing are Tassilo's reminiscences of Vienna, "Grüss mir mein Wien," the tender duet "Schwesterlein, Schwesterlein" between Tassilo and Lisa, the exquisite duet between Lisa and Tassilo "Sag' ja, mein Lieb, sag' ja," and two contrasted comedy numbers for Zsupán and Lisa, "Ich möchte träumen" and the invitation "Komm mit nach Varasdin."

With Lehár and Straus writing for Berlin, Kálmán was now the star composer at the Theater an der Wien, which was experiencing difficult times. Hubert Marischka, long the leading man of Viennese operetta, was also the theatre's director, and from Kálmán he commissioned a show with yet another dashing role for himself. Although it had fewer songs that could stand alone, and did not rival Kálmán's previous success in popular esteem, *Die Zirkusprinzessin* (The Circus Princess, 1926) is in some ways his most consistently satisfying score. Acts 1 and 2 are set in St. Petersburg, where Prince Sergius Wladimir (Richard Waldemar), nephew of the Tsar, has had his advances rejected by beautiful, widowed, and wealthy Princess Fedora Palinska (Betty Fischer). He seeks revenge by tricking her into marriage with a common circus artist, the mysterious and daring "Mister X" (Marischka). In his circus act, Mister X stands masked, thirty metres above the heads of the audience, where he first plays a romance on the violin and then jumps through the air into a chute from which he is propelled onto the back of a galloping horse! Unfortunately for the Prince, the common circus rider turns out to be the genuinely aristocratic Fedja Palinski, who had turned to the circus after being disinherited by his uncle precisely because he had taken a fancy to Fedora. Thus Fedja is reunited with both his lover and his fortune.

Like *Die Bajadere, Die Zirkusprinzessin* sought to cater for contrasted tastes, with fiery Russian themes interspersed with Viennese nostalgia in such numbers as "Wo ist der Himmel so blau wie in Wien?" This is sung by the comedy couple—Toni (Fritz Steiner), a Viennese hotelier's son in the St. Petersburg audience, and "Mabel Gibson" (Elsie Altmann), a Viennese singer/bare-back rider who performs under an American name. As further homage to the current fashion for American culture, English expressions are to the fore, with the romantic couple addressing each other in a duet "My darling, my darling, muss so sein wie Du!" There are also echoes of earlier Kálmán successes, most notably in "Die kleinen Mäderln im Trikot," Toni's lilting portrayal of the circus girls in frilly skirts with legs like marzipan, which recalls "Die Mädis vom *Chantant*" in *Die Csárdásfürstin*. The big number is the tenor's "Zwei Märchenaugen," representing Mister X's vision of beauty: two white arms, a red mouth, and fairy-tale eyes. "Zwei Märchenaugen" showed that Kálmán, too, could write a "Tauber song."

It was when *Die Zirkusprinzessin* was later produced in Berlin that Kálmán met Arthur Hammerstein (the uncle of Oscar II) and was persuaded to supply some melodies which Herbert Stothart worked up into the score for a musical called *Golden Dawn* for Hammerstein's Theatre in New York in 1927. This seems to have given Kálmán a taste for America that he and his librettists Brammer and Grünwald put to use in their next show for the Theater an der Wien, *Die Herzogin von Chicago* (The Duchess of Chicago, 1928). The piece deals specifically with the clash between traditional Viennese waltzes and modern American jazz dances. Rita Georg played wealthy American Mary Lloyd, who visits a Budapest dance hall and is infuriated when Crown Prince Sándor of Sylvarien (played by Marischka) requests the band to strike up a Viennese waltz when she would rather do the Charleston. She ends up using her wealth to take over Sylvarien, and the Crown Prince too. The number that achieved greatest success was the leading-lady's "Ein kleiner Slow-Fox mit Mary."

Viennese audiences could also still get their nostalgia undiluted, most particularly from Edmund Eysler. He had continued to compose cosily enjoyable pieces without achieving much more than ephemeral success. That was until the Theater an der Wien produced *Die gold'ne Meisterin* (The Lady Goldsmith, 1927), which was to prove Eysler's most durable score. The Brammer and Grünwald libretto was set in sixteenth-century Vienna, the woman of the title being Margarethe (Fischer), the socially ambitious widow of a goldsmith. When she dances with an attractive stranger at a ball, she is horrified to discover that he is in fact her new employee Christian (Marischka). Out of pique she transfers her attention to Count Jaromir von Greifenstein (Fritz Steiner), whom Christian exposes as a gold-digging impostor, and a married man to boot. Margarethe and Christian are finally united in the third act, set in the Klosterneuburg monastery, thanks to the worldly-wise Brother Ignatius (Richard Waldemar). Christian's waltz "Du liebe, gold'ne Meisterin" and the duet "So tanzt man nur in Wien" served to rekindle memories of Viennese operettas of old; a further touch of nostalgia was added by cameo appearances from the veteran Viennese stars Mizzi Zwerenz as the housekeeper and Franz Glawatsch as a penniless nobleman.

Other composers besides Kálmán sought to demonstrate that Vienna was not trapped in a time warp. Bruno Granichstaedten (1879–1944) had tasted international success with traditional works such as *Bub oder Mädel?* (Boy or Girl? 1908), *Majestät Mimi* (Her Majesty Mimi, 1911), and *Auf Befehl der Kaiserin* (By Order of the Empress, 1915); but during the 1920s he followed the trend towards more modern dance styles and jazz-influenced sounds. He had a fine success in *Der Orlow* (1925), which further advertised its modernist leanings by being set in America, where the exiled Russian Grand Duke Alexander is now plain Alex

The finale of Weill's *Dreigroschenoper,* with Erich Ponto, Roma
Bahn, Harald Paulsen, and Kurt Gerron, 1928
Photo: AKG London

Doroschinsky (played by Marischka), working in a car factory owned jointly by
John Walsh (Richard Waldemar) and Jolly Jefferson (Fritz Steiner). The show
takes its title from the immensely valuable Orlov diamond that Alex has smuggled
out of war-torn Europe and the action revolves around the retention of the diamond and the securing of the hand of beautiful Russian ballerina Nadja Nad-
jakowski (Fischer). Granichstaedten's score calls for jazz instrumentation and features the shimmy, tango, and fox-trot, producing its biggest hit in Alex's cigarette
song, "Ein kleines bissel Nikotin." Granichstaedten collaborated on the libretto
with Hubert Marischka's brother Ernst (1893–1963), and the same partnership
was also responsible for another work in a consciously modern vein, *Reklame!*
(Advertising! 1930).

But the most forward-looking scores among the German-language works of the time were those of Kurt Weill (1900–1950), a classically trained composer of serious contemporary works. His Berlin theatre scores were anything but escapist, romantic operettas and owed more to the biting edge of Berlin cabaret than to Viennese operetta. *Die Dreigroschenoper* (The Threepenny Opera, 1928) was a collaboration with Marxist playwright Bertolt Brecht on an anticapitalist updating of John Gay's *The Beggar's Opera*. Harald Paulsen played the lecherous thief Macheath, Roma Baum his wife Polly Peachum, Kurt Gerron the corrupt London police chief Tiger Brown, and Lotte Lenja (later Lenya) the prostitute Jenny. The music made use of deliberately harsh modern harmonies. Although time has served to blunt the work's contemporary edge, it remains a classic of the musical theatre. Part of the concept was to use contemporary dance rhythms and jazz-band orchestrations, and Weill provided it with dance tunes such as Macheath's "Moritat" (Mack the Knife), Polly's "Seeräuber-Jenny" and "Barbara-Song," Jenny's "Salomon-Song," and other numbers completely lacking the sugary sentiment of operetta.

The work's reception inspired a sequel, although, like so many sequels, it was inferior both artistically and commercially. In fact it was a flop—partly because Brecht delegated much of his work. Yet the lasting popularity of Weill's theatre songs has ensured that *Happy End* (1929) has been much revived in modern times. Its story of Salvation Army girl Lillian Holliday (played by Carola Neher) and Chicago gangster Bill Cracker (Oskar Homolka) makes it a distant thematic relation of *The Belle of New York,* though the pieces could scarcely be more different in style. The most famous Brecht-Weill songs in it include the "Bilbao Song," the "Matrosen-Tango" in tango rhythm, the "Song von Mandelay," and, above all, Lillian's tear-jerker about blind love, "Surabaya Johnny."

In such works, Central European composers were showing their awareness of changing popular theatre trends at a time when operetta's grip on international audiences had weakened. Works by Messager, Hahn, Christiné, and Yvain found a lasting place in the native French repertory but made little impression elsewhere. If the works of Lehár and—to a lesser extent—Straus, Fall, and Kálmán remain more familiar internationally, it is very largely due to recordings of their major numbers rather than to any international stage currency.

Chapter Twelve
The Troubled 1930s

As European composers reacted to the increasing influence of American songs and rhythms, the result was, if anything, an even greater diversity of works during the 1930s than during the 1920s. While some composers readily sought to embrace the new musical styles, others were more inclined to stick to the old traditions. In France, for instance, Reynaldo Hahn was still trying to revive the spirit of the classical opéra-comique. *Brummel* (1931) was set in Regency England and was constructed around the character of Beau Brummel, with an evocative equestrian song "A dada." *Malvina* (1935) was another historical piece, set in 1830, with a leading role for operatic baritone Roger Bourdin.

In addition, Hahn also collaborated again with Sacha Guitry, now divorced from Yvonne Printemps, on a further comédie musicale for the Bouffes-Parisiens. *O mon bel inconnu* (Oh, My Handsome Stranger, 1933) tells of a hatter, who, bored with his wife and daughter, places a personal ad for a soul mate. His wife and daughter are among those who reply, as well as a supposed countess who is in fact his maid. The highlight of Hahn's cultured and graceful score is the Act 2 title waltz in which the three women each muse on the rendezvous to which he invites them, none knowing that the others have also been invited.

The classical tradition that Hahn sought to maintain was followed also by the veteran Gabriel Pierné (1863–1937), another composer renowned for more serious works. Like Hahn's *Brummel* and several of Lehár's later works, his *Fragonard* (1933) featured a historical character. In this case it was the painter Fragonard, on whose inability to resist the ladies the plot revolves. The piece was admired by musicians as an elegant continuation of the operetta tradition, but attracted less enthusiasm from the general public.

Much more to the public taste was an operetta with music by symphonic and operatic composer Arthur Honegger (1892–1955), who was recruited by Albert Willemetz when the latter became director of the Théâtre des Bouffes-Parisiens. *Les Aventures du Roi Pausole* (1930) was adapted by Willemetz from an erotic 1901 novel by Pierre Louÿs about the immoral kingdom of King Pausole, who has a different wife for every night of the year. His daughter Aline, by contrast, has received a chaste upbringing. One day she runs away with the head of a dance troupe that has come to entertain the royal family, believing the dancer to be a man. In fact, it is a female, Mirabelle, in disguise. The erotic tension increases when the King's page Giglio takes part in the lovemaking of Aline and Mirabelle, in addition to deputising for the King with Queen-of-the-day Diane. Giglio eventually wins the hand of the Princess from the King, who has so exhausted himself that he declares the kingdom a republic in order to get some rest. Honegger's score was the refined mix of modern and traditional elements to be expected from a serious classical composer, and the frank eroticism of the piece was sufficient to ensure an excellent run.

At the same time the French song-and-dance musical comedy continued to prosper, particularly in a series of pieces by the songwriter Vincent Scotto (1876–1952). Born into a Neapolitan family in Marseilles, he came to prominence with songs such as "La Petite Tonkinoise" and "Sous les ponts de Paris." His first book musicals were a series of "opérettes marseillaises," featuring characters and subjects associated with that city, designed as a vehicle for Scotto's son-in-law,

Honegger's *Les Aventures du Roi Pausole* at the Théâtre des Bouffes-Parisiens, 1937
Copyright Lipnitzki-Viollet/Roger-Viollet, Paris

singer Henri Alibert (1889–1951), who also wrote the books. Their venture was encouraged by the success of Marcel Pagnol's Marseillais plays and by *La Revue marseillaise*, which ran for two seasons at Paris's Moulin de la Chanson. The same location was venue for *Au pays du soleil* (In the Land of the Sun, 1931), in which Alibert played the impoverished Titin, who is wrongly accused of murder but eventually cleared and united with his lover Miette. What mattered more than the story was the Marseillais ambience and the catchy rhythms of such numbers as the title song and two of the duets, the fox-trot "Miette" and the romantic "J'ai rêvé d'une fleur."

Two successors in similar vein featured Alibert as one of a trio of male friends. In *Trois de la marine* (Three from the Navy, 1933) the three were French sailors on shore leave in Toulon. In *Un de La Canebière* (One from La Canebière, 1935) they were fishermen in the Marseillais port of Vallon des Auffes, dreaming of owning a sardine factory. This was the most successful of the series, less for the sardines than for the songs: the introductory "Les Pescadous," the slow fox-trot "J'aime la mer comme une femme," the trio's lively "Cane-, Cane-, Canebière," and, above all, the especially popular "Le plus beau tango du monde." After *Les Gangsters du Château d'If* (1936) the series faded away.

As a whole, in fact, the light French song-and-dance musical comedy of the 1920s had given way to the attractions of film, music-hall entertainments, and imported musical shows. The most significant native development of 1930s French book musicals was the "opérette à grand spectacle." This was to Paris what the works of Sigmund Romberg were to New York and those of Ivor Novello to London, namely an attempt to recapture the romantic spectacle of earlier days, albeit without the same elaborately developed comic opera scores. These opérettes à grand spectacle reached their peak in productions of the ever-resourceful lyricist Albert Willemetz, in collaboration with book author André Mouëzy-Eon (1879–1967), for Maurice Lehmann, director of the huge Théâtre du Châtelet. The three even worked with Romberg himself on a work composed specifically for the Châtelet—*Rose de France* (1933), with baritone Roger Bourdin. But the outstanding native opérette à grand spectacle of the 1930s was *Au soleil du Mexique* (1935), whose score was provided by that erstwhile exponent of jazz-age musical comedy, Maurice Yvain. The story featured baritone André Baugé as bullfighter Nino Chicuelo, who is forced to flee Mexico after killing a man in a brawl. Fanély Revoil played Chicuelo's girlfriend Juanita, for whom he cannot resist returning secretly to Mexico to show off his bullfighting skills at a fiesta. After being whisked off to Waikiki on a yacht, he is enabled by a revolution to meet up again with Juanita, who has meanwhile been immured in a convent in Guadeloupe. As befitted the "grand spectacle" tag, the piece had sixteen sets, featured a volcanic eruption and an earthquake, and paraded a range of dances, with comedy provided by popular entertainer Bach. Lehmann kept such works running not just at the Châtelet but also at the Mogador up to the outbreak of World War II, helped by imports from London (Posford's *Balalaika*), Vienna, and Berlin.

Meanwhile, in German-speaking countries, even the most internationally successful material began to have an end-of-era look about it. For Tauber, Franz Lehár continued revising his previous hits, but with decreasing success. *Endlich*

Scotto's *Un de La Canebière,* with Henri Alibert (third from left), at the Théâtre des Variétés, 1936
Copyright Martinie-Viollet/Roger-Viollet, Paris

allein of 1914 became *Schön ist die Welt* (Beautiful World, 1930), with the lovers who spend Act 2 alone atop the mountain now elevated to the status of royalty. Besides additional numbers for Tauber, Lehár acknowledged contemporary dance styles by adding a tango, a slow fox-trot, and a rumba for the comedy couple. Then came *Der Fürst der Berge* (The Prince of the Mountains, 1932), a revision of *Das Fürstenkind,* with bass-baritone Michael Bohnen in the title role.

Lehár's final creation, *Giuditta* (1934), was composed not for a commercial theatre but for the Vienna State Opera and starred Tauber and Czech opera singer Jarmila Novotna. Although it may have helped satisfy Lehár's creative aspirations, it also demonstrated that traditional operetta was becoming something of a museum piece. The story was reminiscent of *Carmen:* a temptress flourishes while bringing about the ruin of an army officer she has persuaded to desert on her behalf. The work was not quite grand opera; it interspersed singing and dialogue, and there were dance numbers for the comedy pair. However, there was some 50 percent more music than usual (a full two hours), and much of the writing for the leading couple was of considerable difficulty. The work was meticulously scored for a large orchestra, with fine arias for Tauber: "Du bist meine Sonne," "Schönste der Frauen," and "Freunde, das Leben ist Lebenswert!" Best known is Giuditta's "Meine Lippen, sie küssen so heiss," in which she describes how men fall for her charms.

Lehár retired after *Giuditta,* but Emmerich Kálmán continued composing throughout the 1930s, though his later works achieved no more than critical success. His final collaboration with librettists Julius Brammer and Alfred Grünwald turned to the Paris of Murger and Puccini for *Das Veilchen vom Montmartre* (The Violet of Montmartre, 1930). Murger (played by Robert Nästlberger) was one of the characters, along with composer Hervé (Ernst Tautenhayn) and painter Delacroix (Walter Jankuhn). The leading ladies were the model Ninon (Anny Ahlers) and street singer Violetta (Adele Kern), who in Act 3 ends up starring in an apocryphal operetta collaboration between Hervé and Murger. The show's hit was the Moon Song ("Du, guter Mond, schaust zu").

Kálmán was ill at ease with the French style, however, and he returned to familiar ground with librettists Rudolf Schanzer and Ernst Welisch for *Der Teufelsreiter* (The Devil's Rider, 1932). Set in early nineteenth-century Vienna and Bratislava, it featured Hubert Marischka as a Hungarian cavalry captain, Count Sándor, who falls in love with the daughter of his political opponent Metternich. Still heard is the ballet music "Grand Palotás de la Reine," which was played at a ball in Act 3.

By 1932, the Theater an der Wien, which had been home to the major Viennese operetta hits for more than half a century, was losing the battle against political, artistic, and economic reality. One of the rare successes of Marischka's later regime came from an unexpected quarter. *Sissy* (1932) was described as a Singspiel rather than an Operette, meaning that it was a light comedy interspersed with songs, with music underscoring the dialogue in places. The book was written by Marischka himself, in collaboration with his brother Ernst, and was a fictionalised account of the events leading up to the marriage of the Empress Elisabeth and the Emperor Franz Joseph of Austria. Marischka, now turned fifty, was no longer the heroic lead but played Sissy's father, Count Max of Bavaria.

Nostalgia for the Habsburg past keeps this piece on the Austrian stage to this day, helped by the charming and unassuming score of violin virtuoso Fritz Kreisler. In fact, little of the score was actually written for *Sissy:* Kreisler incorporated many of his popular violin pieces into it, including "Schön Rosmarin," "Liebesfreud," "Liebeslied," "Caprice viennois," and "Marche miniature viennoise." Even the main attraction, "Ich wär so gern einmal verliebt," had appeared in the

Paula Wessely and Hans Jaray in Kreisler's *Sissy,* 1932
Photo: AKG London

1919 American operetta *Apple Blossoms*—and reappeared once more as "Stars in My Eyes," sung by Grace Moore in *The King Steps Out,* the American film adaptation of *Sissy.*

In the face of mounting difficulties the Theater an der Wien staged one other work by a composer who was better known as a performer. Although the modern world remembers him as a great tenor, Richard Tauber was also a conductor and no mean composer. In *Der singende Traum* (The Singing Dream, 1934) he and co-star Mary Lossef appeared in a work whose location switched from Marseilles to New York and Capri. Unlike Kreisler's work, Tauber's has not survived on the stage, but "Du bist die Welt für mich," the big Act 2 solo that Tauber wrote for himself, has endured in the repertory of operetta tenors alongside the more famous Tauber songs of Lehár.

In 1935 the Theater an der Wien finally went into liquidation, along with the associated Karczag publishing firm. Kálmán and others now looked towards Zurich, which, with the rise of Hitler, was by then a safer city than Vienna for Jews. Kálmán's *Kaiserin Josephine* (1936) was thus first produced at

Zurich's Municipal Theatre. The Nazi annexation of Austria prevented a production in Vienna, and the work has remained little known apart from the beautiful "Glücklich am Morgen." Kálmán himself felt safer emigrating to America. There he collaborated with Lorenz Hart on a work that failed to reach the stage, and more fruitfully with Viennese refugee Karl Farkas (1898–1971) on a Viennese nostalgia piece, *Marinka* (1945). Back in Europe after the war, his last work was the posthumously produced *Arizona Lady* (1954), a cowboy piece set in the Prohibition era.

Oscar Straus was another who was forced by the political tensions of the 1930s to seek asylum first in Zurich and then in wartime America, returning to Europe after the war. Following his 1928 Guitry collaboration *Mariette,* Straus had maintained his prolific output not only for the theatre but also for films, whose influence he acknowledged in his operetta *Hochzeit in Hollywood* (Wedding in Hollywood, 1928). The most successful of his stage works during the next six years was *Eine Frau, die weiss, was sie will* (A Woman Who Knows What She Wants, 1932), a light musical comedy for Fritzi Massary. It achieved an English production, and two of its numbers were internationally successful in their time, the title song and the worldly-wise "Jede Frau hat irgendeine Sehnsucht" (Every Woman Thinks She Wants to Wander). It was the last show Straus was able to put on in Berlin before he, his librettist Alfred Grünwald, and leading lady Massary were forced to leave Germany.

Like Kálmán, Straus took his work to Zurich's Municipal Theatre, where his most successful operetta of the 1930s was produced. *Drei Walzer* (Three Waltzes, 1935) is another of those pieces that, like Kollo's *Wie einst im Mai,* followed the fortunes of several generations. Act 1 is set in Vienna in 1865 and concerns a dancer, Fanny Pichler, and her ill-starred love for Count Rudi Schwarzenegg. The second act, set in 1900, tells of Fanny's operetta-star daughter Charlotte, whose romance with Rudi's son Otto is also thwarted. Finally, the two families are united in Act 3 when Charlotte's movie-star daughter Franzi portrays her grandmother in a film that Rudi's grandson objects to. He arrives on the set to complain and is roped in to play his grandfather. Romance develops.

The novelty of *Drei Walzer* was that the music of Act 1 incorporated themes by Johann Strauss the elder, while Act 2 used themes by Johann Strauss the younger. Oscar Straus provided new music for Act 3. *Drei Walzer* had relatively little success in its German original, but, when Albert Willemetz adapted it in France as a vehicle for Yvonne Printemps and her current partner Pierre Fresnay during the Exhibition Year of 1937, it became a big hit. The three acts were reset in Paris during the Exhibition years of 1867, 1900, and 1937. Printemps turned the Act 1 waltz "C'est la saison d'amour" (after Johann I), the Act 2 "Je t'aime" (after Johann II), and the Act 3 "Mais c'est le destin peut-être" and "Je ne suis pas ce que l'on pense" (the last added especially for her) into standards that have been sung by generations of French prima donnas.

Straus, who had moved to France in 1939, now took out French nationality and collaborated with Willemetz on *Mes amours* (1940). He remained active after the war, with a revised version of his classic *Ein Walzertraum* and two final operettas. *Die Musik kommt* (The Music Comes, 1948) was staged in Zurich and then revised for Munich as *Ihr erster Walzer* (Her First Waltz), where his final score, *Bozena* (1952)—completed in his eighties—was also staged.

Another composer affected by the political developments of the 1930s was Robert Stolz (1880–1975). His first short operetta, *Studentenulke* (Student Pranks, 1901), had been produced in Marburg (now Maribor in Slovenia), where he began his conducting career as well. In 1907 he had moved to the Theater an der Wien, where he took over as conductor of *Die lustige Witwe* and conducted for the original production of *Der Graf von Luxemburg*. His Viennese operettas began with *Das Glücksmädel* (The Lucky Girl, 1910), starring Alexander Girardi. Subsequent works included *Der Favorit* (The Favourite, 1916), which produced the soprano aria "Du sollst der Kaiser meiner Seele sein." His first international success was *Der Tanz ins Glück* (The Dance into Happiness, 1920), about a valet who exposes his employer—a hairdresser masquerading as a count—in order to win the hand of a hatmaker, only for true love to win out after all. The piece was seen in London as *Whirled into Happiness* and in New York as *Sky High*. Hardly less successful were *Die Tanzgräfin* (The Dancing Duchess, 1921) and *Mädi* (1923), which became *The Blue Train* in London. But it was during the 1930s, when Stolz became a prolific composer of songs for German films, that he also produced the stage scores for which he is remembered.

Wenn die kleinen Veilchen blühen (Wild Violets, 1932) was a turn-of-the-century tale set in Bacharach on the Rhine. A play within a play re-creates an incident in which a headmistress's nephew, Paul Gutbier, disguises himself as a teacher, kisses one of the pupils, and ends up at a champagne party. The incident is recalled years later by the daughter of one of the servants as a piece of gentle blackmail that allows her to marry Paul's son. Noteworthy among Stolz's lightly tripping songs are the opening chorus "Im Bacharach am Rhein," the student number "Ich hab' ein Mädel gern" (both of these reprised repeatedly throughout the evening), the title song, and the romantic duet "Du, du, du, schliess' deine

Auge zu." After moving to Zurich, Stolz created the romantic *Venus in Seide* (Venus in Silk, 1932), whose title refers to a painting of the Princess Jadja Milewska-Palotay. Her fiancé is kidnapped on the way to the wedding, prompting an exceedingly complex story of misidentifications and misunderstandings before the two are formally united. Like the story, the score was more substantial than that of *Wenn die kleinen Veilchen blühen*. Best known is the leading lady's entrance "Spiel auf deine Geige."

Next came a German stage adaptation of a movie musical for which Stolz had provided songs. *Zwei Herzen im Dreivierteltakt* (Two Hearts in Waltz Time, 1933) was also known as *Der verlorene Walzer* (The Lost Waltz), both titles summarising the dilemma of composer Toni Hofer, who needs to produce a waltz for a new operetta but who can't write unless he's in the middle of a new love affair. Both materialise courtesy of his librettist's young sister Hedi. Central to the stage score were the film's two big hit numbers—the bouncy title waltz and smoochy fox-trot "Auch du wirst mich einmal betrügen."

Stolz's next work was not only mounted in Zurich, it featured local colour. Set in Lake Constance, *Grüezi* (Hi! 1934) concerned the competition between a Swiss hotelier and his three sons for the attentions of their secretary. Things really heat up when film director Harry Hell arrives and promptly becomes suitor number five. Fortunately, enough young women are brought into the plot for five happy couples to be paired off at the final curtain. The hit numbers were the comedy duet "Jedes kleine Mädel hat eine kleine Lieblingsmelodie" and, above all, the pseudo-folk song "Auf der Heide blüh'n die letzte Rosen." Berlin saw the piece as *Himmelblaue Träume* (Sky-Blue Dreams, the title of one of its duets), and Vienna as *Servus, Servus*. Stolz was soon after on his way to temporary exile in America via Paris, where he composed additional numbers for the Paris production of Posford's *Balalaika*. He returned after the war to enjoy a prolonged autumn to his career as composer, conductor, and recording artist.

One German Jew who emigrated permanently to America was Kurt Weill, who followed *Die Dreigroschenoper* and *Happy End* with various theatrical works, none of which fall into conventional categories. The one nearest to operetta was *Der Kuhhandel* (The Cow Business), which was never staged in Germany but which was produced in London in substantially diluted form as *A Kingdom for a Cow* (1935) while Weill was passing through. The piece was satirical without being bitter. As such it was something of a 1930s equivalent of Offenbach, as well as a European counterpart to the Gershwins' *Strike up the Band!* It concerned shady dealings on an imaginary Caribbean island shared by two republics, which an American businessman persuades to declare war on each other as a way to promote his arms business. Modern performances of the original German score have revealed it as full of lilting melodies and rousing rhythms in the best Weill style. After this, Weill moved on to America, and to American works which will be discussed later.

Weill's 1920s use of contemporary dance rhythms was echoed in the more conventional European operetta field by the Hungarian Pál (Paul) Ábrahám (1892–1960). During a brief musical career he created three international successes in which contemporary dances and American characters and expressions were mixed with remnants of Viennese operetta in exotic orchestrations reminiscent of Kálmán. He began as an operetta conductor and composer in Budapest and sprang to world attention with *Viktória* (1930), first produced in Hungarian but more familiarly known in the German version of Alfred Grünwald and Fritz Löhner-Beda as *Viktoria und ihr Husar* (Victoria and Her Hussar). Hussar captain Stefan Koltay and his batman Janczi have been sentenced to death in war-torn Siberia but manage to escape to Tokyo, where they take refuge in the American embassy. There Stefan discovers that Viktória, wife of Ambassador John Cunlight, is the lover from whom he was separated by the war. To stay close to her he risks death by accompanying the ambassador to his new posting in St. Petersburg; the latter eventually obligingly steps aside in the final act, set in the Hungarian countryside. Best remembered from the score is the slow waltz "Pardon, Madame" and the tenor's "Reich mir zum Abschied noch einmal die Hände"; but there are also garishly orchestrated numbers for a comedy duo of Viktória's brother Count Ferry Hegedüs and his half-French, half-Japanese bride Lisa San. She engagingly explains that "Meine Mama war aus Yokohama," while their giggling duet "Mausi, süss war du heute Nacht" was such a sensation that Oszkár Dénes, Count Ferry in the original Hungarian production, was able to repeat the role in German and English productions and as far afield as Australia.

Ábrahám's next work was premièred in Germany and was only slightly less successful. For *Die Blume von Hawaii* (The Flower of Hawaii, 1931) the exotic settings were Honolulu and a Monte Carlo cabaret, with twanging Hawaiian guitars and saxophones adding to the exoticism of the orchestration. The story concerned a Hawaiian attempt to prevent American annexation of the island. This is achieved by smuggling the exiled Princess Laya onto the island and marrying her to her cousin, the ruling Prince Lilo-Taro, whom the Americans are trying to marry to the governor's niece Bessie Worthington. Anny Ahlers and Alfred Jerger created the leading Hawaiian roles, with Harald Paulsen as the American gover-

The cast of Ábrahám's *Viktoria und ihr Husar,* Theater an der Wien, 1930
Photo: AKG London

nor's secretary John Buffy. The sultry "Ein Paradies am Meeresstrand," reprised throughout the score, was a hit, along with the tenor's ardent title song. Popular too were cabaret vocalist Jim-Boy's catchy "My Golden Baby" and his black-face "Bin nur ein Jonny"—deliberate attempts to trade on the appeal of Al Jolson.

Ábrahám's third hit proved less enduring. The action of *Ball im Savoy* (Ball at the Savoy, 1932), was divided between Venice, Nice (the Savoy Hotel of the title), and Paris. Hungarian coloratura soprano Gitta Alpár played a honeymooning marquise and sang the big number, "Toujours l'amour," while the comedy pair of Oszkár Dénes as Turkish attaché Mustapha Bey and Rózsi Bársony as jazz composer Daisy Parker were entrusted with the lively dance numbers that were an integral part of Ábrahám's formula. Alas, Ábrahám's star faded as quickly as it had risen. Forced to leave Germany, he moved first to Vienna—where he created *Märchen im Grand-Hotel* (Fairy Tale in the Grand Hotel, 1934), *Dshainah, das Mädchen aus dem Tanzhaus* (Dinah, the Girl from the Dance-Hall, 1935), and the football show *Roxy und ihr Wunderteam* (Roxy and His Wonder Team, 1937) —and then to Budapest. Owing to the political situation, these works stood little chance of international dissemination, and Ábrahám himself was compelled to leave Europe altogether: he spent the war years scraping a living in America as a pianist. He finally returned to Europe shortly before his death in 1960.

German-language operetta was at the crossroads, not just politically but artistically, as it attempted to reconcile the traditional and the new. The more the newer trends took hold, the greater the nostalgia for the past, and there were various attempts to satisfy it by overhauling the operetta hits of the nineteenth century. In 1923 Johann Strauss's *Eine Nacht in Venedig* was staged at the Theater an der Wien as a vehicle for Richard Tauber, with revisions to the book by Ernst Marischka and to the score by Erich Wolfgang Korngold (1897–1957). For a Max Reinhardt production in 1929 the same pair revised Strauss's *Die Fledermaus,* with a male Orlofsky. They then went one further with a work that, along the lines of Oscar Straus's *Drei Walzer* some years later, used music by both the Johann Strausses. In this case the story was about the two composers: it concerned the family rivalry that surrounded the younger Strauss's first concert in 1844. *Walzer aus Wien* (Waltzes from Vienna, 1930) was something of a committee creation: Julius Bittner (1874–1939) shared the arranging credits with Korngold, and A. M. Willner and Heinz Reichert were co-librettists with Ernst Marischka. Hubert Marischka created the role of the younger Strauss, Willy Thaller played the father. Betty Fischer was the seductive Countess Olga Baraskaja, and veteran Mizzi Zwerenz appeared in a character role. In its original form the operetta had limited success; but it proved the basis for repeated adaptations and readaptations worldwide, becoming a favourite in France and providing material for Broadway and Hollywood as *The Great Waltz.*

If Johann Strauss emerged from the *Nacht in Venedig* and *Die Fledermaus* reworkings with his scores relatively unscathed, Carl Millöcker was less fortunate. A *Gasparone* revision by Paul Knepler and Ernst Steffan, produced in 1933, contained some semblance of fidelity to the original, though its score and libretto were extensively reordered and supplemented by extraneous material. But a revision of another Millöcker work, *Gräfin Dubarry,* effectively created a new work on the same historical subject, with Millöcker's melodies rearranged into quite different form. Yet, if *Die Dubarry* (1931) was not really Millöcker, it was an undoubted success. The new book was by Paul Knepler and Ignaz M. Welleminsky (1882–1941) and the musical adaptation by Theo Mackeben (1897–1953). Hungarian coloratura soprano Gitta Alpár played the milliner who catches the eye of Count Du Barry and ends up in the bed of Louis XV. Her role included two first-rate solos in the insinuating "Ich schenk mein Herz" and the glittering "Ja, so ist sie, die Dubarry." The show's triumphant progress around the world received extra publicity in London when the red-haired leading lady Anny Ahlers (the original Princess Laya in *Die Blume von Hawaii*) jumped to her death from the window of her lodgings a few days after Goebbels was elected minister of culture in her native Germany.

When she was still performing in Germany, Ahlers had also appeared in yet another of the works that made use of melodies by the younger Johann Strauss. In *Casanova* (1928) Ahlers played the first of the featured conquests of the great eighteenth-century seducer. The show was a seven-scene spectacular staged by producer Erik Charell (1895–1974), with a book by Ernst Welisch and Rudolf Schanzer. The music was arranged by Ralph Benatzky (1884–1957), a theatre conductor who for almost twenty years had been putting together scores for Vienna and Berlin that achieved little more than local attention. Operatic bass-baritone Michael Bohnen played Casanova, whose conquest of the virginal nun Laura (sung by Anni Frind) in the third scene gave the work posterity through the celebrated Nuns' Chorus that was adapted from Strauss's operetta *Blindekuh*.

Benatzky's major claim to fame came with his score for Erik Charell's next spectacular, *Im weissen Rössl* (White Horse Inn, 1930). With its catchy tunes and almost unremitting high spirits, it was a show that captured the mood of the moment as no other, owing its success as much as anything to its setting in the famous inn on the edge of the lake at St. Wolfgang in the Austrian Salzkammergut. The show was in fact an adaptation of a romantic play produced back in 1897 about a headwaiter, Leopold (played in the operetta by light comedian Max Hansen), in love with his landlady, Josefa, who instead prefers visiting city lawyer Otto Siedler. While Josefa tries to provide Siedler with various home comforts, Leopold does all he can to upset things, leading ultimately to his dismissal. It takes a visit from the Emperor Franz-Joseph (Paul Hörbiger) to make Josefa realise that rustic Leopold is the right man for her.

As the show's principal composer, Benatzky contributed the title waltz, Leopold's serenade "Es muss was wunderbares sein," and the thigh-slapping "Im Salzkammergut." But various other hands helped prepare the piece for opening night. Robert Stolz provided the romantic "Die ganze Welt ist Himmelblau" and "Mein Liebeslied muss ein Walzer sein," and Bruno Granichstaedten set Leopold's reflective "Zuschau'n kann i net." Even the librettist Robert Gilbert (son of composer Jean Gilbert) turned his hand to composition for the comedy character Sigismund's "Was kann der Sigismund dafür?" For later productions, both in German and translation, even more songs were interpolated; Stolz's "Adieu, mein kleiner Gardeoffizier," from the film *Das Lied ist aus,* appeared in the English and French adaptations. *Im weissen Rössl* remains the most frequently performed musical to come out of 1930s Berlin.

Eduard Künneke was another contributor to *Im weissen Rössl;* he did the vocal arrangements. Though his international career was now behind him, Künneke retained his position throughout the 1930s as the senior composer of German operetta. *Liselott* (1932), a revised version of *Die blonde Liselott* (Blonde Liselott, 1927), was one of his successes, with the popular Käthe Dorsch as a royal Austrian and Gustaf Gründgens as her brother-in-law, the King of France, whom she dissuades from declaring war on her country. However, it was another work the same year that was to prove Künneke's most enduring success after *Der Vetter aus Dingsda. Glückliche Reise* (Happy Journey, 1932) fell in the bright modern dance-band mode and concerned two expatriate Berliners, Robert von Hartenau and Stefan Schwarzenberg. Tiring of life in Brazil, they are enticed back to Berlin by Robert's pen-friendship with Monika Brink, a self-styled society woman. In fact, Monika is nothing of the sort. Moreover, her side of the correspondence has been conducted by her colleague Lona Vonderhoff. Sufficient confusion is created to keep the piece bubbling merrily along until the four young people pair off happily and fly back to Brazil. The merriment is helped by such numbers as the young men's tango "Drüben in der Heimat," Monika's blues "Das Leben ist ein Karusell," and the title march. Walter Jankuhn and Lizzi Waldmüller had the starring roles of Robert and Monika.

Though Künneke's output varied between such up-to-the-minute dance-band works and quasi-operatic scores, he always maintained old-fashioned standards of musicianship. Moreover, as an Aryan, he was not subject to the persecution suffered by so many Jewish artists, not all of whom were able to escape across the Atlantic. In 1933 Alfred Rotter, producer of Künneke's *Liselott,* as well as Lehár's *Friederike, Das Land des Lächelns,* and *Schön ist die Welt,* was murdered with his wife in Liechtenstein. Fritz Löhner-Beda, co-librettist of the same three Lehár shows, was among those who later died in Auschwitz.

Künneke's first work under the Goebbels regime was an unsuccessful Dickens adaptation, *Klein-Dorrit* (Little Dorrit, 1933). But then came one of his happier creations. *Die lockende Flamme* (The Alluring Flame, 1933) boasted a biographical libretto written by Paul Knepler in collaboration with Ignaz M. Welleminsky that featured the poet E. T. A. Hoffmann. To Hoffmann was given the show's big number, the elegant "Ich träume mit offenen Augen," and Spanish dancer Dolores exerted her charms on him in the lively "In meiner Heimat,

Gustav Gründgens and Käthe Dorsch in Künneke's *Liselott*
Photo: AKG London

in Andalusien." There was also a highly successful comedy song, "Künstlerball bei Kroll."

In 1935 Künneke scored two successes, one in Zurich, *Herz über Bord* (Heart Overboard), and another in Berlin, *Die grosse Sünderin* (The Great Sinner) at the State Opera. Though styled "Operette," this latter was Künneke in quasi-operatic mode: a demanding score accompanied a spectacular costume piece. Like Lehár's *Giuditta,* it required classically trained opera singers. Helge Roswaenge and Tiana Lemnitz shone in the tenor's "Das Leben des Schrenk," the soprano's "Ich bin eine grosse Sünderin," and the duet "Immerzu singt mein Herz immerzu." Of Künneke's last works, *Zauberin Lola* (Enchantress Lola, 1937), *Hochzeit in Samarkand* (Wedding in Samarkand, 1938), and *Traumland* (Dreamland, 1941) were the most noteworthy, and each of them produced songs that are still heard in Germany. The first was a musical comedy about the nineteenth-century dancer Lola Montez and her relationship with Bavarian King Ludwig II, the second a spectacularly staged piece that proved to be Künneke's farewell to Berlin, and the third a modern fantasy set against a movie background with some popular comedy numbers. Thereafter, wartime and illness kept him largely quiet.

Künneke's pre-eminent position in 1930s Berlin operetta was challenged only intermittently by various younger composers who had moved from their native Austria to the new centre of German-language entertainment. It was another operetta with a topical plot about the movies that gave success to Nico Dostal (1895–1981), who had for some years pursued a career as a theatre conductor and arranger. *Clivia* (1933) concerns film star Clivia Gray, who goes to the South American republic of Boliguay to make a movie, becomes involved in various political complexities, and ends up marrying the Boliguayan president. Walter Jankuhn played the tenor role of the president, and Lillie Claus (who later married Dostal) was Clivia. She had the two big numbers: the introductory "Man spricht heut' nur noch von Clivia" and the reflective "Ich bin verliebt." The latter echoed the title of a number by Lehár, on whom Dostal had modelled his style.

Dostal followed this with a series of similarly well-received works, among them *Die Vielgeliebte* (The Well-Loved One, 1935), *Monika* (1939), *Die ungarische Hochzeit* (The Hungarian Wedding, 1939), and *Manina* (1942). Most successful was *Die ungarische Hochzeit,* about a Hungarian Count's attempt to organise brides for a group of settlers. His manoeuvres threaten to leave everyone married to the "wrong" partner, until the Empress comes along and sorts everything out. The work has challenged *Clivia* as Dostal's most successful piece, and the Hungarian-flavoured soprano number "Spiel mir das Lied von Glück und Treu" has helped keep Dostal's name in international circulation.

Fred Raymond (born Raimund Friedrich Vesely, 1900–1954) took his modishly American-sounding name when he began his career as a singer pianist. Outstandingly popular among his early compositions was "Ich hab' mein Herz in Heidelberg verloren," which remains Heidelberg's theme song to this day. In 1927 he used it as the basis for a stage work of the same title and then followed it during the 1930s with scores for stage and screen. The former were mostly revue-operettas written for Berlin's Metropoltheater in collaboration with librettist and impresario Heinz Hentschke (1895–1970). These reached their apogee in *Maske in Blau* (Mask in Blue, 1937), a lively piece about a young artist who travels from San Remo to Argentina in search of the subject of the painting that gives the show its title. The most successful numbers were the romantic tenor title song, the soprano's exotic "Frühling in San Remo," and the lilting comedy numbers "Im Gegenteil," "Ja, das Temp'rament," and "Die Juliska aus Budapest." Nearly as popular was Raymond's *Saison in Salzburg* (1938). This was reminiscent of *Im weissen Rössl* in both its setting and its story of village innkeeper Toni and the waitress Vroni who is the best baker of Salzburger nockerln (a sweet soufflé) in the village. Jolly songs such as "Wenn der Toni mit der Vroni" and "Und die

Musik spielt dazu" were in much the same style as in the earlier show. Raymond had less success with *Die Perle von Tokay* (The Pearl of Tokay, 1941). Rather more expressive of the mood of the time was his wartime song "Es geht alles vorüber, es geht alles vorbei" (It's all passing, it's all over).

Rudolf Kattnigg (1895–1955) was a theatre conductor before making his debut as a composer with *Der Prinz von Thule* (1936) and *Kaiserin Katharina* (1936). The former was distinguished by the tenor aria "Juble mein Herz." Later came *Mädels vom Rhein* (Girl from the Rhine, 1938) and, after the war, *Bel Ami* (1949), a vehicle for matinée idol Johannes Heesters that was based on a story by Guy de Maupassant. In between came his biggest success, *Die Gräfin von Durazzo* (1937), later known under the catchier title of *Balkanliebe* (Balkan Love). The story of the attempts of a deposed prince to regain his throne, it was set variously in the Balkan mountains, Venice, and the Austrian Alps. The Venetian scene provided Kattnigg with his greatest individual song success in the lovely barcarole "Leise erklingen Glocken vom Campanile."

The youngest of the important German operetta composers of the time was Swiss-born Friedrich Schröder (1910–72). Like Raymond's *Maske in Blau*, Schröder's first theatre score, *Hochzeitsnacht im Paradies* (Wedding Night at the Paradise, 1942), had a text by Heinz Hentschke. Schröder had been working as assistant conductor at the Berlin Metropol and composing film songs such as "Ich tanze mit dir in den Himmel hinein" when he got the commission. *Hochzeitsnacht im Paradies* was a musical comedy with a sub-Feydeau plot of mistaken identities in matrimonial suites and a conclusion set picturesquely at a gondoliers' festival in Venice. Johannes Heesters was the tennis-playing bridegroom whose wedding night is spoilt by the appearance of an old flame. The show gave Heesters his theme song, "Es kommt an die Sekunde an," as well as providing other hits in "Ich hab' mir einen Stundenplan" and "Ein Glück, dass man sich so verlieben kann."

If the works of French and German composers of the 1930s retain at least a toehold on their countries' respective repertories, the international significance of the shows was largely transitory as far as the English-speaking world was concerned. It was, at all events, largely to satisfy nostalgia for older musical traditions that the German works of the time enjoyed any international currency. Ultimately it was the rise of the Nazis and their persecution of Jewish artists that struck European operetta the killer blow from which it would never recover.

Chapter Thirteen
European National Schools

By comparison with the international popularity of the quasi-operatic scores of nineteenth-century operetta, European works of the interwar years found increasingly restricted markets; they were forced to rely instead on the appeal of subjects, effects, and songs geared to the talents of local performers and the tastes of local audiences. Indeed, after World War II, continental European musical theatre virtually disappeared from the international scene. Yet in individual countries it was far from dead. In France, for example, with the exception of Offenbach, the composer whose works are most often performed today is not Lecocq, Messager, Christiné, or any of the others who boasted worldwide success in the nineteenth century, but a man who emerged only after the Second World War.

Francis Lopez (1916–95) was born in eastern France, but his ancestry was South American on both sides, and he was brought up in Basque country. He trained as a dentist, writing songs on the side, until 1945, when his first stage score was hastily put on at Christmastime in place of a cancelled show at Paris's Casino-Montparnasse. The timing proved opportune and, like *Phi-Phi* after World War I, *La Belle de Cadix* (The Belle of Cadiz) offered the sort of escapist entertainment to which war-weary audiences readily responded. A surprise success, it ran way beyond its intended fifty performances. The book had been rescued from the drawer of Marseillais lyricist Raymond Vincy (1914–68), a contributor to Vincent Scotto's 1930s Marseilles operettas, and its star was handsome tenor Luis Mariano. Mariano played film star Carlos Médina, who is on location in Spain. The film crew recruit a real Gypsy king, and Médina becomes involved in what he believes is a staged marriage to his Gypsy co-star; it turns out to be not just for reel but for real. Only after various complications typical of operetta do the two decide to ditch their previous lovers and stay married. Mariano's matinée-idol appeal, allied to Lopez's romantic music, made the title song an enormous hit.

This Lopez success was by no means an isolated phenomenon. Maurice Yvain, whose toe-tapping scores had helped define French musical theatre in the 1920s and who thereafter graduated to the larger-scale opérette à grand spectacle, used his talents to similar effect in the lush, romantic *Chanson gitane* (1946) for the Gaîté-Lyrique. The tenor André Dassary played an aristocrat who marries a Gypsy and then must choose between her and his elegant social life. The Gypsy song of the title, "Sur la route qui va," had already been popularised by a film, and Yvain's attractive score also offered the animated "Au pas du petit poney" and an ardent tenor solo, "Tant que le printemps." *Chanson gitane,* Yvain's last important work, continues to be popular in France.

Vincent Scotto, though lacking Yvain's technical proficiency, adapted to the new formula and produced his own most enduring stage score and another classic of postwar Parisian musical theatre, *Violettes impériales* (Imperial Violets, 1948). Staged at the Mogador, the operetta was adapted from a screenplay about a Seville flower seller named Violette, whose lover Don Juan, the comte d'Ascaniz, leaves her for the aristocratic Eugénie de Montijo at the urging of his mother. Learning of Don Juan's love for Violette, Eugénie sets him free, which makes her available for the future Napoléon III. Violets feature prominently, not only in the heroine's name but in two of her major songs, "Qui veut mon bouquet de vio-

Scene from Lopez's *Andalousie,* with Luis Mariano and Gise Mey, at the Théâtre du Gaîté-Lyrique, 1947
Copyright Lipnitzki-Viollet/Roger-Viollet, Paris

lettes?" and "Valse des violettes." The baritone hero was created by Marcel Merkès, who with his wife Paulette Merval enjoyed a long career in French operetta. *Violettes impériales* ran for two years, prompting Scotto to write two more scores for the Mogador, *La Danseuse aux étoiles* (The Star Dancer, 1949) and the posthumously produced *Les Amants de Venise* (The Venetian Lovers, 1953). Both ran for around five hundred performances, though neither has lasted.

Although most of the composers and lyricists who now appeared on the Parisian musical theatre scene vanished after a hit show or two, Lopez and Vincy went on and on. *Andalousie* (1947) at the Théâtre du Gaîté-Lyrique featured the ubiquitous Albert Willemetz as co-librettist and was in the exotic-romantic vein of *La Belle de Cadix.* Set once more in southern Spain, it also starred Luis Mariano, now playing a poor Andalusian pot seller named Juanito who becomes a great bullfighter. He sets off for an engagement in Caracas, vowing to return to his sweetheart Dolores, but does so only after some dramatic encounters with Venezuelan politics and dirty dealing. Lopez's easily accessible music, along with the smouldering performances and opulent staging, kept audiences coming for a full year, and the show is still revived.

As if to prove that there was more to them than spectacular staging and Mariano's sex appeal, Lopez and Vincy next turned out a piece on a much smaller scale. *Quatre jours à Paris* (1948) was a sort of latter-day *La Vie parisienne,* a highly amusing piece about what happens when Gabrielle Montaron comes up from the country for four days and gets involved in the complicated love-life of a dashing Parisian hairdresser. It too ran for a year, and it too is frequently revived.

Also written for the intimate Théâtre Bobino were *Monsieur Bourgogne* (1949) and *Soleil de Paris* (1953), neither of which had the appeal of *Quatre jours.* Meanwhile, at the Châtelet, Lopez and Vincy's large-scale pieces went from strength to strength. *Pour Don Carlos* (1950) was set in a Pyrenees spa; Egyptian-born tenor Georges Guétary played the matinée-idol leading man. *Le Chanteur de Mexico* (1951) again starred Mariano, as a singer from Lopez's own home town of Saint Jean-de-Luz who goes to Paris, where he wins a place on an operetta tour of Mexico and conquers the heart of pretty Cri-Cri. Lilo, the original Cri-Cri, later starred on Broadway in Cole Porter's *Can-Can.*

La Route Fleurie (1952), which became another popular favourite in France, was another more intimate piece. Georges Guétary played a penniless Mont-martre composer who sets off for the Côte d'Azur with a couple of friends, played by blonde soubrette Annie Cordy and music-hall comedian Bourvil. *A la Jamaïque* (1954), yet another long-running success, was written for comedienne Jane Sourza. The characters are transported to the Caribbean for the colourful second act. The Châtelet's *La Toison d'Or* (The Golden Fleece, 1954) put tenor André Dassary into a story about Middle Eastern oilfields. Then, in *Méditerranée* (1955), Corsican movie and music-hall singing star Tino Rossi played . . . a Corsican singing star. Throbbing tenor arias and Mediterranean settings were all that fans of Rossi and Lopez needed to ensure another long run.

Lopez next tried his luck in Madrid, producing three Spanish-language shows—*El aguila de fuego* (The Fiery Eagle, 1956), *La canción del amor mio* (1958) and *S. E. la Embajadora* (Her Excellency the Ambassador, 1958). His Paris pro-ductions then included *Le Secret de Marco Polo* (1959), with Mariano as the fa-mous explorer, *Visa pour l'amour* (1961), teaming Mariano with Annie Cordy, and *Le Prince de Madrid* (1967), with Mariano as the artist Goya. Mariano bowed out with *La Caravelle d'or* (The Golden Caravel, 1969), set in Portugal. It was his suc-cessor Rudi Hirigoyen who starred in *Viva Napoli!* (1969), a historical piece set during the Napoleonic era, and young tenor José Todaro who had the lead in *Gypsy* (1971), about the Austro-Hungary of Emperor Franz Joseph.

Lopez's works continued to appear in Paris almost until his death: the last, *Les Belles et le gitan* (The Beauties and the Gypsy), was premièred in 1993. His forty-odd shows over a period of as many years became as much a Parisian institution as the Folies-Bergère and the Moulin Rouge, even though they were increasingly relegated to the suburban Elysée-Montmartre and Eldorado rather than the fashionable Gaîté-Lyrique or Châtelet. Parisians who had grown up on Lopez's shows apparently didn't mind that over the years the quality became weaker or that the small print in the programme indicated that the songs were sometimes by his wife Anja or his son Rodrigo. Nonetheless, the Lopez shows that are most often revived are his earlier works, whose fluent melodies retain their freshness and originality and are matched by Raymond Vincy's cleverly constructed books and sophisticated lyrics.

But postwar Paris had long since ceased to set the international musical theatre fashion. With their old-fashioned style rooted in European dance rhythms and their old-fashioned lyricism, Lopez's shows did not stand a chance in New York or London. The sole French work produced overseas in the early years after World War II was a musical that employed more modern song styles, confined itself to a small instrumental ensemble, and dealt with an earthy subject. Its composer, Marguerite Monnot (1909–61), was a student of Nadia Boulanger and had been a concert pianist herself before becoming cabaret singer Edith Piaf's chief songwriter, composing such standards as "Mon Légionnaire" (1936), "Hymne à l'amour" (1951), and "Milord" (1956). It was with a Piaf vehicle, *La P'tite Lili* (1951), that Monnot made her theatre debut; but it was *Irma la Douce* (1956) that brought her international acclaim.

The piece portrayed the seedier side of Parisian life; it was inspired by a short story by Alexandre Breffort published in the satirical newspaper *Le Canard enchaîné*. It paraded "poules" (whores) and "mecs" (pimps), as they were called in Parisian street slang, and it featured a narrator, the owner of a bar in the back streets of the Pigalle. This tour guide to the red-light district also explains the slang and introduces the characters. First is law student Nestor-le-Fripé (played by Michel Roux), who falls for kindhearted prostitute Irma la Douce (Colette Renard) and takes an apartment with her. He desperately tries to persuade her to quit whoring—going so far as to disguise himself as a wealthy elderly customer named Oscar, who demands her exclusive services. However, Nestor has to take a job to earn the money that "Oscar" pays Irma, and the strain of working at both

Colette Renard, René Dupuy, and Michel Roux in Monnot's
Irma la Douce, Théâtre Gramont, 1956
Copyright Lipnitzki-Viollet/Roger-Viollet, Paris

his job and his studies eventually proves too much. So Nestor "kills off" Oscar, for which he is arrested, convicted of murder, and sentenced to the penal colony on Devil's Island. At the end, all is sorted out and Nestor and Irma are reunited. The romantic duet "Avec les anges" and the bouncy "Ah! Dis-donc, dis-donc" helped the piece run for five years in Paris and London and achieve more than five hundred performances on Broadway.

Just as French works of the early postwar years almost never found an international audience, so the musical theatre pieces of other traditional European centres tended to stay in their own countries. In Vienna, Robert Stolz, who remained active into his nineties, enjoyed renown until the 1970s as the last of the great operetta composers. Memories of both his and the city's past glories were captured above all by *Signorina* (1955), revised for the Bregenz Festival's lake stage as *Trauminsel* (Dream Island, 1962), and *Frühjahrsparade* (Spring Parade, 1964), a reworking for the Vienna Volksoper of Stolz's songs for a 1940 Deanna Durbin musical, which he had composed while exiled in Hollywood.

More ephemeral works in the same tradition were composed by younger men, such as Gerhard Winkler (1906–77), who wrote the operetta *Première in Mailand* (Première in Milan, 1950), Norbert Schultze (1911–), composer of the song "Lili Marlene" and the musical comedy *Käpt'n Bay-Bay* (1957), and Peter Kreuder (1905–81), creator of 1930s movie songs and the musical comedy *Madame Scandaleuse* (1958). In West Germany songwriter Just Scheu (1903–56) and composer Ralph Maria Siegel (1911–72) entered the musical comedy field with *Blumen für Gloria* (1949). That a balance could be struck between traditional and modern was demonstrated by the long run of the pop musical *Elisabeth* (1992), by Sylvester Levay and Michael Kunze. Like Kreisler's *Sissy*, it was about the Habsburg Empress Elisabeth.

Only one postwar German-language work made it overseas. This had a curiously lengthy evolution: it originated between the wars as a Swiss circus comedy, which was subsequently adapted by librettist Jürg Amstein and composer Paul Burkhard (1911–77) as the musical play *Der schwarze Hecht* (The Black Pike, 1939). When it was revived in Zurich in 1948, director Erik Charell recognised its possibilities for the spectacular style of production he had used for *Im weissen Rössl*. The result was *Feuerwerk* (1950), a highly original story concerning a family gathering at the sixtieth birthday of its patriarch, Albert Oberholzer. Enter the black sheep, Albert's brother Alexander, who has become a circus manager and whose tales of his extraordinary life tempt Albert's daughter Anna to run away to the circus. This leads to a colourful second act at the circus, before Anna finally returns to her conventional existence. What made it a hit internationally was not just the unusual subject matter but the song "O mein Papa," which outlasted the show.

In the postwar Communist bloc, musical theatre gained a more extended life not only from state subsidies but from the fact that overt American influences and thus imported American works were long frowned on. Native talents were thus encouraged, albeit that their style inevitably owed much to international popular musical styles. East Germany especially enjoyed a local tradition epitomised by the works of Gerd Natschinski (1928–), who was for a time director of East Berlin's Metropoltheater, where he had major success with *Mein Freund Bunbury* (1964). This was a musical adaptation of Oscar Wilde's *Importance of Being Earnest*, apparently a popular subject in German-speaking countries: Paul Burkhard's *Bunbury* was produced in Basle just twelve months later.

The Soviet Union also contributed significantly to the repertory of Eastern bloc countries. Between the wars the main exponents of the Soviet school had

Scene from Shostakovich's *Moskva, Cheryomushki*
Society for Cooperation in Russian and Soviet Studies, London

been the composers Isaak Dunayevsky (1900–1955) and Yury Milyutin (1903–68). Dunayevsky had classical training but mainly wrote popular songs and theatre and film music. His march for the 1936 film *Tsirk* (Circus) became familiar as the call-sign of Moscow Radio, and his operetta scores *Zolotaya Dolina* (Golden Valley, 1937), *Volny Veter* (Fair Wind, 1949), and *Belaya Akatsiya* (The White Acacia, 1955) contain exhilarating and attractive music. Milyutin was likewise a songwriter and film composer, his operetta successes including *Devichy Perepolokh* (Search for a Wife, 1945), *Trembita* (1949), and *Potseluy Chaniti* (Juanita's Kiss, 1957). By far the most talked-about Soviet operetta was a political-satirical musical comedy by none other than symphonic composer Dmitry Shostakovich (1906–75). *Moskva, Cheryomushki* (1959) was produced at the Moscow Operetta Theatre; it concerned three couples who move from central Moscow to the new high-rise housing estate of Cheryomushki, during the course of which they encounter political greed and corruption. Shostakovich's reputation ensured that this example of Soviet operetta would be heard in the West: it was even staged in Britain in 1994.

In investigating the essentially local schools of operetta that were encouraged by political developments after World War II, we should also note that national pockets of operetta had always existed alongside the operettas of international currency. These pockets would comprise works by local practitioners who never quite made it onto the international stage. Though usually deliberately echoing the styles of imported works of their time, there would inevitably also be some local flavour imposed by the individual styles of their creators and the particular circumstances of their creation. We have ignored these national schools hitherto because their contribution to operetta as an international phenomenon was negligible. However, in closing our survey of European operetta, it is worth casting a look backwards—sometimes as far back as the nineteenth century—at some of the more significant of these local schools.

National schools had certainly existed in every European country. For every Lehár or Kálmán who entered the international mainstream, there had always been as many composers who remained at home. Among those in southeast Europe were the Romanian Ciprian Porumbescu (1853–83), composer of *Crai Nou* (New Moon, 1882); the Czech Rudolf Piskáček (1884–1940), who wrote *Slovácká princezka* (The Slovak Princess, 1918) and *Perly panny Serafinky* (Miss Serafinká's Pearls, 1929); and the Croatian Ivo Tijardovic (1895–1976), composer of *Mala Floramye* (Little Floramye, 1926) and *Splitski Akvarel* (Split Watercolour, 1928). In northern Europe, Danes hold the operetta *Farinelli,* by Emil Reesen (1887–1964), in especial esteem.

Even Italy, for all its love of grand opera, had a national operetta school that grew out of the imported French, Viennese, and British works of the nineteenth century. During the twentieth century it flourished through the remarkable activities of Carlo Lombardo (1869–1959), who as actor, producer, director, librettist, and composer contributed to numerous works during the first three decades of the century. Born in Naples, Lombardo became a songwriter and later musical director and principal comedian of a touring operetta company. He set up his own operetta company, for which he initially turned out Italian versions of foreign operettas. When Italy and Austria found themselves on opposite sides in World War I, copyright conventions broke down, and Lombardo seized the opportunity to create operettas of his own, using music from here and there. The score for *La Duchessa del Bal Tabarin* (1917), set in Paris, was a reworking of Bruno Granichstaedten's music for *Majestät Mimi;* attributed to "Leon Bard" (a near-anagram of "Lombardo"), it gave no credit to its original composer. In fact, it is largely through this adaptation that Granichstaedten's music has survived, since *La Duchessa del Bal Tabarin* has long been available in a Spanish recording.

Lombardo had similar success when he cobbled together the score for *Madama di Tebe* (1918), set in a Paris nightclub. Here the basic source was *Flup..!* (1913), the light-hearted Belgian musical comedy by the Polish-born Joseph Szulc, but the biggest hits of Lombardo's score can be traced back to such diverse sources as Franz Lehár's *Der Rastelbinder* and a Spanish work by Vicente Lleó (1870–1922). Elsewhere, Lombardo made acknowledged use of material by Italian composers, adapting music by the Neapolitan songwriter Pasquale Mario Costa (1858–1933) for *Il re di Chez Maxim* (The King of Maxim's, 1919).

When Lombardo tried to interest Pietro Mascagni (1863–1945) in a similar pastiche, using music from Mascagni's less popular operas, Mascagni insisted instead on composing a new score. The result was *Sì* (1919), whose title was the name of a Folies Bergère dancer who found it a good deal easier to say "yes" than "no." She is thus the ideal choice for a marriage of convenience to bon vivant Luciano, who will inherit a fortune if he marries and settles down. He believes that, by marrying Sì, he can get around the second condition; but eventually he finds a spiritually more satisfactory relationship elsewhere. Mascagni's score mixes Italian lyricism with Viennese sensuousness and French vivacity; especially appealing is the title song. *Sì* enjoyed more success than many of Mascagni's operas after *Cavalleria rusticana*.

Lombardo also tried to make an arrangement with Franz Lehár, who readily consented to refurbishing the unsuccessful *Der Sterngucker* with a new Lombardo book concerning one Charles, Duke of Nancy, who acquires a Duchess in the course of some amateur theatricals. The resultant *La danza delle libellule* (The Dance of the Dragonflies, 1922) contained a new Lehár hit, "Gigolette," in a more modern dance style, as well as other ingratiating numbers such as the duet "Bambolina." Again Lombardo's adaptation proved more successful than its source; it was adapted back into German as *Libellentanz,* in which form it was produced in Budapest and Paris, and it also appeared in English in London as *The Three Graces*. It survives on Italian stages to the present day.

Lombardo also collaborated with Italian composers on operettas that mixed traditional lyricism with twentieth-century blues and fox-trots. Mario Costa composed an original score for his *Scugnizza* (Neapolitan Urchin, 1922), a tale of a "Neapolitan Salome" and the amorous complications caused when an American millionaire, his daughter, and his secretary visit an Italian town. But perhaps the epitome of the Italian operetta was Lombardo's collaboration with violinist, conductor, and chamber music composer Virgilio Ranzato (1882–1937). In *Il Paese dei Campanelli* (1922), various intrigues between the locals and visiting naval cadets are set against a picture-postcard Dutch countryside. It became hugely successful in Italy, above all through the fox-trot "Luna tu." Later Lombardo collaborations with the same composer included *Cin-ci-là* (1925), which is set in Macao and concerns a sexually naive prince and princess who consummate their marriage only when a more knowledgeable Parisian couple shows them how.

Another of Lombardo's collaborators was Giuseppe Pietri (1886–1946), a graduate of the Milan Conservatory. Like Mascagni, he tried his hand at opera before switching to operetta. Before he teamed with Lombardo, he wrote *Addio*

Sheet-music cover for Costa's *La Scugnizza*
Kurt Gänzl Collection

giovinezza (1915), about a love affair between a student and a dressmaker; the popular *La donna perduta* (The Lost Lady, 1923), with its nostalgic Bell Duet; and the outstanding *Acqua cheta* (Still Water, 1920), about the love lives of two sisters in early nineteenth-century Florence; its score captures the spirit of Tuscany. Pietri's two collaborations with Lombardo were *Primarosa* (1926) and *L'isola verde* (1929).

Yet the richest of all these peripheral schools of operetta right back to the earliest days was undoubtedly that of the Spanish zarzuela. The term *zarzuela* implies a potpourri or mish-mash, and that's exactly what this combination of song, dance, verse, and dialogue was. The form may be traced back to the first half of the seventeenth century and takes its name from La Zarzuela, the hunting lodge near Madrid where King Philip IV indulged his taste for theatrical music. For a time zarzuela became submerged by the fashion for Italian opera, and it was only

Interior of Teatro de la Zarzuela, Madrid
Photo by Chicho. Courtesy the Ministerio de Cultura, Madrid/Centro de Documentación Teatral.

with a renewed demand for popular musical entertainment around the middle of the nineteenth century that the genre began to take on a new life. Italian operatic influences were now balanced by French, most notably in the libretti, many of which were derived from fashionable French opéras-comiques or Italian operas. Such was the case with Joaquín Gaztambide (1822–70) and his *El valle de Andorra* (1852, after an opera by Halévy), *Catalina* (1854, on Meyerbeer's *Etoile du nord*) and *Un día de reinado* (King for a Day, 1854, after Verdi's opera). So it was too with Francisco Asenjo Barbieri (1823–94) and *Los diamantes de la corona* (1854, after Auber's opera), and Emilio Arrieta (1821–94) with *El dominó azul* (1853, after Auber's *Le Domino noir*).

At the same time Spanish subjects were not ignored: for example, Barbieri's *Jugar con fuego* (Playing with Fire, 1851) and *El postillón de la Rioja* (1856), by Cristóbal Oudrid (1825–77). Such was the success of this new wave of works that in October 1856 the Teatro de la Zarzuela, still today the principal home of zarzuela, opened. Little by little the newly rejuvenated genre spread not only throughout Spain but also to South and Central America and to Mexico.

The abiding popularity of Arrieta's *Marina* (1855) was such that in 1871 the composer turned it into a full-scale opera at the request of the Italian tenor Enrico Tamberlik. Tamberlik's interest stemmed from the fact that, despite being set on the Costa Brava in the fishing village of Lloret de Mar, its music was decidedly Italianate. During the 1870s, however, zarzuela composers increasingly attacked the Italian influence on their native genre. Led by Barbieri, they produced works that attempted to be more authentically Spanish. A prime mover was Barbieri's *El barberillo de Lavapiés* (1874), a tale of political intrigue during the reign of Carlos III. This work is blessed with a score that from start to finish comprises a succession of glorious Spanish melodies and rhythms. Its opposition to Italian influences is declared in various ways, from setting Barbieri's little barber in a poor suburb of Madrid compared with Rossini's more grandiose operatic barber of Seville, to such specific episodes as the smashing of Italianate street lamps. Produced just eight months after the classic Viennese operetta *Die Fledermaus,* Barbieri's work has become no less the classic nineteenth-century zarzuela.

Historical subjects were prevalent at the time. Barbieri's other successes include *Chorizos y polacos* (Sausages and Poles, 1876), which took its peculiar title from the names of rival eighteenth-century theatrical claques. Manuel Fernández Caballero (1835–1906) attracted particular attention for two pieces with seventeenth-century political settings—*La marsellesa* (The Marseillaise, 1876) and *El salto del pasiego* (The Highlander's Leap, 1878). His other hits included *Los sobrinos del Capitán Grant* (The Nephews of Captain Grant, 1877), based on Jules Verne. Around the same time there emerged one of the most versatile and distinguished composers of whole genre: Alicante-born Ruperto Chapí (1851–1909). Noteworthy among his successes were the one-act *Música clásica* (1880) and various three-act works: *La tempestad* (1882), *El milagro de la Virgen* (The Miracle of the Virgin, 1884), *La bruja* (The Sorceress, 1887), *Las hijas de Zebedeo* (The Daughters of Zebedee, 1889) and *El rey que rabió* (The King Who Raged, 1891).

Though most of these works fit comfortably into the comic opera category, some were in a more serious mould. At the other extreme, a major development of the time lay in the popular one-act comedies of the *genero chico* (small kind), which combined Spanish settings, characters, and popular songs and dances and included in the orchestration native instruments such as the barrel organ, guitar, and mandolin. The music was important but the dialogue equally so, and many works had extended nonmusical scenes. This has contributed to their remaining virtually unexportable, despite their enormous popularity in Spain.

The composer whose music above all typifies the slightness, lightheartedness, tunefulness, and essentially Madrilenian nature of the genero chico is Federico Chueca (1846–1908). Composing in collaboration with Joaquín Valverde (1846–1910), Chueca turned the taste for this type of creation into a craze, above all with *La gran vía* (The Main Road, 1886). In truth, this was little more than a topical revue: its characters include not only a trio of rats but also Madrid's Lyceum Dance Hall and the streets and alleyways that were due to be cleared away so a new main road could be built through the city.

Chueca's melodies went right to the hearts of the Spanish people, so much so that a march from *Cádiz* (1886) became an unofficial national anthem during the Spanish-American War in 1898. His music is invigorating and captivatingly direct, achieving its individual effect not just through melody and rhythm but by incorporating unusual onomatopoeic effects, as in the refrain "bar ra bá ba bas ti-ri-rín tin tin tin tin ta-ra-rán tan tan tan tan ti-ri-rín tin tin tin tin ta-ra-rán tan tan tan tan" in the washerwomen's "Seguidillas" in *El chaleco blanco* (The White Vest, 1890). Elsewhere, in *Agua, azucarillos y aguardiente* (Water, Sweets, and Liquor, 1897), the street cry of the show's title is called out during the overture, while later a character's snores are incorporated into the vocal exchanges. Chueca's other one-act successes include *El año pasado por agua* (The Past Year in Water, 1889), *La alegría de la huerta* (The Joy of the Orchard, 1900), and *El bateo* (The Baptism, 1901).

The demand for the genero chico became so great during the 1890s that no fewer than eleven Madrid theatres were staging them, and many hundreds of pieces were written to fill the bills. Other classics of the genero chico include *La verbena de la Paloma* (The Night of the Festival of the Dove, 1894), with music by Tomás Bretón (1850–1923), and Chapí's *La revoltosa* (The Rebel, 1897), a tale of jealousy and intrigue in a Madrid tenement building. Chapí's other genero chico successes included *El tambor de granaderos* (The Grenadier Drummer, 1894), *Las bravías* (The Wild Ones, after Shakespeare's *Taming of the Shrew*, 1896), *La chavala* (The Lass, 1898), *El barquillero* (The Wafer Seller, 1900), *El puñao de rosas* (The Bunch of Roses, 1902), and *La patria chica* (The Little Homeland, 1907).

Caballero, too, produced several one-act classics, among them *El dúo de la Africana* (The Duet from *L'Africaine*, 1893), about backstage intrigues during a performance of Meyerbeer's opera. Others were *El cabo primero* (The Commander in Chief, 1895), *La viejecita* (The Little Old Lady, 1897, based on *Charley's Aunt*), *El Señor Joaquín* (1898), and *Gigantes y cabezudos* (Carnival Giants and Bigheads, 1898), which featured traditional Spanish carnival figures. Further prolific contributors to the genero chico included Jerónimo Giménez (or Jiménez, 1854–

1923), who added colourful orchestration to a rich melodic invention similar to Chueca's. Perhaps Giménez's best work is *La tempranica* (The Precocious Girl, 1900), which uses much the same book as Manuel de Falla's *La vida breve*. Other pieces still remembered for their delightful overtures and *intermedios* are *El baile de Luis Alonso* (Luis Alonso's Ball, 1896) and *La boda de Luis Alonso* (Luis Alonso's Wedding, 1897).

Among composers who began contributing to the zarzuela around the turn of the century, one who made an indelible mark was Amadeo Vives (1871–1932). A Catalan, he was a cultured musician who started out as an organist, choirmaster, and teacher. His first big success was the three-act *Don Lucas del Cigarral* (1899), set in the sixteenth century, and he confirmed his standing with the one-act *Bohemios* (1904), a piece with a Parisian setting inspired by Murger's *Vie de bohème*. This last was so highly regarded that it was at various times adapted by other hands into an opera and a full-length zarzuela. Vives dedicated the score to his friend Giménez, with whom he collaborated on several pieces, including *El húsar de la guardia* (The Hussar of the Guards, 1904), set in Napoleonic France, *La gatita blanca* (The White Kitten, 1905), and *La generala* (The Lady General, 1912), a contemporary piece set in a castle in Oxford. As we see in *Bohemios, El húsar de la guardia,* and *La generala,* the creators had by then turned away from the exclusively Spanish subjects that typified the genero chico of the 1890s towards more romantic pieces in the mood of the Viennese operettas of Lehár. Indeed, *La generala* was specifically styled an *opereta.*

Having thus given distinction to the one-act zarzuela, Vives turned his attention back to three-act zarzuelas, which he developed into what he termed "lyric comedies." *Maruxa* (1914) was a sentimental piece set in Galicia, and his acknowledged masterpiece was *Doña Francisquita* (1923). A model of refined lyricism based on the classical playwright Lope de Vega's *La discreta enamorada,* it has come to be regarded as the quintessential twentieth-century zarzuela. Its successor, *La villana* (The Peasant Woman, 1927), was similarly based on a Lope de Vega play, *Períbañez y el comendador de Ocaña.*

Further demonstrating the diversification of the zarzuela during the early twentieth century was *La corte de faraón* (Pharaoh's Court, 1910), with music by the Valencian Vicente Lleó. The big hit, "Son las mujeres de Babilonia las más ardientes," was the song Carlo Lombardo appropriated for the Italian operetta *Madama di Tebe* mentioned previously. Otherwise Lleó was notable chiefly for revue-style shows and for adaptations of imported works such as Lehár's *Der Graf von Luxemburg.* It was another Valencian, José Serrano (1873–1941), who after

Vives was the second major force to emerge in the twentieth century. Though he composed lighthearted *sainetes* such as *El amigo Melquíades* (Friend Melquíades, 1914), written in collaboration with the younger Joaquín Valverde (1875–1918), Serrano specialised in big, broad, sensuous themes such as graced his one-act pieces on Spanish subjects—*La reina Mora* (1903), *Moros y Cristianos* (1905), *Alma de Dios* (1907), *La alegría del batallón* (The Joy of the Batallion, 1909), and *El trust de los Tenorios* (1910). Later works used Italian settings: Venice for *El carro del sol* (The Carriage of the Sun, 1911), Sorrento for *La canción del olvidó* (The Song of Oblivion, 1916), and Tuscany for *Las hilanderas* (The Spinsters, 1927). Serrano returned to Spanish settings for three of his later successes: *Los de Aragón* (The People of Aragón, 1927), *Los claveles* (The Carnations, 1929), and *La dolorosa* (1930).

Manuel Penella (1880–1939), the son of a director of the Valencia Conservatory, concentrated on more ambitious, quasi-operatic scores. These included *El gato montés* (1916), a piece with a *Carmen*-like story that is largely remembered for a pasodoble based on its themes. Perhaps the most admired of Penella's stage works is *Don Gil de Alcalá* (1932), about an eighteenth-century Spanish adventurer. The more ambitious side of zarzuela was evident also in scores by two Basque composers of symphonic music. In *Las golondrinas* (The Swallows, 1914) the short-lived José Maria Usandizaga (1887–1915) created a piece about a company of travelling players that has gained particular favour among musicians, while Jesús Guridí (1886–1961) produced another classic in *El caserío* (The Village, 1926), set in his native Basque country.

Like Serrano, Pablo Luna (1879–1942), a musical director of the Teatro de la Zarzuela, varied his settings. His *Molinos de viento* (Windmills, 1910) was set in Holland, *Los cadetes de la Reina* (1913) in an imaginary operetta country, and *El asombro de Damasco* (The Terror of Damascus, 1916) in Syria. *El niño judío* (The Jewish Boy, 1918) took place in Madrid, Aleppo, and India, while *La pícara molinera* (The Sly Miller Woman, 1928) was set in the mountains of Asturias. The same lyrical, richly melodic style was also taken up during the 1920s by two composers who worked in collaboration. Reveriano Soutullo (1880–1932) and Juan Vert (1890–1931) achieved note first for *La leyenda del beso* (The Legend of the Kiss, 1924), but *La del Soto del Parral* (The Girl from El Soto del Parral, 1927) is regarded as their masterpiece, while *El último romántico* (1928) produced the beautiful tenor serenade "Bella enamorada." Both Soutullo and Vert died prematurely.

Other composers who emerged during the 1920s were noted for their big, broad, colourfully orchestrated melodies, which they used for Spanish revues as well as zarzuelas. Francisco Alonso (1887–1948) sought through his zarzuelas to pay homage to various parts of Spain, as in *La linda tapada* (The Veiled Lady, 1924), set in Salamanca; *La calesera* (1925), a costume piece set in 1830s Madrid; *La parranda* (The Revel, 1928), set in Murcia province; and *La picarona* (The Jade, 1930), set in Segovia. With a similarly opulent melodic style, Jacinto Guerrero (1895–1951) ranged more widely in his settings. *La Alsaciana* (1921) was set in nineteenth-century Alsace, *La montería* (The Hunt, 1922) in England, and *Los gavilanes* (The Sparrow Hawks, 1923) in Provence. Guerrero did not ignore his native Spain, however; *El huésped del Sevillano* (The Sevillan's Guest, 1926) concerned the writer Cervantes and was set in seventeenth-century Toledo; *La rosa del azafrán* (The Saffron Rose, 1930) was set in La Mancha; and the posthumously produced *El canastillo de fresas* (The Basket of Strawberries, 1951) in Aranjuez.

The huge popularity of the zarzuela in Spain was mirrored in Latin American countries and even spawned a few original works there. Thus, for instance, the Cuban composer Ernesto Lecuona (1896–1963) wrote *El cafetal* (The Coffee Plantation, 1934) and *María la O* (1953) for production by his own zarzuela company in Havana. As with other European schools of operetta, however, the zarzuela and its offshoots largely disappeared after the Second World War. That the genre has endured as well as it has is partly due to two long-lived composers who survived to make recordings of their works. Federico Moreno Torroba (1891–1982), the scion of a musical family, brought rare elegance to his scores. He tended to set his zarzuelas in his native Madrid. His first major success was *La Marchenera* (The Girl from Marchena, 1928), but this was easily outclassed by *Luisa Fernanda* (1932), a romantic piece set against the background of the overthrow of Queen Isabel II in 1868. Its searingly beautiful score was almost matched by that for *La Chulapona* (The Girl from Madrid, 1934) which, despite its three-act formula, recalled the Madrilenian style of the genero chico. Moreno Torroba's successes extended until after World War II with *María Manuela* (1957).

The last of the major zarzuela composers was the Basque Pablo Sorozábal (1897–1988), who was one of those who preferred a variety of settings. *Katiuska* (1931) was set in the Ukraine at the outset of the Russian Revolution, while the lighthearted *Adiós a la Bohemia* (1933) and *La del manojo de rosas* (The Girl with the Bunch of Roses, 1934) were both set in Madrid. Sorozábal's masterpiece is *La tabernera del Puerto* (The Landlady of the Port Inn, 1936), which takes place in an imaginary Spanish fishing village. Of his later works, *Don Manolito* (1942) was set in the mountains around Madrid and *Los burladores* (The Libertines, 1948) in Madrid itself.

That the zarzuela remains so little known outside Spanish-speaking countries is one of the great anomalies of the musical theatre. The extent of its repertory, and the range and brilliance of its invention, raise it fully to the level of French and Viennese operetta. Alas its local subjects, references, and dance rhythms, together with its individual mix of drama, song, and dance, mean that it does not translate well outside its native Spain. For those prepared to meet it on its own terms, the stage productions, recordings, and videos available in Spain offer the potential for profound and endless enjoyment.

Part IV

The Musical Since World War II

Chapter Fourteen
The Golden Age of the American Musical

Just as the First World War gave the United States a chance to export the jazz-age sounds that made such a contrast to the traditional European strains, so the Second World War helped the mature American musical affirm its position as the dominant force around the world. In this and the following two chapters we look at what, in retrospect, increasingly seems to have been the golden age of the American musical. As throughout the book, the focus is on the various creative teams in turn, rather than necessarily on dealing with key works in chronological sequence.

The route to maturity was signposted not only by productions such as

Show Boat and *Porgy and Bess.* Progress toward acceptance of thought-provoking works that were more than just vehicles for catchy songs was assisted not least by the contribution of Kurt Weill after his arrival in America as a refugee from Nazi oppression. It is a measure of Weill's mastery that he, alone of the European refugees, succeeded in establishing himself as a major creator of American as well as European musicals.

Weill's first work for the American stage was *Johnny Johnson* (1936), in collaboration with the playwright Paul Green, a serious antiwar parable that incorporated typically inventive Weill songs into a formally experimental but also profoundly American musical. More recognisably in the commercial American tradition was *Knickerbocker Holiday* (1938), with book and lyrics by Maxwell Anderson (1888–1959). A tale of Old New York, it featured operatic baritone Ray Middleton as Washington Irving (the author of "Rip Van Winkle"), who spirits himself back to seventeenth-century New Amsterdam, where he prevents Governor Pieter Stuyvesant from hanging the show's hero, knifegrinder Brom Broeck. In the role of Stuyvesant, Walter Huston croaked through the celebrated September Song, which was to remain Weill's most famous American song. (Mack the Knife was written in German.) Here, as throughout his Broadway career, Weill orchestrated his own score, something no American composer since Victor Herbert had done.

A more striking achievement still was Weill's third American show, *Lady in the Dark* (1941). It had all the right auspices from the start: staging at the prestigious Alvin Theatre, a book by playwright Moss Hart, and (following George Gershwin's tragically early death) lyrics by Ira Gershwin. Like *Johnny Johnson,* the work conformed to no musical comedy precedent. Gertrude Lawrence played Liza Elliott, a New York magazine editor whose sessions with a psychoanalyst provide the story. The musical contribution is almost entirely in the form of three extended dream sequences, in the third of which up-and-coming comedian Danny Kaye as a circus ringmaster sings a breakneck nonsense patter-song ("Tschaikowsky"), consisting of a recitation of the names of forty-nine Russian composers. Lawrence had some especially fine numbers in "One Life to Live," "The Saga of Jenny," and the beautiful "My Ship." This last, the only song that occurs outside the dream sequences, provides the clue to Liza's neuroses, which disappear when she is able to sing the whole song through.

Weill returned to something more in the American musical theatre tradition for *One Touch of Venus* (1943), a reworking of the Pygmalion story, which had already been popularized in Franz von Suppé's *Die schöne Galathé* and Edward

Gertrude Lawrence in Weill's *Lady in the Dark*
Papers of Kurt Weill and Lotte Lenya, Yale University Music Library.
Used by permission. Photo by Richard Tucker.

Everett Rice's *Adonis*. The statue of Venus that comes to life here was played by soubrette Mary Martin, who sang the showstoppers "I'm a Stranger Here Myself" and the seductive "Speak Low." The lyrics were by Ogden Nash (1902–71) and the book was a collaboration between Nash and humorist S. J. Perelman. The whimsical humour sustained the show through 567 performances—the longest run of Weill's career.

He followed it with one of the shortest. In spite of lyrics by Ira Gershwin and staging at the Alvin, *The Firebrand of Florence* (1945), about sculptor Benvenuto Cellini, failed to attract. Nothing daunted, Weill proceeded to his most ambitious Broadway creation, a work that, like *Show Boat* and *Porgy and Bess,* achieved opera-house status. Indeed, like *Porgy and Bess, Street Scene* (1947) was specifically designed as a Broadway opera. Based on Elmer Rice's play of the same title, its score superbly captures the atmosphere and varying emotions inside a steamy New York tenement torn apart by jealousies. As with *Porgy and Bess,* the music merges contrasted styles into a seamless whole: the arioso "Somehow I Never Could Believe," the declamatory "Ain't It Awful the Heat," the delicious Ice-Cream Septet, the lightly dancing "Moon-faced, starry-eyed," and the swinging "Wouldn't You Like to Be on Broadway?"

Like Sullivan's *Ivanhoe* and Gershwin's *Porgy and Bess, Street Scene* achieved an initial run (148 performances) that was remarkable by operatic standards but inadequate for commercial success. And, like *Porgy and Bess* (but unlike *Ivanhoe*), it has been increasingly admired as time has gone on. So too have Weill's final two Broadway scores, *Love Life* (1948) and *Lost in the Stars* (1949). The former was a whimsical piece that boasted lyrics by the young Alan Jay Lerner (1918–86); in it, a couple's relationship is viewed from the perspective of various periods of time from 1791 to the 1940s. *Lost in the Stars,* set in South Africa, was a powerful adaptation of Alan Paton's anti-apartheid novel *Cry, the Beloved Country.*

Ironically, Weill's greatest Broadway success came after his early death when, in 1954, *Die Dreigroschenoper* was staged as *The Threepenny Opera.* The success of *Threepenny,* twenty-six years after it was written, is typical of the reception of Weill's music, which has generally been better appreciated by posterity than by contemporary audiences. Certainly, historians are increasingly acknowledging Weill's importance as an innovative force in the Broadway musical. What Weill brought to the American musical in the original treatment of challenging subjects should not be underestimated, and it is hardly surprising that he became somewhat annoyed when the first Rodgers and Hammerstein collaboration, *Oklahoma!* (1943), was hailed as trailblazing. Inventive it certainly was, from the moment the curtain rose not on the traditional chorus but on cowhand Curly's exultant "Oh, What a Beautiful Mornin'." Yet there was scarcely more new in *Oklahoma!* than had appeared in any Weill work. What it had in spades that Weill's shows lacked was popular appeal.

Oklahoma! combined for the first time the well-tried talents of Richard Rodgers, no longer teamed with Lorenz Hart (who died shortly after the opening), and Oscar Hammerstein II, who had been cast adrift by Jerome Kern's move to Hollywood. The show was an adaptation of Lynn Riggs's play *Green Grow the Lilacs,* and it was set in the wide-open spaces of Oklahoma. Its enduringly romantic story concerns Laurey Williams (played by Joan Roberts), who hopes to be taken to the local dance by handsome cowhand Curly (Alfred Drake) but along the way becomes embroiled with bitter and dangerous Jud Fry (Howard Da Silva). There is a fine comic turn by Ado Annie Carnes (Celeste Holm), the girl

The original and tenth-anniversary casts of Rodgers and Hammerstein's *Oklahoma!*
Beinecke Rare Book and Manuscript Library, Yale University

who "cain't say no"—and especially can't resist cowboy Will Parker (Lee Dixon). All this is set off by a superb score in which Rodgers's fluent, operatically shaped melodic lines and Robert Russell Bennett's quasi-symphonic orchestrations adorn brilliantly imaginative Hammerstein lyrics.

Oklahoma! was indeed a development of what Hammerstein and Bennett had helped Kern pioneer in *Show Boat:* the luxuriant trappings of European operetta are wedded to a story of credible everyday characters living ordinary lives and speaking everyday language. By comparison with Hart's witticisms, Hammerstein's lyrics offer a portrait of rural Oklahoma, where "the corn is as high as an elephant's eye." From the romantic "People Will Say We're in Love" and "Out of My Dreams" through the jaunty "The Surrey with the Fringe on Top" and such comic songs as Will's innocent description of the modernity of "Kansas City" and Ado Annie's confession "I Cain't Say No" to the exultant hailing of the new state of "Oklahoma!" the score is a triumph. Adding to its appeal is the choreographical innovation of Agnes de Mille, who used the all-American language of the square dance to express the characters' feelings. With an initial 2,212 performances, the show smashed Broadway's long-run record and firmly established the integrated musical on the American stage. What Kern and Gershwin had experimented with as far back as the 1920s—a piece that was not just a collection of catchy numbers, but a fusion of drama, song, and dance—became a reality in 1943.

Those same elements were even more daringly developed to scarcely lesser success in *Carousel* (1945), an adaptation of a Hungarian play by Ferenc Molnar, now set on the New England coast. Where *Oklahoma!* had opened with Curly's "Oh, What a Beautiful Mornin'," *Carousel* no less daringly opened with an orchestral prelude that was no mere potpourri but a waltz that evoked a carousel. The hero, Billy Bigelow (played by John Raitt), is a good-for-nothing carousel barker who falls for the innocent Julie Jordan (Jan Clayton). She becomes pregnant, and, to provide for his future child, Billy attempts a robbery. This goes wrong, and Billy is killed. In the second act, which takes place many years later, he is allowed back to earth (in a manner reminiscent of Maurice Yvain's *Là-haut*) to watch over his teenaged daughter. The fantasy, far from being lighthearted, has a darkly serious, moralising aspect, exemplified in Billy's gospel-style "You'll Never Walk Alone." Yet the whole is enlivened by such glorious numbers as the romantic duet "If I Loved You," the joyful chorus "June is Bustin' out All Over," the dreamy "When the Children Are Asleep" for the secondary couple Carrie Pipperidge and Enoch Snow, and Julie's enchanting "What's the Use of Wond'rin'?"

Even more than *Oklahoma!* had done, *Carousel* seamlessly integrated song, dance, and dramatic action. There are two extended musical sequences, "If I Loved You" and Billy's "Soliloquy," in which he contemplates the birth of his child. Stephen Sondheim has characterised these—along with the opening of *Oklahoma!*—as key moments in Rodgers and Hammerstein's works and in the development of the integrated musical as a genre, noting especially the way the "Soliloquy" changes the nature of the drama. Take it out of *Carousel,* and you can't tell the story.

With original interpretations preserved on cast recordings, long-running productions in New York and London, and (later on) hugely successful film versions, *Oklahoma!* and *Carousel* pushed the American musical into the fore-

Jan Clayton as Julie Jordan and John Raitt as Billy Bigelow
in Rodgers and Hammerstein's *Carousel*
Beinecke Rare Book and Manuscript Library, Yale University

front of international popular culture. It mattered little that the next Rodgers
and Hammerstein collaboration, *Allegro* (1947), was a relative flop. It served merely
to concentrate the creators' minds and led to another blockbuster, *South
Pacific* (1949). Based on James A. Michener's *Tales of the South Pacific,* it is the
story of Nelly Forbush, a young nurse from Little Rock, Arkansas, stationed in
the South Pacific, and her wartime lover, the middle-aged French tea planter
Emile de Becque.

Less daring than *Carousel, South Pacific* was written especially for the
sparkling Mary Martin and the operatic bass Ezio Pinza, whose disparate vocal
capabilities led to the unusual situation in which a romantic musical couple
never actually sing together. Martin revelled in joyful numbers such as "A Cock-
eyed Optimist," "A Wonderful Guy," and "I'm gonna wash that man right outa
my hair," in which dramatic realism decreed that she actually wash her hair at
every performance. Pinza sang the resonant "Some Enchanted Evening" and
"This Nearly Was Mine." Yet the success of the piece was due not just to the
colourful South Seas setting and opulent romanticism but also to the cast of supporting characters: de Becque's two half-Polynesian children (who sing "Dites-
moi"), the dollar-loving Tonkinese Bloody Mary ("Bali Ha'i"), her prospective

son-in-law Lt. Joseph Cable of the U.S. Navy ("Younger Than Springtime"), and the crew of sex-starved sailors, who bring down the house with "There Is Nothin' Like a Dame."

Rodgers and Hammerstein next delighted their public with a show based on the true story of nineteenth-century Britisher Anna Leonowens, who became governess to the children of the King of Siam. After the manner of Franz Lehár's *Das Land des Lächelns*, it tells of the clash of Western and oriental cultures, though in this case Anna's influence on the King is more successful in moderating the ruthlessness of the absolute ruler. The piece was geared to the talents of Gertrude Lawrence, its numbers tailored specially for her limited vocal range in "I Whistle a Happy Tune," "Hello, Young Lovers," and her invitation to the King, "Shall We Dance?" The role of the King made a star of non-singing actor Yul Brynner, who, with his shaven head, became so closely associated with the role (thanks especially to the film version) that he appeared in revivals of it for the rest of his life. Not the least important element in the success of both the stage show and film was the contribution of the King's numerous children, with their March of the Siamese Children.

While the hugely successful film versions of their hit shows kept the names and songs of Rodgers and Hammerstein before the public throughout the 1950s, their next few stage shows failed to produce the same magic. *Me and Juliet* (1953), a backstage piece, produced a hit in the tango "No Other Love," but *Pipe Dream* (1955) foundered on a tale of some rather uninspiring marine biologists. *Flower Drum Song* (1958), directed by dancing legend Gene Kelly, disappointed only by the high standards of previous Rodgers and Hammerstein shows; it is set in San Francisco's exotic Chinatown and introduced such perennial favourites as "I Enjoy Being a Girl" and "Sunday." *Cinderella* (1958) was an American television musical that was later adapted for the London stage.

What finally brought Rodgers and Hammerstein back before the public —and constituted their greatest commercial success—was *The Sound of Music* (1959), produced only nine months before Hammerstein's death. Set in 1930s Salzburg, it once more owed much of its popularity to the presence of children; this time there are seven of them, the children of the widowed Baron Von Trapp (played by Theodore Bikel). He hires as their governess Maria Rainer (Mary Martin), whose intention to become a nun has been thwarted by her unnunlike high spirits. She takes in hand not only the baron's children—turning them along the way into a popular singing troupe—but in due course the baron himself. As ever in their most successful works, Rodgers and Hammerstein complemented the human story with melodic songs that the public worldwide took to its heart: the title number, Maria's "My Favorite Things," "Do-Re-Mi," and "The Lonely Goatherd," the baron's more-spoken-than-sung "Edelweiss," the romancing of the eldest Von Trapp daughter, who is "Sixteen Going on Seventeen," the nuns' expression of despair about the over-exuberant "Maria," and the abbess's encouragement to Maria: "Climb Ev'ry Mountain."

Rodgers and Hammerstein had not only written this remarkable run of successes; they had produced each musical. And as producers they were also associated with yet another of the major successes of the early postwar years. Brother and sister Herbert and Dorothy Fields had proposed to them a show about legendary sharpshooter Annie Oakley. Since the show's vaudevillesque musical comedy requirements were at odds with the romantic style of Rodgers and Hammerstein, they originally intended Jerome Kern to provide the score for Dorothy Fields's lyrics. Kern's sudden death put an end to that idea. In his place, Rodgers and Hammerstein hired Irving Berlin, already a veteran of more than thirty years of writing immensely successful songs for Tin Pan Alley, Broadway revues, and Hollywood musicals. Since Berlin always wrote his own lyrics, the Fields siblings ended up writing only the book.

Hitherto, Berlin's Broadway offerings had largely been for revues rather than book musicals, the only two exceptions being *Face the Music* (1932) and *Louisiana Purchase* (1940). But in *Annie Get Your Gun* (1946) Berlin succeeded beyond anyone's wildest dreams. The story features larger-than-life show business characters, including Buffalo Bill Cody and his entire Wild West show, and the songs have a vaudevillian catchiness, an effect that is heightened by numerous reprises throughout the evening. Ethel Merman played brash, confident Annie, and Ray Middleton was the handsome shooting star she challenges and ultimately wins. Berlin's songs are as rich a collection of hits as any musical ever had — "Doin' What Comes Natur'lly," "The Girl That I Marry," "You Can't Get a Man With a Gun," "There's No Business Like Show Business," "They Say that Falling in Love Is Wonderful," "My Defenses Are Down," "I Got the Sun in the Morning," and "Anything You Can Do."

Alongside the more ambitious Rodgers and Hammerstein dramas, *Annie Get Your Gun* created a second, more vaudevillian prong to the new phase of American musicals that were to take an even firmer hold on not just the English-speaking public but the world market. Berlin himself had little success with *Miss Liberty* (1948), his replacement for the Imperial Theatre about the attempt by a newspaper to find the woman who modelled for the Statue of Liberty. However,

Ethel Merman and James Michener backstage
at Berlin's *Annie Get Your Gun*
Freidman-Engerler photograph used by permission of the New
York Public Library for the Performing Arts. Crawford Theatre
Collection, Manuscripts and Archives, Yale University.

he hit the jackpot again for the Imperial with *Call Me Madam* (1950). The book, by Howard Lindsay (1889–1968) and Russel Crouse (1893–1966), features a Washington hostess (played by Ethel Merman) who becomes ambassador to the tiny European duchy of Lichtenburg. That Berlin could match the number of hits he had in *Annie Get Your Gun* is hardly to be expected; but there is wonderful material in "The Hostess with the Mostes'," "Washington Square Dance," and, above all, "You're Just in Love," in which two independently established melodies are played in counterpoint—a device favoured by Arthur Sullivan in more straight-laced days. A serendipitous hit was "They Like Ike," which became Dwight Eisenhower's 1952 campaign song.

Berlin's sole remaining show was for another Lindsay-Crouse book, *Mister President* (1962), which is partly set in the White House and features a fictitious president. The real-life American president then was John F. Kennedy, and the world was very different from that in which Berlin—now aged seventy-four—had made his name. The show was not a success. Berlin provided some numbers for a 1966 revival of *Annie Get Your Gun* but wrote little more. He preferred to devote himself to painting, and reached the age of 101 before his death in 1989.

Berlin's more musical comedy orientated style of postwar work was favoured also by Cole Porter. Even though his shows had consistently reached four hundred performances on Broadway, the likes of *Du Barry Was a Lady* (1939), *Panama Hattie* (1940), *Let's Face It* (1941), *Something for the Boys* (1943), and *Mexican Hayride* (1944) had few lasting numbers among them. Further, since a riding accident in 1937, Porter had had to walk with the aid of sticks and had been in almost constant pain. He seemed to be well past his peak, until 1948, when he produced the work that revived his own fortunes and gave the American musical another worldwide success. *Kiss Me, Kate,* with a book by Bella and Sam Spewack, exploited the show-within-a-show concept. Alfred Drake and Patricia Morison played leading couple Fred Graham and Lilli Vanessi, divorced members of a theatre troupe. The two are thrust together for a musical based upon *The Taming of the Shrew*. They start reminiscing; but Fred's interest in starlet Lois Lane (played by Lisa Kirk) makes Lilli so jealous that she spoils their stage performance, leading Fred to administer a totally in-character spanking. Ultimately, true to the *Shrew* story, Lilli is tamed and reunited with Fred.

The flexibility of the show-within-a-show concept gave Porter the opportunity for a range of musical styles and a rich supply of tunes. For a leading lady who was an opera singer by training, Porter provided her (as Lilli) with the richly lyrical and romantic "So in Love" to balance her venomous declaration (as Kate) "I Hate Men." Meanwhile Fred, as Petruchio, ponders his philandering life in "Where Is the Life that Late I Led?" Fred and Lilli's nostalgic remembrances of their earlier career, "Wunderbar," was intended as a burlesque of the Viennese waltz but was taken by the public as a serious romantic piece. The theatrical company provides lively relief with "We Open in Venice" and "Another Op'nin', Another Show," and a pair of comic gangsters (reminiscent of *Anything Goes*) have fun with Shakespearian titles in the rousing "Brush up Your Shakespeare." Porter departed momentarily from his custom of writing all his own lyrics by adding a slight reworking of Kate's actual speech in Shakespeare's *Taming of the Shrew* in "I Am Ashamed That Women Are So Simple."

Even more than Berlin had with *Annie Get Your Gun*, Porter used this success as the springboard for renewed recognition. To be sure, *Out of This World*

(1950) was no great commercial success, but connoisseurs prize it as one of his wittiest creations. Based on the Amphitryon legend, it starred George Jongeyans (later known as George Gaynes) as Jupiter, who assumes the shape of a honeymooning American in order to bed the latter's new wife. The key role of Juno was played by long-legged comedienne Charlotte Greenwood, who later achieved international familiarity as Aunt Eller in the film of *Oklahoma!* Porter wrote some brilliantly clever songs for her, including a sly reflection on her active youth, "I Sleep Easier Now," and the consequent lament "Nobody's Chasing Me," in which she showed off her high kicks. There is also a splendid "catalogue" quartet, "Cherry Pies Ought to Be You." Perhaps the piece was just a little too clever for the general public. Or perhaps it was just a little short of hummable tunes, following the dropping of "From This Moment On" during previews.

As with Berlin, disappointment merely spurred Porter. *Can-Can* (1953) proved a much more approachable piece, with a cast of more conventionally romantic characters and the almost sure-fire setting of a turn-of-the-century Montmartre dance hall. This is run by La Môme Pistache, played by French chanteuse Lilo. The plot revolves around her relationship with high-minded judge Aristide Forestier (played by Peter Cookson), who seeks to shut down the dance hall but finds himself falling for the proprietress. The songs that appealed most were Pistache's "I Love Paris" and "C'est magnifique," and Aristide's "It's All Right with Me." The subsidiary characters include a dancer named Claudine, played by a young performer who was later to earn top billings—Gwen Verdon.

If the success of Porter's final stage score, *Silk Stockings* (1955), was more domestic than international, he was able to end his career with his reputation at its peak thanks to his hit-packed scores for the films *High Society* (1956) and *Les Girls* (1957). His stage works had never shown the pioneering qualities of Kurt Weill or Rodgers and Hammerstein, but their well-developed books, witty lyrics, and richly tuneful songs made their own contribution to the American musical's post–World War II success.

Another composer who had come to the fore before the war was Harold Arlen (1905–86). His background was as a jazz pianist and singer, and during the early 1930s he attained considerable success with revue songs, including "Get Happy" (1930), "I've Got the World on a String" (1932), "Stormy Weather" (1933), and "It's Only a Paper Moon" (1933). Later, with lyricist E. Y. ("Yip") Harburg (1898–1981), he composed "Over the Rainbow" and other songs for the movie *The Wizard of Oz* (1939). His stage musical debut was with a college story, *You Said It* (1931), followed six years later by *Hooray for What!* (1937), a vehicle for comedian Ed Wynn with a book by Howard Lindsay and Russel Crouse and lyrics by Harburg.

Then came *Bloomer Girl* (1944), a period piece in the *Oklahoma!* mould, with an Agnes de Mille ballet and a leading role for Celeste Holm, the original Ado Annie. In *Bloomer Girl,* Holm played Amelia Jenks Bloomer, who reformed women's garb and bequeathed her name to bloomers. The lyrics were again by Harburg, the most catchy number being the satirical "Sunday in Cicero Falls." Also noteworthy is "The Eagle and Me," introduced by Dooley Wilson, who a few years earlier had secured immortality with his performance of "As Time Goes By" in the film *Casablanca*. Arlen himself played a supporting role.

Meanwhile, Arlen had provided additional songs for the 1943 film version of *Cabin in the Sky* (1940), whose original score by Russian-born composer Vernon Duke (1903–69) and lyricist John LaTouche (1917–56) included the song "Taking a Chance on Love," which was introduced by Ethel Waters. Arlen went on to compose three musicals of his own with black casts. *St. Louis Woman* (1946) has lyrics by Johnny Mercer (1909–76) and concerns a jockey, Little Augie, whose attention to the advances of free-and-easy Della Green earns him a beating up from her bar-owner lover Biglow Brown. Rouben Mamoulian, director of *Porgy and Bess,* directed. The hit was the leading couple's declaration of love, "Come Rain or Come Shine," and there were a couple of songs for Pearl Bailey, who was making her Broadway debut as the barmaid Butterfly. Bailey also appeared with Juanita Hall and Diahann Carroll in the much admired *House of Flowers* (1954), which had lyrics by Truman Capote (1924–84) and features a trade war between two brothel keepers. The less impressive *Jamaica* (1957), with lyrics by Harburg, was primarily a vehicle for Lena Horne.

A close contemporary of Arlen's was Harold Rome (1908–93), who was an architectural draftsman and summer-camp officer before gaining attention on Broadway with songs for the amateur revue *Pins and Needles* (1937), produced by the International Ladies' Garment Workers' Union. His book musical *That's the Ticket* (1948) closed out of town, but he had better luck with *Wish You Were Here* (1952), in which he put to use his experience in summer camps for a show that featured an onstage swimming pool. The title song became popular among crooners. The book was co-written by *South Pacific* director Joshua Logan (1908–88), who also collaborated on Rome's first major success, *Fanny* (1954). This was but a skeleton of Marcel Pagnol's original trio of Marseillais plays (*Marius, Fanny,* and *César*), replacing the French atmosphere, pace, and characterization with an all-purpose American romanticism. But, at the height of Rodgers and Hammer-

Harold Rome and the cast of Rome's *Pins and Needles*
Harold Rome Papers, Yale University Music Library. Used by permission.

stein fever, those were just the qualities that suited the American public. In retrospect, the production was perhaps most noteworthy for providing the Broadway debut of producer David Merrick.

For his next musical, Rome tried another film adaptation, this time of the 1939 *Destry Rides Again,* in which Marlene Dietrich had so memorably sung "See What the Boys in the Back Room Will Have." Rome's stage adaptation (1959) produced nothing of similar durability, but the songs help along a gently comic story about peace-loving Tom Destry (Andy Griffth) who, as deputy sheriff of outback town Bottleneck, triumphs over all manner of violent wrongdoers and wins the love of dance-hall girl Frenchy (played by Dolores Gray). Then, for his third major score, Rome returned to the garment industry that had launched him in 1937. *I Can Get It for You Wholesale* (1962) was based by Jerome Weidman on his own novel about brash, unprincipled, charming Harry Bogen, who sets up his own company to exploit a labour strike that is affecting his former boss, dress manufacturer Maurice Pulverstein. When the competition becomes too strong, he sells half of what he knows will become a worthless company to his best friend Tootsie Maltz, and then woos away Pulverstein's most valuable employees to set up yet another new company of his own, always remaining one step ahead of trouble. The show gained special note for the Broadway stage debut of Barbra Streisand, whose individual style was displayed to great effect in "Miss Marmelstein."

Notwithstanding these successes, Rome never wrote a major hit song. Burton Lane (1912–97) had better luck, although, like others of the time, he initially found it easier to make his mark in Hollywood. Apart from a few revue songs, his Broadway debut was an Al Jolson vehicle, *Hold on to Your Hats* (1940). Then came his successful collaboration with E. Y. Harburg on the stage musical *Finian's Rainbow* (1947), a whimsical piece about an Irish father and daughter who arrive in America from Glocca Morra. They bring with them a crock of gold they have supposedly stolen from the leprechauns and which they expect will multiply if they plant it in the ground near Fort Knox. Somehow this formula captured the fancy of the American public, assisted by songs that include "Look to the Rainbow," "Old Devil Moon," "When I'm Not Near the Girl I Love," and the undisputed hit, "How Are Things in Glocca Morra?"

The show's American success was repeated in the movie version as well as in a 1960 stage revival, but Lane composed no further stage musicals until *On a Clear Day You Can See Forever* (1965). This includes a dream sequence and a multigenerational theme in a piece that centres heavily on its two major characters—heroine Daisy (Barbara Harris on Broadway, Barbra Streisand on film) and psychiatric lecturer Mark Bruckner (Louis Jourdan in tryout, John Cullum on Broadway, Yves Montand on film). It is the title song that has endured. Lane composed only once more for the theatre, on the short-lived *Carmelina* (1979).

Lane's lyricist for *On a Clear Day* was Alan Jay Lerner, who had been Kurt Weill's lyricist on *Love Life* but who really made his name through an enormously productive partnership with composer Frederick Loewe (1904–88). The latter was the Berlin-born son of operetta singer Edmund Loewe, who had appeared in leading roles in Berlin, Vienna, and New York before settling in the United States in the 1920s. Frederick Loewe worked as a pianist, making various attempts to break into Broadway before teaming up with Lerner for *What's Up?* (1943) and *The Day Before Spring* (1945). Their major breakthrough came with a fantasy piece in *Finian's Rainbow* style, *Brigadoon* (1947). Set in Scotland, it concerns a village that comes to life once a century. The hero stumbles on the village on that particular day whilst on a hunting trip. He falls in love with a villager, and it is when he returns to find her again that he succeeds in lifting the spell the village had been under. The treatment is lighthearted and charming, and nobody could take exception to such delightful songs as "Waitin' for My Dearie," "The Heather on the Hill," and the big romantic duet "Almost Like Being in Love." This last attracted an international public through exposure on the air waves, and audiences outside America embraced *Brigadoon* as well.

The reputation of Lerner and Loewe was strengthened by a similarly lightly handled story about gold miners, *Paint Your Wagon* (1951). The gold is discovered by lonely widower prospector Ben Rumson, who settles down in Rumson Town with his daughter Jennifer. Ben finds a wife in newly arrived Mormon divorcée Elizabeth, while Jennifer falls for the handsome Mexican Julio. Amorous fluctuations go hand in hand with the economic ups-and-downs of the town, but love ultimately endures longer than the seams of gold. What have also lasted are Julio's ballad "I Talk to the Trees," Ben's reminiscence of his dead wife, "I Still See Eliza," and his reflective "Wand'rin' Star." The bustling spirit of a booming gold-mining town was superbly captured in the choruses "I'm on My Way" and "There's a Coach Comin' In," while Agnes de Mille's dance routines added to the appeal.

Anglophile Lerner and Berlin-born Loewe frequently favoured less intrinsically American subjects. Their next work was based on a George Bernard Shaw play, and it came to overshadow everything they had written before—or were to write afterwards. *My Fair Lady* (1956) may fairly claim to be the most successful stage musical ever, its music penetrating where the musical had rarely gone before, thanks not just to theatrical productions but to radio, recordings, and, later, a film. It is a sign of the maturity the American musical had now achieved that it could so readily embrace not just a work whose composer had grown up in Europe and a librettist-lyricist educated in England but, more particularly, an English source, English setting, English lead players, and music that consciously sought to capture the atmosphere of English society and the English music-hall era.

The show is an adaptation of Shaw's *Pygmalion*, a Cinderella story about Cockney flower seller Eliza Doolittle. Taken under the wing of linguistic tutor Professor Henry Higgins, she is given an upper-class accent and launched into English society, with the inevitable problems that arise from taking her out of her own social class. Young English singer Julie Andrews played Eliza, with two richly melodic songs in "Wouldn't It Be Loverly" (in the Cockney dialect) and the tripping "I Could Have Danced All Night." English movie star Rex Harrison spoke, rather than sang, "I've Grown Accustomed to Her Face" and his elocution lesson with Eliza "The Rain in Spain." Stanley Holloway played the low-comedy role of Eliza's Cockney dustman father Alfred Doolittle and provided to perfection the English music-hall style needed for "A Little Bit of Luck" and "Get Me to the Church on Time." Period music of a different type comes with the Ascot Gavotte, played at the ball at which Eliza is launched into society. Romantic interest is provided by the baritone character of Freddy Eynsford-Hill, whose rapturous "On the Street Where You Live" is a prelude to his ultimate proposal of marriage to Eliza. *My Fair Lady* ran for 2,717 performances at Broadway's Mark Hellinger Theatre and 2,281 at London's Theatre Royal, Drury Lane. The former was easily a Broadway record, the latter was unbeaten for a London theatre of such size.

By the time the show came off in either location, Lerner and Loewe had provided an attractive collection of songs for the film *Gigi* (1958) as well as the score for the stage musical *Camelot* (1960). The latter is a retelling of the story of King Arthur and the knights of the Round Table, but in a whimsical fashion that presents an immature Arthur and innocent Guinevere as unable to maintain the ideals for which Camelot stands. The show could not hope to match its predecessor's success, but it did well on its own terms, not least because of the presence of Shakespearean actor Richard Burton—speaking, rather than singing, in the manner popularised by Rex Harrison in *My Fair Lady*—and Julie Andrews, now famous from her Eliza Doolittle creation. The most successful numbers are Arthur's title song and his "How to Handle a Woman." *Camelot* was to be the last Lerner and Loewe stage creation. Claiming ill-health, but perhaps convinced that he could not live up to what was expected of him after *My Fair Lady,* Loewe retired from composition, leaving Lerner to find collaborators elsewhere.

Another creator of postwar hit shows was English-born composer Jule Styne (1905–94). Styne started out as a dance-band pianist, arranger, and vocal coach, doing little composing until he was in his mid-thirties, when success with songs for wartime films led him to try his hand on the stage. His first effort, *Glad to See You* (1944), didn't even reach Broadway. But the old-fashioned, inconsequential *High Button Shoes* (1947) did so to some effect, helped by lyrics by Sammy Cahn (1913–93) and by the performance of comedian Phil Silvers as a New Jersey conman. There was also a Keystone Kops ballet choreographed by Jerome Robbins, one of the truly original influences of the postwar American musical.

What really established Styne's brassy, big-band sound was *Gentlemen Pre-*

fer Blondes (1949). Based on Anita Loos's 1920s comic novel, with lyrics by Leo Robin (1900–1985), the piece introduced to the public a blonde bombshell with an appealingly raucous voice. Carol Channing played Lorelei Lee, a woman from Little Rock, Arkansas, who is supplied with diamonds and other comforts by Gus Esmond (Jack McCauley), heir to a button-manufacturing fortune. Pressing business prevents Gus from joining Lorelei on a voyage to Europe, and instead she is accompanied by showgirl Dorothy Shaw (Yvonne Adair). On the boat, Lorelei meets Josephus Gage (played by George S. Irving), the owner of the patent for the new-fangled zip fastener, which seems likely to put buttons (and thus her Gus) out of business. Lorelei's tangled attachments ultimately lead to a merger of the two businesses, which wins her the approval of Gus's father, while Dorothy decides to abandon her true-love principles and likewise marry into money. Stein set off this lighthearted story with a lilting and tuneful score, distinguished above all by "Diamonds Are a Girl's Best Friend." This proved ideally suited for popular vocalists of the time, before becoming inseparably linked with Marilyn Monroe through the film version.

Styne next worked with writers Betty Comden (1915–) and Adolph Green (1915–) on the revue *Two on the Aisle* (1951), which became famous mainly for the off- and onstage feuds between its two stars, Bert Lahr and Dolores Gray. He followed up with the book musical *Hazel Flagg* (1953), which alas duly flagged. Then came Styne's second big success, *Bells Are Ringing* (1956), with book and lyrics again by Comden and Green. Judy Holliday played the amiably dotty Ella Peterson, who works for an answering service. Unfortunately, she gets far too deeply involved with the problems of her unseen clients. Her particular efforts to assist playwright Jeffrey Moss (played by Sydney Chaplin) lead ultimately, of course, to their pairing off at the final curtain. The score produced two numbers that were to become standards, "Just in Time" and "The Party's Over," as well as other strong numbers in "Long Before I Knew You" and "I'm Goin' Back."

In their various ways Berlin, Porter, Loewe, Styne, and more minor figures had consolidated the reputation of the American musical as an entertainment with credibly developed story, characters, and song that incorporated dance and film-style underscoring into an integrated whole. If none of these composers attained the same innovative musical level as Weill or Rodgers, there were others who certainly did. One was Leonard Bernstein (1918–90), who by the time he composed his first stage score had already won fame as a symphonic conductor. Like Weill, he had thoroughly absorbed jazz and popular music influences. Like Weill, too, he

Judy Holliday as Ella Peterson in Styne's *Bells Are Ringing*
Theatre Guild Records, Beinecke Rare Book
and Manuscript Library, Yale University

brought to his theatre scores a grasp of symphonic and operatic composition that enabled him to produce—and orchestrate—works of sizzling intensity.

Bernstein began his popular theatre career with a jazz-tinged ballet, *Fancy Free* (1944), choreographed by Jerome Robbins. The same theme was then developed, with a completely new score, into the musical *On the Town* (1944), a collaboration with librettists-lyricists Betty Comden and Adolph Green, who also appeared. Though basically a song-and-dance show, its musical substance far exceeds what is traditionally associated with that description. The story is in some ways a sequence of revue turns, telling (somewhat after the fashion of Scotto's *Trois de la marine*) the adventures of three sailors on shore leave. Ozzi, Gabey, and Chip have only a twenty-four-hours' leave to enjoy New York and to track down a young woman who has taken Gabey's fancy from a poster proclaiming her "Miss Turnstiles" of the month. The action moves speedily, as Chip (played by Cris

Alexander) gets picked up by a sex-mad taxi driver, Hildy (Nancy Walker), who invites him to "Come up to My Place" and insists that "I Can Cook Too." Meanwhile, Ozzi (Adolph Green) gets "Carried Away" by a crazy anthropologist (Betty Comden), and Gabey (John Battles) reflects on New York as a "Lonely Town" before expressing himself as "Lucky to Be Me" when he believes that he has caught up with Miss Turnstiles. *On the Town* was, like Weill's musicals, ahead of its time. Jazzy, full of modern harmonies, it is now recognised as one of the classic scores of the American musical theatre.

Bernstein's conducting and compositional commitments severely limited his subsequent output for the popular theatre. *Wonderful Town* (1953) again had lyrics by Comden and Green but was very different in character from its similarly titled predecessor. Based on the successful 1940 play *My Sister Eileen,* its leading characters are two sisters from Ohio who seek fame and fortune in the literary and theatrical worlds, respectively, of New York. The piece tells of their encounters with the often eccentric inhabitants of Greenwich Village and was a personal triumph for Rosalind Russell as Eileen's elder sister, Ruth. The score is less ambitious than that of *On the Town,* but it has effective numbers, including the brilliant "Conversation Piece" for a dinner party at which the two sisters entertain their boyfriends.

On a much more highly developed scale altogether was Bernstein's next stage work, *Candide* (1956). A musical version of Voltaire's sexually explicit satire, it is styled a "comic operetta" and contains an extended score that is lighthearted and fluent in the operetta tradition and satirical in the manner of an old-fashioned opéra-bouffe, but with a thoroughly modern coating. Its big number is Cunégonde's parody of an operatic coloratura aria, "Glitter and Be Gay," while the effervescent overture has become a popular concert item. Yet, as a stage piece, it failed to take off. Perhaps the "comic operetta" tag confused the audience; but equally, Bernstein and a succession of collaborators had difficulty condensing Voltaire's epic into a viable stage musical. Bernstein continued to work on revisions of the work right up to his death, and there have been yet more revisions since.

Then came the work that established Bernstein's musical theatre stature. For all its modern harmonies and uncompromising lyrics by the young Stephen Sondheim (1930–), whom we shall consider in more detail in a later chapter, *West Side Story* (1957) was not only a critical but also a huge public success. The plot is a modernisation of the Romeo and Juliet story, with the rival houses of the Capulets and Montagues replaced by rival New York street gangs. Tony (played by

Rita Moreno in the film version of Bernstein's *West Side Story*
Prints and Photographs Division, Library of Congress, Washington, D.C.

Larry Kert) was once the leader of a white gang calling itself the Jets, and trouble flares when he falls in love with Maria (Carol Lawrence), sister of Bernardo, the leader of the rival Puerto Rican gang, the Sharks. The Jets' current leader, Riff, is killed by Bernardo, who in revenge is killed by Tony. He and Maria plan to flee together, but when Bernardo's girlfriend Anita (Chita Rivera) tells the Jets that Maria has been killed by a Puerto Rican rival for her affections, Tony emerges from hiding and is shot dead.

With its modern dances choreographed by director Jerome Robbins and interwoven into a sharp-edged, forceful score, *West Side Story* made a strong contrast to the traditional musical show. The tragic tale, as well, built on the precedents of *Porgy and Bess* and *Carousel* in departing from the happy endings that dominated musical theatre. By this time, indeed, the theatre-going public increasingly accepted and in some ways even preferred musicals with a serious content. What helped make the work a popular success was the fact that Bernstein's score, while seamlessly integrated into the plot, also contained individual songs that became huge successes. Tony's tender expression of delight on learning the name of his beloved ("Maria"), his love duet with Maria ("Tonight"), Maria's self-admiring "I Feel Pretty," the lyric-ballet interpolation "Somewhere," and the mocking comedy song for the Jets, "Gee, Officer Krupke!" proved hugely popular when they were played on the radio along with hits from the very different, but equally popular, *My Fair Lady*.

With the uncompromising musical and dramatic standards of *West Side Story*, the American musical had undeniably come of age as an artistic entity that might justly claim to be the true inheritor of the role previously occupied by opera. Bernstein thereafter concentrated on conducting, permitting himself only one final Broadway effort, *1600 Pennsylvania Avenue* (1976). This sought to offer a servants'-eye view of life in the White House from George and Martha Washington to Theodore Roosevelt but proved a disastrous flop.

In *On the Town* and *West Side Story*, Bernstein had created shows that ranked with the best of Rodgers and Hammerstein, Lerner and Loewe, Berlin, and Porter as part of a new musical theatre repertory that for the public at large made all that had gone before outdated. In the next chapter we shall meet some of the other creators who contributed to attaining that status.

Chapter Fifteen
Lyricists' Musicals in the Golden Age

While Kurt Weill and Leonard Bernstein were developing the integrated musical by musical means, others were doing the same thing from the point of view of the lyricist. Prominent among them was Frank Loesser (1910–69). The son of a piano teacher, he worked as a nightclub pianist but began his creative career as a lyricist, writing words for film songs such as "Says My Heart" (1938) with Burton Lane, "Two Sleepy People" (1938) with Hoagy Carmichael, and "The Boys in the Back Room" (1939) with Frederick Hollander. Loesser, though, had been in the habit of setting his lyrics to his own dummy tunes, and, when he managed to get some of these accepted for performance and publication, he thereafter collaborated only with himself. "On a Slow Boat to China" (1949) was one of his biggest hits, by which time he had also made his debut as composer and lyricist on Broadway. *Where's Charley?* (1948) was an adaptation of the 1892 British farce *Charley's Aunt,* designed as a vehicle for dancing comedian Ray Bolger. It served the purpose admirably, as well as producing two hits in the song and dance "Once in Love with Amy" and the love duet "My Darling, My Darling."

If there was nothing especially innovative about Loesser's songs for *Where's Charley?* his next show most emphatically made up for it. *Guys and Dolls* (1950) was described as a "musical fable of Broadway" and was based on the short stories of Damon Runyan and the quirky underworld characters who populated them. The idea came from the *Where's Charley?* production team of Cy Feuer and Ernest Martin, and the result was one of the most remarkable shows of American musical history. The book by Abe Burrows is based largely on Runyan's "The Idyll of Miss Sarah Brown," featuring gambler Nathan Detroit (played by Sam Levene) who runs "the oldest established permanent floating crap game in New York." For fourteen years he has been promising his nightclub "chantoosie" fiancée Adelaide (Vivian Blaine) that he will give it all up and settle down with her. His latest reason for postponing that happy day is the arrival in town of high-stakes gambler Sky Masterson (Robert Alda). In order to win the stake money for a game large enough to satisfy Sky, Nathan bets Sky that the latter cannot convince Sarah Brown (Isabel Bigley), a member of the Salvation Army, to accompany him on a trip to Havana. By promising to supply Sarah with "souls" to save at her mission sessions, and with the help of spiked drinks, Sky wins the bet but falls in love with Sarah. The next day, after defeating the other gamblers at the big game, Sky brings them to the mission. He agrees to marry Sarah, and Nathan too is forced to give up his crap game and marry Adelaide.

The show depends to a large extent on its lyrics to convey the flavour of Runyan's characters, and the importance of the songs lies in the way they are not just attractive settings of romantic, witty, or sophisticated words, but advance the mood, the action, and the characterisation. The opening number is a harmonisation of racing tips ("Fugue for Tinhorns"), after which the crap players comment on the influence of women in the exhilarating title song. Miss Adelaide then demonstrates her talents as a chantoosie in "A Bushel and a Peck" and, suffering a psychosomatic nose-drip brought on by frustration, bemoans Nathan's unwillingness to marry in "Adelaide's Lament." At the missionary session the typically Runyanesque Nicely-Nicely Johnson (Stubby Kaye) habitually stops the show with his "Sit Down, You're Rocking the Boat." So well integrated are the numbers

Eve Withers as Adelaide in Loesser's *Guys and Dolls*
Crawford Theatre Collection, Manuscripts
and Archives, Yale University

that even the joyous love songs "I've Never Been in Love Before" and "I'll Know" lose a dimension when detached from the show.

Loesser went on to create highly popular songs for Danny Kaye as Hollywood's *Hans Christian Andersen* (1952) and then returned to Broadway with a work that advanced the integration of book, dialogue, lyrics, song, dance, incidental music, and underscoring even further. So seamless is *The Most Happy Fella* (1956) that it was given the unique compliment of an original cast recording that, apart from one essentially visual scene, contained the complete musical, on three long-playing records. The show is an adaptation of Sidney Howard's play *They Knew What They Wanted* and tells of a portly, middle-aged Napa Valley winegrower, Tony Esposito (played by opera baritone Robert Weede), who takes a fancy to young San Francisco waitress Amy (Jo Sullivan). He leaves her a note with his address, from which a romantic correspondence develops. However, when Amy requests a photograph, he sends her a picture of his handsome young foreman Joe. An engagement results, and when Amy turns up for the wedding, complications develop. Amy becomes pregnant by Joe but ultimately finds happiness with Tony. For all its integrated quality, Loesser's score did not lack songs that could stand on their own, among them Tony's title song, the lighthearted English lesson "Happy to Make Your Acquaintance," the rousing (and vocally demanding) duet "My Heart Is So Full of You" and "Standing on the Corner (Watching All the Girls Go By)" for four ranch hands.

Loesser wrote three more musicals. In *Greenwillow* (1960) he failed with an idyll of bygone rural America, while *Pleasures and Palaces* (1965) did not even reach New York. In between, he created one further work that showed how the American musical had moved on from the period charm and set numbers of *Annie Get Your Gun* and *Kiss Me, Kate*. The title itself said as much—*How to Succeed in Business Without Really Trying* (1961). The idea of a musical about the business world was something that not even Loesser initially saw as promising; but he finally agreed to join the team of producers Feuer and Martin and book author Abe Burrows (his partners in *Guys and Dolls*). *How to Succeed in Business* had a run of 1,417 Broadway performances and probably would have been a success even without the music. But Loesser contributed a number of appealing songs, including "The Company Way" and "The Brotherhood of Man." Robert Morse played ambitious office window-cleaner J. Pierpont Finch, and ex-crooner Rudy Vallee was company president J. B. Biggley.

If Loesser's own theatrical output was not huge, he was instrumental in encouraging other writers who likewise specialised in integrated shows with essentially American subjects. Two particularly successful musical comedies of the 1950s originated from the short-lived partnership of two young composer-lyricists. Richard Adler (1921–), the son of a musician, took to songwriting after wartime navy service and in 1950 teamed up with Jerry Ross (1926–55). Loesser helped them get their chance on Broadway writing songs for a revue, and then came their first big hit with a book musical. This was *The Pajama Game* (1954), an adaptation by George Abbott and Richard Bissell of the latter's novel of romance and intrigue between bosses and trade union representatives in a pajama factory. John Raitt played Sid Sorokin, the factory foreman, and Janis Paige was the provocatively named Babe, the boss of the union's Grievance Committee. The modern setting was matched by the bright, brassy orchestral sounds of songs such as Babe's "I'm Not At All in Love," the duet "Small Talk," Sid's soliloquy into his dictaphone "Hey There (You With the Stars in Your Eyes)," and the Act 2 tango "Hernando's Hideaway." The piece was notable for introducing to the Broadway musical not only Adler and Ross but other big names of the future: Harold Prince (a member of the production team), Jerome Robbins (in his first directorial, as opposed to choreographical, role), and choreographer Bob Fosse.

Except for Robbins, the same creative team was present for the follow-up.

Ballplayers in Adler and Ross's *Damn Yankees*
Fosse/Verdon Collection, Music Division, Library of Congress

Damn Yankees (1955) is another sports musical, this time about baseball, but it is also a version of the Faust legend. To help the local baseball team win the pennant, Joe Hardy (played by Stephen Douglass) sells his soul to the devil (Ray Alton), after which he is transformed from paunchy middle-aged spectator to all-conquering baseball hero. Eventually, he concludes that less elevated ambitions provide greater rewards. The devil's assistant was played by Gwen Verdon, singing to great effect the tango "Whatever Lola Wants, Lola Gets." There is also a marvellous comedy number in which the baseball players unconvincingly profess themselves immune to such distractions as booze and women when they are thinking about "The Game." However, the big hit of the show was the players' declaration "(You've Got to Have) Heart." *Damn Yankees* was an even greater success than *The Pajama Game* and ran for more than 1,000 performances. Though its co-author and director George Abbott was already in his late sixties, he was still around in 1994 to be involved at the age of 107 in a major Broadway revival of the musical. By contrast, just six months after the première, the show's co-author Jerry Ross died from a long-term lung ailment at the age of only twenty-nine. Richard Adler wrote the scores for three more musicals—*Kwamina* (1961), *A Mother's Kisses* (1968), and *Music Is* (1976)—but none achieved more than minor acclaim.

The most obvious successor to *The Pajama Game* and *Damn Yankees,* but one that ultimately outclassed them, came from a composer a generation older than Adler and Ross. Meredith Willson (1902–84) had been a flautist in the Sousa Band and the New York Philharmonic during the 1920s, a musical director on the radio during the 1930s, and a composer of band, orchestral, and film music during the 1940s. *The Music Man* (1957), staged at the Majestic Theatre, home of several of the Rodgers and Hammerstein shows, was his first stage musical. The big hit, "Seventy-Six Trombones," a throwback to (and updating of) Sousa marches, became widely known beyond the show. Yet those who know only that number know little of *The Music Man.* What is remarkable about Willson's score is its variety of musical styles and the degree of integration of words and music. The tenderly reflective "Goodnight, My Someone" and the beautifully lyrical duet "Till There Was You" contrast with the liltingly rhythmic "Gary, Indiana" and the barber-shop quartet's "Sincere" and "Lida Rose." There is something Sullivanesque in the way Willson combines the men's "Goodnight Ladies" with the "Pick-a-Little, Talk-a-Little" ensemble for gossipy townswomen. The latter is a fine example of Willson's musical onomatopoeia, which is used even more remarkably in the opening number, where the conversation of a group of travelling salesmen is set to the rhythm of the train wheels.

The show helped further the reputation of soprano Barbara Cook (fresh from *Candide*) as the innocent young librarian Marian Parco. However, the show revolves around the character of conman and would-be "Professor" Harold Hill, a traveller in musical instruments. Its creator, Robert Preston, had no previous experience in musicals and no pretensions to singing ability; but Willson wrote melodies suited to Preston's limited range and songs that used a kind of half-spoken patter, as in his opening number "Trouble." Significantly, it was Frank Loesser who suggested that Willson should create a musical from his boyhood reminiscences of his native Iowa. Not without reason has it been said that "if *Guys and Dolls* is the most New York of Broadway musicals, *The Music Man* is surely the most American."

Having distilled the product of many years' inspiration into *The Music Man,* Willson could scarcely be expected to repeat its success. On its own terms *The Unsinkable Molly Brown* (1960) is a worthy piece, with a similarly American story about a real-life Colorado woman (played by Tammy Grimes), an uncultured nouveau riche who fails in her attempts to be accepted in Denver's high society. Only when she happens to cross the Atlantic on the *Titanic* and, in surviving its sinking, becomes accepted as a heroine, does she finally achieve the so-

Tammy Grimes in Willson's *The Unsinkable Molly Brown*
Theatre Guild Records, Beinecke Rare Book and Manuscript Library, Yale University

cial recognition she sought. In a fashion that outdid Novello's *Glamorous Night* and anticipated a later Broadway show, the sinking of the *Titanic* is portrayed on stage. Willson's score produced enjoyable echoes of the brilliance of *The Music Man* in the rousing "I Ain't Down Yet," the gentle "Chick-a-Pen," and the "Pick-a-Little, Talk-a-Little" soundalike "Keep-a-Hoppin'." It enjoyed a fine run and was made into a movie, but it never challenged its predecessor's great success. Still less did *Here's Love* (1963) and *1491* (1969)—the latter of which did not even reach Broadway.

The demise of the partnerships of Rodgers and Hammerstein and Lerner and Loewe effectively ended their style of romantic American musical. However, Jule Styne continued his trademark brassy musicals. *Say, Darling* (1958) was a comical backstage piece based on a novel by Richard Bissell (creator of *The Pajama Game*) about turning a novel into a musical. The lyrics were by Betty Comden and Adolph Green. Instead of an orchestra, the show used two pianos to represent the atmosphere of rehearsals, providing a foretaste of the sixties break with traditional orchestral trappings that was part inspirational, part sheer economic reality.

Styne then achieved his greatest success in partnership with lyricist Stephen Sondheim, *Gypsy* (1959). Based on the memoirs of legendary stripper Gypsy Rose Lee, the action actually centres around the stripper's mother, Rose, a part designed especially for Ethel Merman. Rose seeks to attain through her two daughters the glory she never achieved herself, and she tours them in an undistinguished act of her own devising. Her prime hope is the younger, Baby June; but June escapes her mother's clutches by eloping with a fellow performer. This leaves Louise, who, when a top-billed stripper fails to turn up, steps in and strips off to huge acclaim as Gypsy Rose Lee. That the show has survived better than Styne's other scores may partly reflect Sondheim's contribution; but the score also contains two of Styne's strongest showstoppers in Rose's raucous "Everything's Coming up Roses" and the all-purpose "Let Me Entertain You," which is shamelessly reprised throughout the evening.

Styne returned to Comden and Green for *Do Re Mi* (1960) and *Subways Are for Sleeping* (1961), both of which were produced by David Merrick. The former had comic duo Phil Silvers and Nancy Walker, though the hit number, "Make Someone Happy," was sung by romantic baritone lead John Reardon. The show managed a decent run, which was more than could be said for *Subways Are for Sleeping,* whose poor reviews provoked Merrick into hyping it with eulogistic quotes from members of the public who happened to have the same names as well-known critics. The ruse failed to make much difference.

Success returned for Styne three years later with a work he collaborated on with Bob Merrill (1921–98), who had made a name in the early 1950s as writer of novelty songs such as "If I Knew You Were Comin' I'd've Baked a Cake" (1950), "My Truly, Truly Fair" (1951), "How Much Is that Doggie in the Window?" (1953), and "Where Will the Dimple Be?" (1955). He then turned to Broadway, providing music and lyrics for *New Girl in Town* (1957), an adaptation by George Abbott of Eugene O'Neill's *Anna Christie*. With Gwen Verdon in the title role it ran for a year, as did another O'Neill adaptation, *Take Me Along* (1959), though neither added significantly to Merrill's list of hit songs. Then came *Carnival* (1961), for which Merrill again provided music and lyrics to a book by Michael Stewart that was an adaptation of the screenplay (based in turn on a Paul Gallico story) for the highly successful 1953 film *Lili*. This is the tale of an orphan who finds work in a circus and, through her love for a team of puppets, eventually falls in love with their creator. The parts played on film by Leslie Caron and Mel Ferrer were re-created for the stage by Anna Maria Alberghetti and Jerry Orbach. David Merrick, as producer-choreographer, contributed greatly to the success of the piece with his circus effects; but no less important was Merrill's varied score, which produced a big hit in the gentle waltz "Love Makes the World Go Round."

Instead of building on this success as composer-lyricist, Merrill allied his lyric-writing ability to Jule Styne's musical style for the song-and-dance musical comedy *Funny Girl* (1964). A romanticised version of the career of 1920s Ziegfeld Follies star Fanny Brice, the musical was built around her on-off relationship with shady-dealing sometime husband Nick Arnstein. The latter role was played by Sydney Chaplin, but his contribution was overshadowed by the overwhelming performance of Barbra Streisand in the title role. The show ran for more than three years, helped by the worldwide success of Streisand's two big numbers, the reflective "People" and the barnstorming "Don't Rain on My Parade."

Funny Girl proved to be not only the longest-running Broadway success for both Styne and Merrill but also the last major success for either. Styne went on writing new shows virtually up to his death at the age of eighty-eight, but only two had significant runs. *Hallelujah, Baby!* (1967) had a book by Arthur Laurents and lyrics by Comden and Green and was an ambitious attempt to portray racial issues over a period of sixty years. For *Sugar* (1972), Styne and Merrill teamed up once again for an adaptation of the Billy Wilder film *Some Like It Hot*. This had been a major success for Marilyn Monroe, as well as for her co-stars Jack Lemmon and Tony Curtis as two 1920s Chicago jazz musicians who witness the notorious gangland slaying the St. Valentine's Day Massacre and feel obliged to "disappear" by disguising themselves as women. But the musical version achieved only modest acclaim.

By the 1960s Styne and Merrill and others of their era were in turn being eclipsed by a new generation of Broadway writers, who eschewed the romantic, realistically staged works of the Rodgers and Hammerstein variety in favour of moving the action along at a slicker pace, with swift changes of all-purpose scenery. Among the leading composers of this new wave was Jerry Bock (1928–), who studied music at the University of Wisconsin, where he wrote material for college and camp shows and later for radio, television, and revues. He reached Broadway as a collaborator with lyricist Larry Holofcener (1926–) for shows that included *Mr. Wonderful* (1956), of which George Weiss was co-composer. This was less a book musical than a vehicle conceived by Jule Styne (as producer) for the song-and-dance talents of Sammy Davis, Jr. The weakness of the book and of Davis's acting was less important than a score that included two numbers—the title song and "Too Close for Comfort"—that were big hits not only for the original cast but for the likes of Peggy Lee, Sarah Vaughan, and Eydie Gorme.

Shortly after the show's opening, Bock was introduced to lyricist Sheldon Harnick (1924–), who became his regular collaborator. Their first joint effort was a none-too-successful piece about prize fighters entitled *The Body Beautiful* (1956), but the songs impressed George Abbott sufficiently for him to hire the pair to write a musical about Fiorello H. La Guardia. La Guardia had been a successful lawyer, who unexpectedly rose on an anticorruption ticket to Republican membership of the House of Representatives before ousting New York mayor "Jimmy" Walker. His name lived on through the New York airport named after him.

In the musical *Fiorello!* (1959) the part of La Guardia made a star of little-known Tom Bosley, specially chosen because of his uncanny physical resemblance to La Guardia. But even more notable was the way that Bock and Harnick captured the period flavour and the double-dealing world of New York politics in a brassy, jazzy score that in its lighthearted contrasting of virtue and corruption bears similarities to that of *Guys and Dolls*. Right at the start any suggestion of sanctimoniousness is removed when La Guardia's employees sing their tongue-in-cheek declaration of being "On the Side of the Angels." Then comes a delightful chorus, "Home Again," and two charming romantic numbers, "'Til Tomorrow" and "When Did I Fall in Love?" for strike-leader Thea, who becomes La Guardia's first wife. What especially stand out in the score are two splendidly satirical numbers for New York Republican leader Ben Marino (Howard da Silva) and his supporters. In "Politics and Poker" they consider candidates for the apparently hopeless Republican ticket in the forthcoming elections, while in "Little Tin Box" they react to suggestions of financial corruption by describing how, by such means as returning empty bottles to the grocer for the deposit and going without lunches for a week, they saved up their small change.

Like the Gershwins' *Of Thee I Sing, Fiorello!* was awarded a Pulitzer Prize. The whole venture was deemed so successful that the team of producers Harold Prince and Robert E. Griffiths, book authors George Abbott and Jerome Weidman, and songwriters Bock and Harnick was kept intact for a successor, *Tenderloin* (1960). This was an even more straightforward period piece, with lively vaudeville elements capturing the New York of the 1890s. Maurice Evans was the crusading Rev. Andrew Brock, who seeks to wipe out the immorality and corruption of the area of New York known as the Tenderloin. It proved an amiable, enjoyable, but ultimately unremarkable piece, despite such promotional efforts as getting the original cast album on sale within forty-eight hours of recording and within eight days of the New York première.

Things picked up again for Bock and Harnick with an adaptation of a 1937 Hungarian play about two workers in a perfume shop who heartily dislike each other without realising that they are involved in a lonely hearts correspondence with each other. The piece had already had two Hollywood adaptations, as *The Shop Around the Corner* (1940) and *In the Good Old Summertime* (1949). For its 1963 stage musical adaptation as *She Loves Me* the piece was reset in New York, but with the Hungarian flavour retained by having the shop run by Hungarian immigrants. Barbara Cook played Amalia Blash, Daniel Massey her apparently incompatible co-worker George Nowack, and Jack Cassidy the scheming, two-timing Steve Kodály, whose eventual sacking helps move matters along the path to happiness. There is also a Hungarian flavouring to the score, which includes two charming numbers for the heroine ("Ice Cream" and "Dear Friend") and a lively title song for the hero. Another effective touch is a brief chorus, "Thank You, Madam," which is repeated throughout the piece whenever a sale is completed.

The reputation of *She Loves Me* grew after its original production, earning an abridged British television production in the 1980s and revivals on both sides of the Atlantic in the 1990s. By contrast, the success of the next Bock-Harnick creation was immediate. Indeed, it was to prove not only their own biggest hit but one of the greatest international musical successes of its time. *Fiddler on the Roof* (1964) is based on the stories of the Russian-American humorist Sholom Aleichem and concerns the breakdown of traditional ways of life among Jews in the Russian village of Anatevka in the early twentieth century. Tradition is represented by dairyman Tevye and his wife Golde; the desire for change, by their five daughters, who reject the marriage partners arranged for them. Into this largely generational dispute come the pogroms, which finish off the village and force the remaining family members to emigrate to America. Zero Mostel was the first of a series of performers around the world who were to make their names with the role of Tevye, with his philosophical hit song "If I Were a Rich Man." Future operatic soprano Julia Migenes created the supporting role of Hodel, one of the daughters whose appeal to the "Matchmaker" to bring her a suitable husband added to the show's wide-ranging popularity, along with the haunting chorus "Sunrise, Sunset." As well as winning a host of awards, the show's 3,242 Broadway performances set a new record and prefaced worldwide popularity on stage and screen.

If Bock and Harnick could scarcely top this, their two further collaborations did confirm their reputations. *The Apple Tree* (1966) was a clever compilation of three one-act pieces in very different styles, with the linking theme of temptation and with leading characters played by the same two performers, Alan Alda and Barbara Harris. That the show could overcome public aversion to one-act pieces sufficiently to achieve 463 Broadway performances was a mark of its quality. Next Bock and Harnick turned to another overtly Jewish theme in *The Rothschilds* (1970). Based on Frederic Morton's history of the international banking family, it featured Hal Linden as the founder of the dynasty, Mayer Amschel Rothschild, whose five sons build up branches in various European capitals and, after their father's death, help abolish the Frankfurt ghetto and its exclusionary laws. Though the sophisticated and wealthy Rothschilds were never going to excite popular sympathy as readily as the downtrodden peasants of Anatevka, the show still managed more than five hundred performances.

    The Rothschilds was the final collaboration for Bock and Harnick. Still in his early forties, Bock decided to concentrate on writing his own lyrics, but he never succeeded in getting another show produced. Harnick, by contrast, became one of a series of lyricists in the third phase of the career of the remarkably durable Richard Rodgers. Following the death of Oscar Hammerstein in 1959, Rodgers sought to write shows in a more modern idiom, at first adding to his roles of composer and producer that of lyricist. In *No Strings* (1962) Diahann Carroll and Richard Kiley played a black woman and white man who maintain and eventually end a relationship with no strings attached. Rodgers took up the current fashion for the "concept" musical by eliminating the orchestra in the pit and introducing a small onstage ensemble that, quite literally, had no strings. Besides the elegant title song, the score produced another hit in "The Sweetest Sounds."

    In spite of the satisfaction of being able to awaken at 4 A.M. and go to work on a song without waiting for some outside lyricist to provide words, Rodgers did not remain his own lyricist. Instead, he collaborated next with Oscar Hammerstein's protégé Stephen Sondheim, who already had under his belt the lyrics to *West Side Story* and *Gypsy,* and both lyrics and music to *A Funny Thing Happened on the Way to the Forum* and *Anyone Can Whistle.* The romantic Rodgers and cynical Sondheim were opposites who increasingly regretted their collaboration. But, just as conflicts of personality were no hindrance to success for Gilbert and Sullivan, so the collaboration of Rodgers and Sondheim beneficially served to tone down the extremes of both. The result was an endearing comic-romantic piece that paid homage to Venice with some of the success of *The Gondoliers* three-quarters of a century earlier. *Do I Hear a Waltz?* (1965) was based by Arthur Laurents on his play *The Time of the Cuckoo,* about an ageing woman who finds love with a married man while on holiday in Venice. As a straight play with Shirley Booth and a film with Katharine Hepburn, it had enjoyed popular acclaim. As a musical with Elizabeth Allen as the leading lady and Sergio Franchi as the Venetian with whom she has a brief affair, the show was less successful commercially. However, the score contains two fine numbers in the title song and the beautiful "Moon in My Window," and its collaborators' eminence has enabled the show to survive and demonstrate its charms to a later generation.

Rodgers's final three scores were each a succès d'estime but little more. *Two by Two* (1970) had lyrics by Martin Charnin (1934–), who had played one of the Jets in the original *West Side Story.* The new work was an adaptation of a Noah's Ark story by Clifford Odets, with Danny Kaye as a six-hundred-year-old Noah. Alas, Kaye increasingly usurped the show to satisfy his ego, not least when, after tearing ligaments in his ankle, he continued to appear, in a wheelchair and on crutches. Rodgers afterwards had his sole collaboration with Sheldon Harnick on the short-lived *Rex* (1976), which owed its early demise to an unwieldy book about the relationships of Henry VIII (played by Nicol Williamson) with his various wives and (in the second act) his daughter Elizabeth. Martin Charnin was again one of the lyricists on Rodgers's final score, the charmingly old-fashioned *I Remember Mama* (1979), about an immigrant Norwegian mother raising a family during difficult times in turn-of-the-century San Francisco. By the end of 1979, however, Rodgers—one of the most enduring and inventive of theatre composers —was dead.

Another of the American musical's creative partnerships began when journalist-lyricist Lee Adams (1924–) teamed up in 1950 with Charles Strouse (1928–), a composition student of Nadia Boulanger's in Paris. Together they wrote songs for television and nightclubs, and acquired Broadway exposure through the small-scale revues of Ben Bagley: *The Littlest Revue* (1956) and *Shoestring '57* (1957). Then they collaborated with book author Michael Stewart on *Bye Bye Birdie* (1960), a piece that had its roots in the rock-and-roll phenomenon of Elvis Presley. Pop idol Conrad Birdie has just achieved cult status when he is drafted into the army. His manager Albert Peterson (played by Dick Van Dyke) is under pressure from his secretary-girlfriend Rosie (Chita Rivera) to get a steady job, but he insists on staging one last promotion, in which Conrad will bid farewell to his fans by kissing fifteen-year-old Kim McAfee. Unfortunately, after he does it, her boyfriend knocks him out and Conrad is arrested for consorting with a minor. Albert finally throws the pop business over and seek a more peace-

Susan Watson as Kim and Dick Gautier as Conrad in
Adams and Strouse's *Bye Bye Birdie,* 1960
Photo by Friedman-Abeles. Wisconsin Center for
Film and Theater Research.

ful life with Rosie. The delightfully tongue-in-cheek book was helped by a score
that included such catchy songs as the fans' "We Love You, Conrad" and two
numbers that became big individual successes: Albert's encouragement to the fans
to "Put on a Happy Face" and Conrad's acknowledgement that he'd got "A Lot of
Livin' to Do."

Though this refreshingly original show won its authors a Tony award and
a sizeable run, none of their jointly created successors was to attain the same
heights. *All American* (1962) was a vehicle for Ray Bolger, with a book by comedy
writer Mel Brooks, about a Central European professor who arrives in America
and puts all sorts of intellectual slants on the most basic aspects of modern America. Numbers such as the nostalgic ballad "Once Upon a Time" were insufficient to give the show more than a modest run. There were mixed reviews, too,

for *Golden Boy* (1964), an adaptation of a 1937 Clifford Odets play, which owed its 569-performance run largely to the appeal of Sammy Davis, Jr., as gifted but sensitive Joe Wellington, who bets his future on his ability as a boxer. Then Strouse and Adams sought to find a counterpart of the "pop" world that had given them early success by turning to the Superman comic strip. *It's a Bird, It's a Plane, It's Superman* (1966), with Jack Cassidy in the title role, proved an undisguised flop.

The show that finally gave the Strouse-Adams partnership a second major success ten years after the first was *Applause* (1970), for which Betty Comden and Adolph Green were book authors. It was an adaptation of Joseph L. Mankiewicz's screenplay for the 1950 cult film *All About Eve,* which had starred Bette Davis and Anne Baxter. In the musical another screen idol, Lauren Bacall, played the part of ageing star Margo Channing. Her status is gradually usurped by young fan Eve Harrington (Penny Fuller), who works, contrives, and sleeps her way into a starring role that was to have been Margo's. The latter's consolation comes first from the knowledge that she herself would have done much the same twenty years earlier, and second from the reassurance given by her faithful partner Bill (Len Cariou). Bacall won a Tony award as Best Actress and the show was voted "Best Musical." The most successful number was the title song, performed by a subsidiary character and the show's dancers, about the kick a performer gets from applause.

Strouse and Adams wrote three more shows together—*I and Albert* (1972) for London, followed by *A Broadway Musical* (1979) and a final attempt to cash in on their earliest success with *Bring Back Birdie* (1981). None lasted more than a few performances, and Adams never had another hit. Strouse, though, went on to his greatest triumph in collaboration with Martin Charnin. *Annie* (1976) was seen first at the Goodspeed Opera House, a restored Victorian theatre in East Haddam, Connecticut, which had become a breeding ground for new musicals as well as a place to revive forgotten musicals of old.

Annie was based on the cartoon strip *Little Orphan Annie,* which had been enchanting readers of the *Chicago Tribune* and other newspapers since 1924. Annie (played by Andrea McArdle) is a precocious little orphan, who is anxious to escape from the home run by tyrannical Miss Hannigan (Dorothy Loudon). She eventually succeeds by being chosen to spend a luxurious Christmas with the bald, wealthy, and powerful Daddy Warbucks (Reid Shelton). She charms him so much that he is moved to broadcast an appeal for the parents Annie believes would gladly rescue her permanently from the orphanage. No one answers, but Annie finds herself a worthy replacement father in Warbucks himself. The book

Goodspeed Opera House, East Haddam, Connecticut
Photo by Diane Sobolewski. Courtesy of Goodspeed Opera House.

by Thomas Meehan was pitched to appeal to adults and children alike, as were the old-fashioned songs: Annie's dream of her missing family ("Maybe"), her optimistic declaration that the sun will come out "Tomorrow," the orphan children's agreement that "It's a Hard-Knock Life," and the radio station's 1930s-style radio jingle "You're Never Fully Dressed Without a Smile." The show ran for 2,377 performances on Broadway, was staged around the world, and spawned a successful film. However, Meehan, Charnin, and Strouse had little success with an unimaginatively titled sequel *Annie 2* (1990), even after they revised it as *Annie Warbucks* (1992). Nor did Strouse do any better with a range of collaborators on shows that included *Dance a Little Closer* (1983) with Alan Jay Lerner, *Rags* (1986) with Stephen Schwartz, and *Nick and Nora* (1991) with Richard Maltby, Jr.

By the time this new generation of songwriters had emerged around 1960, the economics of Broadway had undergone radical changes. Postwar prosperity had increased the costs of major productions to the point where lengthy runs were needed to make a profit. The alternative was to cut costs and to stage on a smaller scale in less prestigious surroundings. This was the origin of the off-Broadway show, which had an early success in *Once Upon a Mattress* (1959), a small-scale burlesque retelling of "The Princess and the Pea." The appealing score, headed by such endearing numbers as "In a Little While" and "Shy," was by Mary Rodgers (1931–), daughter of Richard Rodgers. Rodgers emulated her father by collaborating with Stephen Sondheim on songs for the revue *The Mad Show* (1966), but soon thereafter declared herself disenchanted with Broadway.

The off-Broadway show par excellence was *The Fantasticks* (1960), which got its economics so right with its small cast, two-piano and percussion accompaniment, and word-of-mouth publicity that, at the time of writing—40 years later—it is still running. The piece had a sound literary source in Edmond Rostand's *Les Romanesques,* which was adapted by book author, lyricist, and performer Tom Jones (1928–), with music by his college-student colleague Harvey Schmidt (1929–). The piece tells of the romantic ins-and-outs of childhood sweethearts Matt (played by Kenneth Nelson) and Luisa (Rita Gardener) before they are finally united. The success of the show was cemented by a couple of charming duets, "Soon It's Gonna Rain" and "They Were You," and above all a song performed by compère-tempter El Gallo (Jerry Orbach) at the start of the show —the gentle "Try to Remember."

The show's success led to Schmidt and Jones being signed up for Broadway. Their *110 in the Shade* (1963) was an adaptation by N. Richard Nash of his play *The Rainmaker,* about Lizzie Curry (Inga Swenson), a country girl whose family's livelihood is threatened by drought. She falls for the blandishments of Starbuck (Robert Horton), who claims to be able to make the rain fall—for a price. He is, of course, a complete charlatan; but at least Lizzie enjoys a brief romance with him. This surpasses anything she can get from divorced sheriff File (Stephen Douglass), but she has to settle for the latter when Starbuck is drummed out of town. Then the rain comes of its own accord. Schmidt and Jones produced an atmospheric score with agreeable numbers such as Starbuck's "Rain Song," his quarrel duet with Lizzie "You're Not Fooling Me," and the tender "Is It Really Me?" which Lizzie sings in his arms just before he is revealed as an impostor. For all its quality, the show achieved only a modest run.

For their next show Schmidt and Jones contrived to combine characteristics of each of their two earlier pieces. Though produced for a regular Broadway theatre, the cast was even smaller than that of *The Fantasticks*—just two performers. But the two were stars who, since *South Pacific* and *The Music Man,* re-

Cast of Schmidt and Jones's *Fantasticks,* 1960
Photo by Bender. Wisconsin Center for Film and Theater Research.

spectively, had been leading lights of the American musical theatre. *I Do! I Do!* (1966) was an adaptation of Jan de Hartog's play *The Fourposter,* with Mary Martin as Agnes and Robert Preston as Michael. It covered their fifty years of marriage, with the same bed and bedroom being the scene of a youthful marriage, two childbirths, successes, infidelities, and various other difficulties, before the departure of the children leads to a final marital contentment. The songs brilliantly captured the contrasted feelings of the couple in the loving duet "My Cup Runneth Over," the marital nit-picking of "Nobody's Perfect," and the expression of parental ambitions, "When the Kids Get Married." The show had a run of 561 Broadway performances, as well as several foreign productions, but it was the last of the Schmidt-Jones successes. *Celebration* (1969) ran for 110 performances, and several attempts to make a success of *Colette* (1970), about the French novelist, proved abortive.

A greater individual, if isolated, success was achieved by Mitch Leigh (1928–) through his musical adaptation of Cervantes's *Don Quixote*. *Man of La Mancha* (1965) was another work that began at the Goodspeed Opera House before moving on to Broadway. The immediate source was a television adaptation of the book by Dale Wasserman, with dramatic structure provided by the play-within-a-play concept. Richard Kiley and Irving Jacobson played the parts of Cervantes and Sancho Panza, acting out the story of the fanciful knight and his rotund vassal before fellow prisoners as they wait their turn to be called before the Inquisition. Ray Middleton had a supporting role as an innkeeper, with opera singer Robert Rounseville as a priest. The show ran for 2,328 performances on Broadway and achieved international currency matched only by the likes of *My Fair Lady* and *Fiddler on the Roof.* This was helped by its classical European setting and by a Spanish-guitar–flavoured score that proved a welcome departure from the all-American subjects currently popular in the Broadway musical. Don Quixote's expression of his personal philosophy, "The Impossible Dream," became an international hit, and the score had enough lyrical content to make it one of the few musicals welcomed into opera houses.

One way and another, these shows of the 1960s onwards were providing an altogether more varied approach to staging than the traditional romanticised shows that had survived through the 1950s in the creations of Rodgers and Hammerstein, Cole Porter, and the like. In part the changes were encouraged by the economics of the period, which increased the cost of traditional theatrical resources (human and otherwise) at a time when the cinema and television were also making audiences more demanding. In part, too, they were a product of the far greater freedom of expression that pervaded the straight as well as musical theatre at a time of greater sexual openness.

So far we have examined various teams that flourished in this new environment, whilst ignoring the most creative minds of all, whom we shall now consider in the next chapter.

Chapter Sixteen
Coleman, Kander and Ebb,
Herman, and Sondheim

The quarter-century from 1943 to the late 1960s was perhaps the core period of the development of the American musical. Besides those composers and lyricists already considered who emerged during the 1950s, there are four other creative influences who stand out for the works they produced in the latter part of that core period and since: composer-lyricists Stephen Sondheim and Jerry Herman, the team of composer John Kander and lyricist Fred Ebb, and (with various lyricists) the composer Cy Coleman.

Coleman (1929–) early on revealed his versatility as a brilliant pianist. Classically educated, in his twenties he moved in the jazz world as well, performing with his own trio. Jazz influences have always come naturally into his songwriting from his first big success, "Witchcraft" (1957). This he wrote in collaboration with Carolyn Leigh (1926–81), who was also the lyricist for his first Broadway musical. *Wildcat* (1960) concerns a brash young woman named Wildcat Jackson, who bluffs her way around the oilfields of the American South seeking to earn money to support her crippled sister. Having attracted the attention of foreman Joe Dynamite, she contrives through a combination of jealousy and good luck to make her fortune with a successful oil strike, winning Joe at the same time. The show was written for television star Lucille Ball, and its run was curtailed when she left the cast. Her role has a down-to-earth, breezy quality that is reminiscent of Annie Oakley in *Annie Get Your Gun*. *Wildcat's* attractively varied numbers include "Give a Little Whistle" and an instruction on how to act like a lady ("Tippy, Tippy Toes"); but everything was dwarfed by the popularity of her encouragement to her lame sister, "Hey, Look Me Over!"

A second Coleman-Leigh musical was an adaptation by comic playwright Neil Simon of a Patrick Dennis novel that burlesqued stage autobiographies. The title character of *Little Me* (1962) is ageing Belle Poitrine (Nancy Andrews), who is dictating her memoirs, which tell in flashback her progress from humble beginnings via a succession of liaisons to a kind of social eminence. Apart from George Musgrove, the man who pursued her from the start and finally ends up with her, her various lovers were played by a single comic performer—television comedian Sid Caesar. Coleman produced another varied score that burlesques various showbiz styles and has three big hits: Belle's "The Other Side of the Tracks," George's "I've Got Your Number," and above all the leading man's big production number, "A Real Live Girl." The show's attractions were heightened by Bob Fosse's choreography.

Coleman's next musical again saw him working with Simon and Fosse, but his lyricist was now the veteran Dorothy Fields. The result was Coleman's greatest success. *Sweet Charity* (1966) was based on the award-winning Federico Fellini film *Nights of Cabiria,* about a curiously innocent, generous, and ever-optimistic Roman prostitute. Softened for the Broadway stage, it tells of Charity Hope Valentine, a dance hostess in a seedy New York ballroom who is anxious to settle down in a steady relationship. She finds her ideal man in tax accountant Oscar Linquist, whom she meets when they are trapped in an elevator. Having led him to believe that she works in a bank, she worries about being exposed as a liar,

Gwen Verdon, Helen Gallagher, and Thelma Oliver
in Coleman's *Sweet Charity*
Fosse/Verdon Collection, Music Division, Library of Congress

but in fact he knows all about her background and believes that he wants to marry her anyway. Eventually he cannot bring himself to do so, leaving Charity to pick up the pieces and resume her former life.

The musical was a showcase for Fosse's wife Gwen Verdon, star of such hit shows as *Can-Can* and *Damn Yankees*. It was hugely popular and became an equally successful film with Shirley MacLaine. Coleman's brassy, jazz-tinged, rhythmically invigorating score is blessed with several stirring numbers. In "Big Spender," Charity and some of the other girls at the Fandango dance palace parade their services; in "If My Friends Could See Me Now," Charity marvels at the sumptuous apartment she finds herself in after she is picked up by film star Vittorio Vidal; in "The Rhythm of Life," she is taken by Oscar to the Rhythm of

Life Church; and in the strutting "I'm a Brass Band," Charity expresses her elation that Oscar wants to marry her. Nowhere has Coleman's invigorating style been shown to better advantage.

It was seven years before Coleman came up with his next stage score, for which he added the role of producer of the original-cast recording. *Seesaw* (1973) again had lyrics by Dorothy Fields and was a similarly brassy piece based on a 1950s play, *Two on a Seesaw*, which featured just two characters, originally played by Henry Fonda and Anne Bancroft. In its musical adaptation it underwent a great deal of change and much tribulation; new characters were added, representing various aspects of trendy New York, including a group of Puerto Ricans performing *Hamlet*. Its central story is of sober, besuited, provincial Jerry Ryan, who comes to New York and falls in love with Bohemian Gittel Mosca. If this bears some resemblance to the basic plot of *Sweet Charity*, so does a score that brought forth song standards in the leading lady's "Nobody Does It Like Me" and the showstopping chorus "It's Not Where You Start." The choreography of Michael Bennett and his assistant, Tommy Tune, won a Tony award.

Recognising the economic realities of the time, Coleman's next score was on a much smaller scale, featuring just four characters plus an onstage orchestra of four musicians who wander into and out of the story. *I Love My Wife* (1977) was a lighthearted commentary on the permissive age. A piece about wife-swapping —or, at any rate, *attempted* wife-swapping—it shows how the attempts of the two male characters to set up an extramarital foursome for some festive fun come to nothing both because of their inexperience and their eventual recognition that they love their wives.

For his next show Coleman finally won his first Tony award for what was a far from typical score. *On the Twentieth Century* (1978) boasted a book and lyrics by Betty Comden and Adolph Green; it was based loosely on a 1932 play (and a later film) about a luxury train that travelled between New York and Chicago. Coleman supplied the piece not with the pseudo-1930s dance music that might have been expected but with a burlesque comic-opera style. John Cullum played flamboyant impresario Oscar Jaffee, who books a compartment on the train next to his former protégée and mistress Lily Garland (played by Madeline Kahn). He plans to woo her back to his management for a spectacular production to be financed by an elderly religious fanatic (Imogene Coca), and the hilarious episodes before Oscar finally gets the girl include the discovery that his backer is an escaped lunatic. Sharing the honours were director Harold Prince, designer Robin

Wagner (whose train set moved and opened up to splendid effect) and understudy Judy Kaye, who deputised to such storybook effect that Kahn was asked to stand down in her favour.

Much more in the usual brassy Coleman mode was another show-business piece, based on the career of legendary showman P. T. Barnum. *Barnum* (1980), with lyrics by Michael Stewart, offered a partly realistic, partly stylised representation of the circus environment, including a variety of circus acts and exhibits, from the dwarf General Tom Thumb to the famous soprano Jenny Lind. The show required leading man Jim Dale to walk a tightrope and introduced future movie star Glenn Close as his wife. Coleman's score is at its best in Barnum's duet with his wife, "The Colors of My Life," and in the jazzy, swinging march "Come Follow the Band."

Coleman had a flop with *Welcome to the Club* (1988), later revised hardly more successfully as *Exactly Like You* (1998). However, with lyricist David Zippel, he struck gold again with *City of Angels* (1989). This time there was a jazzy 1930s score for a story set in the era of the silent movies. Gregg Edelman played Stine, a writer who has been lured to Hollywood to turn his detective novel about a private eye named Stone into a screenplay. Apart from the ballad "With Every Breath I Take," the score contains no really outstanding number, but it helps along a brilliantly contrived and witty book by Larry Gelbart in which screenplay and real life intermingle to hilarious effect.

For *The Will Rogers Follies* (1991), Coleman was reunited with lyricists Comden and Green, as well as with director-choreographer Tommy Tune. Like *Barnum,* the piece is a showbiz biography, covering the appearances in Ziegfeld's spectacular revues of the Wild West cowboy and raconteur Will Rogers. Alas, Rogers's life was insufficiently eventful to provide another *Barnum,* and the complex dramatic structure failed to work as successfully as it did in *City of Angels.* Yet, with Keith Carradine in the starring role, it provided unpretentious entertainment and won another "best musical" Tony award. In his most recent show, *The Life* (1997), Coleman offered a salute to the former theatre district of 42nd Street during its sordid depression years of the 1980s.

If John Kander (1927–) has not matched Coleman's versatility and originality as a composer, he has produced snappy, attractive songs, and has been blessed with a long-lasting lyricist partnership. Kander began his musical theatre career as pianist, musical director, and arranger of dance music for shows that included Jule Styne's *Gypsy.* His first Broadway score, *A Family Affair* (1962), written with brothers James and William Goldman, had a modest run. Then he teamed up with lyricist Fred Ebb (1932–), with whom he has worked ever since. Their early output included songs recorded by Barbra Streisand before they tried their hand at a Broadway show. With Harold Prince as producer, George Abbott as director and book co-author, and Liza Minnelli in the title role, *Flora, the Red Menace* (1965) had all the elements for success. However, the Kander and Ebb songs, linked to a story of an art student involved with young communists, were insufficient to give the show immediate appeal, though their subsequent fame has led to various revivals. The favourite number was Flora's "A Quiet Place."

Then came the work that has ensured their place in the musical's gallery of fame. *Cabaret* (1966) was based by book-author Joe Masteroff on John van Druten's play *I Am a Camera,* an adaptation of Christopher Isherwood's stories of life in 1930s Berlin. The setting is a decadent Berlin cabaret presided over by a leering Master of Ceremonies (played by Joel Grey). The sexually permissive plot revolves around Sally Bowles (Jill Haworth), a girl from Chelsea, London, who is working as a singer at Berlin's Kit-Kat Club. Sally moves in with young American writer Cliff Bradshaw in a boarding house run by Fräulein Schneider, a part created by Kurt Weill's widow Lotte Lenya. Fräulein Schneider is engaged to the Jewish Herr Schulz (Jack Gilford), which creates problems when the politics of the period intrude. Cliff is beaten up after unwittingly couriering Nazi funds. He therefore departs for Paris, leaving Sally to continue at the cabaret, which is clearly poised for the political upheaval that is to follow. The score's romantic numbers were outclassed in popularity by those capturing the rhythms and sounds of Berlin of the 1930s, for instance Sally's title song and "Don't Tell Mama" (about her debauched existence), plus catchy numbers for the Master of Ceremonies— the multilingual greeting "Willkommen," the tongue-twisting "Two Ladies," and "The Money Song." New songs were added for the show's film version, which even more securely established it as a classic.

The follow-up show, *The Happy Time* (1968), had a French-Canadian setting; it was a much more modest success. Then came *Zorba* (1968), an adaptation of the Nikos Kazantzakis novel that in 1964 had been made into a popular film starring Anthony Quinn. The stage version was given the same show-within-a-show format as Leigh's *Man of La Mancha,* the framing provided this time by a narration by the leader of a bouzouki group. The Greek-flavoured score and jolly songs such as "Life Is," "The Top of the Hill," and "No Boom Boom" helped the show do reasonable business, without ever challenging the popularity of the film or its score by Manos Hadjidakis.

Even less successful initially was *70, Girls, 70* (1970). The title didn't help,

Cast of Kander and Ebb's *Cabaret*
Photo by Bob Marshak. New York Public Library for the Performing Arts.

being an obscure play on the showman's way of proclaiming the number of performers on display—except that in this case "70" referred not to the number of
performers but to their age. The piece was an adaptation of an English play about
the residents of an old folks' home who become safecrackers. It had been a mild hit
as the film *Make Mine Mink,* but, despite lively numbers such as "Old Folks" and
"Coffee in a Cardboard Cup," it was only after a 1989 revival with new songs that
the show delighted audiences to any great extent on both sides of the Atlantic.

The work that has most closely rivalled *Cabaret* in its style and success is
Chicago (1975), for which Berlin cabaret and low life are replaced by American
vaudeville and crime. When Roxie Hart (played by Gwen Verdon) shoots her ex-
lover, she hires lawyer Billy Flynn (Jerry Orbach). He wins public support for
her through sympathetic front-page news coverage, squeezing out fellow-
murderer and would-be vaudeville performer Velma Kelly (Chita Rivera) who
has until now been getting the press coverage. Roxie is acquitted, only to find
herself in turn superseded as front-page news after a sensational multiple murder.
This leaves her free to join Velma in a double act on the vaudeville circuit. The
score appealed for Velma's "All That Jazz," Roxie's "Funny Honey," Billy's "All I
Care About," and Roxie's husband Amos's showstopping "Mr. Cellophane." The

production was notable for the way it continued to break down musical theatre conventions. The story unfolded on a multiple-purpose set as a sequence of vaudeville turns, with the traditional pit orchestra replaced by a jazz band perched high above the action. The conductor announced each of the turns, which included important dance sequences by director-choreographer Bob Fosse.

The next Kander and Ebb show, *The Act* (1977), was nothing more than a vehicle for Liza Minnelli, playing Michelle Craig, an ex-film star who is now a Las Vegas nightclub singer. The show stood or fell on Minnelli's appeal, and it stood admirably while she delivered with aplomb such brassy numbers as "Shine It On," "Bobo's," "Little Do They Know," and "City Lights." But, like other star vehicles, it failed when she lost interest. The first sign came when Minnelli tried getting by with prerecorded tapes; soon she had dropped out altogether. Kander and Ebb then turned to a hit movie for their subject. *Woman of the Year,* starring Katharine Hepburn and Spencer Tracy as a pair of newspaper reporters, had won an Academy Award in 1942. For the 1981 musical adaptation the characters were updated into a television hostess and a cartoonist. Tess Harding (played by Lauren Bacall), winner of a "Woman of the Year" award, has used her television show to knock cartoonists, provoking Sam Craig (Harry Guardino) to retaliate by introducing a character called Tessie-Cat into his syndicated cartoon strip. The two meet and, after sparks have flown, fall in love. The stage show repeated the success of the film, running for two years and winning several Tony awards. Sam's lilting "See You in the Funny Papers," Tess's "When You're Right, You're Right" and "One of the Boys," Sam's ballad "Sometimes a Day Goes By," and a showstopping comedy duet "The Grass Is Always Greener" were among the hits.

The Rink (1984) was a small-cast musical that was yet another vehicle for Liza Minnelli. Anna Antonelli (played by Chita Rivera) runs a seaside fairground skating rink. She receives a visit from her daughter Angel (Minnelli), who left home years earlier. A confrontation ensues, but by the end the two come together —as much as anything through the common bond of single motherhood. The piece further typified the way Kander and Ebb musicals not only recognised social issues but accommodated experimental trends and cost-cutting theatrical needs. Here a small gang of wrecker's men who have been sent to pull down the rink appear symbolically on roller skates and play a range of characters in flashback sequences. Angel's "Colored Lights" and her mother's "Chief Cook and Bottle Washer" headed up a score that climaxes as the wreckers skate around "The Rink."

When Broadway producers hesitated to take the next Kander and Ebb show, *Kiss of the Spider Woman* (1990), producers in Toronto and London were happy to step in. Like *The Rink,* it had a book by Terrence McNally and a star-ring role for Chita Rivera. Based on a novel by Manuel Puig that had been turned into a successful movie, it was a serious, emotion-charged work, featuring scenes of torture visited on the homosexual Molina and the political activist Valentin in a grimy South American jail. Songs such as the Latin American "Her Name is Aurora," Molina's "Dressing Them Up" and the title song recaptured the typically forthright appeal of Kander and Ebb songs. So did "Second Chance" in *Steel Pier* (1997), set in Atlantic City in 1933 and featuring the dance marathons that flourished during the Depression era. Their next show, *Over and Over,* based on Thornton Wilder's satire *The Skin of Our Teeth,* was tried out in 1999.

Yet, in spite of their hits, their popularity, and their influence, neither Cy Coleman nor Kander and Ebb have led the musical theatre field in public per-ception in the late twentieth century. Rather, two composer-lyricists whose styles could hardly be more different have dominated international awareness of the American musical since 1960. At one extreme is Jerry Herman (1933–), who, while others have sought innovation and intellectual challenge, has proven him-self a master at providing singable tunes and straightforward plots to delight the general public. At the other end is the intellectually challenging, classically trained Stephen Sondheim, whose shows have never carried the clout with audiences that they have with the critics.

Herman initially aimed for a career as a designer and architect, before writing special material for a range of theatrical performers and songs for off-Broadway revues. His first staged musical was *Milk and Honey* (1961), which ran for more than five hundred performances. An affecting story of a love affair be-tween two middle-aged Jewish-American visitors to Israel—widowed Ruth (played by Mimi Benzell), who is touring with a ladies' group, and Phil (Robert Weede), who is separated from his wife and visiting his daughter—it has a bitter-sweet ending. The couple separate, but the audience is left with the hope that Phil will get the divorce that will enable them to marry. The most successful numbers were the title number and Phil's explanation of the meaning of "Shalom."

An off-Broadway show called *Madame Aphrodite* (1961) was a quick flop; but Herman bounced back with a vengeance with a show whose 2,844 perfor-mances at the St. James Theatre beat the Broadway record of *My Fair Lady* before itself being overtaken by *Fiddler on the Roof. Hello, Dolly!* (1964) was an adapta-tion by Michael Stewart of Thornton Wilder's play *The Matchmaker,* which in turn found its origins in a Viennese piece by Johann Nestroy and an English play by John Oxenford. Yonkers widow Dolly Levi (played by Carol Channing) is the matchmaker, who, when commissioned by wealthy Horace Vandergelder (David Burns) to find him a wife, decides that she herself is the ideal candidate. The show lasted long enough to accommodate a sequence of leading ladies, among them Ethel Merman, and generated a film with Barbra Streisand. An all-black company, led by Pearl Bailey and Cab Calloway, that took over in 1967, helped keep public interest going. As with the part of the King in *The King and I,* the role of Dolly was one that its creator, Channing, almost made into a career. What helped the show above all was the succession of richly melodic musical comedy numbers that Herman provided—Dolly's "I Put My Hand In" and the rousing "Before the Parade Passes By," Vandergelder's "It Takes a Woman," the quartet "Put On Your Sunday Clothes," and the romantic duet "It Only Takes a Moment." Above all there is the title song, whose insistent melody Herman repeats to huge effect in a spectacular showpiece.

His style and a public thus established, Herman provided much of the same mix in a work that, like Coleman's *Little Me,* was based on a novel by Patrick Dennis. In this case the autobiographical story tells of Dennis's zany Auntie Mame, who moves uneasily between affluence and poverty and into whose care Dennis comes after he is orphaned. In the musical version, *Mame* (1966), adapted by Jerome Lawrence and Robert E. Lee, Auntie Mame attempts to balance her eccentricity and her social ambitions with her duties towards her young ward, via disastrous ventures into the theatre, the saddle and other fads. The leading role was played by Angela Lansbury, for whom Herman provided hit numbers in "Open a New Window" and the emotional "If He Walked into My Life," as well as a share in the duet "Bosom Buddies." Above all there are the richly hummable quartet "We Need a Little Christmas" and another of Herman's patented high-stepping title numbers. If the 1,508 performances were little more than half the run of its predecessor, they were still a remarkable achievement.

Herman could scarcely keep up such a record, and the show with which it ended was *Dear World* (1969), a more sophisticated piece based on Jean Giraudoux's *The Madwoman of Chaillot.* Angela Lansbury played another eccentric character; in this instance, she is a woman who is attempting to save her "Dear World" from pollution and destruction. Neither the title song nor the piece as a whole provided the consistently lighthearted entertainment that Herman's fans expected. However, he came close to providing it again with his next show, for which he returned to Michael Stewart as book author. *Mack and Mabel* (1974) concerned the real-life affair between silent film director Mack Sennett (played by Robert Preston) and actress Mabel Normand (Bernadette Peters). In musical

Poster for Herman's *Mame*
Prints and Photographs Division, Library of Congress,
Washington, D.C.

terms it was all that could be wanted, with such irresistibly tuneful numbers as Mack's "When Movies Were Movies," "I Won't Send Roses," and "I Wanna Make the World Laugh," together with the big chorus numbers "Hundreds of Girls" and "Tap Your Troubles Away." However, lacking a workable book and sympathetic characters, the show managed no more than sixty-five performances. The enduring appeal of the songs has subsequently given the show cult status and allowed Herman to present a revised (and only marginally more successful) version in London in 1995.

Herman's next show, *The Grand Tour* (1979), an adaptation of the play *Ja-*

cobowsky and the Colonel, not only marked his shortest Broadway run but failed even to leave behind a treasured score. However, he had another outstanding triumph in *La Cage aux Folles* (1983), based on a French play and film. The curtain goes up on a chorus line in glamorous female garb. At the conclusion of the opening number, however, we discover that half of the "girls" are men. The setting is a French Riviera cross-dressing nightclub run by Georges (played by Gene Barry) and Albin (George Hearn), the latter of whom is the star of the floorshow in his female garb as Zaza. The two are lovers, who share their home with Georges's son Jean-Michel, the product of Georges's one-night aberration with a chorus girl. To complicate matters further, Jean-Michel has fallen in love with Anne, whose father is a leading campaigner against what he deems sexual immorality. In the hilarious denouement, Albin is forced to pose as Jean-Michel's mother before Anne's father is finally exposed as a client of just the sort of establishment he publicly condemns.

With its 1,761 performances, *La Cage aux Folles* came second only to *Hello, Dolly!* among Herman's triumphs. Its score is scarcely inferior, with Albin's defiant declaration "I Am What I Am," the delightfully old-fashioned "With Anne on My Arm," Georges's contemplative "Song on the Sand," and the big ensemble number "The Best of Times" to add to the tap-dancing chorus-line title number. *La Cage aux Folles* is a glittering show that presents a homosexual relationship in an uncomplicated fashion, and it was unfortunate that in London the onset of the AIDS scare caused it to be rejected unseen by a large part of its potential audience. At the time of writing, it is Herman's last Broadway show, though in 1996 he produced a television Christmas special, *Mrs. Santa Claus,* for Angela Lansbury.

If audiences knew they could sit back and enjoy a Jerry Herman show, they were no less aware that anything with music and lyrics by Stephen Sondheim would be a challenging intellectual affair. It was through a family friendship that Sondheim had come under the tutelage of Oscar Hammerstein II and thus gained insight into the art of the lyricist. But he had also studied music, and he combined employment as a television scriptwriter with taking such opportunities as presented themselves for a lyricist and composer. A Broadway production of his first musical score, *Saturday Night,* in 1955 was abandoned when the producer died, and the show ultimately received its first staging (in London) in 1997. However, it gave Sondheim a portfolio of songs, which helped him gain the lyricist's job for Bernstein's *West Side Story,* a collaboration in which Bernstein readily acknowledged the value of Sondheim's musical training. Yet success as a lyricist there and later with Jule Styne on *Gypsy* threatened to typecast him and thwart his attempts to show his ability also as composer. When that opportunity finally arrived, he grabbed it with both hands.

A Funny Thing Happened on the Way to the Forum (1962) was a show for the old Alvin Theatre that lay in the tradition of classical burlesques from Offenbach's *Orphée aux enfers* through Christiné's *Phi-Phi* to Cole Porter's *Out of This World*. True to the spirit of its source in the works of Plautus, it transferred the American vaudeville tradition to the modern stage, with a cast headed by Zero Mostel and Jack Gilford as Pseudolus and Hysterium, two slaves of the woman-chasing Senex. In Senex's absence, his adolescent son Hero offers Pseudolus his freedom if he will help Hero win Philia, a virgin slave recently arrived from Crete. Complications arise first from the fact that Philia has already been sold to Miles Gloriosus, and second when Senex arrives home unexpectedly and is mistaken by Philia for her new owner. All is resolved when Philia and Miles Gloriosus turn out to be brother and sister, stolen in childhood from Senex's neighbour Erronius. Since they cannot marry, and since Philia is freeborn, Hero gets his virgin and Pseudolus his freedom.

In this first staged show with his music, numbers such as the one in which Hero offers to make Pseudolus "Free" provide foretastes of the future Sondheim, with spartan musical lines serving primarily to get the lyric and dramatic content across. Yet the show fell firmly in the grand musical comedy tradition of the Alvin Theatre as well, with a number of memorable tunes—a commodity that Sondheim subsequently rationed more carefully. "Lovely" is not only Hero's view of Philia but descriptive of its melody. Besides "Pretty Little Picture," there are other sparkling vaudevillian numbers for the men in "Everybody Ought to Have a Maid" and "Impossible." Sondheim's lyric and melodic qualities come together to greatest effect in an opening number added at the last minute, "Comedy Tonight." It set the show on the road to success and gave Sondheim one of his most enduring creations.

He followed it with a show that was more consistently anticipatory of the innovative Sondheim, collaborating for the third time in his first four staged shows with book author Arthur Laurents. *Anyone Can Whistle* (1964) had a decidedly weird book about Cora Hoover Hooper (played by Angela Lansbury), mayor and boss of a small town faced with bankruptcy, who seeks to attract tourists by creating a fake miracle in which water flows from a rock. Confusion arises when a group of inmates of the local lunatic asylum, known as the Cookie Jar, escape and mingle with the tourists. In order to sort out who is who, the mayor and her town council enlist the help of a visiting physician, Dr. Hapgood (Harry Guardino), who falls in love with Fay Apple (Lee Remick), a nurse from the mental institution. Hapgood succeeds in separating the tourists and mental patients into two distinct groups, but nobody ever manages to tell which group is sane and which insane. In the end Hapgood himself is unmasked as insane, thus reinforcing the message of the narrow line between brilliance and insanity.

The score contained a catchy title song for Remick, who also had a couple of highly effective numbers in the powerful "There Won't Be Trumpets" and the mock-French duet "Come Play Wiz Me." Lansbury's big number was "A Parade in Town." In a fashion Sondheim was to develop in later works, there were extended, austere, but cumulatively effective, sequences combining song and underscored dialogue. But the treatment of mental affliction (which included a choreographed "Cookie Chase" in which the words "Lock him up, put him away" were sung to a lilting waltz) was seen by many as tasteless. Others were simply bemused by Sondheim's intellectual processes. The show closed after just nine performances, though it has been revived in later years since Sondheim achieved cult status.

After this disappointment and that of his collaboration as lyricist for Richard Rodgers's *Do I Hear a Waltz?* (another Laurents book), Sondheim was silent for some years. From here on, however, he concentrated on setting his lyrics to his own music for an astonishingly varied series of shows that have aimed more at intellectual stimulation than popular appeal. He was forty by the time he achieved his major breakthrough with *Company* (1970). This presents what is really a sequence of character sketches, in which he pursues the theme of personal relationships, contrasting likeable, unmarried Robert (played by Dean Jones) with various married (or almost married) couples. Along the way Sondheim parades a scepticism for conventional relationships, exploring the shortcomings of the various couples' liaisons, as well as of Robert's affairs with various women.

Company enjoyed a substantial commercial success, achieved a run of 705 performances, and won a Tony award. It established Sondheim's reputation, with songs that were original in construction, their musical lines and instrumentation finely tuned to set off his modern, incisive lyrics. "The Little Things You Do Together" sets a declaration of the joys of marriage against a background of bickering; "Another Hundred People" refers scathingly to the people who drift in and out of Manhattan every day; and "Barcelona" retails a stewardess's preoccupation with flight schedules as she climbs out of Robert's bed at 4:30 A.M. "The Ladies Who Lunch," introduced by Elaine Stritch, is a scornful denunciation by a drunken, much married woman of her fellow women, while "Being Alive" is Robert's elated, but transient, acceptance of his married friends' persuasion that he should settle down:

> I'll always be there
> As frightened as you,
> To help us survive
> Being alive, being alive, being alive!

With the Sondheim bandwagon on the road, *Company* was swiftly followed by *Follies* (1971), which similarly analyses the lives of a group of elderly showpeople. They are former members of the spectacular revue company, the Weissman Follies, who have gathered for a reunion to mark the demolition of the theatre in which they used to perform. By means of flashbacks we see the former selves of Sally and Buddy, Phyllis and Ben—two pairings of former showgirls and stage-door Johnnies whose subsequent financial and emotional experiences are contrasted. The score added to Sondheim's emotionally powerful songs with Sally's sadly self-deprecating "Losing My Mind"; Phyllis's sarcastic taunting of her husband in "Could I Leave You?"; the resilient "I'm Still Here," for faded film actress Carlotta (played by Yvonne de Carlo, star of B movies in the thirties); and the tongue-in-cheek pretence of an elderly "Broadway Baby." In capturing the essence of the Weissman (Ziegfeld?) Follies, Sondheim also (for strictly dramatic reasons) had recourse to catchy numbers such as Weissman's opening recollection of the chorus lines of "Beautiful Girls," the ensemble "Waiting for the Girls Upstairs" (for Buddy and Ben, Sally and Phyllis, and their youthful selves, recalling evenings at the stage door), and the former song-and-dance couple's patter song "Rain on the Roof."

Follies too ran for more than five hundred performances and won Sondheim another Tony award. It was followed by what was to become Sondheim's most successful score commercially. *A Little Night Music* (1973) was based on the Ingmar Bergman film *Smiles of a Summer Night*. The romantic content was encapsulated in a score made up of themes in waltz time or derivatives thereof, and the northern setting was reflected by orchestrator Jonathan Tunick in pastel shadings. The story tells of middle-aged lawyer Fredrik Egerman (played by Len Cariou) and his young second wife Anne (Victoria Mallory), who, after months of marriage, is still a virgin. Fredrik meets a former mistress, the touring actress Desirée Armfeldt (Glynis Johns). She has a daughter Fredrika (Judy Kahan) by Fredrik, but is now in the throes of an affair with hussar Carl Magnus Malcolm (Lawrence Guittard). Fredrik is invited to a weekend at the home of Desirée's mother, Madame Armfeldt (Hermione Gingold), along with his teenaged son Henrik and Carl Magnus and his wife. As the show progresses, partners change, with Fredrik ultimately resuming his affair with Desirée, Carl Magnus reconciled with his wife, and the virginal Anne more fittingly paired with young Henrik.

Individual numbers are less important than the cumulative effect of the score, but there are typically clever representations of conflicting emotions in "You Must Meet My Wife" for Fredrik and Desirée and the ensemble number "A Weekend in the Country." However, one ballad has carried Sondheim's name and songwriting talents to a public for which his intellectual style is otherwise unappealing. Despite a lyric whose meaning is less than transparent, the rueful, reflective "Send in the Clowns," sung (or, in the original production, croaked) by Desirée, achieved wide popularity. The show itself played 601 performances on Broadway, won Sondheim another Tony, achieved worldwide performances and, thanks to the drawing power of "Send in the Clowns," proved commercially revivable to an extent largely denied other Sondheim shows.

Thereafter, Sondheim was even more content to ignore commercial considerations for the sake of daringly different, artistically probing pieces. After providing incidental music for a production of Aristophanes' *The Frogs* (1974), his next real musical was *Pacific Overtures* (1976). It told, from a Japanese point of view, of the forcible opening up of Japan in 1852 by Commodore Matthew Perry and an army of Western invaders. It was developed at the instigation of producer Harold Prince from an unperformed play by John Weidman, a student of Asian history and son of Jerome Weidman, author of *Fiorello!* and *I Can Get It for You Wholesale*. *Pacific Overtures* offers not so much a continuous story as a portrayal of changing aspects of Japanese culture in a sequence of sketches. Sondheim set his stall out from the start with orchestrations (again by Jonathan Tunick) that prominently feature traditional Japanese instruments. The concept was reinforced musically by his use of the Japanese pentatonic scale and visually by casting performers of Asian origin and adapting aspects of Japanese Kabuki theatre, such as having men play the female parts. In presenting the conflict of East and West, the Japanese musical elements are fused with traditional Western elements to produce witty but singable numbers such as "Pretty Lady"; a song in which the Shogun is invited to drink some poisoned "Chrysanthemum Tea"; and "Please Hello," which parodies first Sousa, later Gilbert and Sullivan, and finally Offenbach. In "Someone in a Tree," the story of the meeting of the Americans with the Japanese is told from several different perspectives. *Pacific Overtures* struggled through 193 performances and lost its entire investment, but its artistic merit has inspired several subsequent revivals.

Sondheim turned to more conventional theatrical material with a piece that indulged his taste for the macabre in a version of the nineteenth-century legend of *Sweeney Todd* (1979), the "demon barber" of London's Fleet Street who slit his customers' throats and handed them over to his accomplice, Mrs. Lovett, to pickle and pack into meat pies. The story had reappeared periodically in various forms, from the early "penny dreadfuls" to a 1973 version by Christopher Bond that portrayed the action as revenge for what Todd saw as the wrongs of society; this was the version that appealed to Sondheim. In spite of a particularly gruesome resolution, Sondheim's adaptation (with Hugh Wheeler as book author) proved one of his more commercially successful works, winning not only a Tony award for best musical but running for a total of 557 performances. It was an especial success for Len Cariou as Todd and Angela Lansbury as Mrs. Lovett, the pie-shop owner who becomes Todd's accomplice. The subject offered ample opportunity for Sondheim's range of musical parodies, not least in the incongruously lilting song in which Mrs. Lovett extends to Todd an invitation to taste "A Little Priest." The extended score and the lyricism of numbers such as "Johanna" have helped the work gain acceptance in opera houses as well as musical theatre.

Ever seeking something different, Sondheim next turned to George S. Kaufman and Moss Hart's 1934 tale of disillusioned youth, *Merrily We Roll Along*. This offered the novelty of a story that moved in reverse, showing how currently successful people achieved that position over the course of twenty-five years. For the musical version (1982) the story was updated by George Furth, but the piece lasted only sixteen Broadway performances. Not content to let it rest there, Sondheim subsequently produced various revised forms, which underscored the appeal of such numbers as the hymn to "Old Friends" and the ballad "Not a Day Goes By."

By the time of his next show, Sondheim had severed his long-term association with director Harold Prince. The novelty of *Sunday in the Park with George* (1984) lay in the attempt to re-create a celebrated painting on stage. The painting was Georges Seurat's "Summer Sunday on the Isle of La Grande Jatte," and the musical featured the artist himself (played by Mandy Patinkin) and introduced the individual characters of the painting separately before presenting the whole living picture in the Act 1 finale. Sondheim also sought to reproduce Seurat's pointillist style (in which a painting is built up from small dots of colour) both by naming the artist's mistress (played by Bernadette Peters) Dot and also in musical terms. With such complex elements, the work excited critical enthusiasm but also faced charges of pretentiousness. This was heightened by the way the show was extended from a one-act concept piece to full-length stage piece by the addition of an unconvincing second act in which descendants of the original George and Dot comment on the state of art. The piece ran for 604 performances without ever making a profit and, though failing to win a Tony award, carried off a coveted Pulitzer Prize for drama. The score is at its most memorable in "Everybody Loves Louis," "Finishing the Hat," "Sunday," and the Act 2 opening tableau "It's Hot up Here."

Just as Sondheim had previously turned back to traditional theatrical sources in *Sweeney Todd,* so he did for *Into the Woods* (1987). The traditional theatrical elements of James Lapine's book are English-language pantomime characters, neatly encapsulated in the opening words of the show—"Once upon a time," spoken by the ever-present narrator (Tom Aldredge), and "I wish," spoken by Cinderella. Other traditional characters are Cinderella's Ugly Sisters and her Prince, Little Red Riding Hood and the Wolf, Jack (of beanstalk fame) with his Mother, his Cow, and his Giant, and Rapunzel and her Prince. There are also supporting appearances from Sleeping Beauty and Snow White, as well as a further set of characters—a Baker (played by Chip Zien) and his Wife (Joanna Gleason), who are anxious to cast off a curse imposed by a witch (Bernadette Peters) that has prevented them from having children. In the first act the individual stories are developed in conventional form to a happy ending in which the Baker's Wife becomes pregnant; but in Act 2 things begin to go awry. The characters in the various narratives interact, and Jack's Mother, Rapunzel, and the Baker's Wife are killed. When the Giant is finally slain as well, the various characters—dead and alive—come forward to present the morals of their stories. Sondheim's score is appropriately more approachable in style, with agreeable melodic strands running through the title song, "Hello, Little Girl," "Maybe They're Magic," "Giants in the Sky," and "Agony."

Where *Sunday in the Park with George* developed into a full-length Broadway show from a one-act workshop piece, *Assassins* (1991) remained essentially in its short workshop form. The book was by John Weidman and again expressed Sondheim's taste for the macabre, its characters being the killers or would-be killers of American Presidents Abraham Lincoln, James Garfield, William McKinley, Franklin D. Roosevelt, Richard Nixon, John F. Kennedy, Gerald Ford, and Ronald Reagan. Their stories are presented in what is more or less a series of stand-up turns in popular music styles.

Then, for *Passion* (1994), Sondheim offered what was, for him, an unusually romantic subject, albeit a dark one. The source was the Italian film *Passione d'amore,* and the story, set in 1863, tells of the dilemma of a young soldier, Giorgio (played by

Bernadette Peters and cast in Sondheim's *Into the Woods*
Photo by Martha Swope, copyright Time Inc.

Jere Shea), who is torn between his beautiful, sensuous, and undemanding Milanese mistress Clara (Marin Mazzie) and the chronically ill and emotionally tormented Fosca (Donna Murphy). He begins an affair with the latter while posted to an austere army post in a bleak provincial town, but she becomes increasingly demanding. The action moves between the two locations via a series of love letters. It ends with Fosca's death, but with Giorgio emotionally committed to her. The contrasts are conveyed on various levels, from the simple effect of names implying "clear" (Clara) and "gloomy" (Fosca) to a score that conveys the full range of emotions, from the rapturous opening duet, "Happiness," between Giorgio and Clara to its more tender counterpart for Giorgio and Fosca, "No One Has Ever Loved Me."

Coleman, Kander and Ebb, Herman, and Sondheim have each made outstanding contributions to the development of the American musical, not least in bringing it to a higher intellectual plane. Yet, with film musicals having had their day, and television and rock music increasingly the entertainment media of the general public, they have also presided over a period when the stage musical has become a more specialist form of entertainment, less readily appreciated by the public at large.

Chapter Seventeen
Postwar London

As the American musical pushed forward the frontiers of the musical play from World War II onwards, it was the works of Rodgers and Hammerstein, Berlin, and Porter to which British theatregoers, no less eagerly than American, turned. British musical theatre creators were left either to seek to compete with the American musical on its own terms or meet the residual demand for more traditional fare. Such, indeed, was already the case when we left our review of the British musical theatre around the outbreak of World War II, with native works divided between the escapist Ruritanian works of Ivor Novello on the one hand and the song-and-dance musical comedies of Vivian Ellis on the other. By the time Britain emerged from the war, the state of development of the American musical was further ahead of the British than before.

Among native British works, the musicals of Ivor Novello especially remained hugely popular during the 1940s, despite the relative failure of *Arc de Triomphe* (1943), a vehicle for Mary Ellis that traced the professional and amorous adventures of a French opera singer. The only really successful number was "Dark Music," sung by Elisabeth Welch in an incidental role. Much greater success attended *Perchance to Dream* (1945), whose story moved from 1818 to the 1930s. Like Kollo's *Wie einst im Mai* and Straus's *Drei Walzer,* it portrayed successive generations of two families, with unrequited love in the first two generations finding fulfilment in the third. The ancestral home provided the setting for each act. Novello was the non-singing leading man, Muriel Barron the soprano mistress or wife in all the three acts, Roma Beaumont her soubrette rival, Olive Gilbert a contralto supporting performer. Novello's score produced a duet for soprano and contralto, "We'll Gather Lilacs," that almost attained the stature of a folk song, and other delights are the waltz "Love Is My Reason for Living," the contralto's beautiful "Highwayman Love," and the soubrette's "The Night I Curtsied to the King."

Novello's final Ruritanian creation was *King's Rhapsody* (1949). Novello himself played King Nikki of Murania, unwillingly brought back from his Parisian actress-mistress Marta Karillos (played by Phyllis Dare) to rule his country and marry the more politically acceptable Princess Cristiane (Vanessa Lee). Lee's "Some Day My Heart Will Awake" and Olive Gilbert's contralto "Fly Home, Little Heart" were the show's big hits. The cast also featured Phyllis Dare's sister Zena Dare, thus reuniting the two, who had been leading lights of the Edwardian musical shows of almost fifty years earlier. Their reunion was perhaps symbolic: this was virtually the last of the British shows that sought to recapture the style of that earlier period. Novello died suddenly six months into the show's run.

Novello's last score was in stark contrast to his Ruritanian essays. *Gay's the Word* (1951) was a light, bright, tongue-in-cheek piece designed as a vehicle for musical comedy comedienne Cicely Courtneidge at a time when the word *gay* had not yet acquired its present-day meaning. The uncomplicated plot tells of a touring-actress-cum-drama-school-head who thwarts a band of smugglers and stages a successful show with her school into the bargain. The lyrics were by comedy writer Alan Melville (1910–83), and Courtneidge's bright, breezy songs included "Bees Are Buzzin'," "Vitality," and "It's Bound to Be Right on the Night," recalling Novello's revue song "And Her Mother Came Too" of thirty years earlier.

Irreplaceable though Novello was as composer and performer, his romantic formula had also inspired others. Another Welshman, Harry Parr Davies (1914–55), composer-accompanist to the singer Gracie Fields, entered the ranks of theatre composers with fellow composer George Posford in a comedy piece for Courtneidge, *Full Swing* (1942), and he followed it with a highly successful romantic musical play, *The Lisbon Story* (1943). Like Novello's *Dancing Years* of 1939, this was a contemporary wartime drama. It concerns a Parisian leading lady, Gabrielle Girard (played by Patricia Burke), who gives in to the entreaties of a Nazi leader in order to help a French scientist escape with wartime secrets. Since the show ends with her being shot dead on stage by the Nazi, the piece had a forward-looking seriousness; but its score was resolutely in the Novello mould. Burke had a lovely waltz, "Some Day We Shall Meet Again," and there was an impressive tenor aria, "We Must Never Say Goodbye." The enduring hit was an incidental number, "Pedro the Fisherman," given in the show to a quartet of back-up singers who functioned as an audience distraction while the scenery was changed.

Davies's subsequent scores before his early death included another Courtneidge vehicle, *Her Excellency* (1949). It was *Dear Miss Phoebe* (1950), an adaptation of J. M. Barrie's *Quality Street,* that produced his other big musical theatre song hit, the very Novelloish and "olde-Englishe" "I Leave My Heart in an English Garden." As with Novello, Davies's last piece was in more lighthearted style —the farcical *Blue for a Boy* (1950).

George Posford also built upon his prewar work, but with less outstanding success. *Evangeline* (1946) was another attempt at a stage adaptation of the Rodney Brent novel which Cole Porter had used for *Nymph Errant,* while *Zip Goes a Million* (1951) ventured where Jerome Kern had failed in adapting the play *Brewster's Millions.* The latter proved a reasonable success, both with and without its original star, George Formby. The adapter and lyricist was Posford's regular collaborator Eric Maschwitz. The two also produced a stage version of their prewar radio success *Goodnight Vienna* and a quick West End flop, *Happy Holiday* (1954), an adaptation of Arnold Ridley's play *The Ghost Train.*

A good deal of the popularity of Novello's "We'll Gather Lilacs" and Davies's "Pedro the Fisherman" was due to recordings made by Lehár's former star tenor Richard Tauber. One of the many Jewish artists from central Europe who sought refuge in wartime London, Tauber actually appeared in the film version of *The Lisbon Story*. As a composer he also made his contribution to the British stage, providing (with Bernard Grün as co-composer) the score for *Old Chelsea* (1943). This was another piece of unashamed nostalgia, with Tauber somewhat incongruously cast as an impoverished eighteenth-century British composer. His fans were rewarded by another enduring "Tauber song" in "My Heart and I," composed by Tauber himself.

There was a romantic tinge, too, to the postwar works with which Vivian Ellis entertained audiences at the Adelphi Theatre in collaboration with humorous writer A. P. Herbert (1890–1971) and producer Charles B. Cochran. *Big Ben* (1946) was a political piece with a campaign number "I Want to See the People Happy"; but the libretto lacked the lightness of touch necessary to keep the public happy for more than 172 performances. Far different was the fate of its successor, *Bless the Bride* (1947), which had just the right touch of innocence and timelessness to create enduring popularity. Set at the time of the Franco-Prussian War, it tells of Lucy Veracity Willow (played by Lizbeth Webb), who rejects marriage to English nobleman Thomas Trout (Brian Reece) in order to run away on her wedding day with romantic Frenchman Pierre Fontaine (Georges Guétary). Opening the same week as *Oklahoma!* began its London run, the show also held its own for two years against competition from *Annie Get Your Gun,* likewise opening in London at that time. This was helped by national enthusiasm over the real-life marriage of the future Queen Elizabeth II, but there is also a delightful score headed up by the heroine's waltz "I Was Never Kissed Before," the hero's tripping "Ma Belle Marguerite," and his rapturous "Table for Two."

Ellis, Herbert, and Cochran tasted disappointment with the third and last of their light operas. *Tough at the Top* (1949) had opera bass Giorgio Tozzi as its boxer hero, but the piece never established itself as its two predecessors had. Ellis next turned out a score to his own lyrics for *And So to Bed* (1951), built around veteran comedian Leslie Henson as the seventeenth-century diarist Samuel Pepys and recounting a fictional flirtation with the mistress of King Charles II (played by Keith Michell). Ellis showed his thorough musicianship in delightful period-style dances such as the rigaudon and sarabande, as well as in the title duet for Charles and his mistress, the concerted number "Bartholomew Fair," and the madrigal "Gaze Not on Swans."

Ellis turned for the last time to his long-time collaborator A. P. Herbert for an adaptation of the latter's 1930 novel *The Water Gipsies* (1955). This is the story of old Albert Bell (played by Jerry Verno), who lives on a barge on the River Thames with his two daughters, Jane (Pamela Charles) and Lily (Dora Bryan). The plot revolves around the girls' contrasted experiences and expectations of men. Bryan's scatty style—demonstrated in the song "Why Did You Call Me Lily?"—proved the big attraction, and the show folded soon after she left the cast. It was the last mainstream Ellis score to reach the West End, though *Listen to the*

Wind (1954), a children's Christmas piece, was staged at the Arts Theatre in December 1955. *Half in Earnest* (1957), an adaptation of Oscar Wilde's *The Importance of Being Earnest,* saw the light of day in America with Anna Russell as Lady Bracknell and Jack Cassidy as John Worthing.

Noël Coward, meanwhile, produced various postwar musicals that sought to recognise changing styles in the musical theatre, but without ever matching the appeal of the new wave of musicals from America. *Pacific 1860* (1946) reopened London's Drury Lane Theatre after the war and, as its title suggests, was a costume piece. Set on a fictional South Seas island, it follows the ups and downs of the ultimately successful romance between Kerry Stirling (played by Graham Payn), member of a social-climbing family, and his opera-singer girlfriend Elena Salvador (Mary Martin). However, the flimsy story failed to sustain the piece, which included some of Coward's more ambitious music, as well as a typical cabaret number about would-be missionary "Uncle Harry." *Ace of Clubs* (1950), set in contemporary London, intertwined a story about stolen jewels with the romance between a sailor (played by Graham Payn) and a nightclub singer (Pat Kirkwood). Again the most successful numbers included some in Coward's catchy revue style—"Three Juvenile Delinquents" and "Chase Me, Charlie"—together with the leading man's attractively optimistic "Sail Away."

Like Ellis, Coward also tried an Oscar Wilde adaptation, *After the Ball* (1954), based on *Lady Windermere's Fan.* However, this also failed. Nor did Coward do better on the other side of the Atlantic, where his cabaret act had made him a familiar figure. For a New York production, *Sail Away* (1961), he re-used the hit number of *Ace of Clubs* for the title song; the cast was headed by Elaine Stritch as cruise director Mimi Paragon on board the *Coronia,* with James Hurst as passenger Johnny van Mier, who falls in love with her. Johnny had the title song, and Mimi climaxed the second act—set in Tangier—with "Why Do the Wrong People Travel?" Joe the Purser, meanwhile, had a hit with "The Passenger's Always Right." Such success as the piece enjoyed was for its period wit and charm, and much the same could be said of Coward's final show, *The Girl Who Came to Supper* (1963). Likewise composed for a New York premiere, it was an adaptation of Terence Rattigan's *The Prince and the Showgirl,* with José Ferrer as Grand Duke Charles, Prince Regent of Carpathia, and Florence Henderson as showgirl Mary Morgan. One of the highlights was the appearance of vaudevillian Tessie O'Shea as Ada Cockle, providing period London atmosphere with a medley of Cockney songs. However, the show was seen as too obviously derivative of *My Fair Lady* and by no means as good.

With airplanes providing faster travel, transatlantic exchange of performers and creators was ever increasing. With the West End in the grip of American fever, the people who travelled east benefited most. Composer Hugh Martin (1914–) was from Birmingham, Alabama, and had begun his career in the United States as a chorister. With fellow singer-songwriter Ralph Blane, he had composed songs for the Broadway musical show *Best Foot Forward* (1941), as well as for film musicals, of which *Meet Me in St. Louis* was the most outstanding. It was later staged. After the war he composed again for Broadway in *Look Ma, I'm Dancin'* (1948) and *Make Me a Wish* (1951). However, his longest stage runs were achieved when he crossed the Atlantic.

Love from Judy (1952) was a collaboration by Martin with book author Timothy Gray and lyricist Eric Maschwitz on an adaptation of the sentimental 1914 Broadway play *Daddy Long-Legs*. This tells of a girl from an orphanage, Judy Abbott (played by Jeannie Carson), and her mysterious benefactor Jervis Pendleton (Bill O'Connor). She calls him Daddy Long-Legs before she learns his identity, when he turns out to be not nearly as old and paternal as she imagines. The hero's title song is the highlight of a likeable score. Gray and Martin also showed their transatlantic allegiances in New York with *High Spirits* (1964), a musical adaptation of Noël Coward's play *Blithe Spirit*. That it ran longer in New York than Coward's own musicals of the time was due largely to the appeal of the original play and the appearance of revue star Beatrice Lillie as the eccentric spiritualist Madame Arcati. Coward himself directed the production, with Edward Woodward as Charles Condomine and Tammy Grimes as the ghost of his first wife, Elvira.

The two British shows that achieved by far the greatest success during the 1950s were both works that shunned modern theatrical trends. Sandy Wilson (1924–) began writing words and music for small-scale revues; then the tiny Players' Theatre, haven of old-time music hall, commissioned him to produce an affectionate pastiche of the dances, dresses, and poses of 1920s musicals of the *No, No, Nanette* kind. The title of *The Boy Friend* (1953) was adapted from a Rodgers and Hart show, and the result was such a success that it transferred to a regular West End theatre. The plot is a true 1920s concoction about heiress Polly Browne (played by Anne Rogers), a pupil at the Riviera finishing school run by Mme Dubonnet (Joan Sterndale Bennett). Polly has the familiar problem of separating suitors who are interested in her fortune from those who are interested in herself. Eventually, she finds a genuine lover in Tony, a messenger boy who is unjustly accused of theft before finally turning out to be a wealthy aristocrat. Wilson was

Wilson's *The Boy Friend* at the Players' Theatre, 1953
Kurt Gänzl Collection

book author, lyricist, and composer, and his score captured all the characteristics of 1920s songs in "A Room in Bloomsbury," "I Could Be Happy With You," "It's Never Too Late to Fall in Love," and "Won't You Charleston With Me?" The show provided such unaffected joy that it ran for five years and 2,084 performances.

By the time *The Boy Friend* reached the West End stage proper, Wilson had already composed another small-scale piece, *The Buccaneer* (1953), a tale of skulduggery in the world of children's comics that likewise transferred to the West End. He then built upon the success of *The Boy Friend* with a work in a very different vein. *Valmouth* (1958) was an adaptation of the esoteric and somewhat scandalous novels of Ronald Firbank. It had less success with the general public than with connoisseurs, and it has been revived on various occasions. It was designed as a vehicle for American actress Bertice Reading as the outrageous black masseuse Mrs Yaj in the seaside English town of Valmouth. Fenella Fielding was the elderly Lady Parvula Panzoust, anxious to leap into bed "Just Once More" and justifying to her late husband her various indiscretions as "Only a Passing Phase." Mrs Yaj herself had two hit numbers in "Magic Fingers" and "My Big Best Shoes." Wilson also produced a successor to *The Boy Friend* in *Divorce Me, Dar-*

Lloyd Pearson, Derek Holmes, and Virginia Vernon in the piano scene
from Reynolds and Slade's *Salad Days*
Mander and Mitchenson Theatre Collection

ling (1964), but changing musical tastes meant that such later shows as *My Monkey Wife* (1971) were confined to fringe theatres.

The second major British success of the 1950s came when the Bristol Old Vic Company followed up a couple of Christmas revues with a small-scale end-of-season musical by its house team: book author Dorothy Reynolds (1913–77) and composer Julian Slade (1930–). The songs were simple, the accompaniment just two pianos and percussion; but the public were entranced by the unassuming and delightful entertainment, decked out with immediately appealing songs. *Salad Days* (1954) was thereupon earmarked for London, where Bristol's enthusiasm was shared by Londoners, who flocked to see it for almost six years. By the time it was taken off, it had set a new record for a West End musical of 2,283 performances.

The story is the simplest fare, following two newly graduated students,

Jane and Timothy, who go through various unlikely encounters, most particularly with a tramp for whom they undertake to look after a piano called Minnie which has the power to set the world dancing. The concert-party nature of the entertainment was displayed in the way performers took on a variety of roles, with the show's book author in the cast as, inter alia, a richly comic nightclub performer, Asphinxia; the composer played one of the two pianos. Since the performers were not really singers, the vocal writing was undemanding; but, as with Offenbach's *La Vie parisienne* some ninety years earlier, that did not prevent the composer from coming up with a richly tuneful score, in which "We Said We Wouldn't Look Back," "I Sit in the Sun," "Oh, Look at Me," "It's Easy to Sing," "We're Looking for a Piano," and "The Time of My Life" stand out.

The taste for the Slade and Reynolds brand of innocence and simplicity assured them further success with the slightly larger-scale *Free as Air* (1957). Set on one of the British Channel Islands, it portrays a desirable heiress seeking refuge from press and suitor, and finding happiness with a handsome local hero whilst defeating those who are set on developing the island. Reynolds was in the cast again, with a share in a love song, "We're Holding Hands." The most memorable number is the statement of the islanders' philosophy, "Let the Grass Grow Under Your Feet." The Slade-Reynolds bandwagon rolled to less effect in a Christmas piece, *Hooray for Daisy* (1959), and in *Follow That Girl* (1960), before finally coming to a halt after *Wildest Dreams* (1961). With other collaborators, Slade produced further scores, including musical adaptations of three British classics. *Vanity Fair* (1962), based on the novel by William Makepeace Thackeray, was followed by *Trelawny* (1972), based on Arthur Wing Pinero's play *Trelawny of the "Wells."* The latter showed Slade at his most ambitious but less than successful, while *Out of Bounds* (1973), an adaptation of Pinero's *The Schoolmistress*, failed to make it to London. Like Sandy Wilson, Slade retired from the fray in the face of changing tastes.

More modern responses to the American musical were provided by three songwriting teams who produced a number of musicals concentrating on the ordinary working man. David Heneker (1906–) was an army brigadier before success as a popular songwriter encouraged him to resign his commission and concentrate on the theatre. With book author Wolf Mankowitz (1924–98), lyricist Julian More (1928–), and fellow songwriter Monty Norman (1928–), he contributed to *Expresso Bongo* (1958), an adaptation of a newspaper story by Mankowitz. Based on the career of British rock-and-roll star Tommy Steele, it anticipated the later American treatment of similar events in *Bye, Bye, Birdie*. The pop star of the British musical is Herbert Rudge (played by James Kenney), who is discovered by agent Johnnie (Paul Scofield) playing bongo drums in a Soho coffee bar. He becomes famous under the name of Bongo, but, after he meets sexually voracious actress Dixie Collins (Hy Hazell), he acquires an unreliability that condemns him to keep on trying rather than succeeding. The supporting cast included many British stars of the future, including Millicent Martin as a stripper. Among the hits were "I've Never Had It So Good," "Time" and "We Bought It."

Heneker, More, and Norman next provided the lyrics and British adaptation of the French musical *Irma la Douce,* which bore many of the low-life characteristics of their own original works. They then went on to another of Mankowitz's adaptations of his tales of Soho lowlife, *Make Me an Offer* (1959). This was set in the Portobello Road and centred on market stallholder Charlie (played by Daniel Massey), who becomes too attached to the antiques in which he trades. He is particularly torn by a beautiful vase, which he needs to sell in order to support his wife (Diana Coupland) and children, as well to develop his business. The supporting characters included a redheaded market seller (Dilys Laye) who put other temptations in his way, plus assorted market traders and collectors.

Striking out on his own as songwriter, Heneker collaborated with book author Beverley Cross on turning H. G. Wells's 1905 novel *Kipps* into a vehicle for pop singer Tommy Steele. *Half a Sixpence* (1963) proved an enormous hit; it only closed (after almost two years) so that Steele could take the show to Broadway, where the success was repeated. Steele played Arthur Kipps, a humble clerk in a Tunbridge Wells drapery whose girlfriend Ann Pornick (played by Marti Webb) comes from similarly straitened circumstances. The news that he has inherited a fortune causes Kipps to start throwing money around and abandon Ann for a higher station in society. However, society is inclined to welcome him only for his money, which is disastrously invested and promptly lost, forcing Kipps to return to Ann and set up a bookshop. The show provided Steele with songs that achieved widespread popularity, most notably the title song and "Flash, Bang, Wallop."

Heneker consolidated his reputation with songs written in collaboration with John Taylor for an Adelphi Theatre musical comedy that was panned by the critics but loved by the public: it ran for five and a half years and 2,202 performances. *Charlie Girl* (1965) provided unpretentious, undemanding entertainment and had a hit-parade title song in a score that combined traditional music hall with modern pop music. It was one of the periodical versions of the Cinderella story and was originally intended as a vehicle for veteran Cicely Courtneidge. It finally made it to the stage with Anna Neagle as Lady Hadwell, impecunious

Tommy Steele in Heneker's *Half a Sixpence*
Photo by Tom Hustler. Kurt Gänzl Collection.

owner of Hadwell Hall and mother of three daughters, of whom two are ladylike and the third—Charlotte, alias Charlie—is a tomboy. Charlie, of course, is the Cinderella of the piece, her Prince being the rich son of Kay Connor (played by Hy Hazell), an old chorus-girl friend of Lady Hadwell's. The male lead was estate handyman Joe (Joe Brown), while comedy actor Derek Nimmo had a cameo part as a football pools agent who agrees to stand in as butler to impress visitors to Hadwell Hall.

That was to remain the height of Heneker's success. His fox-hunting piece *Jorrocks* (1966), based on the novels of R. S. Surtees, kept audiences entertained for a while, as did *Phil the Fluter* (1969), which mixed Heneker songs with those of the show's central character, the Irish songwriter Percy French. *Popkiss* (1972), an adaptation of the Ben Travers farce *Rookery Nook,* achieved little. More success attended *The Biograph Girl* (1980), a small-scale history of silent-era Hollywood. Heneker returned to the West End just once more at the age of almost seventy-eight with *Peg* (1984), a musical version of J. Hartley Manners's *Peg o' My Heart* in which Heneker's own songs supplemented the 1913 popular song by Alfred Bryan and Fred Fisher.

Heneker's sometime collaborator Monty Norman also contributed to a series of shows that garnered little acclaim before he came to the fore once more with Julian More for *Songbook* (1979). This was a clever parody of the popular 1970s shoestring revues that presented an evening of works by classic songwriters such as Cole Porter and Noël Coward performed by a small cast. The Norman-More show celebrated the fictitious songwriter Mooney Shapiro (played by Bob Hoskins) and was decked out with his supposed compositions, which paraded all the clichés of popular songwriting. Diane Langton, Gemma Craven, and Anton Rodgers presented these intentional non-masterpieces in the cabaret style that typified the revues the show burlesqued.

The second team of songwriters who contributed significantly to the 1960s phase of the British musical was headed by Leslie Bricusse (1931–), who first attracted attention as contributor to college shows at Cambridge University. These included a musical comedy, *Lady at the Wheel* (1953), which was produced professionally in 1958. By then he had also enjoyed a huge success with the song "Out of Town" for the film *Charley Moon* (1956). His first West End show was a collaboration with pop singer Anthony Newley (1931–99), who also starred. *Stop the World—I Want to Get Off* (1961) was little more than a small-scale revue, tracing the career, marriage, fatherhood, infidelities, and disillusionment of one Littlechap. Newley was supported by a single actress (Anna Quayle) playing his wife and all the other women he had loved, a pair of identical twins (played by the Baker twins) as his daughters, and a small chorus of performers dressed as clowns in the circus-ring setting. The appeal of the main character, together with his songs "Gonna Build a Mountain," "One in a Lifetime," and "What Kind of Fool Am I?" and his wife's "Typically English," allowed the show to run for sixteen months in London and even longer in New York. The simplicity of its conception and accessibility of its songs made it an enduring vehicle for star performers, most notably Sammy Davis, Jr.

Bricusse next supplied the lyrics to music by West End conductor and songwriter Cyril Ornadel (1924–) for *Pickwick* (1963), a highly successful adaptation by Wolf Mankowitz of episodes in Charles Dickens's *Posthumous Papers of the Pickwick Club*. The title role was tailored to the portly shape and fine tenor voice of Harry Secombe, who largely left behind his alter ego as a zany radio comedian. If the initial success owed much to Secombe and a fine supporting cast that included Anton Rodgers as Jingle, its continuing popularity is due equally to the perennial appeal of Dickens's story and a genuinely musical score by Ornadel that includes the song "If I Ruled the World," which became Secombe's signature tune. Ornadel went on to compose music for various musical adaptations of the classics, among them *Ann Veronica* (1969), after H. G. Wells; *Treasure Island* (1973), after Robert Louis Stevenson; and *Great Expectations* (1975), again after Dickens. *Treasure Island* provided Christmas fare for several years at the former warehouse in the City of London that actor-producer Bernard Miles converted into the Mermaid Theatre.

Bricusse resumed his collaboration with Newley on *The Roar of the Greasepaint—the Smell of the Crowd* (1964). It was similar to its predecessor in being on a small scale—this time in a pantomime rather than a circus setting—and constructed around a central character. The lead was not initially played by Newley himself (although he later starred on Broadway) but by fall-about comedian Norman Wisdom as the oppressed little Cocky against the all-powerful Sir. The prime attractions of the show were once more the appealing central character, plus songs of which "On a Wonderful Day Like Today" became a popular favourite.

The third Bricusse-Newley collaboration, *The Good Old Bad Old Days* (1972), produced a successful title song, without making anything like the impression of its predecessors. A fourth and final collaboration, *The Travelling Music Show* (1978), was a vehicle for television performer Bruce Forsyth that proved a quick flop. By then Bricusse had established himself as lyricist and composer for such musical films as *Doctor Doolittle* (1967) and *Willie Wonka and the Chocolate Factory* (1971), and his later stage works were generally adaptations of his film scores. *Goodbye, Mr Chips* (1982) was based on a 1968 film adaptation of James Hilton's story about a kindly old schoolmaster, played on stage by John Mills. *Sherlock Holmes, the Musical* (1989) was an adaptation of an aborted screen project, with Ron Moody as Arthur Conan Doyle's celebrated detective. *Scrooge* (1992) was another Dickens adaptation whose 1970 film version had Anthony Newley in the title role. *Victor/Victoria,* for which Bricusse supplied lyrics to music by Henry Mancini (1924–94), featured Julie Andrews as a gender-confused performer in both its 1982 screen and 1995 New York stage versions.

That Dickens was seen as such a fertile source for British musicals was due in major part to the monumental success of one show in particular. Its lyricist-composer was Lionel Bart (1930–99), a Jewish East Ender who made his name in the mid-1950s with pop songs such as "A Handful of Songs" and "Little White

Bull" for Tommy Steele, "Living Doll" for Cliff Richard, and "Do You Mind?" for Anthony Newley. He progressed to the West End via material for the politically committed Unity Theatre, where his *Wally Pone* (1958), a Soho gangster adaptation of Ben Jonson's *Volpone,* was briefly staged. The following year he made his mark in no small way, first with a production by Joan Littlewood's progressive Theatre Workshop company at the Theatre Royal, Stratford, East London. Bart's title song for *Fings Ain't Wot They Used T'Be* (1959) proclaimed the quest for modernity, evident also in the modest orchestra of piano, bass, drums, guitar, alto saxophone, tenor saxophone, and trombone and in a cast of layabout characters. Glynn Edwards and Miriam Karlin played cafe owner Fred Cochran and his longtime girlfriend Lilly Smith, and the supporting cast included several performers who were to enjoy subsequent celebrity, among them Barbara Windsor, George Sewell, and Yootha Joyce. The show's efforts to push back theatrical frontiers earned a rap from the censor: one character was played as openly homosexual, which was unacceptable at that time.

That same year Bart provided lyrics only to a score by Laurie Johnson (1927–) for *Lock up Your Daughters* (1959), an adaptation of Henry Fielding's 1730 tale *Rape upon Rape* with which Bernard Miles opened his ambitious Mermaid Theatre project. The spirit of adventure newly afoot in the London musical was evident in architect Sean Kenny's all-purpose set, and the piece created a ready audience for its Restoration excesses. The rape of Fielding's title never actually occurs, being merely the facade behind which are hidden the sexual adventures of the voluptuous Hilaret (played by Stephanie Voss), her lover Captain Constant (Terence Cooper), her would-be lover Ramble (Frederick Jaeger) and the latter's lover (Hy Hazell), who is the wife of Justice Squeezum (Richard Wordsworth), before whom Ramble and Hilaret are arraigned. Songs such as "When Does the Ravishing Begin?" and the heroine's description of her deflowering on "A Sunny Sunday Morning" as she removes her clothes while seducing the judge indicate the nature of the piece, which proved too indecent for New York.

Bart then composed the Dickens adaptation that started the trend and won him immortality: *Oliver!* (1960). He made his own book from Dickens's *Oliver Twist* and provided songs that are simple but varied and particularly apt for a show in which the novel's villainous excesses are toned down to provide family entertainment. The score contains one hit after another: "Food, Glorious Food" for the boys of the orphanage, the title song for the beadle Mr Bumble, and "Consider Yourself" for the Artful Dodger, Oliver, and the boys. Above all there are "Pick a Pocket" and "Reviewing the Situation" for the now-lovable villain Fa-

Nicolette Roeg as Nancy and Harry Goodier as Bill Sykes
from Bart's *Oliver!*
Mander and Mitchenson Theatre Collection

gin (played by Ron Moody), and a fine set of songs for kindhearted but ill-fated Nancy (Georgia Brown)—"It's a Fine Life," "Oom-Pah-Pah," and the plaintive "As Long As He Needs Me." Sean Kenny's revolving, multipurpose set, combining stairs, arches, and platforms, set the standard for British theatrical design for years. The show ran for six years and 2,618 performances, achieved a longer run on Broadway than any previous British musical, and inspired a successful film and frequent revivals around the world.

On the back of this huge success Bart came up with the spectacular *Blitz!* (1962), which presented a panorama of World War II London and a story of East End racial rivalry against the background of falling bombs. Something of the mood of the piece was portrayed by the pastiche "Who's That Geezer Hitler?" The show clocked up 568 performances and a sixteen-month run. Then, for his next piece, Bart abandoned London settings for Liverpool's dockland. *Maggie*

May (1964) was built by librettist Alun Owen around the old English ballad character of prostitute Maggie May (played by Rachel Roberts), though the central character was not Maggie herself but her childhood sweetheart, docker Casey (Kenneth Haigh). The son of a union worker, he opposes unthinking union action but ends up leading a wildcat strike and dies while seeking to ditch a cargo of arms for South American anti-riot police. The piece had a strong book and colourful characters, who were well served by numbers that ranged from a love song "It's Yourself I Want" to a topical piece for a Beatles-replica pop group.

Alas, Bart was to throw away all he had built up with one act of grandiose folly. This was a feeble burlesque of the Robin Hood legend that became one of the most celebrated flops of musical theatre history. When *Twang!!* (with two exclamation marks) opened at London's Shaftesbury Theatre in 1965 its weakness was apparent to everyone except Bart, who was so convinced of its possibilities that he ploughed his personal fortune into it and ended up bankrupting himself. His personal and financial problems were not helped by the reception of his next stage musical, a version of the film *La Strada,* which achieved just one performance on Broadway in 1969. Apart from a couple of shows produced at the Theatre Royal, Stratford, East London, in 1972, nothing more of Bart's reached the stage, not even an oft-promised musical version of *The Hunchback of Notre Dame.* Bart's financial ruin extended even to losing his share in the income from *Oliver!*

Where Heneker, Bricusse, and Bart were lyricists first and composers second, one other outstanding British work of the 1960s belonged almost entirely to the composer. *Robert and Elizabeth* (1964) stood out in its time for a score of almost comic-opera standard. The composer was Ron Grainer (1922–81), who left his native Australia and made his fortune in London as the composer of themes for the enormously successful television series *Steptoe and Son, Maigret,* and *Dr Who.* His venture into the musical theatre began with a version of the romance between the crippled poet Elizabeth Barrett and the poet Robert Browning, with a book and lyrics by Ronald Miller based on the play *The Barretts of Wimpole Street.* The formidably stern Barrett father, who opposed the romance, was effectively a non-singing role, with John Clements delivering his musical contribution *parlando.* However, the triumphant romantic leading roles were written for popular operatic soprano June Bronhill and the highly capable singer Keith Michell, who had already made a mark in Ellis's *And So to Bed* and was later to take the leading role in Leigh's *Man of La Mancha* in London. Grainer's score is topped by the joyous romantic duet "I Know Now," while the leading lady rejoices in an operatic Soliloquy and the leading man in "The Moon in My Pocket." There is also

O'Brien's *The Rocky Horror Show* at Theatre Upstairs, 1973, with Tim Curry (right)
Photo by Donald Cooper

a delightful daydreaming piece, "The Girls That Boys Dream About," for the numerous Barrett children.

The show ran for 948 performances in London and repeated its success around the British Commonwealth. However, legal difficulties prevented it from being staged on Broadway. Moreover, Grainer's television interests and ill-health prevented him from devoting much more attention to the musical theatre. His later contributions were restricted to the smaller-scale *On the Level* (1966), the pastiche *Sing a Rude Song* (1970), which incorporated popular music-hall songs into a story of the performer Marie Lloyd, and the Dickens adaptation *Nickleby and Me* (1975).

In altogether livelier style was a musical adaptation of Chaucer's bawdy *Canterbury Tales* (1968), with lyrics by scholar Nevill Coghill in simple settings by Richard Hill and John Hawkins. Song titles such as "I Have a Noble Cock" and "Come Along and Marry Me, Honey" exemplify the nature of the piece, whose cast included Nicky Henson (son of musical comedian Leslie Henson), Kenneth J. Warren as the Miller, and Wilfred Brambell as the Reeve. The show clocked up more than 2,000 performances, as later did *The Rocky Horror Show*

(1973), a science-fiction rock musical with 1950s-style pop songs by New Zealander Richard O'Brien (1942–). This ran for more than five years in Chelsea before extending its run in the West End and being filmed.

Another isolated success was a show by film composer John Barry (1933–), whose first stage venture was with *Passion Flower Hotel* (1965). This was a tale of public schoolgirls teaching neighbouring public schoolboys to lose their sexual inhibitions and was notable mainly for the number of future stars who appeared as the schoolgirls (Francesca Annis, Jane Birkin, Pauline Collins) and schoolboys (Bill Kenwright, Nicky Henson). Barry fared better with *Billy* (1974), a 904-performance hit at Drury Lane Theatre. An adaptation of the play *Billy Liar,* by Keith Waterhouse and Willis Hall, *Billy* had lyrics by Don Black (1936–) and told of Yorkshire lad Billy Fisher, a daydreamer who lies his way through every problem he encounters in life. Among his current problems are the fact that he has stolen money from his employer and his inability to choose between girlfriends Barbara and Rita. He seeks to resolve the problems by escaping to London; ultimately, he decides to remain in his native Stradhoughton where his daydreams can continue to flourish. The major attraction was the performance of comic actor Michael Crawford, living out Billy's fantasies in delightfully lighthearted fashion. Elaine Paige also attracted attention as Rita.

The postwar years had thus offered Britain isolated local successes; but from the 1940s to the 1960s only *Stop the World—I Want to Get Off* and *Oliver!* were works that significantly challenged the overwhelming success of the American musical on its own terms. The British musical as a whole proved sadly unable to produce the fusion of dramatic, musical, and directorial vision that in those same years made the American musical such a compelling and highly exportable commodity. Happily, talents were in the wings that would at least give the European product the ability once again to compete with the American during the final quarter of the century.

Chapter Eighteen
Towards the Twenty-First Century

Since the Second World War, the theatre has seen huge changes. Production techniques and musical styles have developed, and above all the economics of the theatre have altered radically. Where pre-Broadway or pre–West End openings formerly offered an opportunity to iron out problems, the decline in large-scale provincial theatres and the increased costs of touring have meant that the same function has to be provided by previews before the formal opening night. No longer are labour and theatre props cheap, and the cost of mounting a spectacular show can be paid off only from a substantial run at high prices. With television an even more potent competitor than the cinema ever was, an evening out has become a special occasion, for which the public at large requires a show that is a proven success. Thus acknowledged successes go on for years attracting a public, while slow starters or badly reviewed productions all too readily sink without trace.

New shows have thus increasingly been divided into two categories. On the one hand, those of modest pretensions seek to cut costs by employing small casts that act as their own chorus, with role-doubling, small orchestras that use electronic instruments, and props that merely suggest the setting rather than elaborate formal sets. On the other hand, extravagant large-scale blockbusters require full houses and long runs to repay their costs.

The blockbuster musical, which sought to counter modern economic reality through worldwide productions and marketing, has become associated particularly with English composer Andrew Lloyd Webber (1948–). The son of a principal of the London College of Music, Lloyd Webber was stagestruck from childhood. As a teenager, he teamed up with aspiring pop musician and lyricist Tim Rice (1944–) on a twenty-minute biblical pop cantata called *Joseph and the Amazing Technicolor Dreamcoat*. First produced at a boys' school, it proved extremely popular for its combination of traditional lyrical writing with more up-to-date pop elements, all suffused with youthful exuberance and innocence. Expanded to thirty-five minutes and recorded in 1968, it attracted sufficient critical acclaim to pave the way for another work that likewise began life as a pop single, then became a two-record set, before finally being staged not in London but in New York.

This was *Jesus Christ Superstar* (1971). Described as a "rock opera," it tells the story of the events leading up to the Crucifixion in modern vernacular and rock terms through the eyes of Judas. The originality of the concept and staging, and a through-composed score combining modern rock songs with traditional elements, proved irresistible. The rock title song and Mary Magdalene's country-style ballad "I Don't Know How to Love Him" gained particular popularity. The stage show had a comparatively modest run of 711 performances in New York, but in London it ran for eight years and 3,358 performances, becoming the longest-running West End musical of all time and spawning productions and recordings around the world.

With such success, it was only a matter of time before *Joseph and the Amazing Technicolor Dreamcoat* likewise made its way into the theatre, playing in London in a double bill with another biblical piece by the team, *Jacob's Journey* (1973). *Joseph* thereafter continued to expand into a form in which it was extensively toured and frequently restaged in London, proving especially popular as family entertainment. Again through-sung, it is a simple retelling of the biblical story of Joseph and his brothers, performed by a small cast (originally all-male, but subsequently introducing Potiphar's Wife and a female narrator) backed by a children's chorus. The popular elements include the portrayal of Pharaoh as a performer in the Elvis Presley mode and Joseph's "Close Every Door to Me," the highlight of a wide range of lively popular musical styles that include country ("There's One More Angel in Heaven"), calypso for the brothers, and the lilting "Any Dream Will Do."

Without Rice, Lloyd Webber next ventured into a very different style of piece. With playwright Alan Ayckbourn he created *Jeeves* (1975), based on P. G. Wodehouse's popular creation, with songs in period style. The attempt proved disastrously misjudged. The show closed after only a few performances, though the project was eventually rescued by revision on a much smaller scale, with almost entirely new songs, as *By Jeeves* (1996). Lloyd Webber returned to Rice, and the pair created their third huge commercial success of the decade.

Evita (1978) is a somewhat sanitised portrayal of the legendary Eva Perón, the country girl who ruthlessly rose to be the wife and power behind President Juan Perón of Argentina, espousing the cause of the poor people and achieving near deification before dying of cancer while still in her early thirties. Again the piece is virtually through-composed and incorporates rock music. However, Lloyd Webber also included more ambitiously developed passages and adapted the same material to be used as the narrator Che Guevara's rock number "Oh What a Circus" (in which he mocks Eva's death), and as the show's emotionally charged hit "Don't Cry for Me, Argentina," which dominated the air waves when the work first emerged as a two-record set in 1976. Altogether, the show contains more popular hit numbers than had become customary in works where dramatic development and integration of speech and action were considered more appropriate. Among them are the tango "On This Night of a Thousand Stars," Eva's plea to Juan, "I'd Be Surprisingly Good for You," as she ousts his current mistress from his bed, and the deposed mistress's equally appealing "Another Suitcase in Another Hall." Che also has another striking number, "High Flying Adored." In the London stage production, Elaine Paige played Evita, Joss Ackland was Juan, the pop singer David Essex was Che, and Siobhan McCarthy was the deposed mistress. Produced by director Harold Prince, the show achieved 2,900 performances in London and 1,568 on Broadway, and was staged around the world.

The Lloyd Webber phenomenon was now fully established. Everything he touched seemed to turn to gold, including a set of classical orchestral variations for his cellist brother Julian Lloyd Webber on Paganini's oft-varied theme, and (with lyricist Don Black) a pop-song cycle, *Tell Me on a Sunday,* about an innocent English girl embroiled in a series of love affairs in Hollywood. With an eye ever open for commercial possibilities, Lloyd Webber combined these two into the stage show *Song and Dance* (1982), with the song cycle sung by Marti Webb and a choreographed version of the variations performed by a team of dancers headed by ballet dancer Wayne Sleep.

Lloyd Webber now had his own company, which mounted his productions in conjunction with rising young producer Cameron Mackintosh. For the testing ground of his private Sydmonton Festival, Lloyd Webber set several of the poems in T. S. Eliot's *Old Possum's Book of Practical Cats.* Uncertain how to develop the idea, he turned to Mackintosh and, together, they assembled a team headed by director Trevor Nunn and choreographer Gillian Lynne who together created a stage piece of dazzling originality. Basically a dance show, *Cats* (1981) is populated entirely by feline characters and has no real dramatic development apart from the climactic ascent of the glamorous Grizabella from a rubbish tip to a new existence in the Heaviside Layer (the layer of the ionosphere able to reflect medium-frequency radio waves). There was luxurious casting in pop singer Paul Nicholas as Rum-Tum-Tigger, television actor Brian Blessed as Bustopher Jones (the white-spatted cat of the gentlemen's clubs), Wayne Sleep as the magical Mister Mistoffelees, Bonnie Langford as Rumpleteazer, and *Evita* star Elaine Paige as Grizabella. Catchily appealing as Lloyd Webber's through-composed score proved to be, everything else was overshadowed by the success of the achingly beautiful "Memory," whose lyric was built up by Nunn from suggestions by Eliot. As a further daring innovation, the show was staged in the round at the experimental New London Theatre. The stage and a section of seating revolved, inspiring the publicity line: "Latecomers not admitted while auditorium is in motion."

Seemingly undeterred by the challenge of coming up with another similarly inventive concept, Lloyd Webber gave life to another underused London theatre when he had the huge Apollo Victoria converted into what was, in effect, a vast roller-skating rink, with wooden tracks encircling the auditorium up to the level of the circle. Instead of cats, the characters of *Starlight Express* (1984) were steam trains played by performers on roller-skates, with a climax in which an old steam train named Rusty (played by Ray Shell) beats more streamlined modern competitors to couple up with a pretty carriage named Pearl (Stephanie

Lloyd Webber's *Cats* at the New London Theatre, 1981
Photo by Donald Cooper: PHOTOSTAGE

Lawrence). Nunn was once more the director, with Richard Stilgoe as lyricist. In order to attract a more youthful audience, the score reverted to Lloyd Webber's more pop-orientated style. But despite an insistent title song and attractive numbers such as "There's Me," there was no major hit; nonetheless, the show settled in for seeming permanence alongside *Cats*, undergoing a major overhaul in 1992 in which routines were modernised and new numbers added.

Meanwhile, Tim Rice's attempt to forge a viable alternative working relationship with composer Stephen Oliver (1950–92) for a show about the Plantagenet troubadour *Blondel* (1983) came to little. That Rice could, however, succeed without his erstwhile partner was proved with the success of *Chess* (1986), written in collaboration with Björn Ulvaeus and Benny Andersson, the male half of the successful Swedish pop group Abba. This had its genesis in the challenge by American chess player Bobby Fischer to the domination of the game by the Soviet Union. The stage was set out as a chessboard, and the Cold War action was set against the background of a World Chess Championship taking place in the mountain resort of Merano in the South Tyrol. The competitors are the American Frederick Trumper (played by Murray Head), accompanied by his girlfriend Florence Vassy (Elaine Paige), and the Russian Anatoly Sergeievsky (Tommy Kor-

Stephanie Lawrence, Chrissy Wickham, Frances Ruffelle,
and Ray Shell in Lloyd Webber's *Starlight Express*
at the Apollo Victoria, 1984
Photo by Donald Cooper: PHOTOSTAGE

berg), who arrives along with a huge back-up team determined to ensure Soviet glory. Propaganda, shady trade deals, and amorous complications lead the Russian to defect; the following year, he successfully defends his title in Bangkok against a new Soviet challenger, but then returns to Russia. As with Lloyd Webber's pieces, the work is through-composed, and it likewise originated in recorded form, producing two hits in the duet "I Know Him So Well" for Trumper's mistress and wife, and Trumper's solo "One Night in Bangkok."

Rice went on to write lyrics for animated Disney films and for *Heathcliff* (1996), a stage vehicle inspired by Emily Brontë's *Wuthering Heights* for pop singer Cliff Richard with a score by John Farrar. Simultaneously, Lloyd Webber's operations expanded into a worldwide marketing and production operation that was for a time a quoted public company. Its shareholders had no reason to complain about his next offering, mounted on an unprecedented scale of opulence and with a degree of romantic indulgence beyond anything heard in the musical theatre for some time. This was *The Phantom of the Opera* (1986), an adaptation of the novel by Gaston Leroux. Lloyd Webber's inspiration had been an earlier adaptation by Ken Hill, author of a number of clever and moderately successful musical pieces with pastiche scores. Lloyd Webber had first planned for his production company to mount Hill's show as a vehicle for his current wife Sarah Brightman, but then he decided to compose his own score. The lyrics were by Charles Hart and Richard Stilgoe.

The Phantom (played by Michael Crawford) is a hideously deformed composer who has hidden himself away in the bowels of the Paris Opéra. He falls in love with the voice and beauty of a member of the chorus, Christine Daaé (Brightman) and frightens the directors of the Opéra into promoting her at the expense of prima donna Carlotta (Rosemary Ashe) in an opera he has composed. Jealous at Christine's love for young Raoul de Chagny (Steve Barton), the Phantom takes her to his dungeon home, but is ultimately unable to keep her away from the man she really loves. Lloyd Webber and his regular co-orchestrator David Cullen produced lush, romantic sounds for a score that boasts a scale of lyricism that had appeared to be long gone from the musical theatre. The principal numbers include the Phantom's haunting monologue "Music of the Night"; his duets with Christine, the title song and "Past the Point of No Return"; her duet with Raoul, "All I Ask of You"; an ambitious ensemble, "Prima Donna"; a similarly huge-scale chorus, "Masquerade"; and a comic duet for two bungling operatic impresarios. Although a triumph for Brightman, it highlighted even more the versatility of Crawford, who, after playing the juvenile lead in the film of *Hello, Dolly!*, became famous as a knockabout television comedy star, starred in *Billy*, performed athletic feats in the title role of the London production of *Barnum*, and now displayed a voice of operatic proportions in a hugely demanding role. Productions around the world confirmed the work as Lloyd Webber's most rounded achievement.

Things could scarcely get better, and indeed Lloyd Webber's subsequent shows in the same romantic style have by his own standards been disappointing both artistically and commercially, albeit triumphs by anyone else's. *Aspects of Love* (1989), based on a novel by David Garnett, was on a more modest scale. Set in France, it concerns handsome young Alex Dillingham (played by Michael

Ball), who battles for the attentions of actress Rose Vibart (Ann Crumb) against his lecherous Uncle George (Kevin Colson), only to conclude that he is better off with his uncle's former mistress Giulietta (Kathleen Rowe McAllen). The lyrics were written by Don Black and Charles Hart, and the big number (trailed, as was Lloyd Webber's custom, before the show opened) was the duet "Love Changes Everything," whose main theme bore an uncanny resemblance to a tune in Offenbach's *Tromb-al-ca-zar*.

Rather more ambitious—certainly in its elaborate stage set—was Lloyd Webber's next work. *Sunset Boulevard* (1993) was adapted from a Billy Wilder film about an ageing film star who refuses to believe that her fame and glamour have faded. Patti LuPone was the first of a succession of distinguished actresses who assumed the demanding leading role, and her numbers included the big hit "With One Look." Don Black this time shared the credits as lyricist with Christopher Hampton. The show had a month's break for revision in the light of experience in the United States and ultimately closed within four years—a comparative failure by its composer's standards. Moreover, Lloyd Webber's follow-up, *Whistle Down the Wind* (1996), another adaptation of a screenplay, written with American lyricist Jim Steinman, was withdrawn for revision after its preliminary, unsuccessful staging in America, but received more favourable reviews when revised for London in 1998. It is still running in London at the time of writing, alongside his three big hits of the 1980s—*Cats, Starlight Express,* and *The Phantom of the Opera*. *Cats* has already passed 6,000 performances in London and has also become Broadway's longest-running show.

After *Cats* the activities of producer Cameron Mackintosh ran largely parallel to, rather than in conjunction with, those of Lloyd Webber. He reinforced his position not only with further productions for Lloyd Webber but through an association with the French team of song-publisher-lyricist Alain Boublil (1941–) and recording-producer-composer Claude-Michel Schönberg (1944–). Seeking to strike out after the manner of Lloyd Webber and Rice, they addressed themselves to French historical epics, initially with the "rock opera" *La Révolution française* (1973), a cavalcade of the events surrounding the French Revolution, which was produced initially as a two-record set and then transferred to the stage in Paris with Schönberg playing Louis XVI.

The pair then turned to Victor Hugo's epic novel for *Les Misérables* (1980), highlighting nineteenth-century Parisian poverty through the struggles of the revolutionary Jean Valjean against the police agent Javert. This likewise graduated from a concept album to stage. As with all other French productions of the time,

Boublil and Schönberg's *Les Misérables* at the Palace Theatre, 1985
Photo by Donald Cooper: PHOTOSTAGE

it might have remained confined to French stages had it not been for a different Boublil venture—an adaptation of songs written by Björn Ulvaeus and Benny Andersson for the pop group Abba into the fairy-tale musical *Abbacadabra*. After the usual long-playing record debut, this was taken up by Cameron Mackintosh as a 1983 family Christmas entertainment for London. The connection thus established, Mackintosh looked at other Boublil works and, in *Les Misérables,* saw possibilities that would probably have remained obscure to anyone else viewing a French epic with a huge cast and an even bigger time span. Under Mackintosh's guidance, the piece was totally overhauled, concentrating more on character than events that were familiar to the French but not to the British. Music was switched between characters, and new songs were inserted, with English lyrics by Herbert Kretzmer (1925–).

The English adaptation (1985) overcame teething problems under the protection of the publicly subsidised Royal Shakespeare Company, but transfer to a commercial venue was a highly risky venture. Yet once in the vast spaces of the Palace Theatre, the show soon became a cult. Vindicating Mackintosh's faith, the audience associated itself readily with the hunted but heroically reformed petty thief Valjean (played by Colm Wilkinson), his vengeful police hunter Javert (Roger Allam), the impoverished Fantine (Patti LuPone), her orphaned child Cosette (Rebecca Caine), the roguish innkeeper Thénardier (Alun Armstrong), his wife, and the young student Marius (Michael Ball). The basic gloom of the piece was relieved by the gloriously forceful momentum of Schönberg's three-hour through-composed score, with such finely varied set numbers as Valjean's Soliloquy ("What Have I Done?"), Fantine's lovely "I Dreamed a Dream," Fantine's emotionally wrenching Death, Marius's wistful "Empty Chairs and Empty Tables," and the roisterously comic "Master of the House" for the Thénardiers. The success was repeated as the show made its way around the world, with seemingly only the French (perhaps understandably seeing the revision as a watered-down version of Hugo's concept) greeting Mackintosh's version with indifference.

Mackintosh returned to the same creators for a follow-up. *Miss Saigon* (1989), with English lyrics by Richard Maltby, Jr., was essentially the *Madame Butterfly* story updated to the Vietnam War. Kim (played by Lea Salonga) is one of the attractions of a Saigon brothel run by "the Engineer" (Jonathan Pryce). She falls in love with one of her clients, the American soldier Chris (Simon Bowman), only to lose him when he is evacuated back to America and marries. When it becomes known that Kim has had a son by Chris, he and his new wife, Ellen, return to what is now Ho Chi Minh City, where Kim commits suicide in order to force Chris to take his son to a better life in America. With spectacular stage effects such as a helicopter taking off, and a marketable hit in the duet "I Still Believe," the show became for ten years another of London's principal tourist attractions, even if its score lacked the onward impulse, emotional involvement, and cohesion of *Les Misérables*.

Almost seven years were to pass before London saw the next Boublil-Schönberg piece, *Martin Guerre* (1996), based on a traditional French story about a returning soldier whose wife isn't sure whether he is really her husband or an impostor. In the musical adaptation much of the dramatic tension was removed by making it clear from the start that the man is an impostor. Faced with public and critical indifference, Mackintosh withdrew the piece and relaunched it with an added rationale for the characters' acceptance of the situation. However, the piece never really settled down and closed in London within two years, thereafter embarking on a national tour in pared-down form.

The need to get everything right before launching a musical on demanding critics and audiences has meant that even a Lloyd Webber is nowadays more likely to have a new production only every four years rather than at Offenbach's rate of four per year. It has also meant that, along with the major musical creators since the 1960s—Sondheim, Coleman, Herman, Kander and Ebb, Lloyd Webber, and Boublil and Schönberg—there have been many others who have achieved only fleeting or intermittent success in the musical theatre.

Back in the 1960s, composer Burt Bacharach (1928–) and lyricist Hal David (1921–) created a string of song standards: "Magic Moments," "Twenty-Four Hours from Tulsa," "What's New, Pussycat?" and "Do You Know the Way to San Jose?" In 1968 they added to this their single contribution to Broadway. *Promises, Promises* had a book by playwright Neil Simon that was based on the Billy Wilder film *The Apartment.* The story concerns bachelor Chuck Baxter (played by Jerry Orbach), who is largely ignored by his bosses at work until they discover he has an apartment they can borrow for their extramarital flings. The arrangement brings Chuck rapid promotion (after the manner of Lieutenant Fritz in *La Grand-Duchesse de Gérolstein*), until he needs the apartment himself when fate brings to it the girl for whom he has long sighed. The show had memorable dance routines by Michael Bennett and provided another Bacharach-David pop hit in "I'll Never Fall in Love Again."

Another isolated success was by Sherman Edwards (1919–81), who majored in American history and was for a while a history teacher before becoming a dance-band pianist and songwriter. He conceived the idea of combining his two interests in a musical depicting as faithfully as possible the events surrounding the signing of the Declaration of Independence. *1776* (1969) overcame preconceptions about the appeal of an almost entirely male cast and historical subject, and audiences were much taken by songs that, without having a specifically eighteenth-century sound, nonetheless contained an appropriate period feel. Howard Da Silva had the starring role as Benjamin Franklin, with Ken Howard as Thomas Jefferson, William Daniels as John Adams, and Virginia Vestoff and Betty Buckley in the two female roles of Abigail Adams and Martha Jefferson. The show was a 1,217-performance hit, and went on to be filmed.

Songwriter Gary Geld (1935–) had a fair success with *Purlie* (1970), a musical comedy version of a play by Ossie Davis about slightly dubious dealing that allows the hero to rebuild a chapel and be installed as preacher. Its Broadway run of almost two years was then bettered by the 1,050 performances of Geld's follow-up, *Shenandoah* (1974). This was a musical adaption of a 1965 film, with John Cullum playing James Stewart's film role of a matter-of-fact farmer in the Shenandoah Valley who vainly tries to prevent himself and his family of six sons and a daughter from being dragged into the Civil War. The score of country-western songs and passionate antiwar declarations proved sufficiently appealing for the show to graduate from the Goodspeed Opera House in Connecticut to New York's Alvin Theatre. However, Geld's third and final Broadway score, *Angel* (1978), based on Thomas Wolfe's *Look Homeward, Angel,* managed just five performances.

Off-Broadway theatres provided opportunities for many pieces that might have struggled to achieve production in more conventional venues. Broadway itself had seen musicals based on comic-strip characters, for instance, in *Li'l Abner,* with lyrics by Johnny Mercer and music by Gene de Paul (1919–88), even before Charles Strouse's *It's a Bird, It's a Plane, It's Superman* and *Annie.* Off Broadway, composer-lyricist Clark Gessner enjoyed a 1,597-performance success with *You're a Good Man, Charlie Brown* (1967), a small-scale, charmingly light-hearted stage representation of Charles Schulz's *Peanuts* comic-strip characters Charlie Brown and his day-dreaming dog Snoopy. The show moved briefly to Broadway itself in 1971, and even enjoyed a revival there in 1999. A later *Peanuts* musical, *Snoopy!!!* (1976), with music by Larry Grossman, was almost equally admired.

Off-Broadway productions also provided opportunities for women creators of musicals. Composer Nancy Ford (1935–) and librettist-lyricist Gretchen Cryer (1935–) met at DePauw University, married fellow students, and made their way to Broadway together. Ford was one of the pianists of the long-running *Fantasticks,* and Cryer appeared in the chorus of Coleman's *Little Me* and Schmidt and Jones's *110 in the Shade.* Their creative partnership began off-Broadway with *Now Is the Time for All Good Men* (1967), with Cryer herself appearing in a piece based on her brother's experience of serving two years in prison as a conscientious objector during the Vietnam War. It was followed by the more lighthearted *The Last Sweet Days of Isaac* (1970), which campaigned against nothing more than excess documentation (tapes and photographs as well as paper). Their debut Broadway piece, *Shelter* (1973), was along similar lines; it concerned a young man's relationships with three women while he is in a television studio with a talking computer. But it was with their next work that they hit the jackpot. *I'm Getting My Act Together and Taking It on the Road* (1978) was once more small scale and autobiographical, dealing with a thirty-nine-year-old recently divorced pop singer who seeks to resurrect her career. The leading role was played by the newly divorced Cryer, and the show captured the current popular mood of sympathy for the single (or newly single) woman. The songs were accompanied by piano, guitar, and drums after the style of the time. The show ran for 1,165 performances and was also produced in London and Berlin. During the run, the lyricist was succeeded in the leading role not only by the composer but also for a time by fellow composer Carol Hall (1936–).

Hall's mother was a piano and violin teacher who ensured her daughter's thorough grounding in the classics. During the 1960s Hall followed the time-worn path of writing popular songs before creating a musical, *Wonderful Beast,* which did not get beyond the tryout stage. She did much better with *The Best Little Whorehouse in Texas* (1977), which captured life in the raw in her native state. It was developed from an article written for *Playboy* magazine by journalist Larry L. King about a real-life brothel where the local farmers paid for their services with chickens. This comfortable arrangement is disturbed by the arrival of a television journalist, who finally succeeds in using the power of television to arouse the "respectable community" into shutting the place down. The show was a 1,584-performance success, thanks to earthy Texan dialogue, skilfully etched characters —who included a compromised governor of Texas and an entire football team who arrive en masse to celebrate an important victory—songs that combined Nashville with Broadway, and dance routines by Tommy Tune. It was later filmed with Dolly Parton and Burt Reynolds, but proved less successful outside the United States.

Country sounds also pervaded the musical *Big River* (1985), whose composer was songwriter Roger Miller (1936–95) of "King of the Road" fame. His musical play was adapted by William Hauptmann from Mark Twain's *Huckleberry Finn* and succeeded better than previous attempts to bring Twain's Mississippi stories to the musical stage, achieving more than 1,000 performances. New York also followed London's passion for adapting Dickens with *The Mystery of Edwin Drood* (1985), which was set inside a performance at a Victorian English music hall and had an appropriate mix of songs by Rupert Holmes (1947–). What was especially original was the way the show dealt with the fact that Dickens had left the story unfinished. The musical paused where Dickens had done, and the audience was invited to vote for its preferred ending, with which the cast then brought the show to a conclusion.

A major preoccupation of the last third of the twentieth century has been the rock musical. In its raw form, the use of rock music is limited by its inability to express deep emotion; but several key works have achieved international renown. The "American tribal love-rock musical" *Hair* (1967) was first produced off-Broadway and shortly afterwards on Broadway itself to huge success. Its 1,442-performance Broadway run was followed by similar acclaim around the world: the run at London's Shaftesbury Theatre was halted after 1,998 performances only because the roof caved in—literally. The piece lacks a coherent story and is essentially a celebration of the youthful "make love, not war" philosophy of the 1960s. That it owes much of its celebrity to its much-publicised nudity should not detract from the appeal of the songs of composer Galt MacDermot (1928–), including the hugely popular "Aquarius." Of MacDermot's several subsequent scores, the most successful was a modern musical comedy version of Shakespeare's *Two Gentlemen of Verona* (1971).

Another huge rock-and-roll success was *Grease* (1972), which was first produced off-Broadway and went on to achieve a record Broadway run of 3,388 performances. It was described as a "new 50s rock 'n' roll musical," and it reproduced the slicked-back hairstyles and drainpipe clothing of the period. Most successful of its clever 1950s-pastiche songs by Jim Jacobs (1942–) and Warren Casey (1935–) was "Summer Nights," which became hugely popular after the show was filmed (with interpolated numbers) with John Travolta and Olivia Newton-John in 1978.

Of all the American composers of rock musicals, the one who has had the most significant career has been Stephen Schwartz (1948–), who achieved youthful fame as composer-lyricist of another work that originated off-Broadway. This was the biblical musical *Godspell* (1971), which combined rock music with country-western and other popular styles for a retelling of the last days of Christ. The tone of the show was youthful, and it attracted young audiences around the world with such songs as "Prepare Ye the Way of the Lord" and "Day by Day."

Schwartz next produced on Broadway an elaboration of a work conceived while he was a college student in music and theatre. *Pippin* (1972) was in the same mould as *Godspell;* it too featured a compère (played by Ben Vereen) who leads a group of white-faced players. They tell the tale of King Charlemagne's son Pippin (John Rubinstein), who undergoes a range of experiences while in search of a personal identity. Songs such as "Magic to Do" and "Corner of the Sky" contributed to a 1,944-performance run and various overseas productions. The similarly long-running *The Magic Show* (1974) was an ingenious vehicle for illusionist Doug Henning as a magician whose act saves a nightclub from being shut down. The songs and small orchestra provide a somewhat incidental attraction to a show whose highlights include the hero sawing his mistress in two and then watching his jealous wife run off with the bottom half. Thereafter Schwartz's shows did less well commercially. For *The Baker's Wife* (1976), based on a French film, he composed a more substantial score, but it failed to reach either Broadway or (after a major rewrite) the West End. *Rags* (1986), for which Schwartz was composer Charles Strouse's lyricist, and another biblical piece, *Children of Eden* (1991), likewise folded quickly.

Composer Marvin Hamlisch (1944–) studied classical piano before, in time-honoured fashion, turning to popular songwriting and working as rehearsal pianist and arranger while awaiting his big breakthrough. This came in 1973 with the title song for the Barbra Streisand film *The Way We Were* and, more especially, for his arrangement of Scott Joplin's ragtime music for the film *The Sting*. Even more noteworthy was his first venture into the musical theatre with the music for *A Chorus Line* (1975). This is the epitome of the "concept" musical; it presents the various personal situations and problems of a group of dancers who have gathered to audition for a place in the chorus of a show. The only real plot development is that, by the final curtain, the dancers have been chosen. The individuals' personal situations are presented with a sexual frankness that would have been inconceivable in the American theatre of earlier days. The auditioners serve as the chorus and appear in everyday clothes. By setting the action in an unoccupied theatre, the production also had the virtue of dispensing with expensive scenery in what had become economically strapped times. The numbers that succeeded most were "What I Did For Love," "At the Ballet," "Nothing," and, above all, "One (Singular Sensation)." The prime characters are the would-be show's choreographer Zach (played by Robert LuPone) and his former lover Cassie (Donna McKechnie); but the choreography of director Michael Bennett, whose concept the show was, had as much to do with the show's success as any other element. For a time, it was the longest-running Broadway show, closing in 1990 after a fifteen-year run.

Hamlisch's next Broadway venture was the small-scale *They're Playing Our Song* (1979). It featured a highly successful songwriter, Vernon Gersh (played by Robert Klein), in search of a new lyricist, whom he finds in the person of Sonia Walsk (Lucie Arnaz)—utterly neurotic, but an indispensable collaborator. By the end of Act 1 they have become lovers. The book was by playwright Neil Simon, and the songs, which included "Fallin'," the ballad "I Still Believe in Love," and the title song, were presented as the characters' creations and performed with the assistance of half a dozen backing singers representing the principals' alter egos. The show gained extra publicity from its genesis in the real-life romance between the composer and his lyricist, Carol Bayer Sager (1946–). Hamlisch failed badly with his next work, *Jean Seberg* (1983), written for the London stage and based on the life of the tragic actress. He fared little better either with *Smile* (1986) or with *The Goodbye Girl* (1993), a schmaltzy piece about a pair of opposites—a single mother and an eccentric bachelor—who are forced to share the same apartment and eventually fall in love. The book was based by Neil Simon on one of his film scripts, and the original lyrics were by David Zippel. New songs with lyrics by Don Black were added for a scaled-down London production in 1997.

London has over the past two decades been generally less receptive to new musical theatre creators. However, excitement was aroused by *The Hired Man* (1984), an adaptation by novelist Melvin Bragg of his Cumbrian family history, with music by Oxford graduate Howard Goodall (1958–). In the event, Goodall's folk music–flavoured score helped make the piece more a cult success than a popular hit. Nor did any greater success attend Goodall's *Girlfriends* (1987), about life in the Women's Royal Air Force in the Second World War, or *Days of Hope* (1992), set during the Spanish Civil War.

By comparison, a somewhat freakish success was achieved by *Blood Brothers* (1983), an updated version of the traditional *Corsican Brothers* melodrama of twin brothers who are separated at birth and brought up in contrasted circumstances and then meet and share adventures without realising their relationship. Here the setting is Liverpool, and the action focuses on the twins' mother, Mrs Johnstone (played by Barbara Dickson), forced to give away one of her sons to a wealthy family. While he achieves a respectable position, the twin reared in poverty ends up in prison. Playwright Willy Russell (1947–) provided his own simple songs, of which "I'm Not Saying a Word" and "Tell Me It's Not True" are the most striking. The show attracted no great attention in its first London production, but, after touring and being produced in Germany and the United States, it returned to London in 1988 for a revival and is still running at the time of writing.

Like the operetta between the world wars, the musical has in recent years often looked back to its glory years, with many works being revised and revived. On occasions, too, film scores have been adapted for the stage. This reversal of the former procedure of turning stage musicals into films has particularly been the case with 1950s film musicals, from which examples include *Singin' in the Rain* (1952; staged 1983), with songs by lyricist Arthur Freed (1894–1973) and Nacio Herb Brown (1896–1964); *Hans Christian Andersen* (1952; staged 1974), with songs by Frank Loesser; *Calamity Jane* (1953; staged 1961), with lyrics by Paul Francis Webster (1907–84) and music by Sammy Fain (1902–89); *Seven Brides for Seven Brothers* (1954, staged 1982), with lyrics by Johnny Mercer and music by Gene de Paul; Cole Porter's *High Society* (1956, staged 1987); and the Lerner and Loewe *Gigi* (1958, staged 1973). Perhaps the most successful of all has been *Forty-Second Street* (1980), a stage version of the 1933 Busby Berkeley film musical. The stage version starred Tammy Grimes and Jerry Orbach in a "song and dance extravaganza" that gathered songs by composer Harry Warren (1893–1945) and lyricist Al Dubin (1891–1945) from various Hollywood musicals. The dramatic announcement at the première's final curtain of the death of director-choreographer Gower Champion helped propel the show to a 3,486-performance run.

This adaptation of films into stage musicals has become an even more prominent aspect of the current Broadway and West End scene through the extravagant musicals based on animated Disney films aimed primarily at children. *Beauty and the Beast* (1994) launched the phenomenon on Broadway, and the show subsequently opened in London as well. Its composer, Alan Menken (1949–), had first come to the fore with a show that, rather than transferring to Broadway itself, remained intentionally off Broadway, where its small scale was more suitably accommodated. *Little Shop of Horrors* (1982) was conceived by the tiny WPA Theatre's co-director Howard Ashman (1951–91) as an intimate burlesque of a 1960 horror movie whose title it took. It went on to achieve a five-year run of 2,209 performances, productions around the world, and a film. Menken then composed the tuneful scores for a string of Disney animated movies—*The Little Mermaid* (1989), *Beauty and the Beast* (1991), *Aladdin* (1992), *Pocahontas* (1995), and *The Hunchback of Notre Dame* (1996). The first two were written with Ashman, the third (after Ashman's early death) with Tim Rice, and the last two with Stephen Schwartz as lyricist. The transition of *Beauty and the Beast* to the stage has been followed by that of *The Lion King*. With lyrics by Rice and music by British songwriter-performer Elton John (1947–), this was staged in 1997 at the historic New Amsterdam Theatre, lovingly restored for the purpose.

Among other Broadway creators to come to the fore during the past two decades has been Maury Yeston (1945–), son of a classical pianist mother and an English father who enjoyed music-hall songs. He was raised in New Jersey and educated at Yale University, where he became a professor of music theory. Composer of a cello concerto and other serious works, he joined the Broadcast Music, Inc. (BMI) Musical Theatre Workshops, which were run by distinguished musical theatre conductor Lehman Engel. Yeston's debut as a composer of musicals was with book author Arthur Kopit on *Nine* (1982), on which he worked for ten years. An adaptation of the Federico Fellini film *8½*, it is a surreal portrayal of megalomaniac film director Guido Contini (played by Raul Julia), trapped in an identity crisis and haunted by his relationships with a range of women. Sparsely staged and intellectually demanding, the piece gained a connoisseur's following, helped by Tommy Tune's involvement as director and by an elegant score that readily demonstrates Yeston's thorough musical expertise.

It was to be fifteen years before another Yeston show reached Broadway, though in the meantime he kept in touch with the musical theatre in various ways. First, with Kopit, he wrote an operetta-pastiche adaptation of Gaston Leroux's novel *The Phantom of the Opera*. Alas, the necessary financial backing evaporated when Andrew Lloyd Webber's opulent setting of the same story was staged in London. Eventually Yeston succeeded in producing it in Houston (1991), since when it has enjoyed success as a touring show. Yeston was more fortunate with an off-Broadway show *1-2-3-4-5* (1987), a lighthearted adaptation of the first five books of the Bible with a successful song called "New Words." He also composed *Goya,* a biographical work about the Spanish painter Francisco Goya. This was conceived as a stage vehicle for Spanish tenor Plácido Domingo, but, because of the latter's operatic commitments, eventually emerged in 1989 as a compact-disc creation, flavoured with guitars and pasodoble rhythms and incongruously starring Domingo opposite pop singer Gloria Estefan.

That same year Yeston also provided additional material for a revision of a musical from the past. This was the work of songwriters Robert Wright (1914–) and George Forrest (1915–99), who had reworked the music of Edvard Grieg for *Song of Norway* (1944), created *Gypsy Lady* (1946) from Victor Herbert's *The Fortune Teller* and *The Serenade,* then worked with the Brazilian composer Heitor Villa-Lobos (1887–1959) on *Magdalena* (1948), and achieved worldwide success with their arrangement of Borodin's music for the oriental show *Kismet* (1953), with its popular hits "Stranger in Paradise," "And This Is My Beloved," and "Baubles, Bangles, and Beads." *At the Grand* (1958) was an original Wright and Forrest creation, based on Vicki Baum's novel *Grand Hotel* and a film of the same title. In its original form it failed to reach New York, but, when remounted as *Grand Hotel* (1989), with additional numbers by Yeston, it enjoyed a good run. David Carroll and Liliane Montevecchi took the roles of hotel thief Felix von Gaigern and ageing ballerina Grushinskaya, played in the 1932 film by John Barrymore and Greta Garbo.

When finally Yeston succeeded in bringing another original work to Broadway in 1997, it was a piece about the fateful first and last voyage of the *Titanic.* Problems with the elaborate technical effects—the ship failed to sink during rehearsals—were finally overcome. With its spectacular staging and a rich score

A scene from Yeston's *Titanic* at the Lunt-Fontanne Theatre, 1997
Dodger Endemol Theatrical Productions, Inc.

incorporating period elements, *Titanic* won several Tony awards, but thereafter went down all too soon.

Among other creators to come to the fore in New York in the last two decades of the century were the team of lyricist Richard Maltby junior (1937–) and composer David Shire (1937–), both of whom have also tasted success independently. Maltby conceived and directed the "Fats" Waller compilation *Ain't Misbehavin'* (1978) and wrote the English-language lyrics for *Miss Saigon,* while Shire's film scores include *All the President's Men* (1976) and *Saturday Night Fever* (1977). Together they failed to get their stage musicals performed on Broadway until they produced a compilation show of their songs, *Starting Here, Starting Now* (1977). This was later followed by another compilation show, *Closer Than Ever* (1989). In between they finally achieved a Broadway book-musical production with *Baby* (1983), about three campus couples facing parenthood. Later they did so less successfully with *Big* (1996), an adaptation of the 1988 film comedy (starring Tom Hanks), about a young boy who wishes to be big, and temporarily becomes grown-up in size but not in attitude.

Composer Henry Krieger (1945–) had two important shows during the 1980s. *Dreamgirls* (1981) was a pop-music saga written in conjunction with lyricist Tom Eyen (1941–91) that was reportedly based on the black female singing group the Supremes. The show ran for more than four years, with the songs "And I'm Telling You I'm Going" and "One Night Only" being the most noteworthy. *The Tap Dance Kid* (1983), another showbiz musical, confirmed Krieger's reputation, but *Dangerous Music* (1988) was less successful. Krieger's eventual return to Broadway came with yet another showbiz musical, the through-composed *Side Show* (1997), written in conjunction with lyricist Bill Russell and having as its theme the experiences of the real-life Siamese twins Violet and Daisy Hilton, who rose to fame on the 1930s vaudeville stage. A highlight was a spectacularly lit number called "Tunnel of Love," in which the twins visit an amusement park at night. However, the show suffered from concentration on their role as freaks rather than exploring their personal feelings.

A remarkable three-generation landmark was reached with the off-Broadway production of *Floyd Collins* (1996). Composer-lyricist Adam Guettel is the son of composer Mary Rodgers and thus the grandson of Richard Rodgers. The work tells the real-life story of a man trapped in a cave in 1925. It gained considerable praise for its originality of approach and its musical score (featuring fiddles, banjos, and discordant strings), but its advanced musical language militated against its popular success.

Another name to emerge in the past few years is that of composer Frank Wildhorn. At one point during 1999 he actually had three shows running simultaneously on Broadway, though this was due to chance rather than any real longevity. *Jekyll and Hyde,* an adaptation of Robert Louis Stevenson's novel, achieved concept recordings in 1990 and 1994 before reaching Broadway in 1997. It found limited favour with the critics, but Wildhorn's big melodies and Leslie Bricusse's simple lyrics ensured that the show was still running two years later. *The Scarlet Pimpernel* (based on Baroness Orczy's novel) likewise began as a concept album in 1992, became a very different Broadway show in 1997, and was further revised for Broadway re-opening in 1998. Wildhorn's dramatic ballad style then found an eloquent outlet in *The Civil War* (1999), with a score blending traditional country, folk, and gospel styles into something more akin to oratorio than true musical theatre.

More consistent critical approval has greeted works by composer Stephen Flaherty (1960–) and lyricist Lynn Ahrens (1948–) who, like Maury Yeston, are products of Lehman Engel's BMI Workshop. Their first small-scale musical,

Lucky Stiff (1988), tells of a shoe salesman who has to take his uncle's corpse to Monte Carlo for a final gambling trip, needing to fulfil various conditions to avoid losing a six-million-dollar inheritance to a dog's home. More successful commercially was *Once on This Island* (1990), which is set in the French Antilles and whose tale is told in song and dance by peasants during a violent storm. The unsuccessful *My Favorite Year* (1992) was based on the film of the same name and, less explicitly, on the 1950s *Sid Caesar Show,* with a lowly member of the show's production team forced to keep a former swashbuckling film-star sober for a "live" sketch on the show. The creative pair have also provided material for the Twentieth Century Fox animated feature *Anastasia* (1997).

The most acclaimed achievement of Flaherty and Ahrens is *Ragtime,* which arrived in New York in late 1997 after a Toronto tryout in 1996. The concept has much in common with the Charles Strouse-Stephen Schwartz musical *Rags,* but in this case the show is specifically based on E. L. Doctorow's novel of the same name, representing a sprawling tapestry of immigration and social and industrial progress against the background of turn-of-the-century America. More specifically it tells the tragic tales of three New York families, the characters including Harlem ragtime pianist Coalhouse Walker (played by Brian Stokes Mitchell) and his wife Sarah (Audra McDonald). The epic score seamlessly combines the contrasts of ragtime and soaring ballads in a show that, along the way, brings in real-life celebrities including Henry Ford and Harry Houdini. The duet "Wheels of a Dream" is an avowal of faith by Coalhouse and Sarah in the opportunities presented by a Model T car, while "Your Daddy's Son" is Sarah's impassioned plea for understanding of why she buried her baby.

Then there is *Rent* (1996), a rock opera with lyrics and music by Jonathan Larson (1960–96). This is yet another reworking of material from Murger's *Scènes de la vie de Bohème,* but with Paris's Left Bank here replaced by New York's East Village, and Murger's Bohemian artists transformed into very up-to-date equivalents. Roger (played by Adam Pascal) is a struggling musician and Mimi (Daphne Rubin-Vega) a junkie. Among their friends are Tom Collins (Jesse L. Martin), a homosexual who falls in love with Angel (Wilson Jermaine Heredia), a transvestite street musician. All four are HIV-positive. Many of Larson's lyrics are wryly observant, and he achieves a particular emotional impact in "One Song Glory," in which Roger expresses the hope of writing "the one song before the virus takes hold." As is generally the case, the music is not so much pure rock music as rock music adapted with more lyrical elements for theatrical consumption. The show won a Pulitzer Prize as well as Tony awards, its success hastened by the huge media attention that surrounded its creator's death from AIDS on the night of the first dress rehearsal.

In its way, *Rent* encapsulates both the changes and the continuity that have occurred in the musical theatre over the past 150 years. By contrast with Offenbach's use of mythological characters to mask attacks on the abuse of privilege and power in the Second Empire, Larson deals openly with the problems of the working classes. The musical style has changed overwhelmingly from something high-flown and nineteenth century to something far more down-to-earth. The two-compact-disc recording of *Rent* exposed it to a larger audience than would have seen or heard any nineteenth-century musical stage work in many thousands of performances. Stage techniques have likewise changed to a huge degree. Yet the show demonstrates a reassuring continuity in adapting a Murger novel that had already inspired not only operas by Leoncavallo and Puccini but operettas as diverse as Vives's *Bohemios,* Hahn's *Ciboulette,* and Kálmán's *Das Veilchen vom Montmartre.*

In 1998 *Rent* reached London and settled down to the unfulfilled expectation of a long run. In both cities it formed part of a richly varied theatrical fare that mixes the blockbuster with the smaller-scale, and new productions with revivals. Like the operetta before it, the American musical has reached a point where works of the past are treated as classics, meriting revival not only in the commercial but also the subsidised theatre, where the classical operettas likewise have long since found a refuge.

For the future, the economics of getting new works staged present an obvious source of concern, and the sheer volume of new works must inevitably be restricted compared with the past. Yet, with some forty theatres in New York and London devoted to musical productions of various types, one can scarcely be anything but optimistic about the future. That this is the case even in the face of competition from television and video discredits any view that the musical theatre is losing its attraction for creators, performers, or public. The same is no less true in any theatrical centre of the world. Moreover, videos, compact discs, and cassettes provide an additional, unprecedented access to the theatrical repertory of the past 150 years. The pattern of musical theatre must inevitably change in the future, as it so gratifyingly has in the past; but there is no reason to doubt that the incalculably rich heritage of those 150 years will be rewardingly developed well into the twenty-first century.

Index

Index

Jankuhn, Walter, 219, 228, 230
János vitéz (Kacsóh), 87
Jay, Isabel, 127–28
Jean Seberg (Hamlisch), 345
Jeeves (Lloyd Webber), 333
Jekyll and Hyde (Wildhorn), 350
Jenbach, Béla, 91, 207
Jerger, Alfred, 224
Jessel, Léon, 203
Jesus Christ Superstar (Lloyd Webber), 332
Jill Darling (Ellis), 188
Joconde (Zeller), 65
John, Elton, 347
Johnny Johnson (Weill), 254
Johns, Glynis, 308
Johnson, J. Rosamond, 180
Johnson, Laurie, 326
Jókai, Mór, 50
Jolie Parfumeuse (La) (Offenbach), 24, 28
Jolly, Alfred, 26–28
Jolson, Al, 157, 167, 225, 267
Jones, Dean, 307
Jones, Sidney, 116, 122–23, 128, 130, 138, 152
Jones, Tom, 291–92, 342
Jones, Trefor, 191
Jonson, Ben, 326
Joplin, Scott, 345
Jorrocks (Heneker), 323
Joseffy, Josef, 55–56
Joseph and the Amazing Technicolor Dreamcoat
    (Lloyd Webber), 332
Joséphine vendue par ses soeurs (Roger), 59
Jour et la nuit (Le) (Lecocq), 29
Jourdan, Louis, 267
Joyce, Yootha, 326
Jubilee (Porter), 183
Judic, Anna, 23–25, 33–34
Jugar con fuego (Barbieri), 243
Juive (La) (Halévy), 8
Julia, Raul, 347
Jumbo (Rodgers), 185
Jung England (Fall), 84
Jungfrau von Belleville (Die) (Millöcker), 54
Juxheirat (Die) (Lehár), 76, 78

Kacsóh, Pongrác, 88
Kahan, Judy, 308
Kahn, Madeline, 297–98
Kaiserin (Die) (Fall), 85
Kaiserin Josephine (Kálmán), 220

Kaiserin Katharina (Kattnigg), 231
Kálmán, Emmerich, 90–92, 153, 167, 208–11, 213,
    219–21, 224, 240, 352
Kander, John, 294, 298–99, 301–2, 312, 341
Kapitän Fracassa (Dellinger), 70
Käpt'n Bay-Bay (Schultze), 238
Karczag, Wilhelm, 76
Karlin, Miriam, 326
Kartenschlägerin (Die) (Suppé), 41
Kartousch, Louise, 79, 84, 86, 90, 206, 209
Katinka (Friml), 165
Katiuska (Sorozábal), 248
Katja, die Tänzerin (Gilbert), 203
Kattnigg, Rudolf, 231
Kaufman, George S., 176–77, 186, 310
Kaye, Danny, 254, 277, 287, 298
Kaye, Stubby, 276
Kazantzakis, Nikos, 299
Kellermeister (Der) (Zeller), 67
Kelly, Gene, 184, 187, 260
Kennedy, John F., 263, 311
Kenney, James, 322
Kennick, T., 134
Kenny, Sean, 326–27
Kenwright, Bill, 330
Kerker, Gustave, 144–45
Kern, Adele, 219
Kern, Jerome, 128, 151–58, 162, 171, 173–76, 178,
    180–81, 189–90, 192, 256, 258, 261, 315
Kert, Larry, 273
Keusche Barbara (Die) (Nedbal), 87
Keusche Susanne (Die) (Gilbert), 72, 203
Kid Boots (Tierney), 156
Kiley, Richard, 286, 293
King, Dennis, 166, 186
King, Larry L., 343
King and I (The) (Rodgers), 303
King Dodo (Luders), 144
King of Cadonia (Jones/Rosse), 128
Kingdom for a Cow (A) (Weill), 223
King's Rhapsody (Novello), 314
Kinokönigin (Die) (Gilbert), 73
Kirk, Lisa, 263
Kirkwood, Pat, 317
Kismet (Borodin/Wright/Forrest), 348
Kiss Me, Kate (Porter), 263, 278
Kiss of the Spider Woman (Kander), 301
Kissing Time (Caryll), 146
Klein, Charles, 139
Klein, Robert, 345

Index